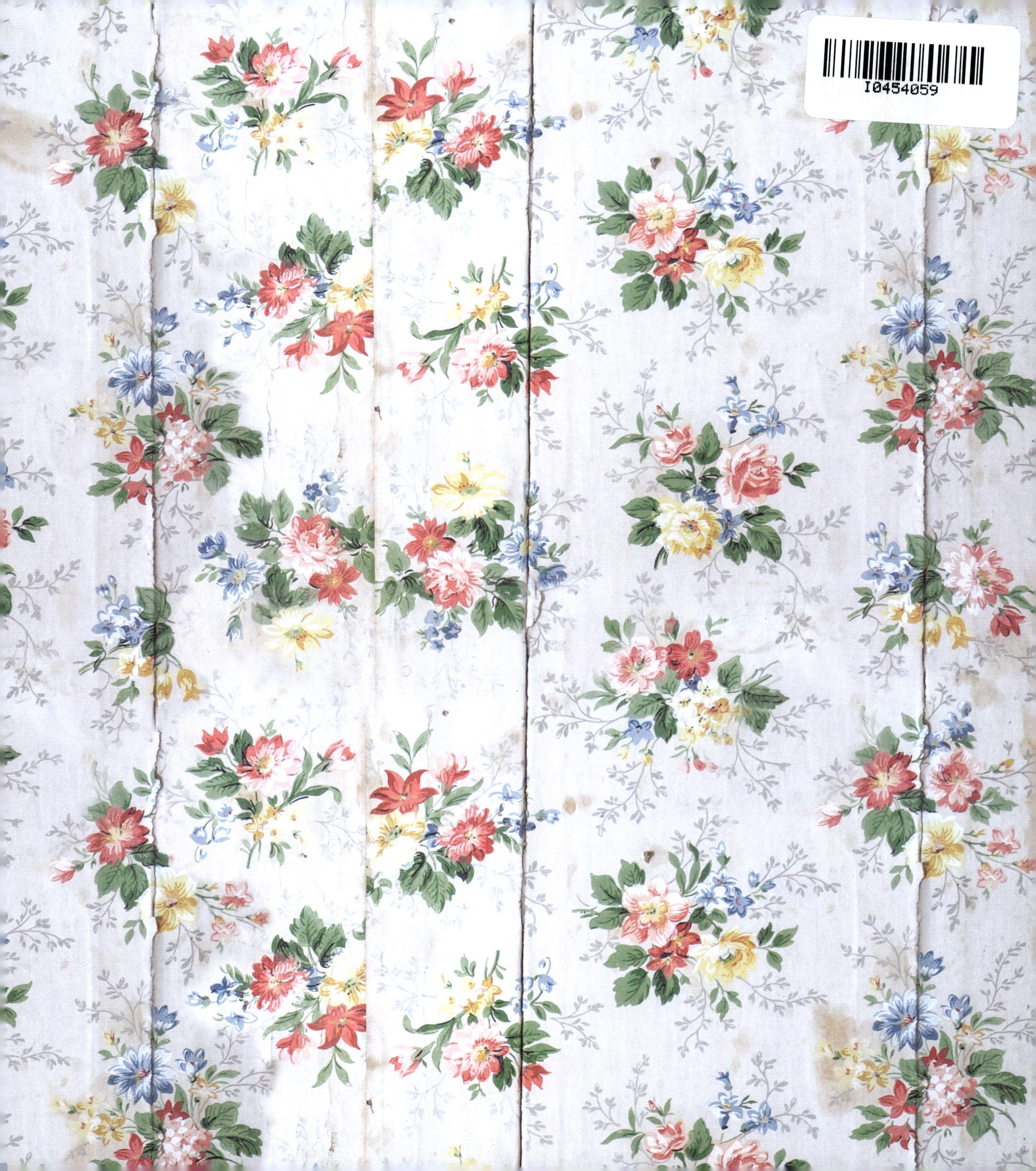

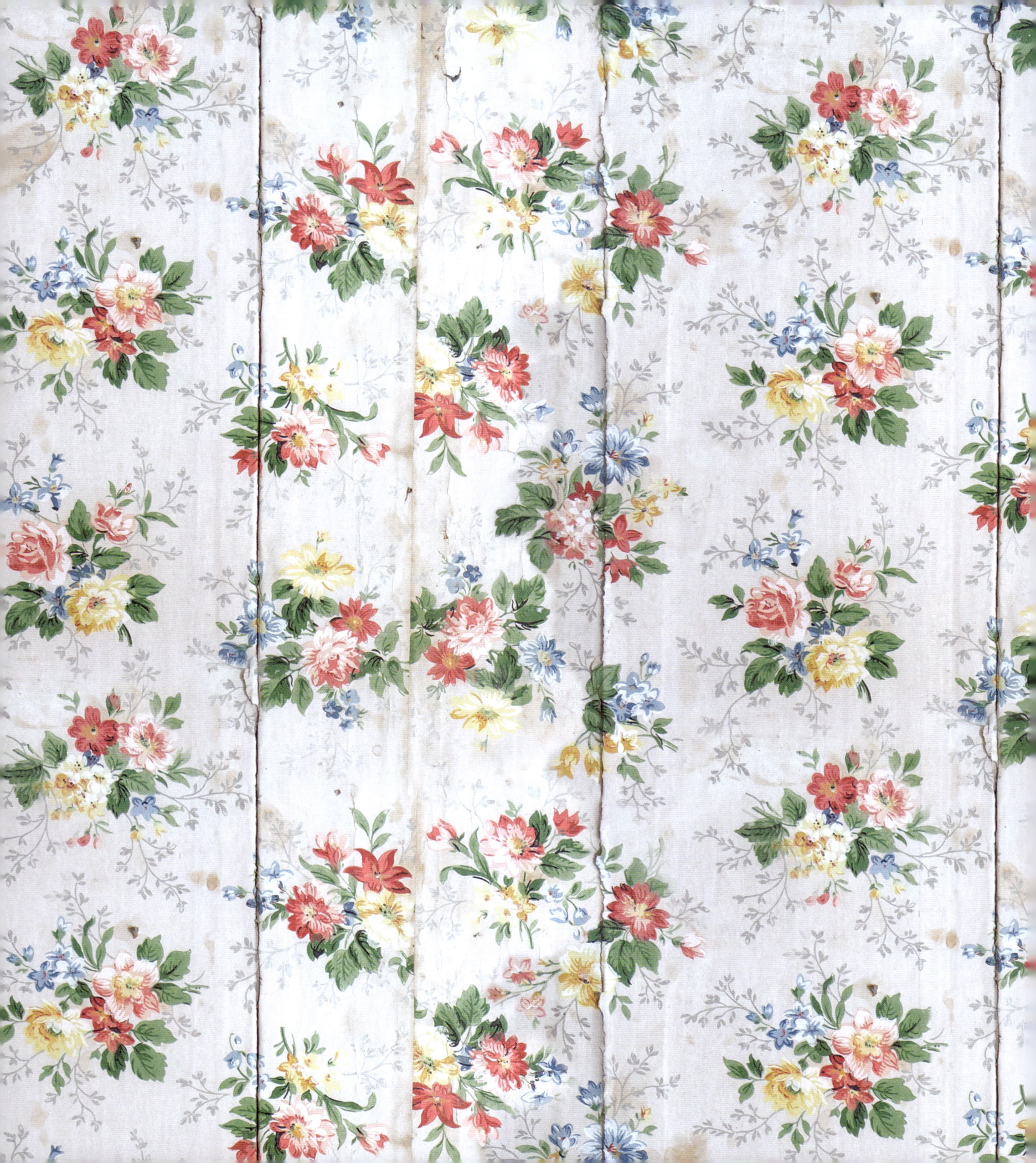

AMERICA
the
ABANDONED

CAPTIVATING PORTRAITS
of DESERTED HOMES

BRYAN SANSIVERO

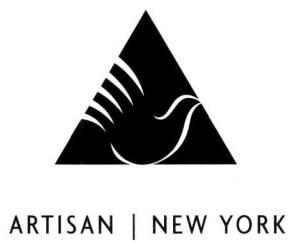

ARTISAN | NEW YORK

Library of Congress Cataloging-in-Publication Data

Names: Sansivero, Bryan photographer
Title: Haunted America : captivating portraits of America's abandoned homes
  / Bryan Sansivero.
Description: New York : Artisan, [2025]
Identifiers: LCCN 2025010172 | ISBN 9781648294389 hardcover |
  ISBN 9781648294402 ebook
Subjects: LCSH: Architectural photography—United States | Abandoned
  houses—United States—Pictorial works | Photography of
  interiors—United States | Ruins in art
Classification: LCC TR659 .S257 2025 | DDC 779/.40973—dc23/eng/20250506
LC record available at https://lccn.loc.gov/2025010172

Design by Jack Dunnington

Artisan books may be purchased in bulk for business, educational, or promotional use. For information, please contact your local bookseller or the Hachette Book Group Special Markets Department at special.markets@hbgusa.com.

The publisher is not responsible for websites (or their content) that are not owned by the publisher.

The Hachette Speakers Bureau provides a wide range of authors for speaking events. To find out more, go to hachettespeakersbureau.com or email HachetteSpeakers@hbgusa.com.

Published by Artisan,
an imprint of Workman Publishing,
a division of Hachette Book Group, Inc.
1290 Avenue of the Americas
New York, NY 10104
artisanbooks.com

The Artisan name and logo are registered trademarks of Hachette Book Group, Inc.

Printed in China (TLF) on responsibly sourced paper

First printing, September 2025

Cover © 2025 Hachette Book Group, Inc.

10 9 8 7 6 5 4 3 2 1

For those close to me whom I've lost over the years.

These photographs show an absence,
and in that quiet absence, the things left behind remind us
of the times we had and the memories we made.
We are never truly forgotten.

INTRODUCTION

I've been photographing abandoned homes for more than ten years. In 2023, I was in a small village in France, documenting abandoned castles and châteaus, and I realized that before I could fully move on to Europe, there were still many places I wanted to visit in the United States. And so *America the Abandoned* was born. This book is a collection of my favorite photos from my travels across the US. Many states are represented here, from Maine to Nebraska, Michigan to Georgia. There are photos in this book that have never been published—many of the interiors, and all of the exteriors.

Though many people assume I make a living traveling the world taking pictures of grand abandoned houses and buildings, this is not my profession. I don't consider myself a photographer of "abandoned buildings" or an "urbex" photographer (someone who takes pictures of derelict forgotten places or ventures into places that are dangerous and forbidden). In the world of social media, urbex photography has become a competitive sport. Some do it for the thrill, others for the photos, and everyone wants to be the first to discover the "most fascinating abandoned place." This is especially true for people who film their adventures and upload them to platforms like YouTube. I, however, consider myself a documentarian and filmmaker before anything else. I've made a documentary about the history of an abandoned hospital, and I've worked on documentaries about people's lives, their struggles, and their will to survive. I love photographing people and capturing the human spirit, and when I photograph old architecture, I find myself documenting the humanity left behind. It's the objects and the stories that keep me going back. With each new discovery and each door that opens, I get a glimpse into the history of not only a building but also a person's life.

I'm often asked about the context of the abandoned homes I document, and many people are surprised to learn that there are approximately 15.1 million vacant homes in the United States alone, according to the Census Bureau as of 2022. Some areas have higher numbers of abandoned homes, and there are many contributing factors as to why. One is the rise of the technology industry and reliance on newer resources. The closing of labor centers such as coal mines in Pennsylvania, steel mills in Indiana, and auto factories in Michigan left many people without jobs, and in the deindustrialization of the 1970s and '80s, millions of people were forced to move from their homes. We will never see many of these homes or even know they existed. They are simply abandoned, then bought and demolished. Very few will end up on the National Register of Historic Places, and even among those that do, many won't survive.

I've explored hundreds of forgotten houses. As a lover of architecture, I am drawn to those with unique exterior features such as grand entryways, large balconies, Gothic windows, and turrets—houses that match the common conception of a "haunted house." Deciding which ones to photograph is easy; conveying the feel of a house through an image is difficult. To get a good photograph, it is critical to travel to the location at the right time of year, at the perfect time of day, and in ideal weather. This is usually when leaves on trees aren't covering the house and when the sun isn't harsh or behind the house. I take all my exterior photographs on square medium-format film, which has a larger negative, a higher resolution, and more detail than regular 35 mm film. Using cameras from the 1950s, such as my Rolleiflex and Yashica, gives the pictures an authentic vintage look. Until I develop the film, I won't know if the pictures I took are any good. There have been times that I've traveled to a house and taken many photos but haven't had a single shot come out. It's frustrating, but not knowing what you're going to get is also a fun part of the challenge.

Taking interior photographs is no less difficult. Many rooms in abandoned homes have very little light or can be overblown with brightness. There are also many physical risks when entering an abandoned property, such as falling through a floor, getting attacked by an animal, or inhaling dust, mold, or other hazardous materials. All of these things have happened to me. I'm often asked if my images are staged, and sometimes they are, but not always by me. I can tell when other photographers have been to a house before me because things seem so perfectly out of place. Some houses are so trashed that you can't even make out what you're looking at, and others so well-preserved that you're seeing them exactly as they were left. I try to touch very little and be very respectful; at most I will prop up a painting or a lamp where it once may have been. A sort of reconstruction to help the object be seen.

My adventures are about so much more than just taking pictures of run-down buildings and collapsing structures. I try to piece together the history of the residents from the things they left behind. I've unearthed everything from family photographs to handwritten letters, clothing and shoes in closets, and even personal relics such as jewelry. Many times these are antiques, unusual items, or pieces with significant value, all left to rot away. Often, the objects seem as if they were left there just yesterday and the owners will one day return. Sadly, this is unlikely, and we will never get answers. But every home and the people who once lived there remind us of a common human connection—that each object we own is temporary and eventually will be forgotten, whether it belongs to a politician, a fashion model, an artist, a famous author, or a criminal, and whether it's in a tiny farmhouse in a southern state or in a large mansion in the Northeast. It doesn't matter how much money you have, or where you come from, or how large your house is. We decay all the same. In every room in every house, someone lived their life, and may have even died. Although they're gone, it's important to me that their memories live on. Someone, whether a mother, father, son, or daughter, lived in these spaces. This is their history. Let this book remind you of the little things we hold so dear, and that they will come and go, like those of others before us.

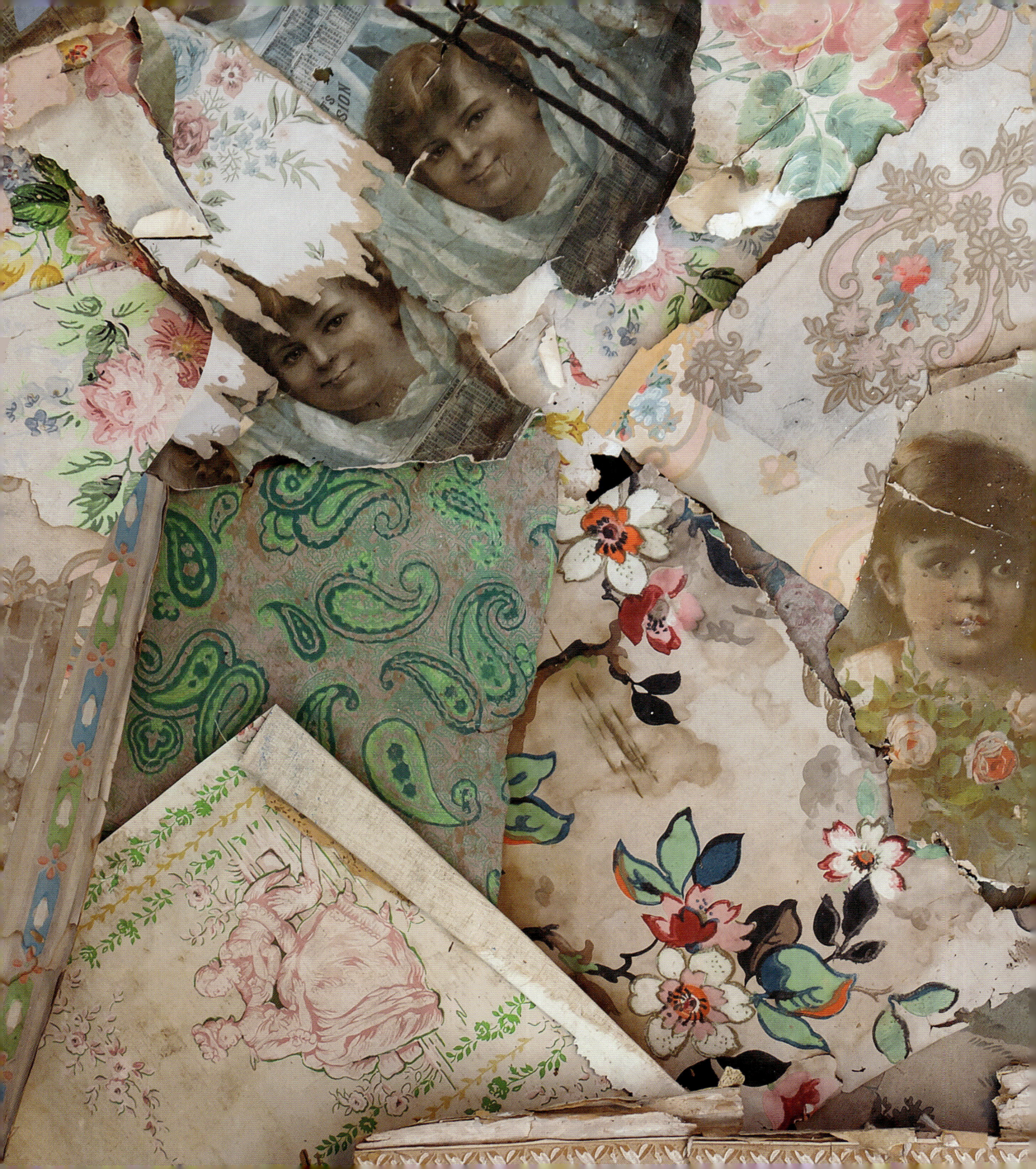

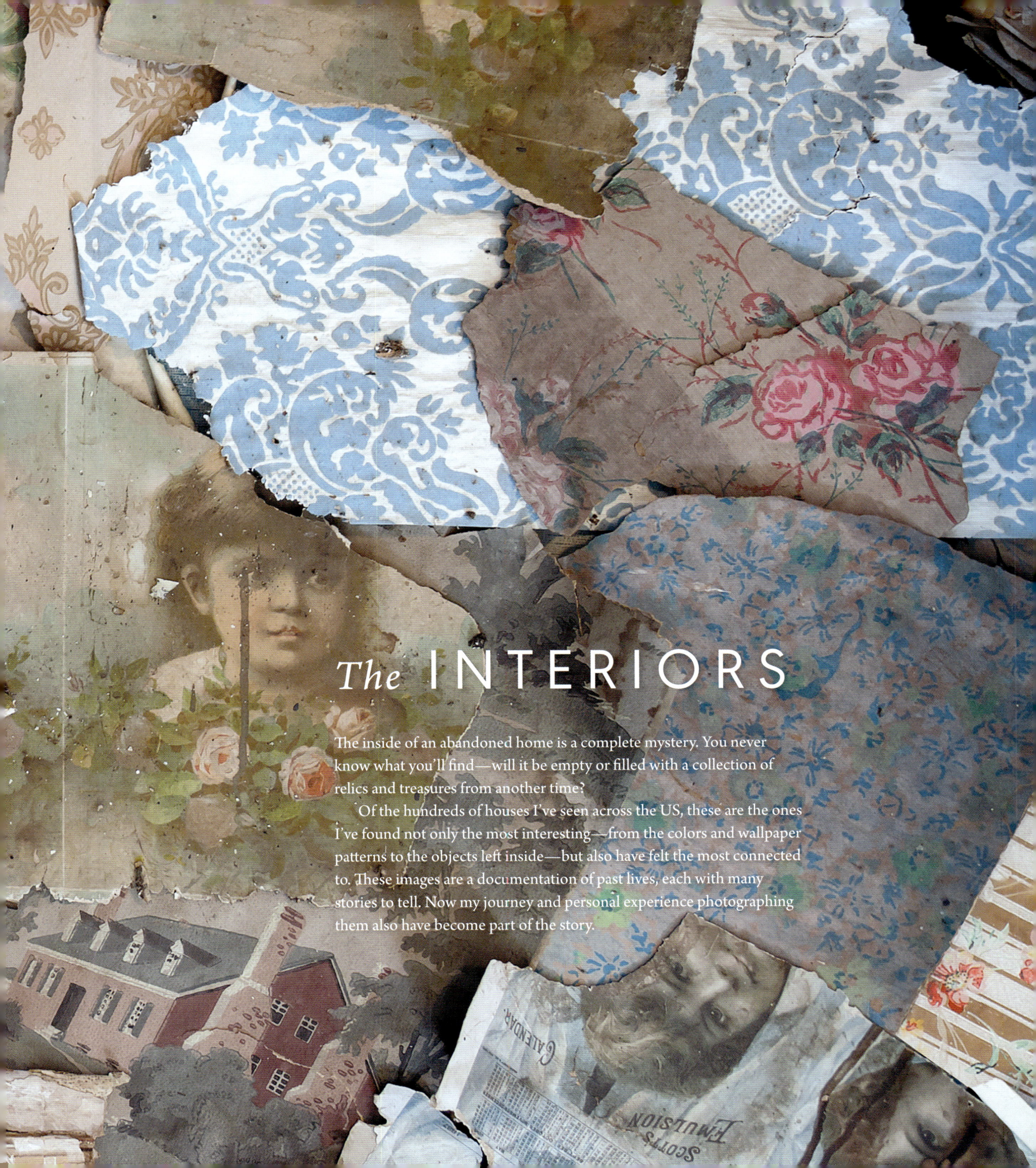

The INTERIORS

The inside of an abandoned home is a complete mystery. You never know what you'll find—will it be empty or filled with a collection of relics and treasures from another time?

Of the hundreds of houses I've seen across the US, these are the ones I've found not only the most interesting—from the colors and wallpaper patterns to the objects left inside—but also have felt the most connected to. These images are a documentation of past lives, each with many stories to tell. Now my journey and personal experience photographing them also have become part of the story.

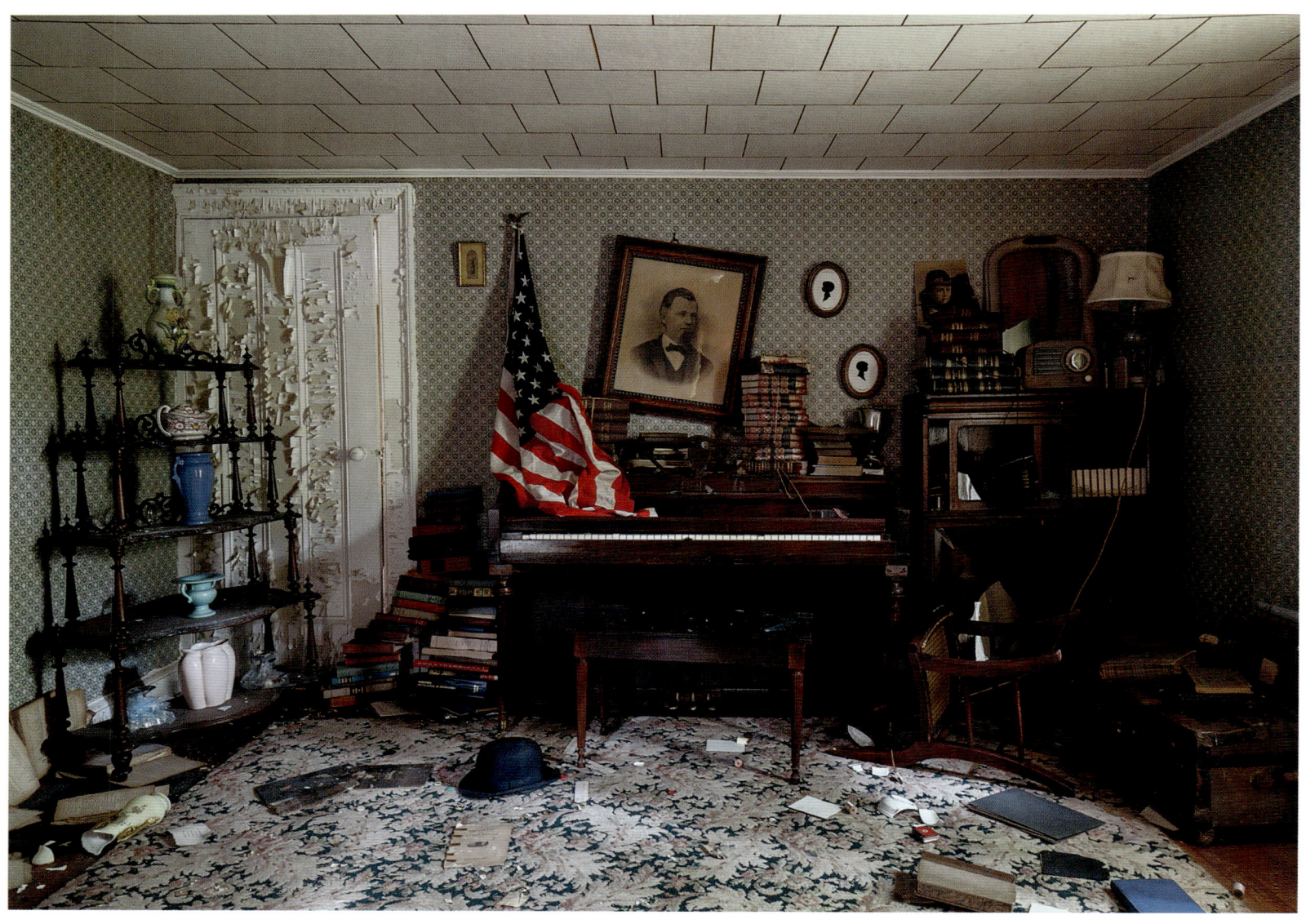

"A PATRIOT'S PIANO"
New London County, Connecticut

Inside this home, I found that almost every room had been ransacked. Only once I made my way to the back did this room with piles of books, a piano, and all kinds of antiques reveal itself to me.

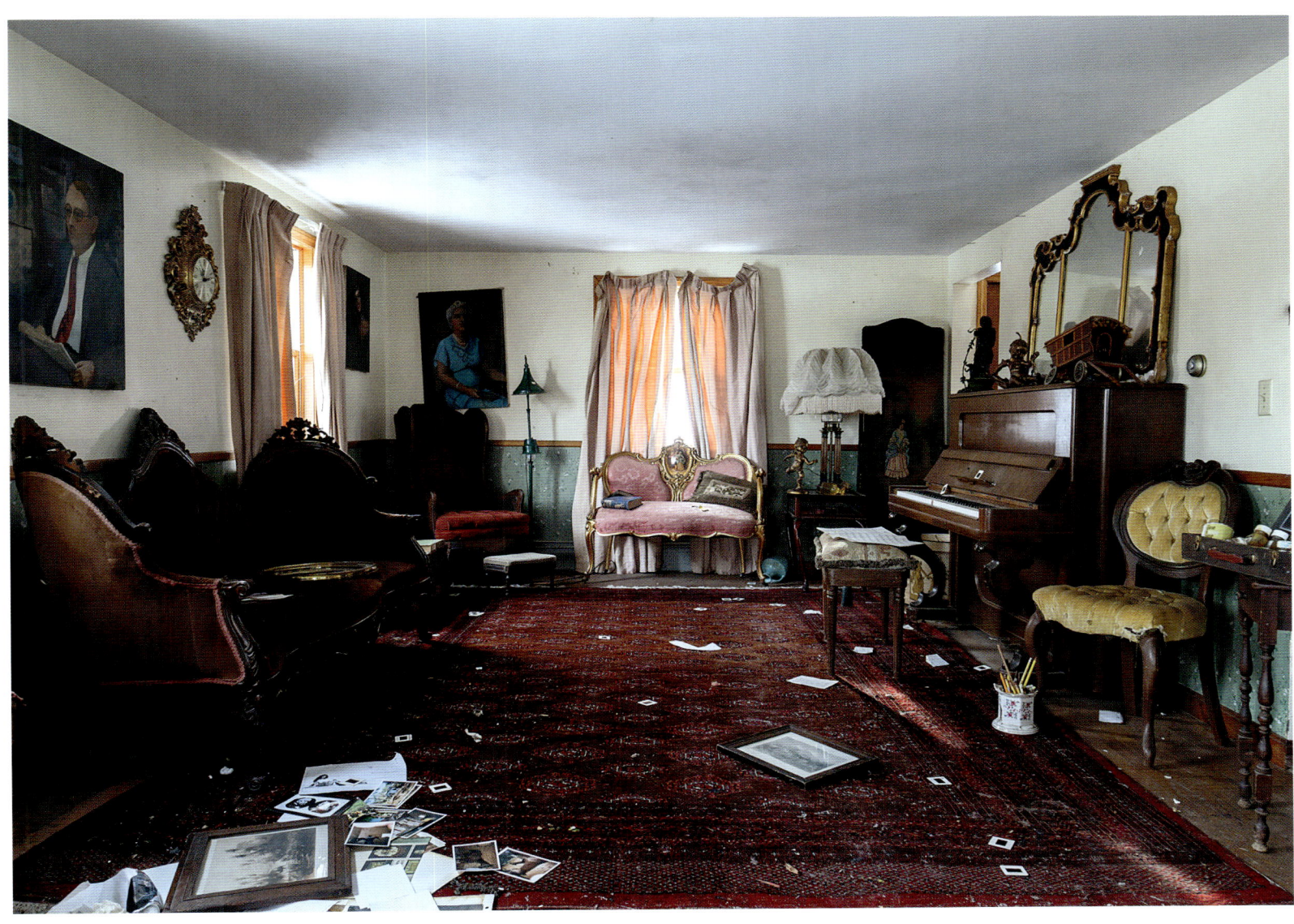

"HER MEMORIES, LEFT BEHIND"
Essex County, Vermont

It was below freezing when I climbed up a steep hill in the snow to photograph this house. An entire family's belongings had been left inside and were damaged from the harsh weather and temperatures. In the garage was an Oldsmobile 442.

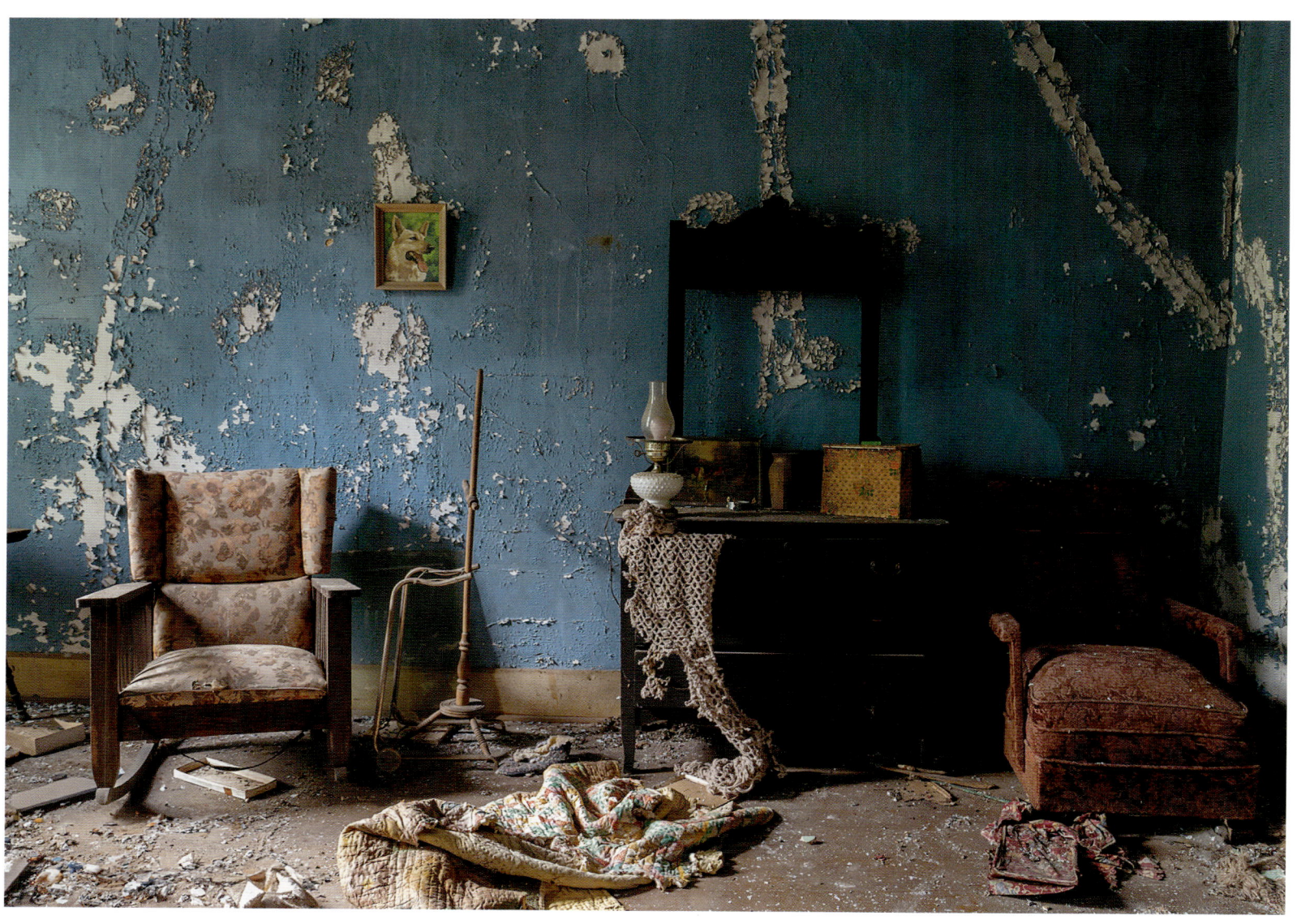

"THE DOG PORTRAIT"
Lee County, Alabama

This is the first room you enter in this large house in the woods. The color of the walls would make anything in the room stand out, but the furniture and portrait add intrigue.

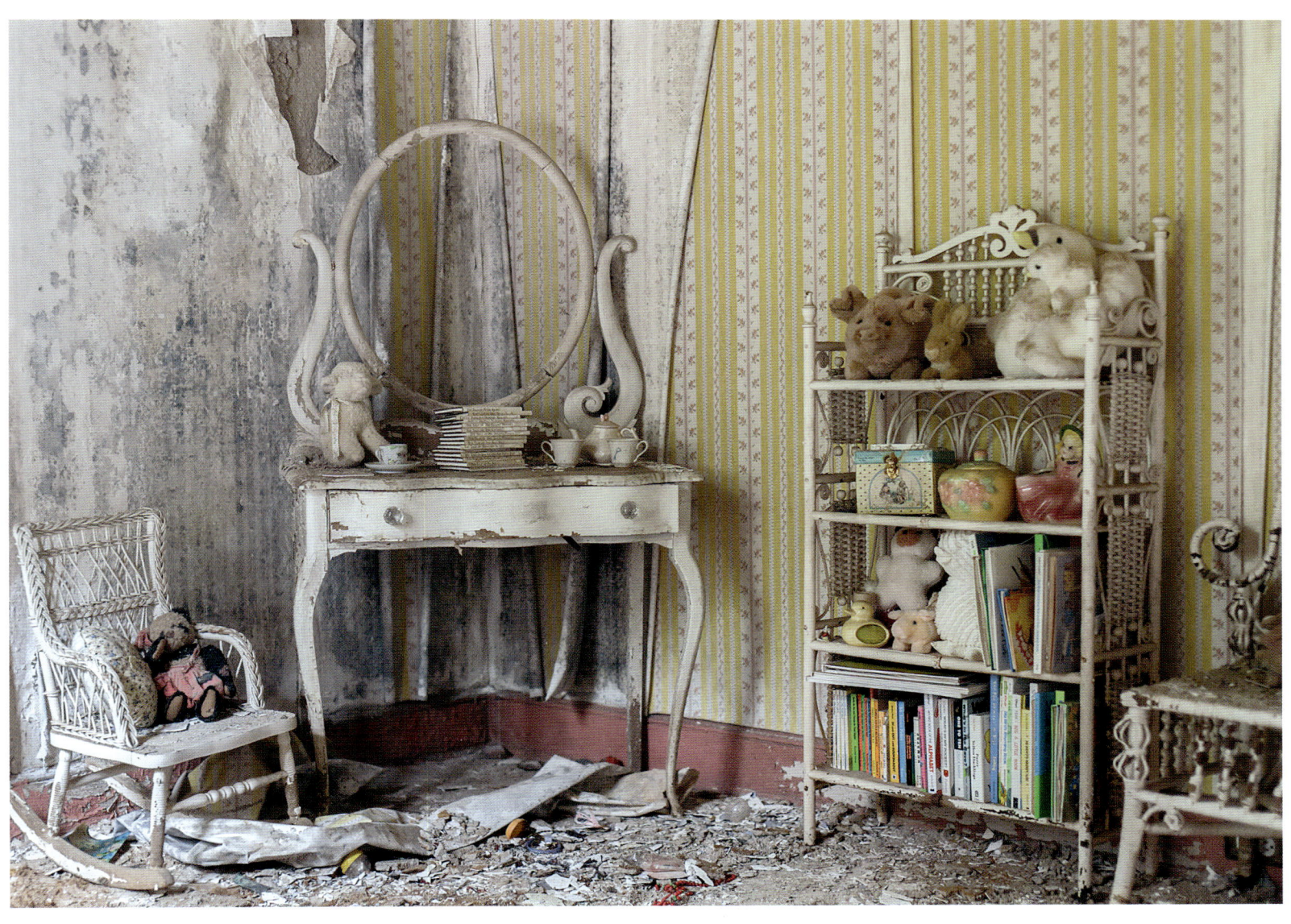

"THE TINY VANITY"
Suffolk County, New York

The story behind this house is tragic, which made seeing these toys all the more heartbreaking. The vanity without a mirror was like a ghost, a piece missing, like the soul of the house.

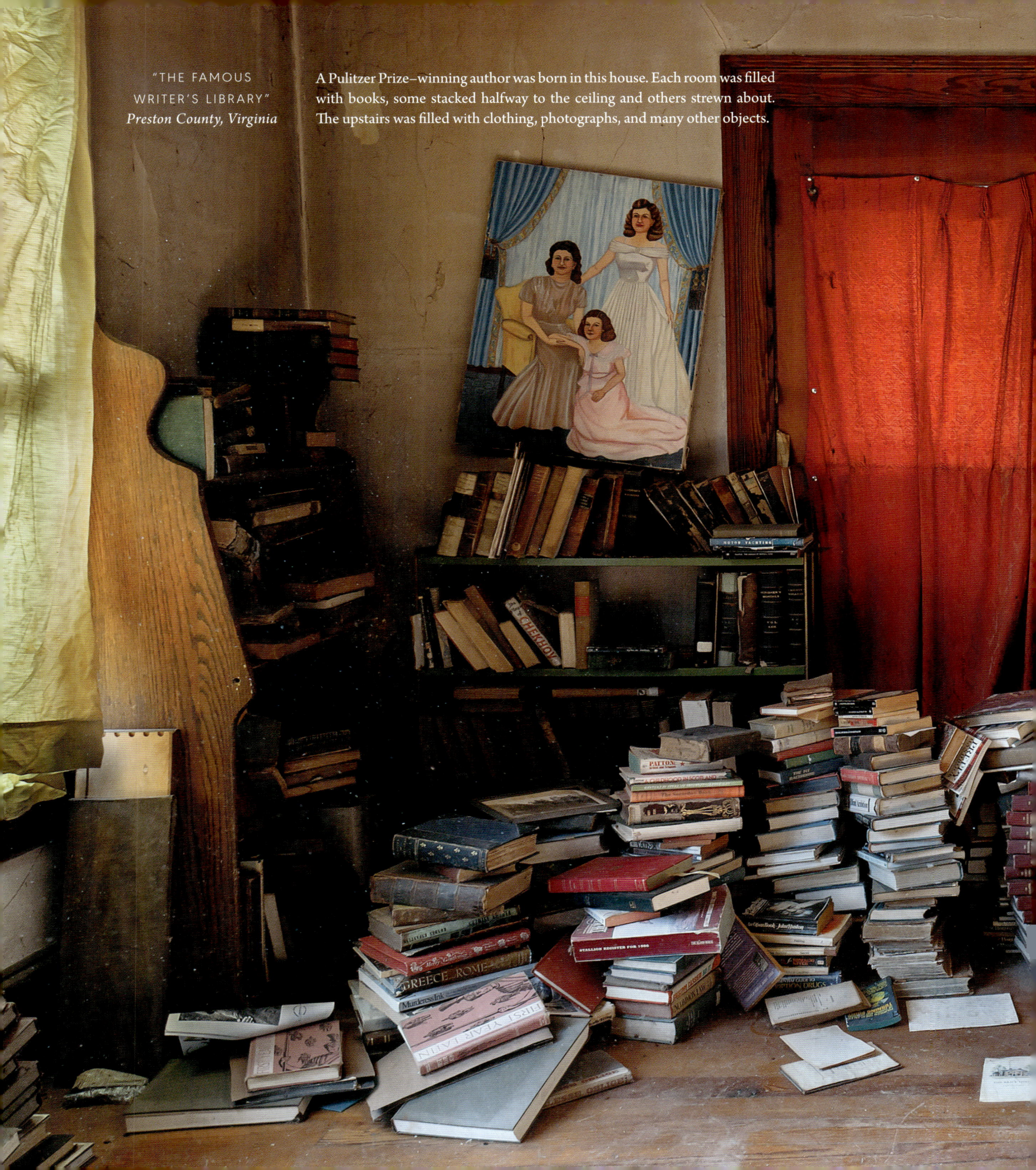

A Pulitzer Prize–winning author was born in this house. Each room was filled with books, some stacked halfway to the ceiling and others strewn about. The upstairs was filled with clothing, photographs, and many other objects.

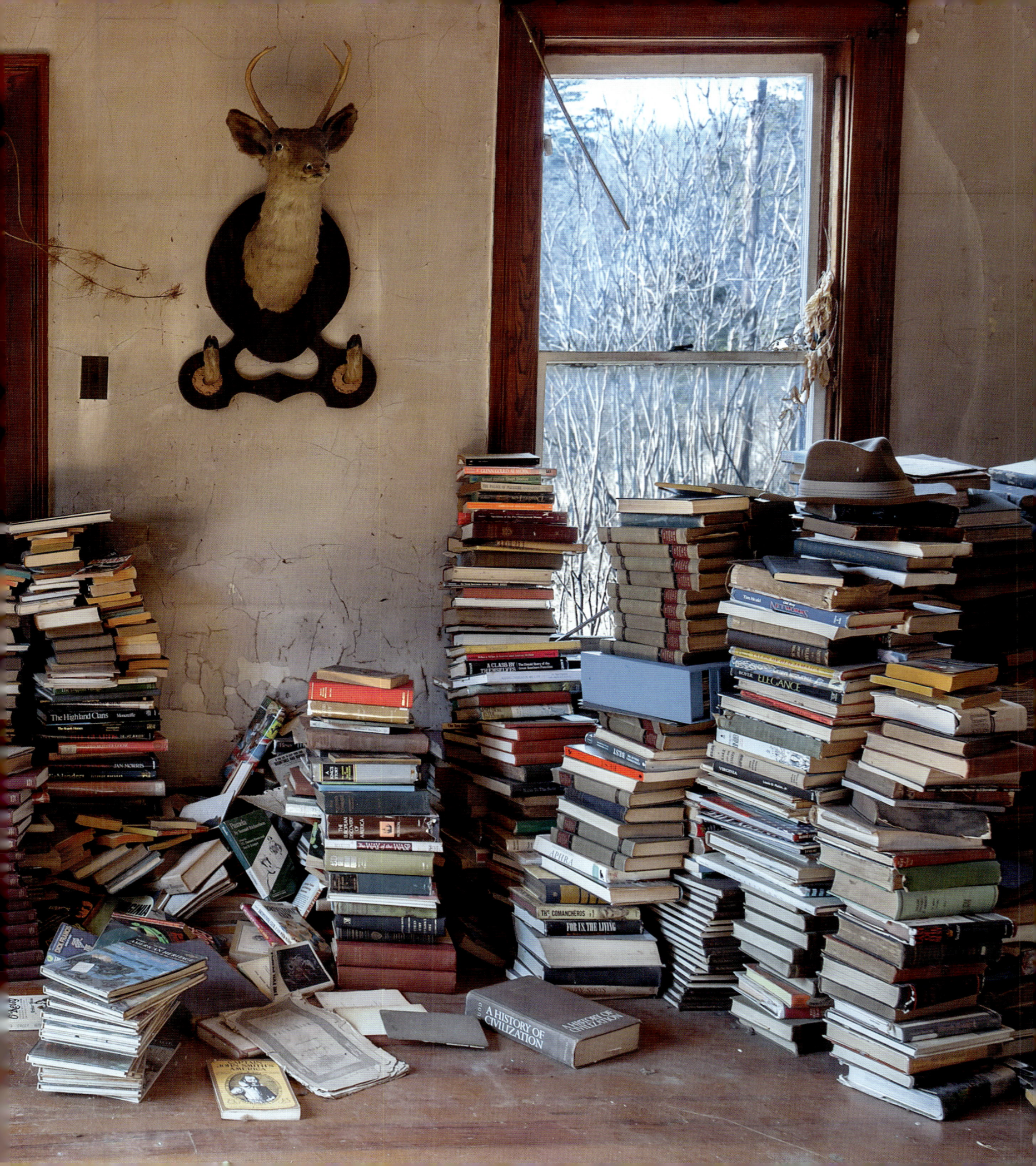

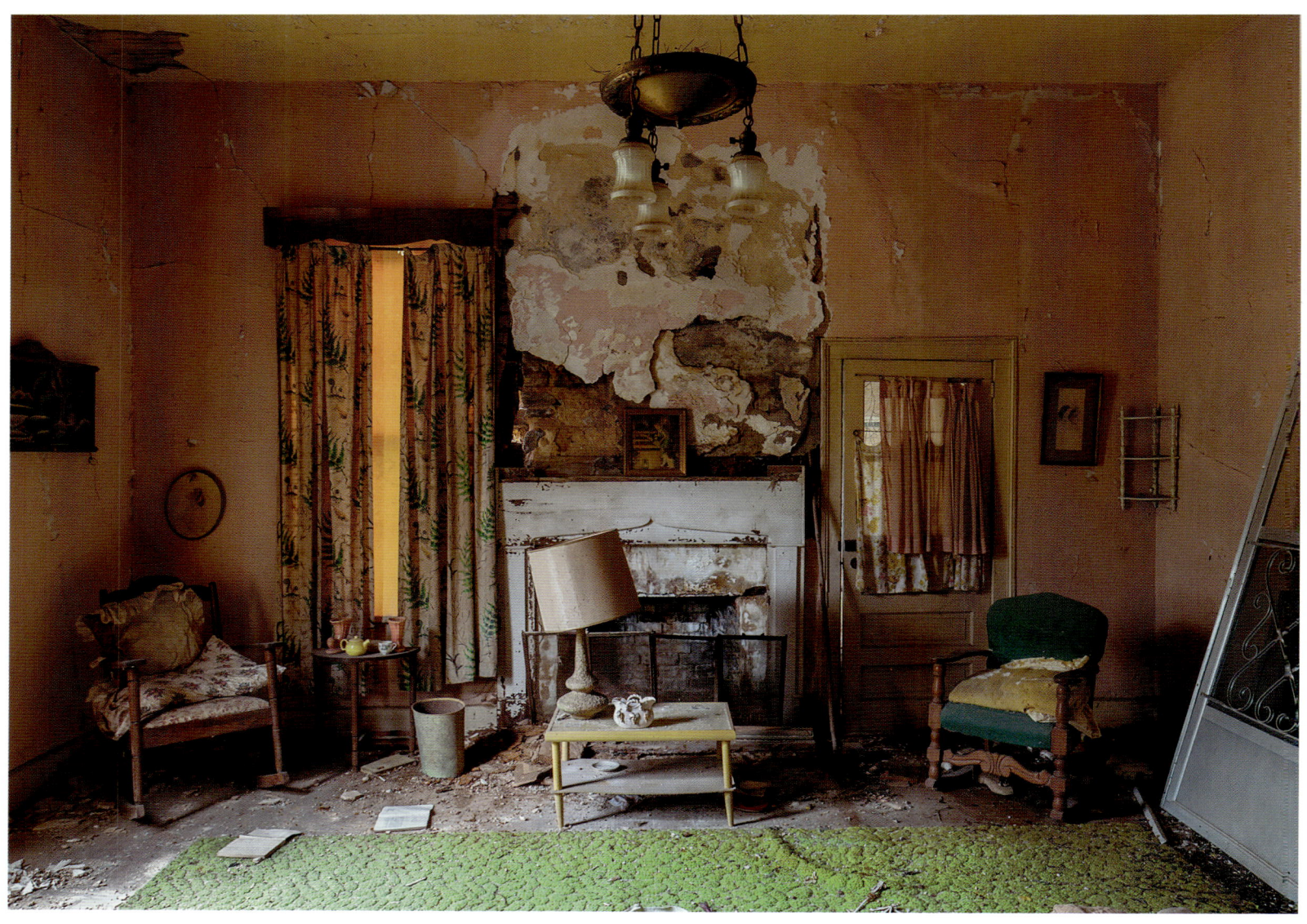

"THE PINK ROOM"
Lee County, Alabama

This room was in the back of this house. The walls were full of paintings, and decor such as vases and lamps was everywhere. Old furniture sits in place, setting the scene for what was certainly once a lively space.

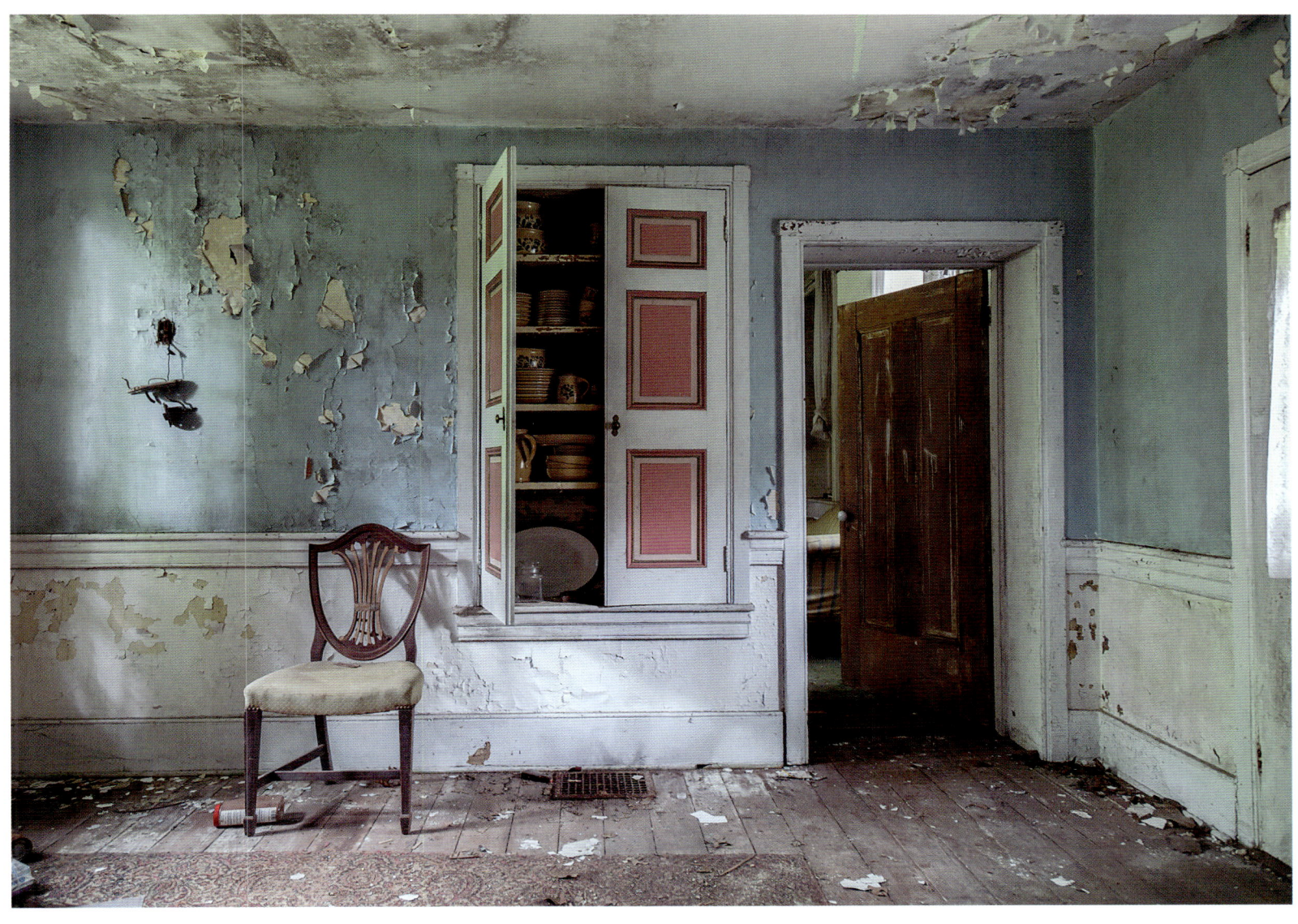

"THE CHINA CABINET"
New Castle County, Delaware

This is the kitchen inside a former politician's home. Behind a closed cabinet was a full china set. To the right, the living room can be seen behind the door.

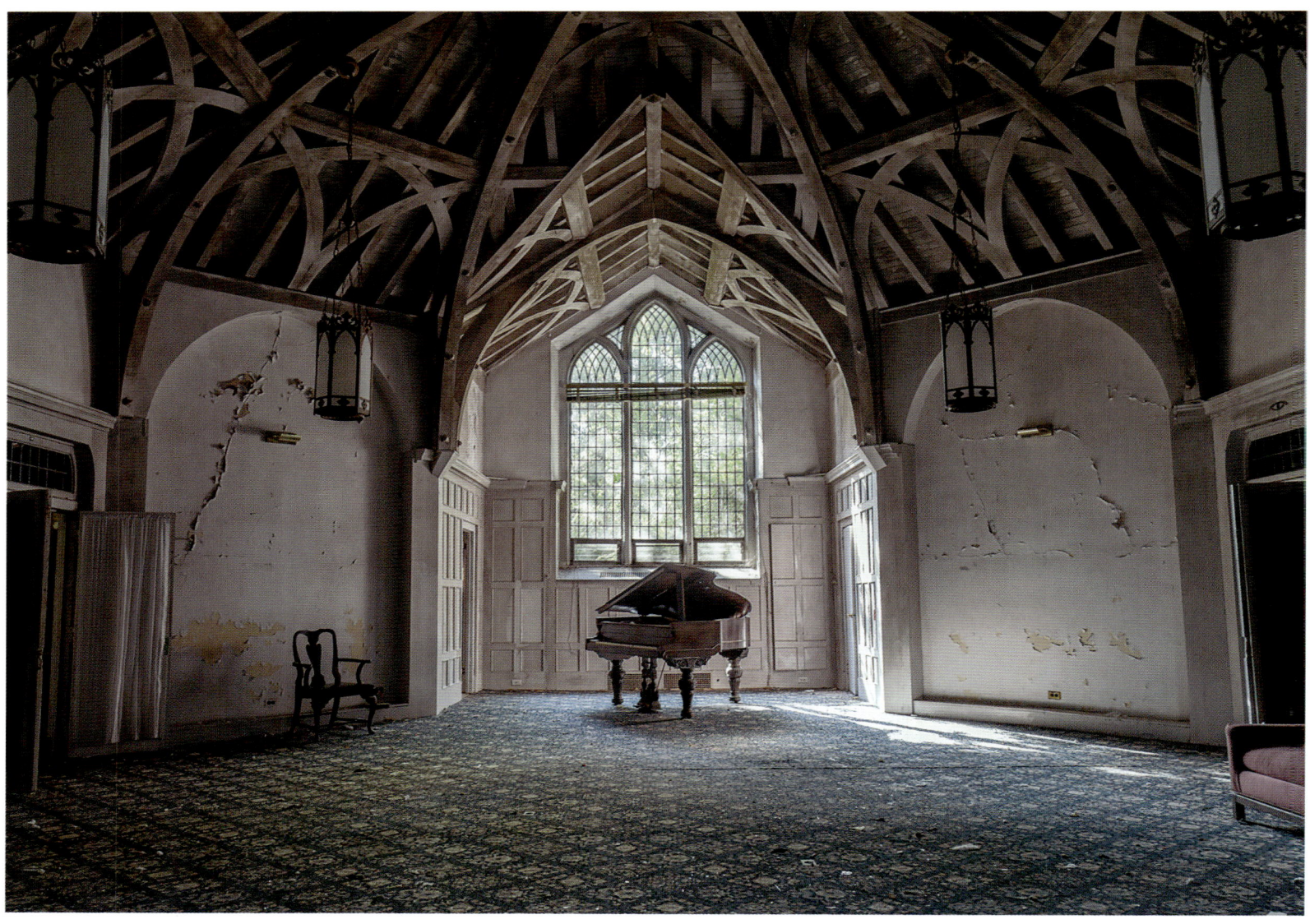

"THE GRAND ROOM"
Sleepy Hollow, New York

Around ten years ago, I was looking for a place to photograph a model when I made a wrong turn. I veered into a driveway to backtrack, but it kept going. Driving among trees, I noticed a large building on the left. It was this huge run-down mansion, completely abandoned.

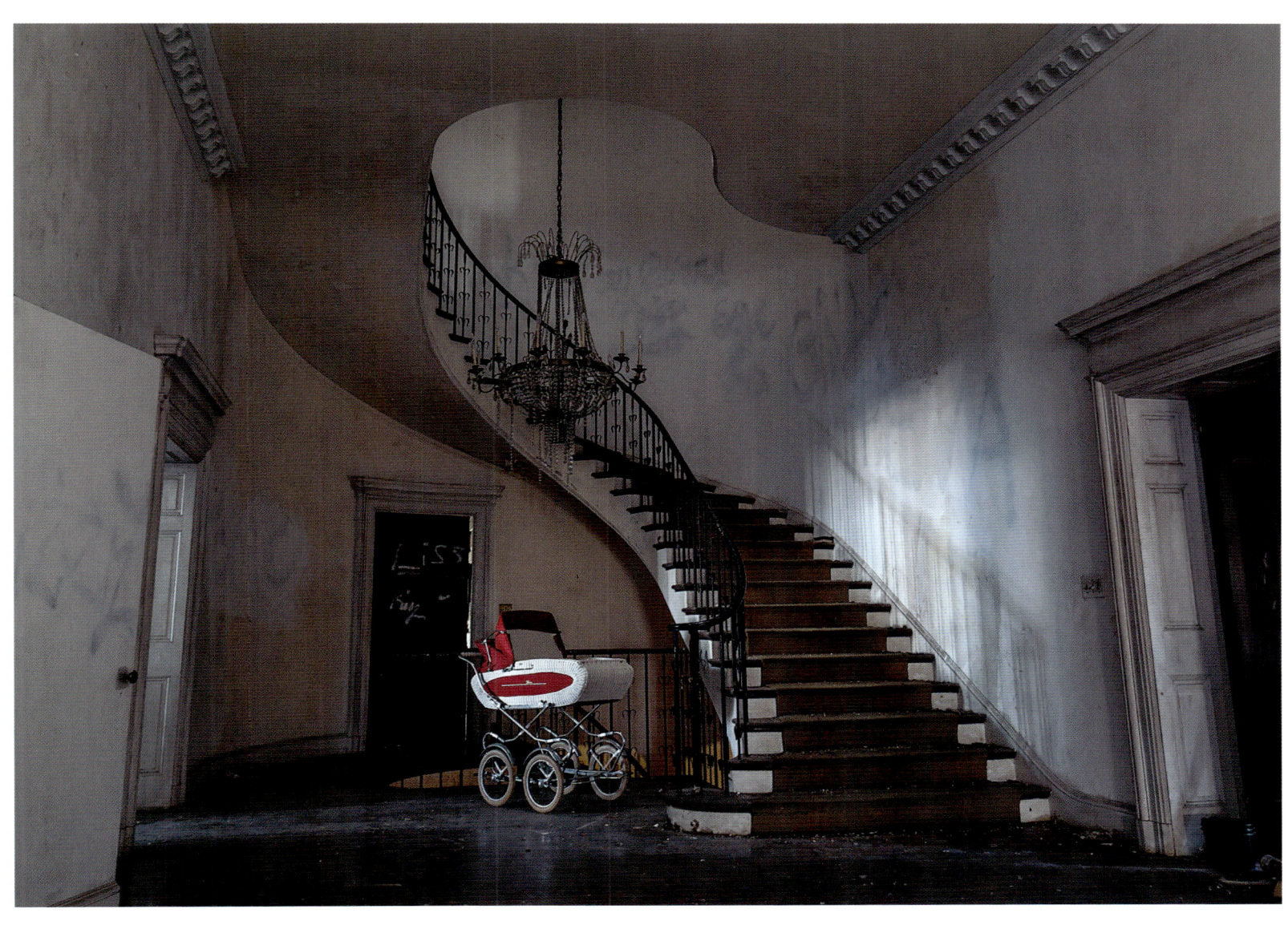

"THE RED PRAM"
Suffolk County, New York

The Gold Coast of Long Island is filled with wealth and spectacular old mansions. This particular mansion on the Gold Coast is featured throughout the book. I hope this pram was once used by a happy family.

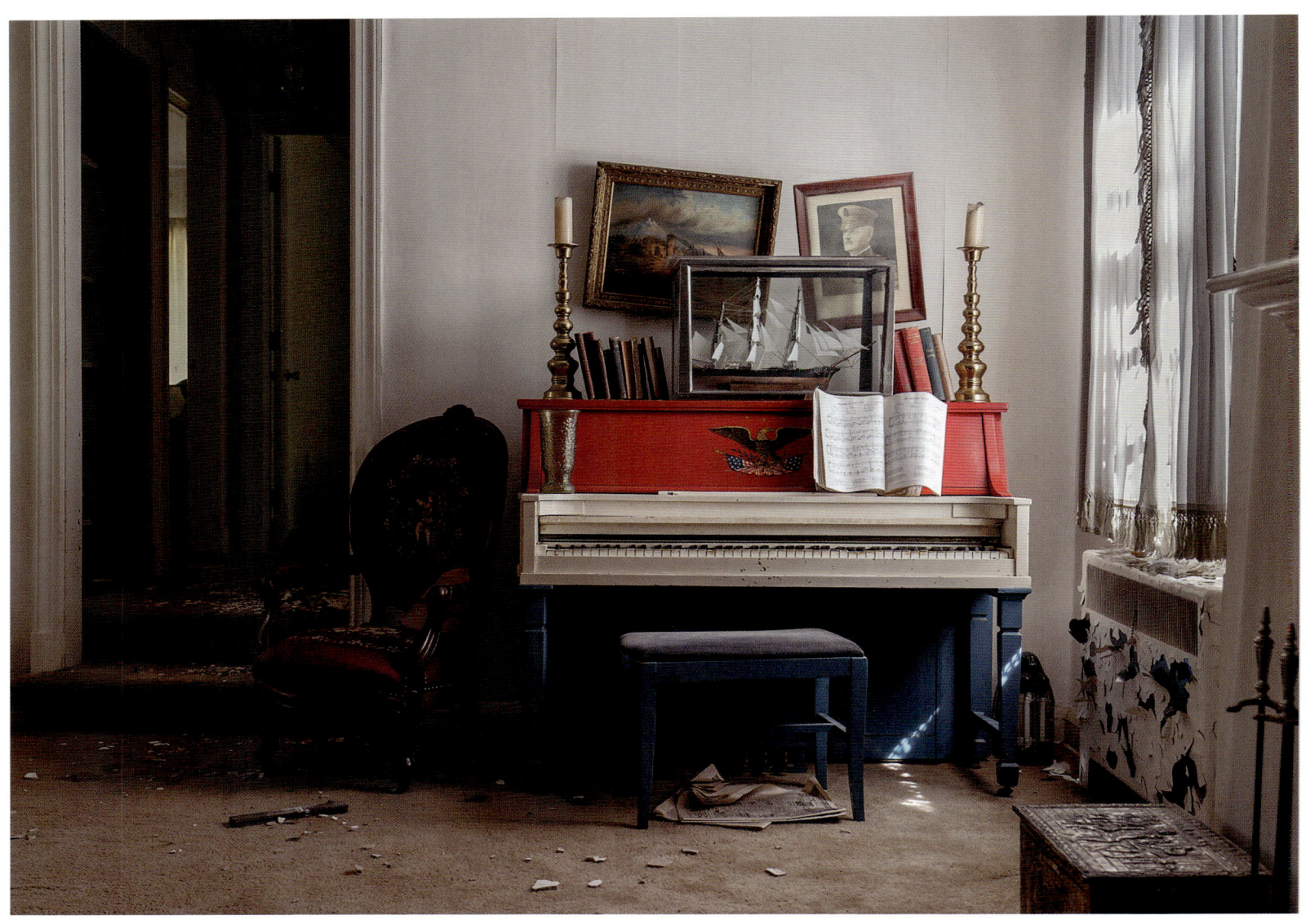

"THE BICENTENNIAL PIANO"
Howard County, Maryland

Now demolished, this house belonged to a music lover and was filled with records, instruments, and a unique piano, which was made in 1976 to celebrate the bicentennial of the United States. A photograph of a military officer and a ship behind glass are representative of the military décor displayed throughout the home.

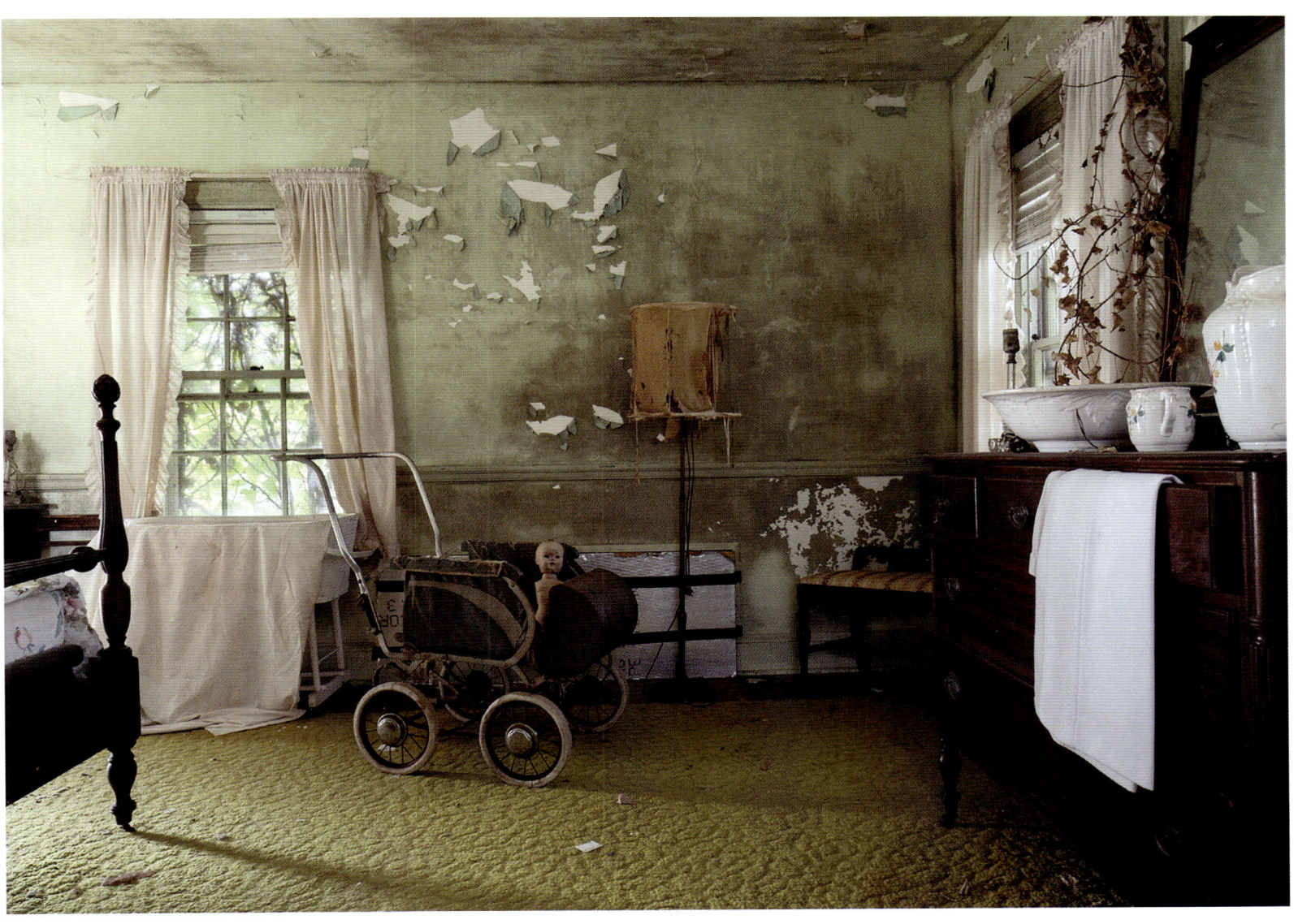

"THE GREEN CARRIAGE"
Caroline County, Maryland

A green palette ran through this house. In the main upstairs bedroom, I found a pram with a doll inside, a crib, and a dollhouse. While vines were growing in from the outside, the fine porcelain basin and pitchers were still perfectly in place atop the dresser.

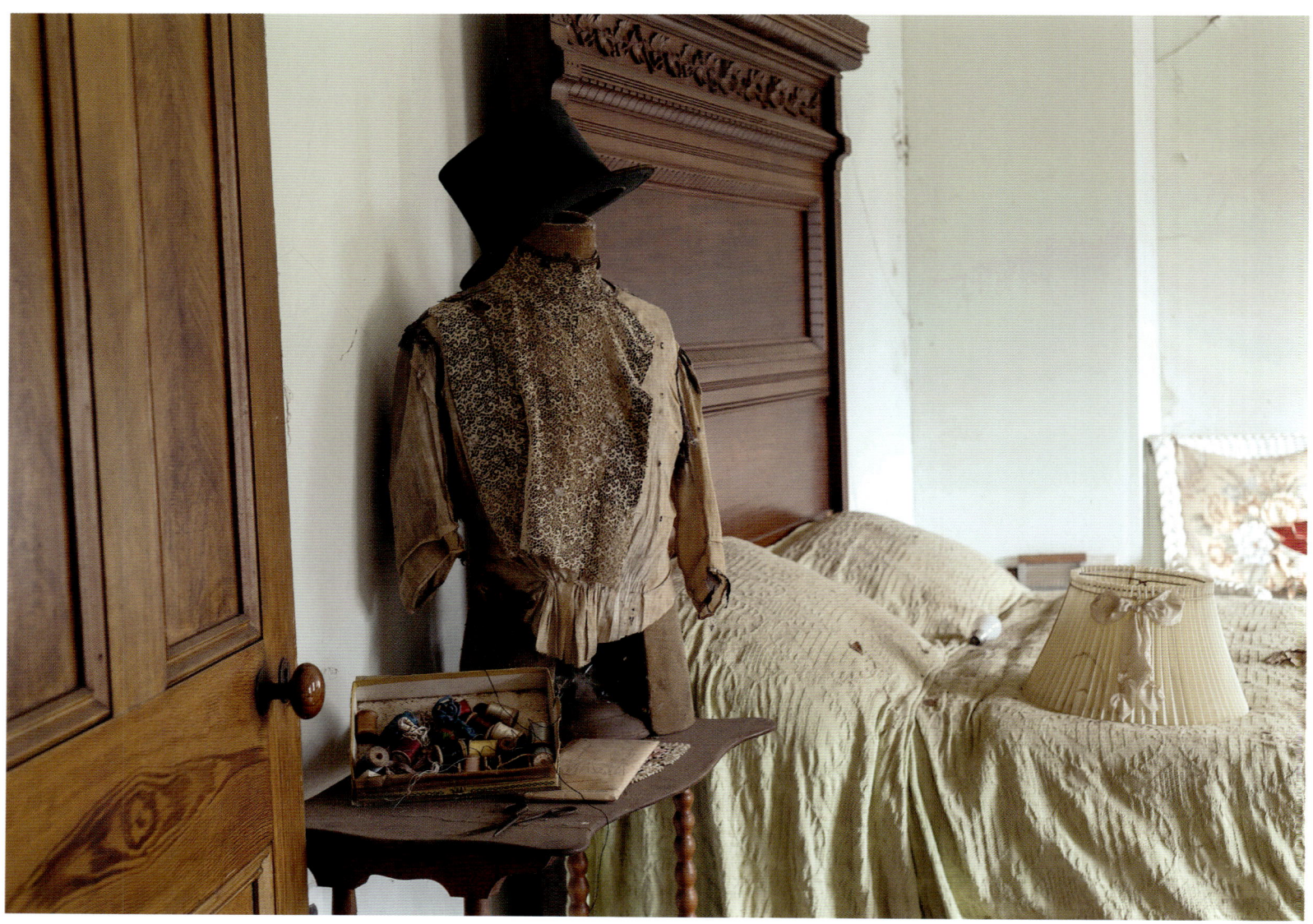

"THE TAILORED
DRESS FORM"
Suffolk County, New York

Many rooms in this abandoned farmhouse were filled with antique sewing items—machines, thread, and dress forms. I can only assume the woman who lived here was a talented seamstress. Some of the items were in such pristine condition, they could be displayed in a museum.

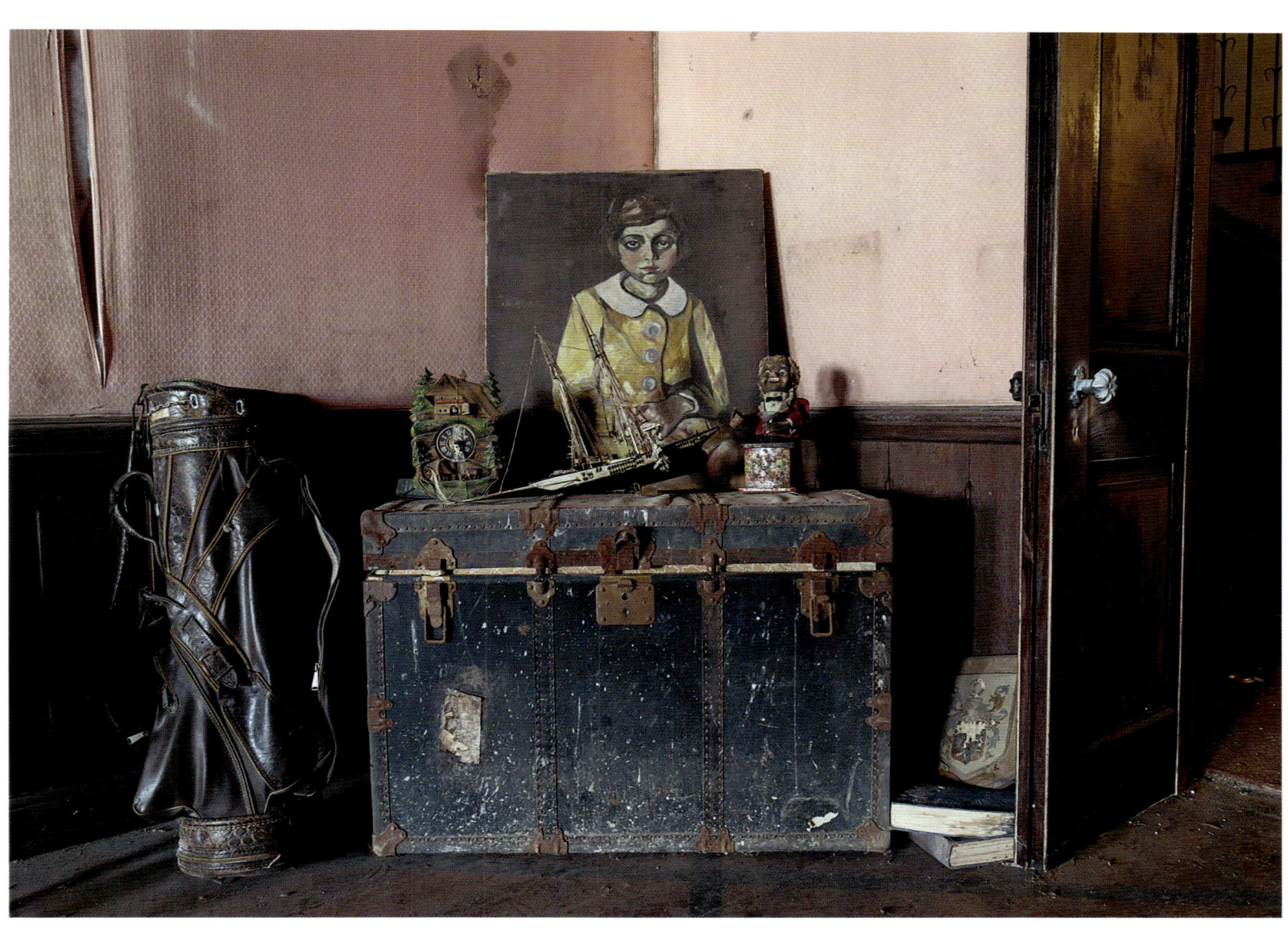

"THE BOY"
Suffolk County, New York

Of all the objects inside this abandoned Gold Coast mansion, this painting of a boy was the most mysterious. Did he once live here? We may never know. I find it sad to see photographs and paintings left behind. In my eyes, these should be cherished, especially if they depict family members.

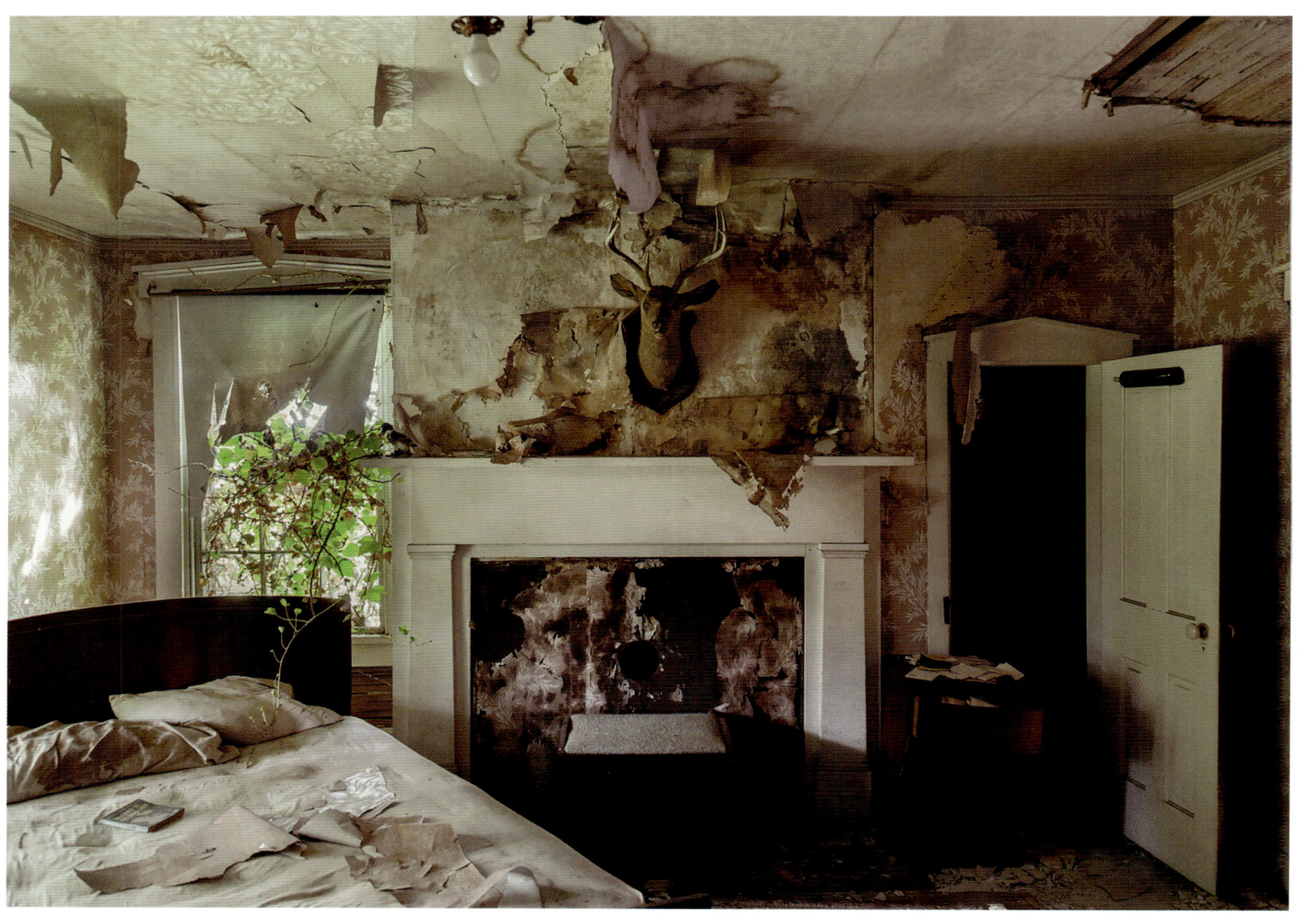

"NATURE TAKES OVER"
Caroline County, Virginia

This house, which dates to the 1850s, was filled with items from the Civil War era. From books to photographs and military and hunting paraphernalia, it was bursting with history. The most unique feature: a family graveyard out front, marking generations of family members.

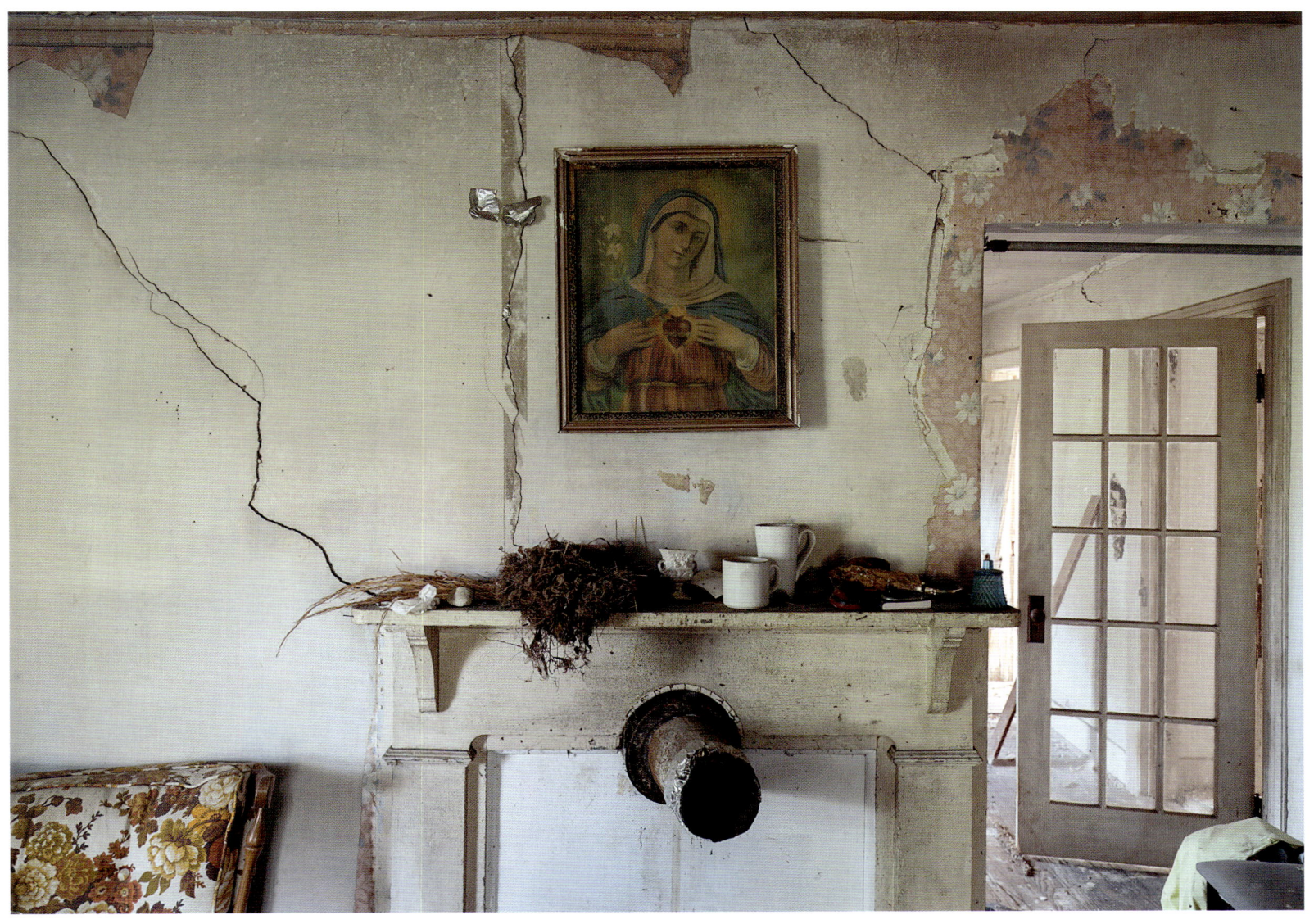

"THE HEART OF MARY"
Westmoreland County, Virginia

This portrait caught my eye, but so did its surroundings. I always find it interesting to see things like bird nests in abandoned homes where nature has reclaimed the space.

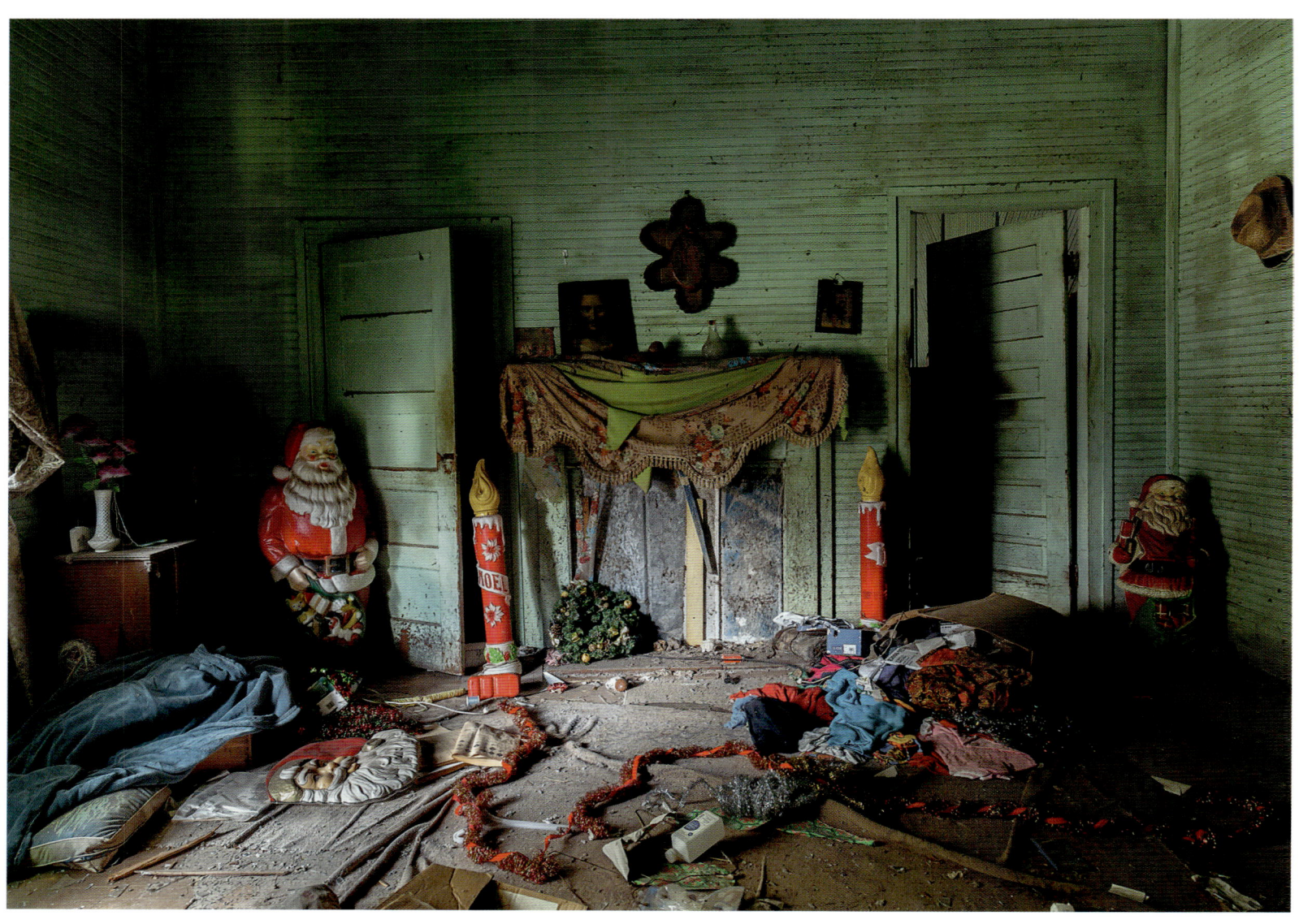

"SILENT NIGHT"
Marlboro County, South Carolina

Walking around this small town in South Carolina, I noticed several abandoned houses, including one with a car still in the driveway. Through the open door of this home, I could see vintage Christmas blow molds thrown about. Further inside, I came upon this living room with a portrait of Jesus, various Christmas items, and a vanity.

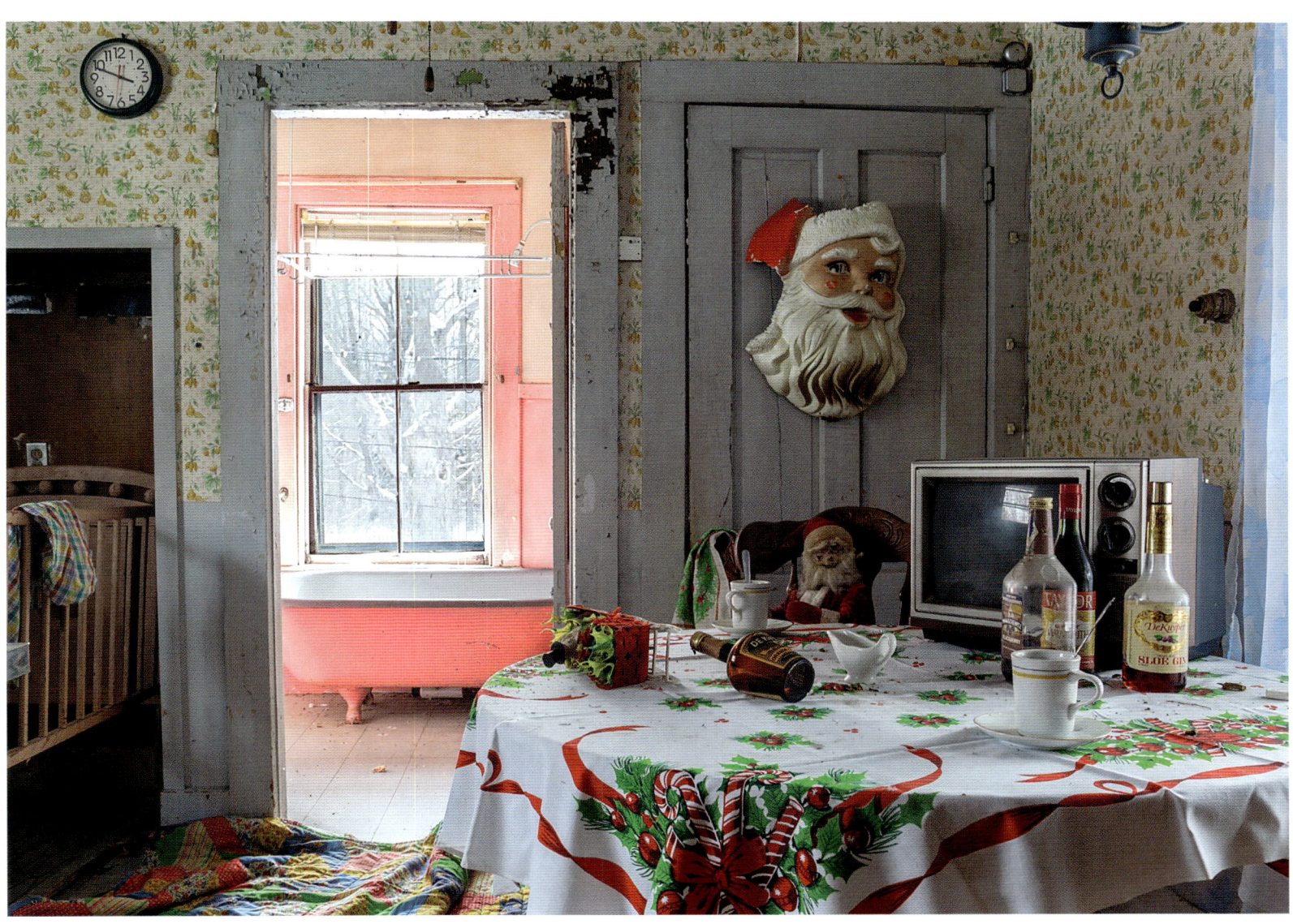

"SANTA CLAUS IS COMING"
Worcester County, Massachusetts

I made my way up a steep, snowy slope to this house high on a hill with a rickety, caving-in front porch. The remains of a deer lay in the snow by a window. I peered inside the home and saw Christmas candles on the windowsill and a table set with mugs and plates. The scene was like an old-time Christmas movie.

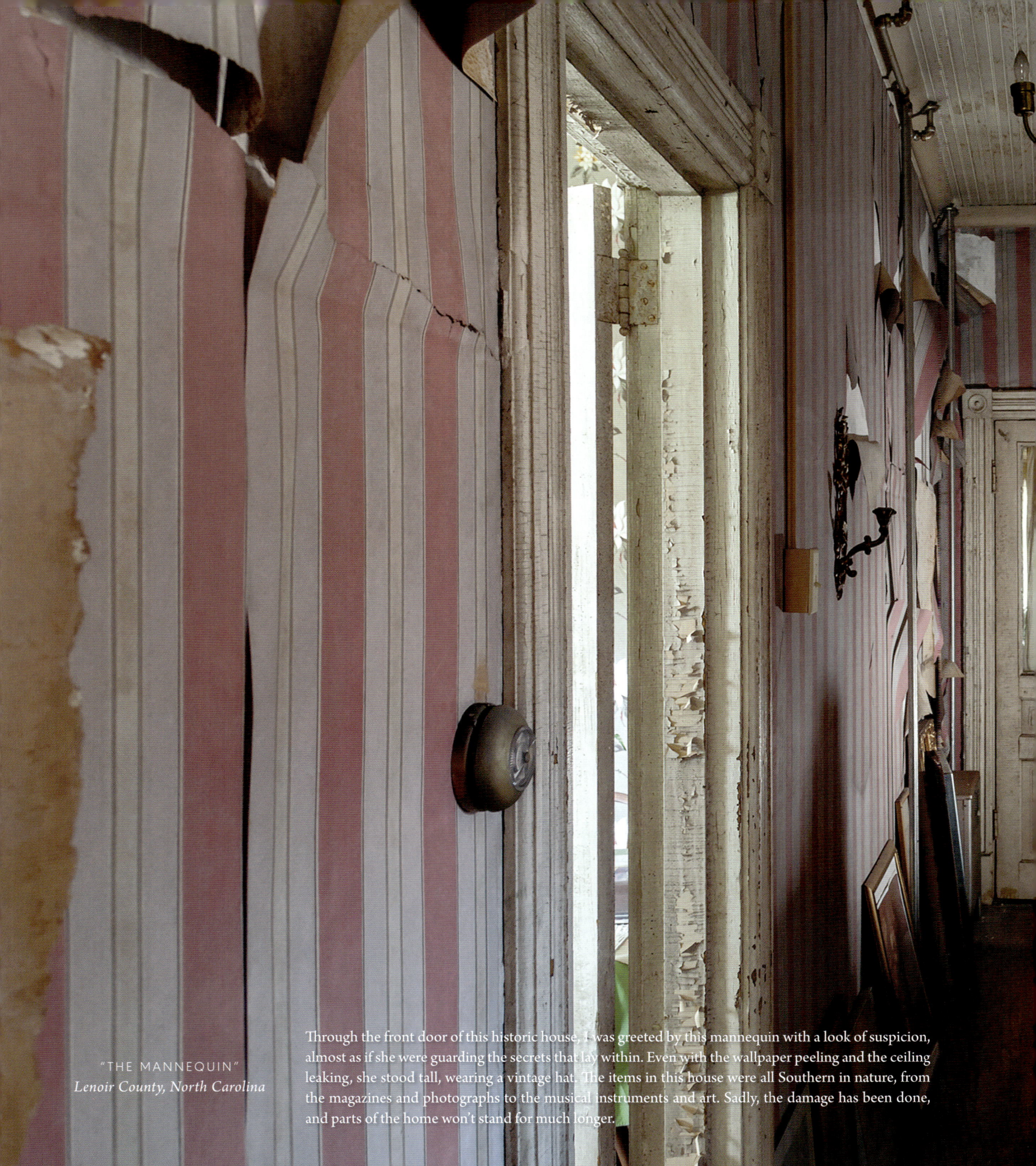

"THE MANNEQUIN"
Lenoir County, North Carolina

Through the front door of this historic house, I was greeted by this mannequin with a look of suspicion, almost as if she were guarding the secrets that lay within. Even with the wallpaper peeling and the ceiling leaking, she stood tall, wearing a vintage hat. The items in this house were all Southern in nature, from the magazines and photographs to the musical instruments and art. Sadly, the damage has been done, and parts of the home won't stand for much longer.

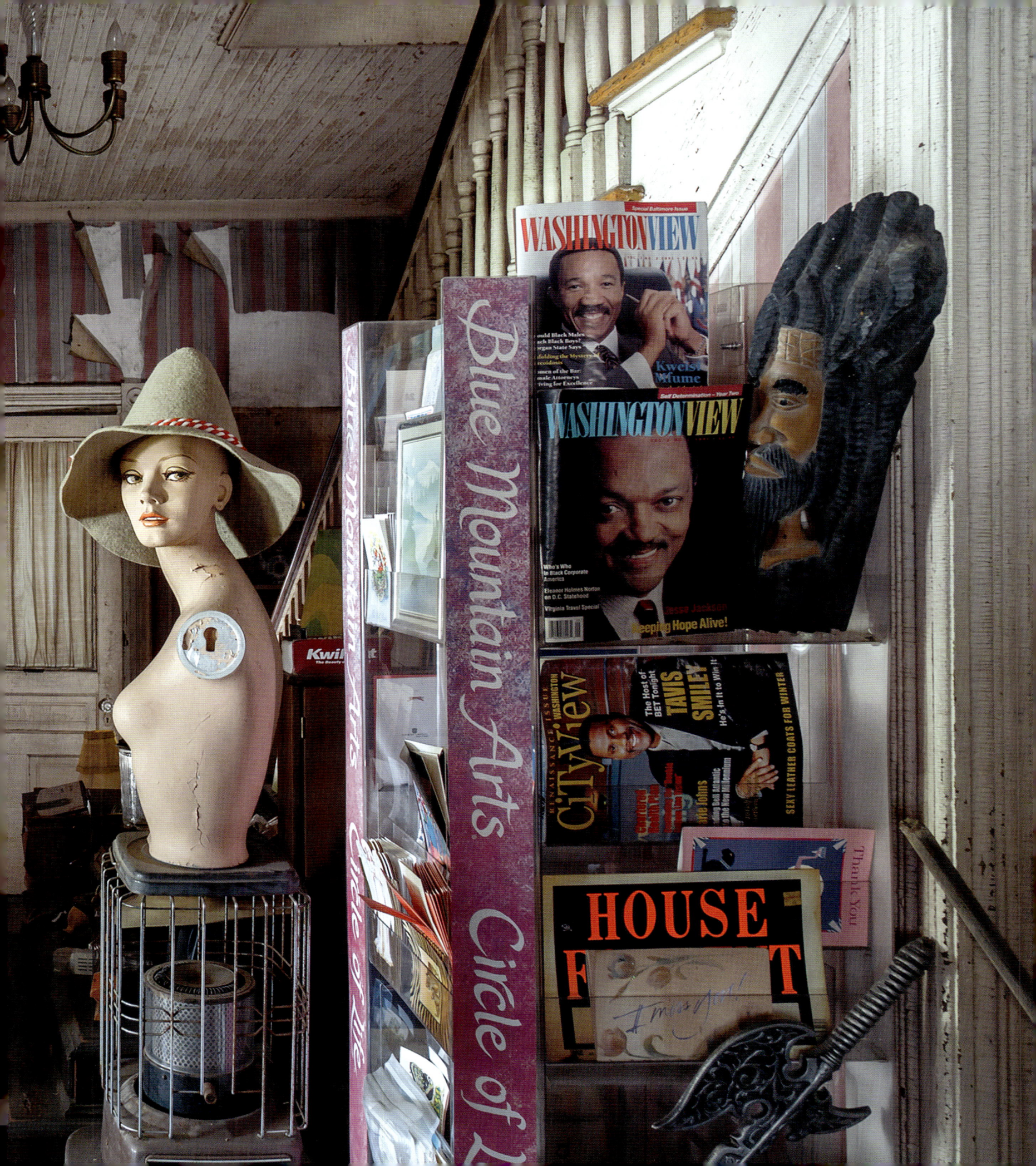

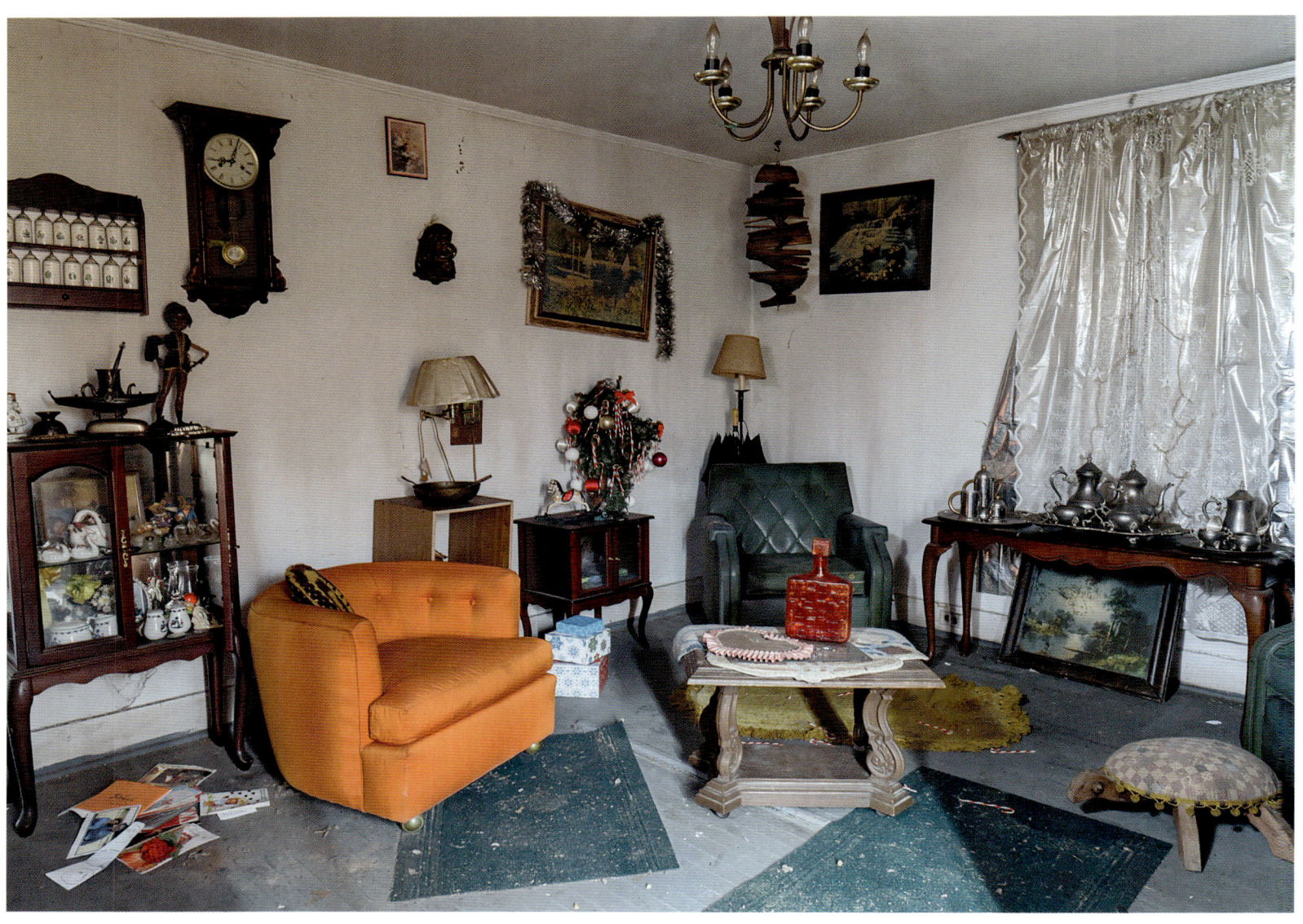

"THE CHRISTMAS HOUSE"
Westmoreland County, Virginia

This house was filled with vintage Christmas items, including a tree with ornaments on it and presents underneath. This small, cozy room had an antique fireplace stove, a cabinet filled with china, and religious items. Like so many abandoned homes, it was very dark inside, and many of the rooms were too dark to photograph. With a long exposure, the colors here came to life.

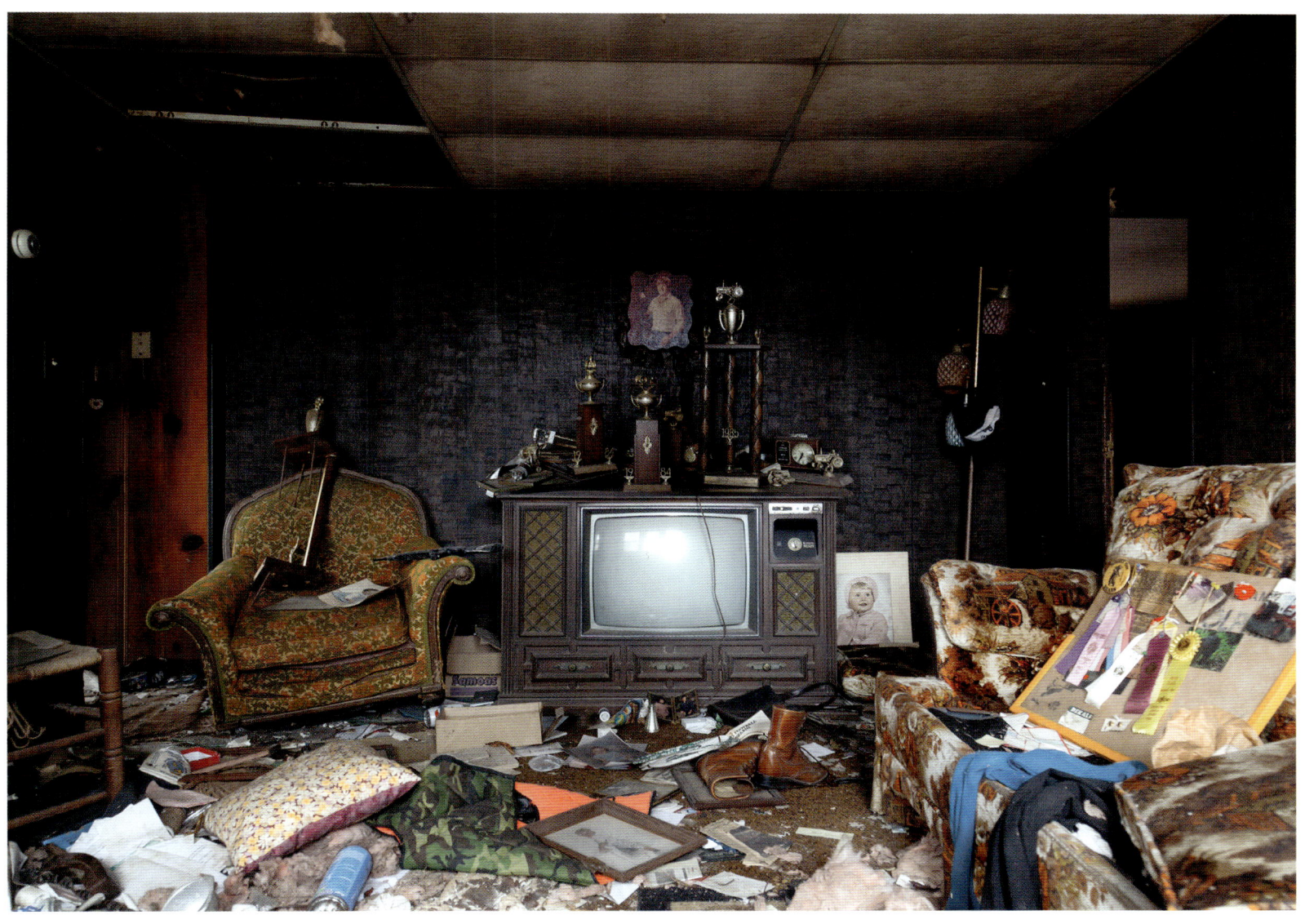

"THE FARMER'S PRIZES"
Harrison County, Ohio

Driving down a road, I noticed a small abandoned house under a tree up on a hill. An old barn sat across the street. I parked my car and made my way around to the back of the house, where I saw an open door. That door led to a living room with a TV covered with farming trophies, with awards for best tractors and prized livestock among them.

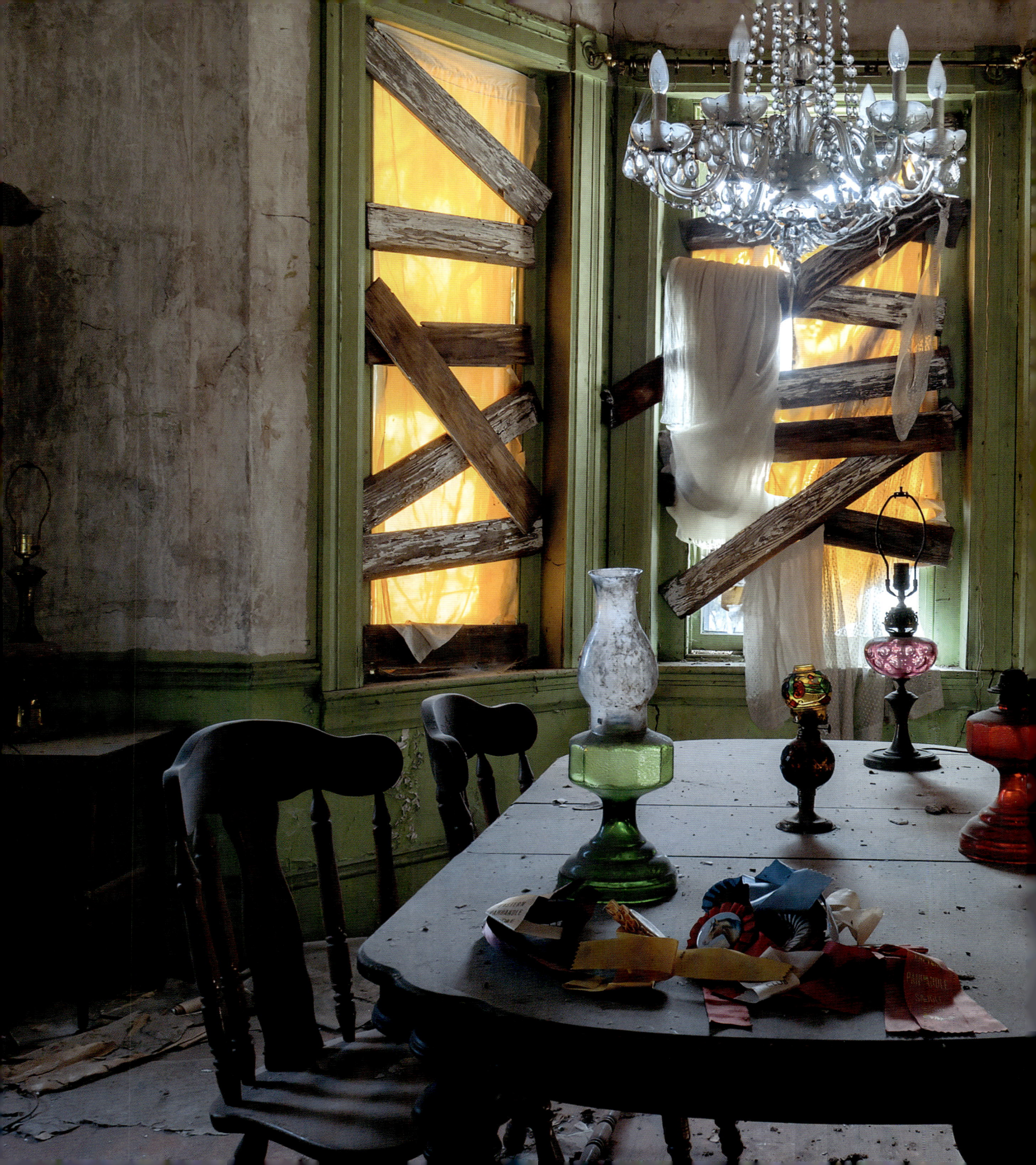

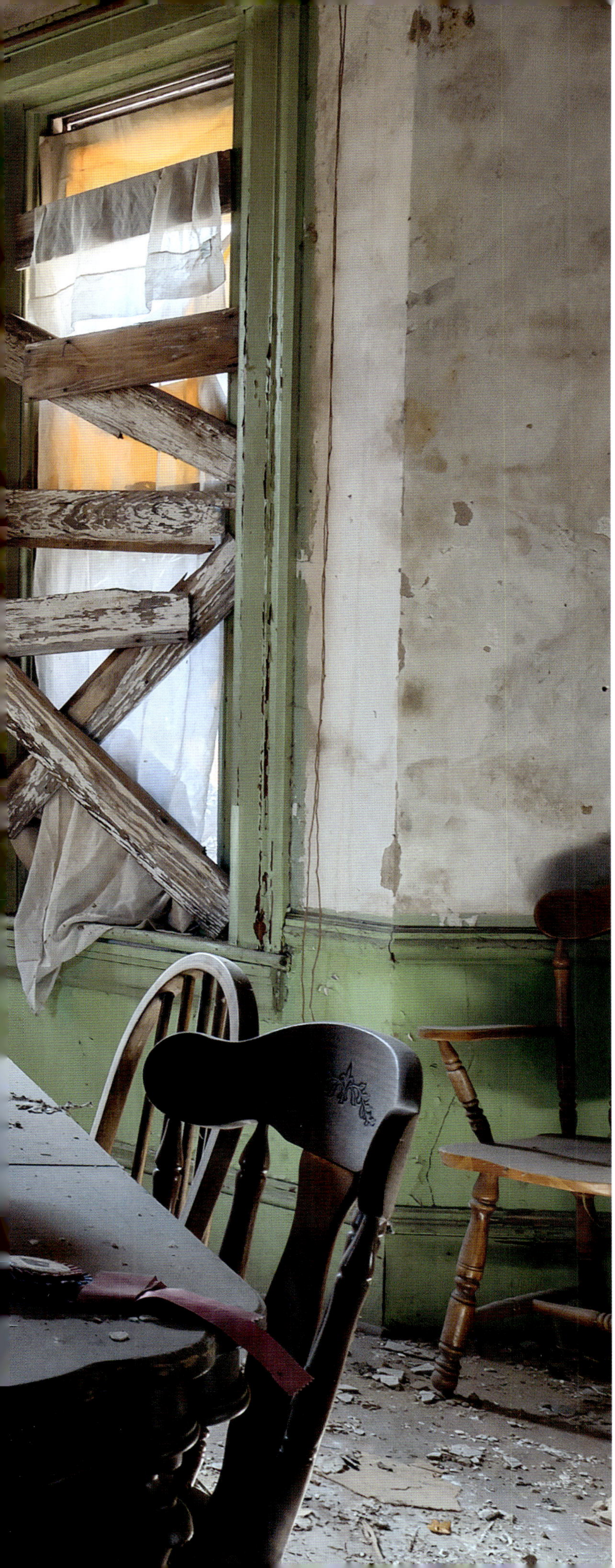

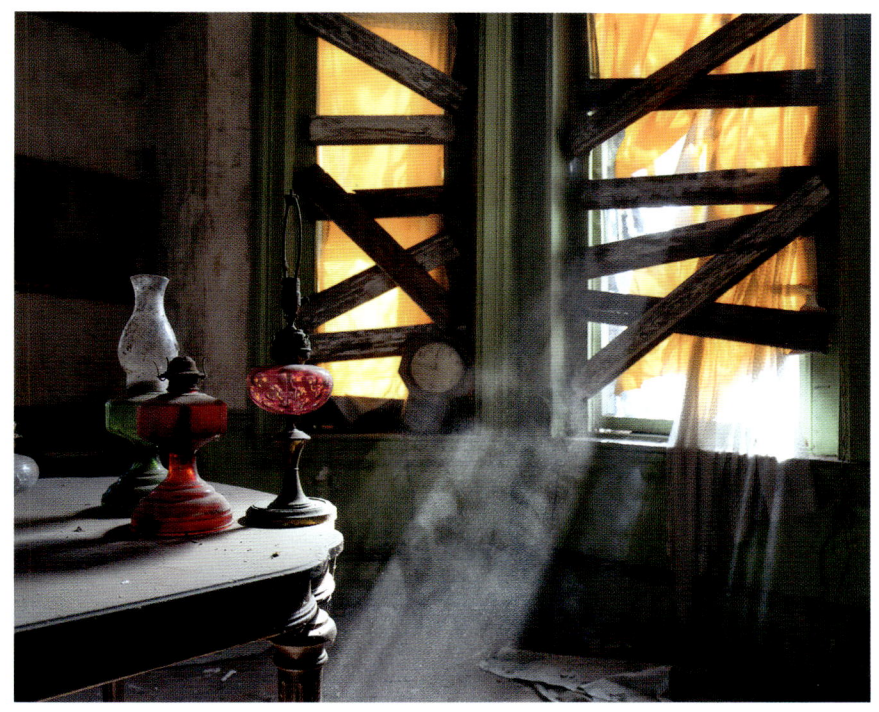

"THE EQUESTRIANS' HOME"
Frederick County, Virginia

I discovered this abandoned house by seeing it from a nearby highway. From the outside, the house was grand in every way, so it was shocking to find this room inside. With the green trim and the colorful lanterns on the table, it's one of my favorites among the rooms I've photographed—the way the windows were boarded up from the inside, behind the curtains, makes it look like the set of a horror film. The course ribbons and paintings are clues that the previous residents were horse owners and likely very competitive equestrians.

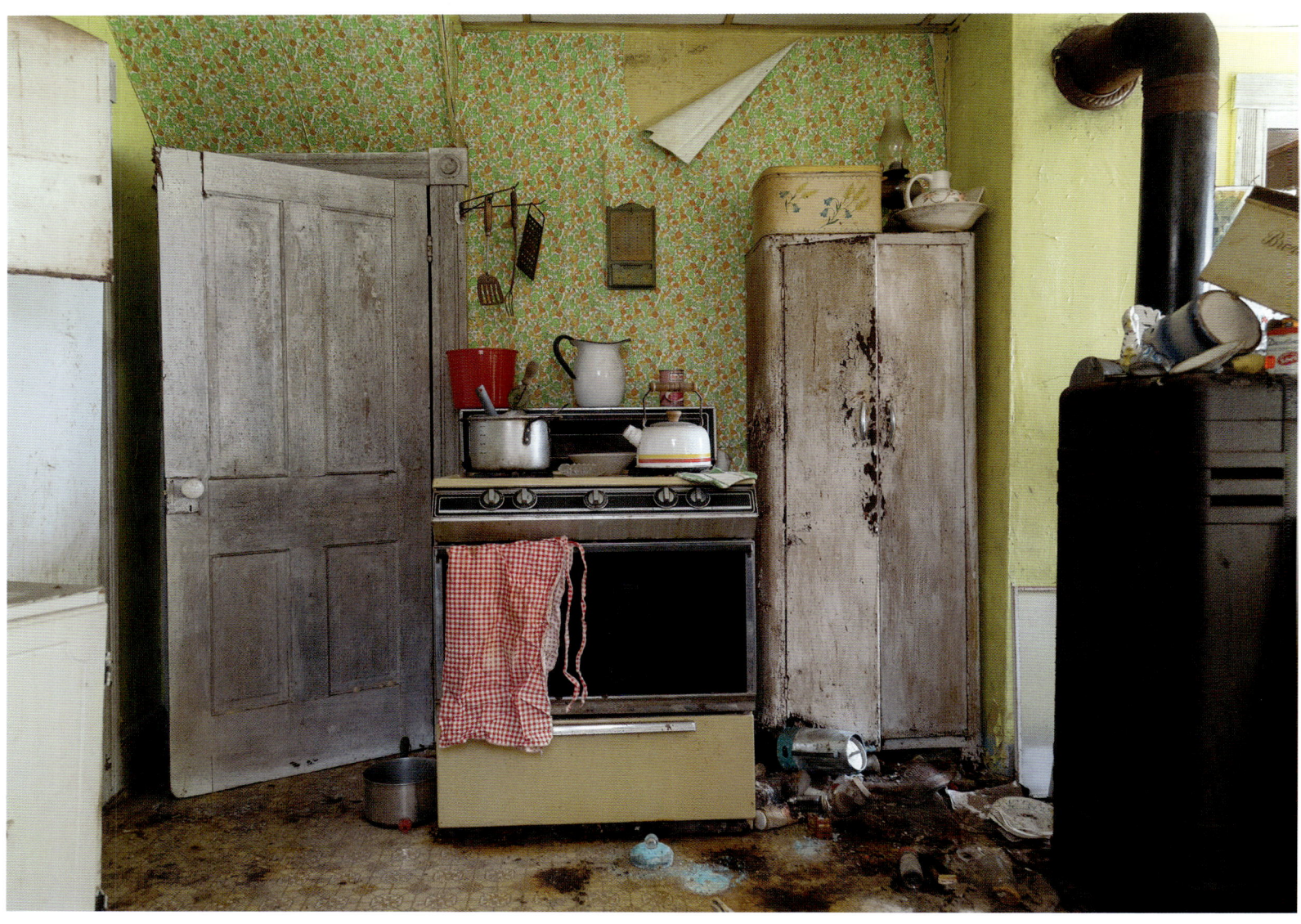

"A COZY KITCHEN"
Kent County, Maryland

This kitchen was filled with appliances from the 1950s or '60s; perhaps that was the last time they were used. A cabinet to the left was filled with mid-century bottles, dishes, and glasses. The floral wallpaper made this the cheeriest kitchen I've come across.

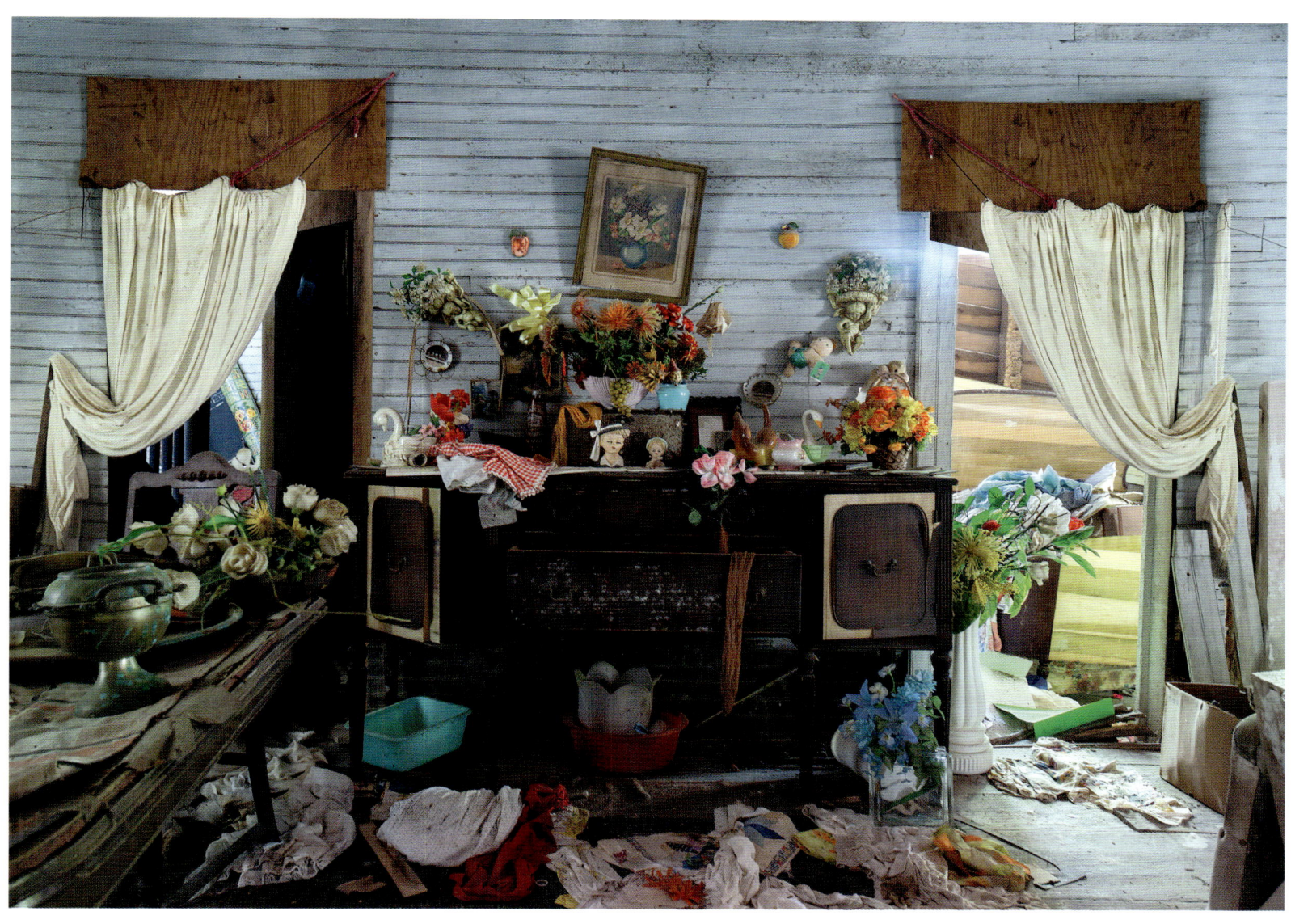

"GRANDMA'S FLOWERS"
Halifax County, North Carolina

There was so much to photograph in this house where an elderly woman once lived. This dining room was the next room over from the living room.

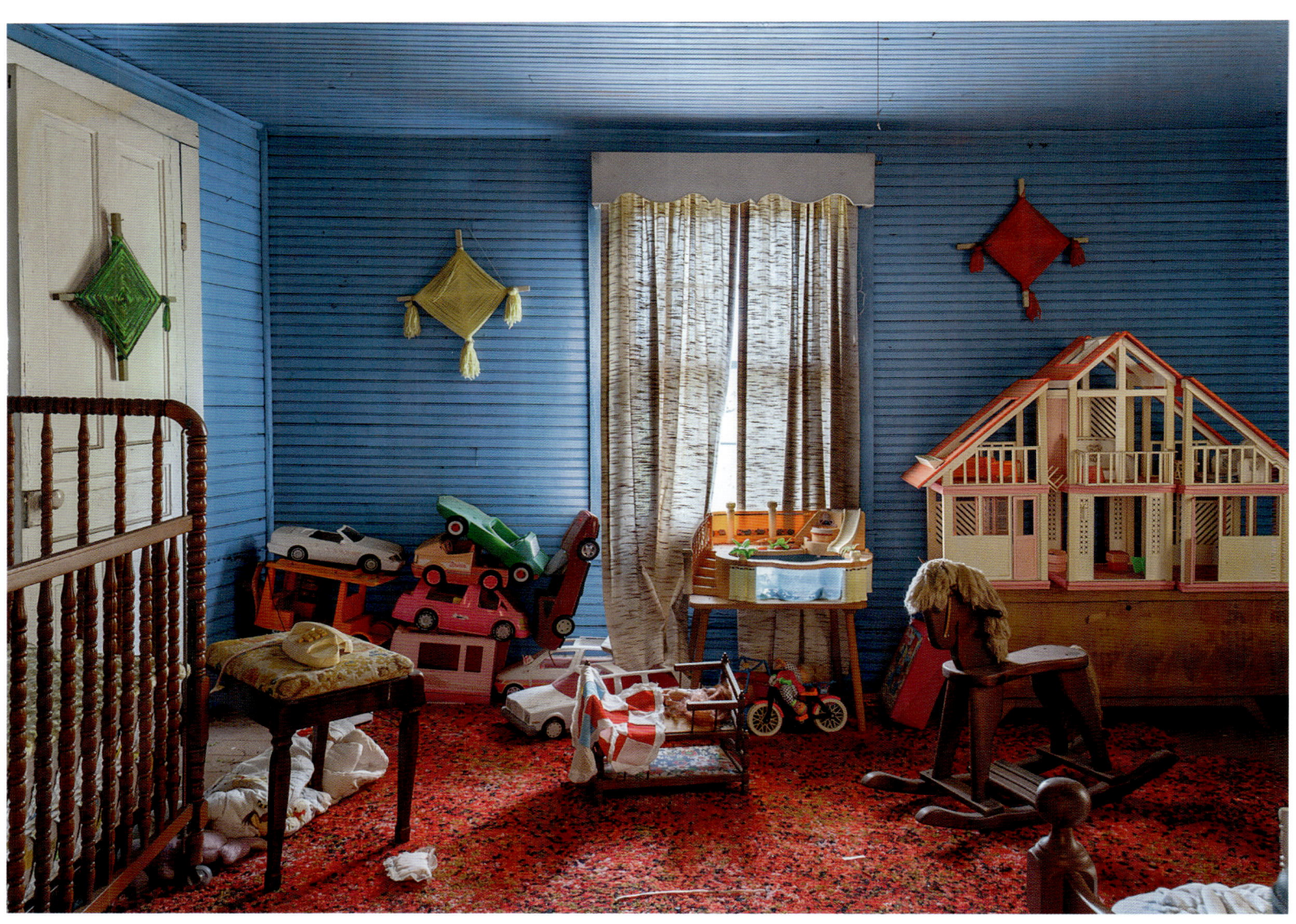

"THE PLAYROOMS"
Pitt County, North Carolina

It's not often that I find rooms filled with such childhood nostalgia as this one, with toy cars, a rocking horse, and a large dollhouse. There was also a door on the left side of the room that opened into a space (opposite) that may have been every child's dream play area. This home is sinking on the first floor, but the upstairs holds a huge collection of toys from primarily the 1970s and '80s.

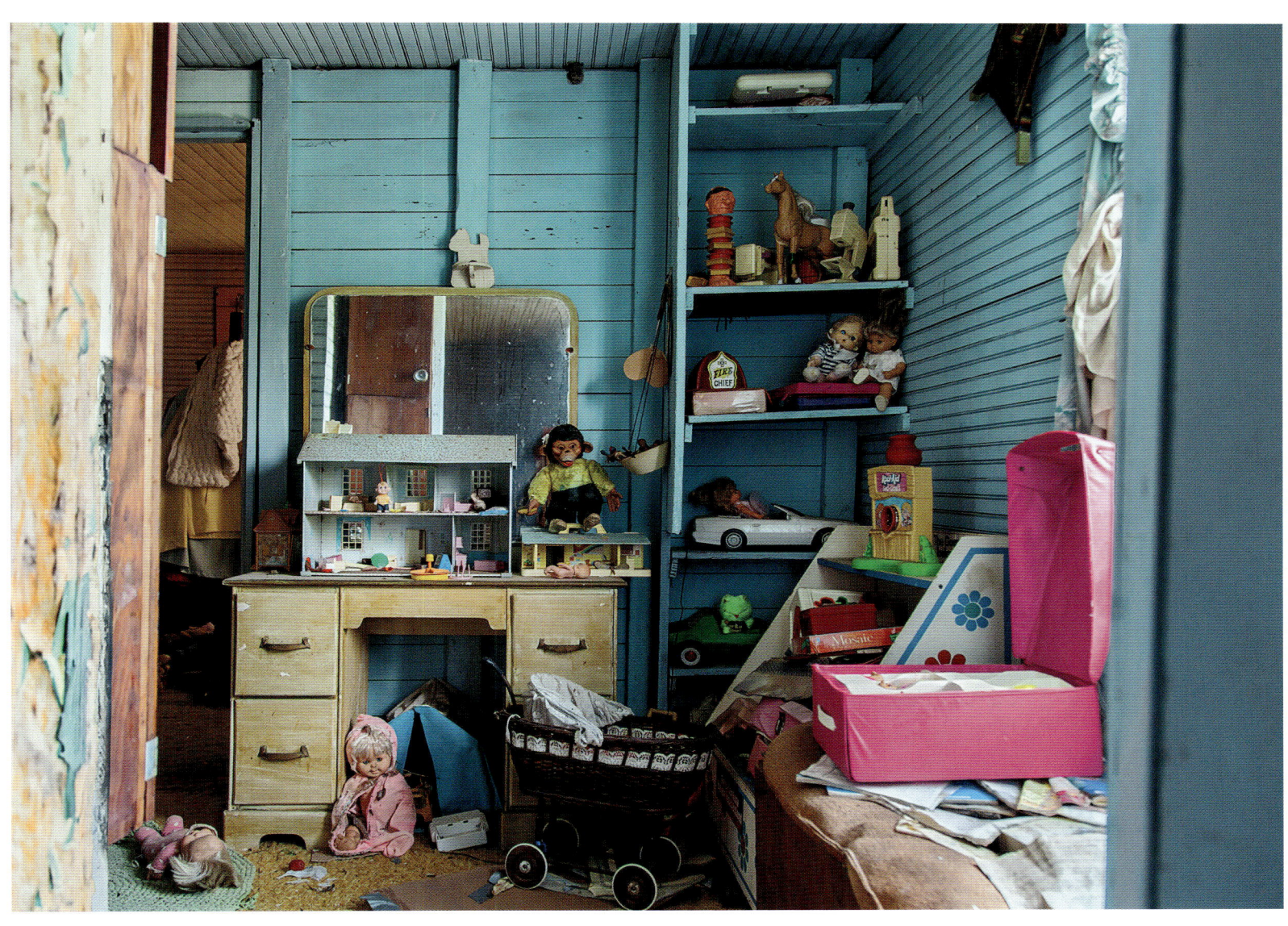

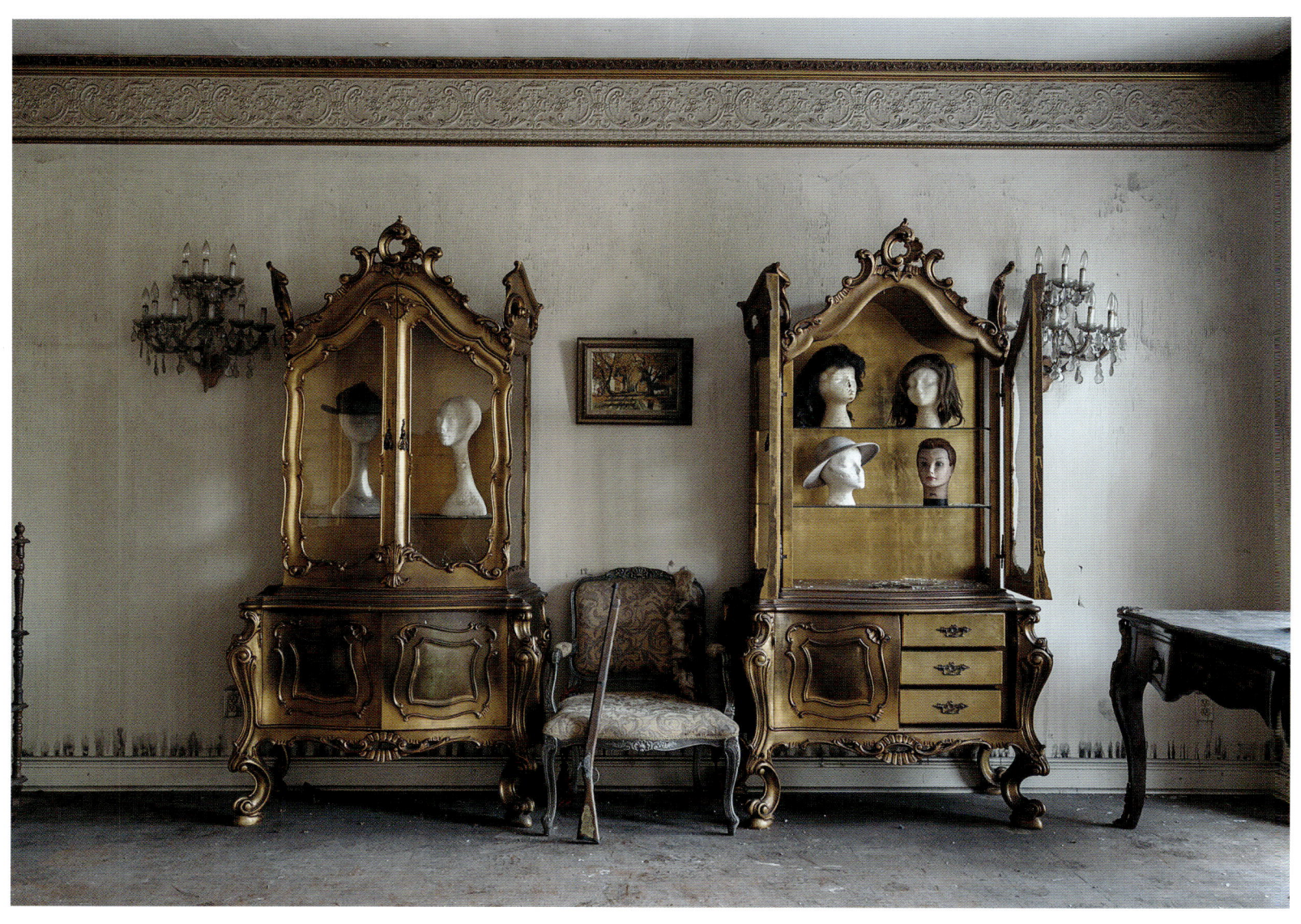

"THE HEAD HUNTER"
Rockland County, New York

This house had experienced a fire, and many valuable possessions were left behind. When I walked in, there were already people inside, taking photos and videos. I assume someone found the mannequin heads in another room and placed them in the cabinets.

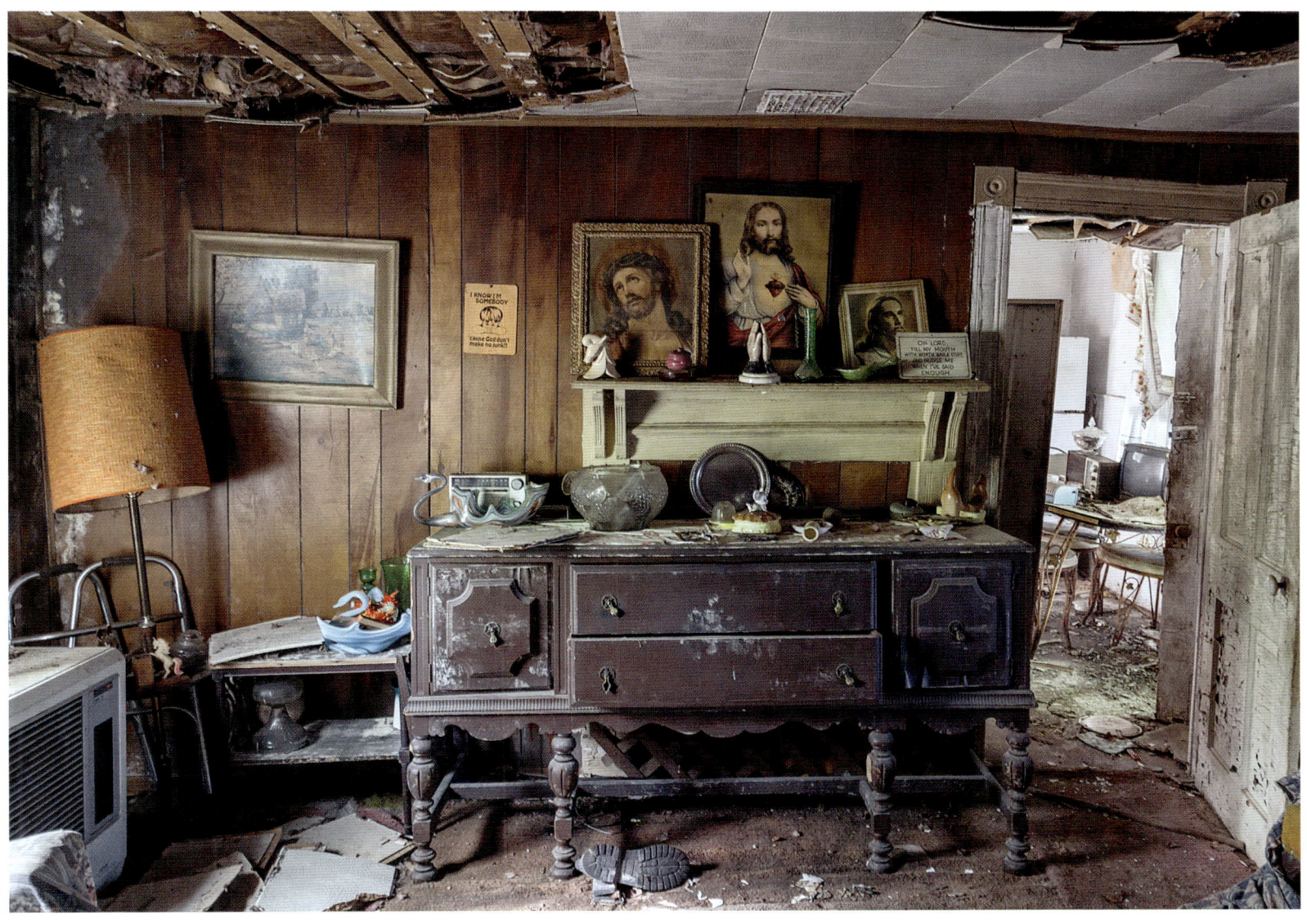

"A WORSHIPPER'S HOME"
Dorchester County, Maryland

This home was filled with religious items like traditional paintings and relics, as well as cheeky sayings. A sign on the mantel reads, "Oh Lord, fill my mouth with worthwhile stuff, and nudge me when I've said enough."

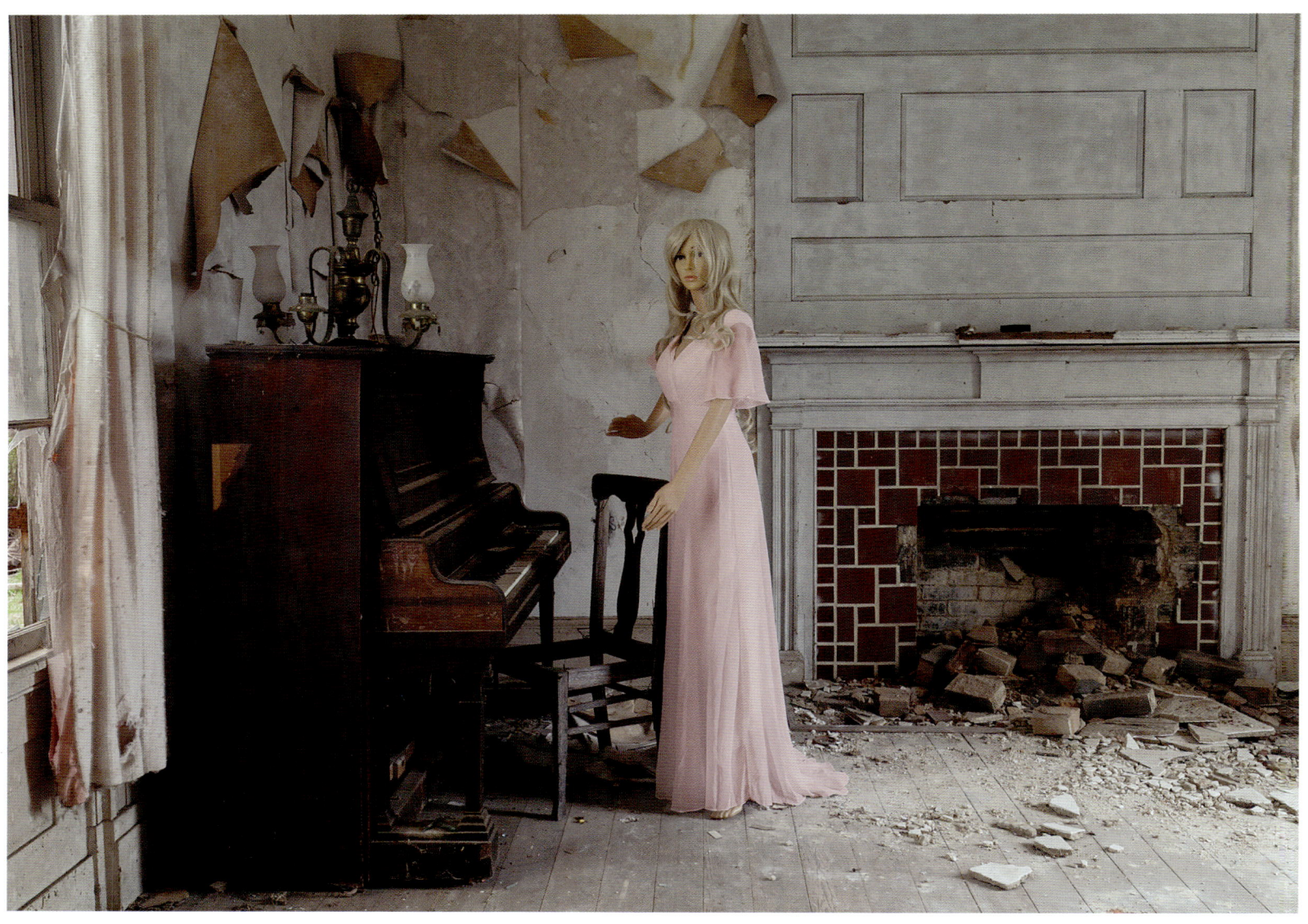

"LADY IN PINK"
Fluvanna County, Virginia

Driving through rural Virginia, I came across a house that looked intriguing from the outside. Inside, it was completely empty except for the objects in this room. It was beautiful yet unsettling.

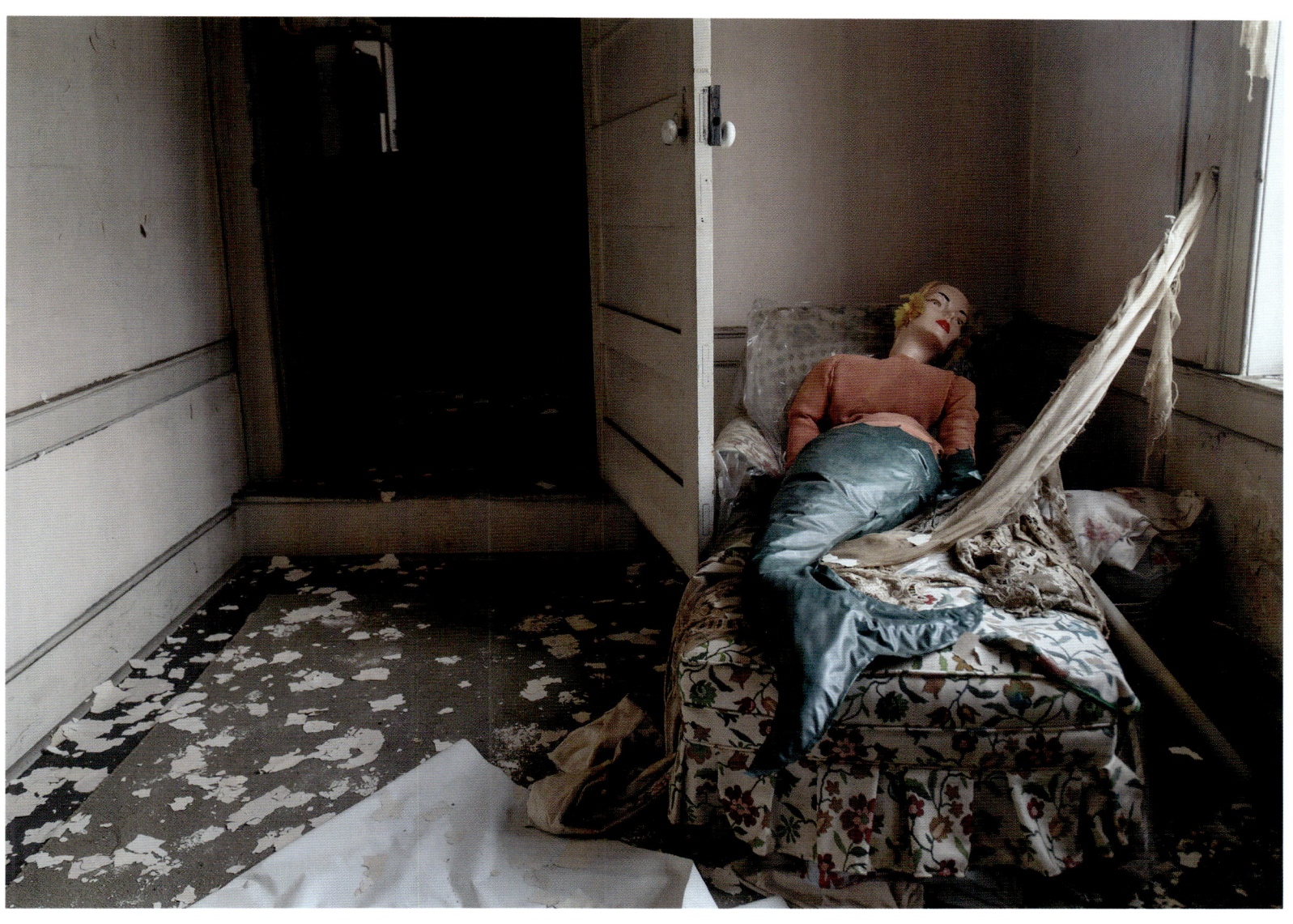

The history of this home is like a real-life movie, involving a serial killer and a famous author. Most items in the house align perfectly with its bizarre backstory, but the connection to the many mermaids found inside is a mystery as deep as the ocean. Why were they lying around everywhere, and even hanging in the closets?

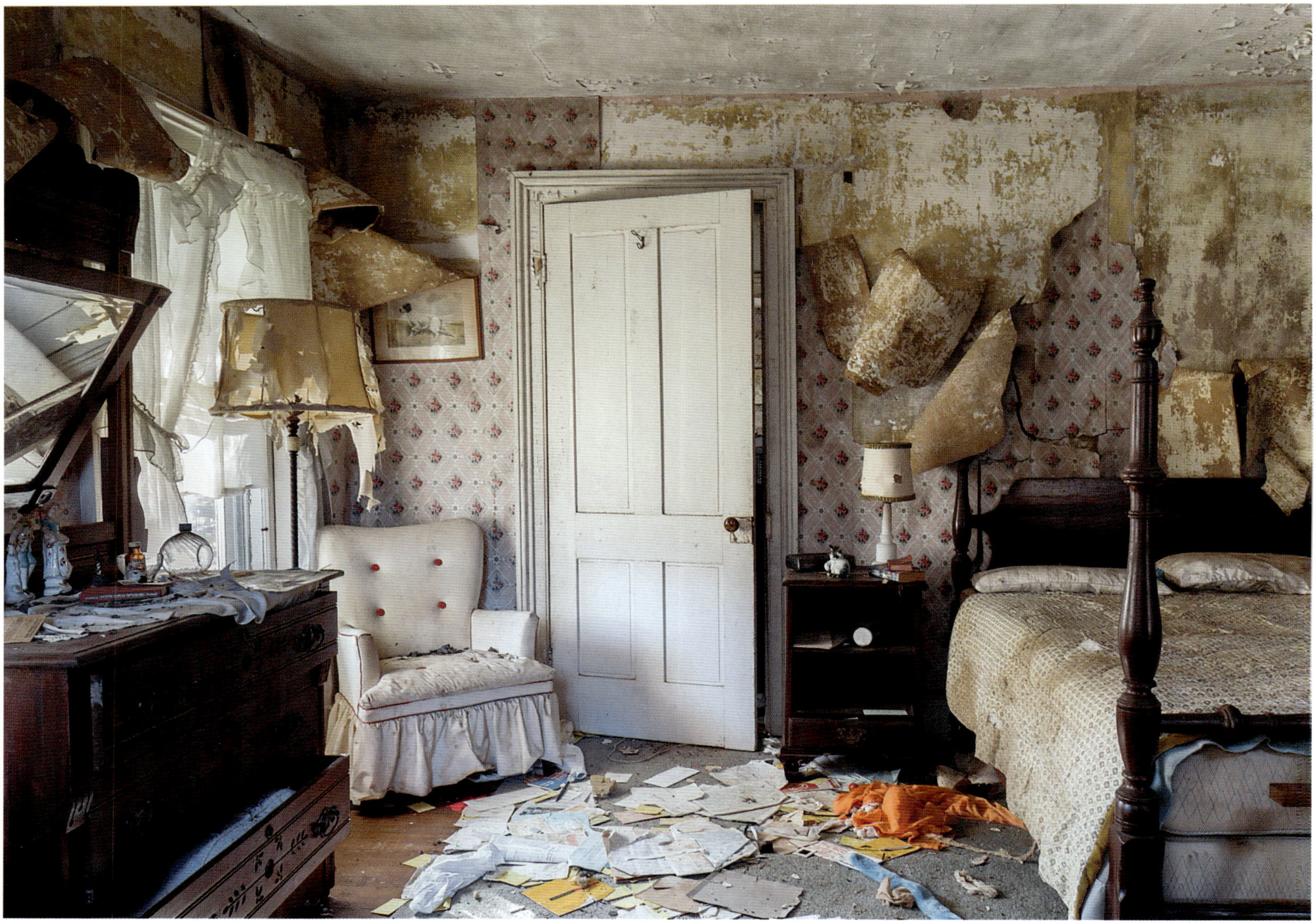

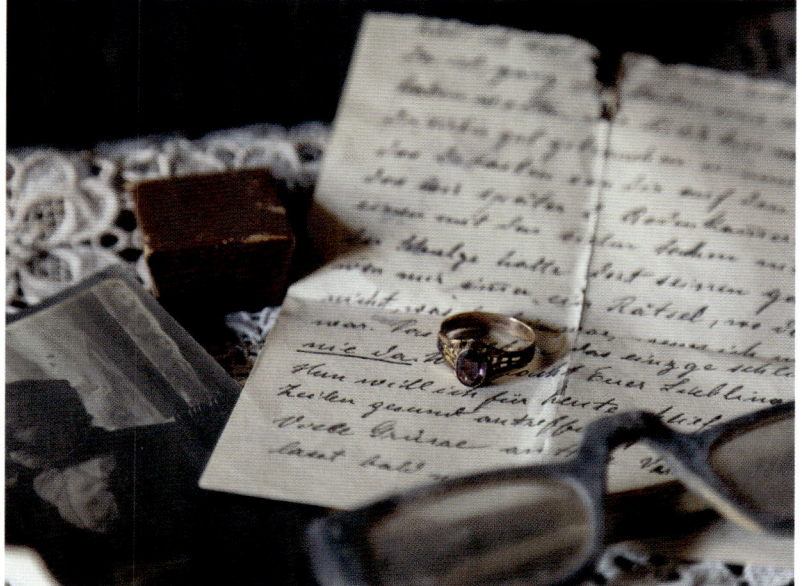

"THE GERMAN FAMILY'S HOME"
Warren County, New Jersey

This was the home of a German American family and it looked like the occupants had left in a hurry, in the middle of packing. Places like this can be unsettling, as if the owners will return any moment.

A portrait of a woman in a Victorian dress, a pair of glasses, a ring, and a handwritten note are all clues about the owners.

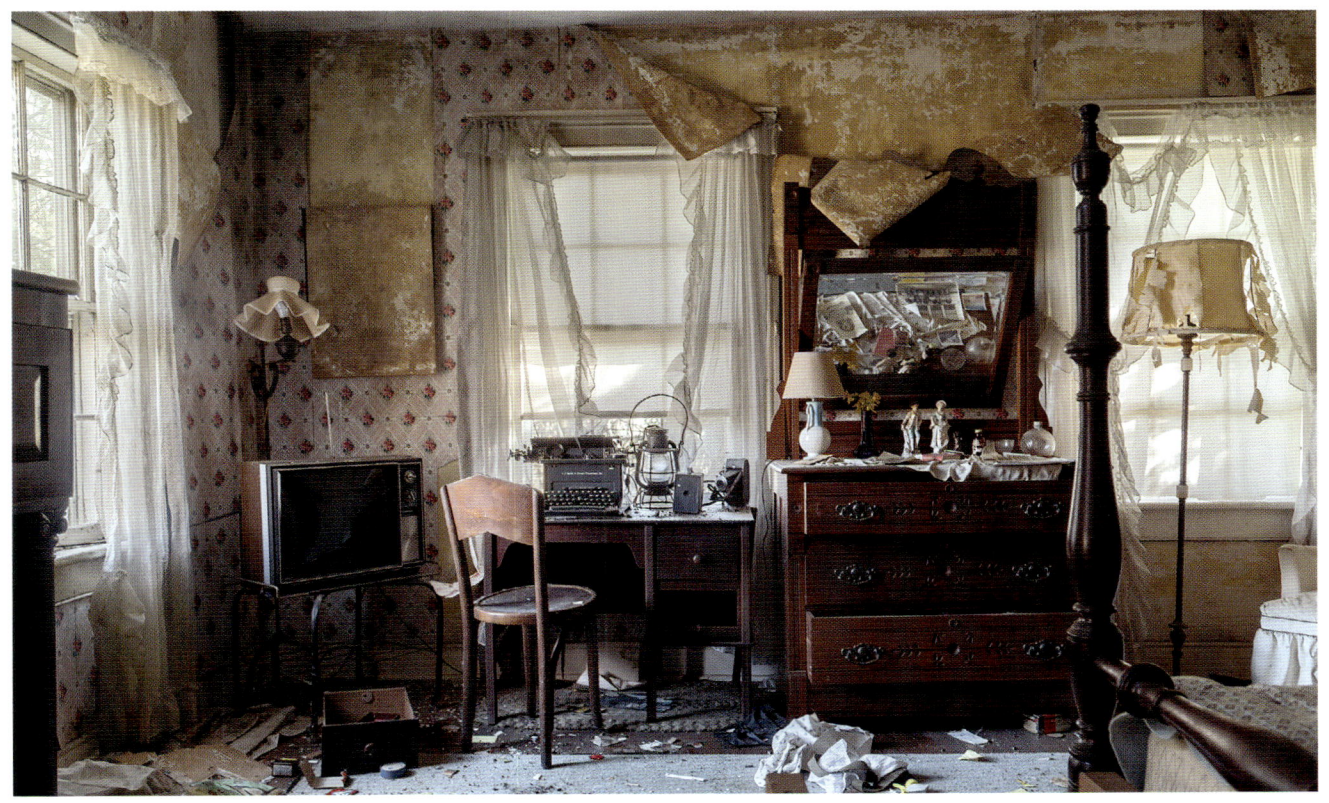

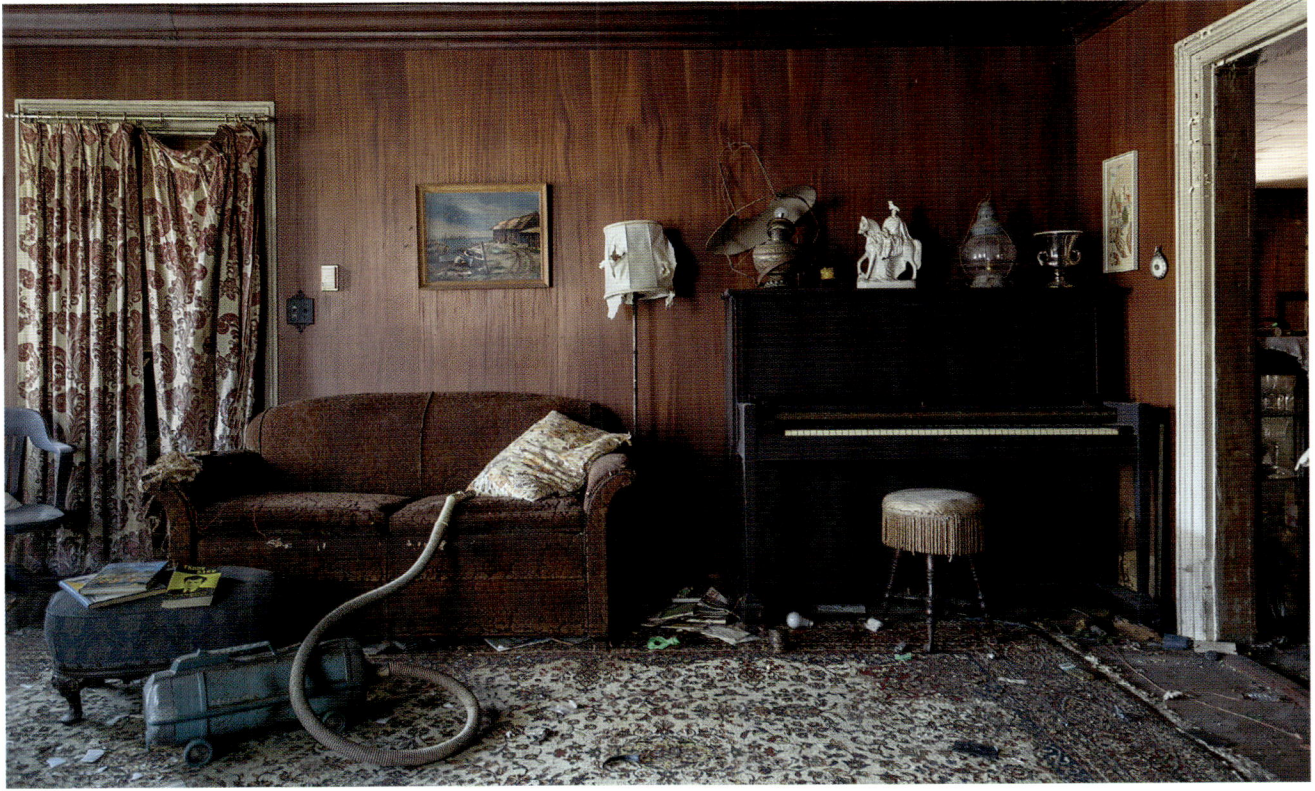

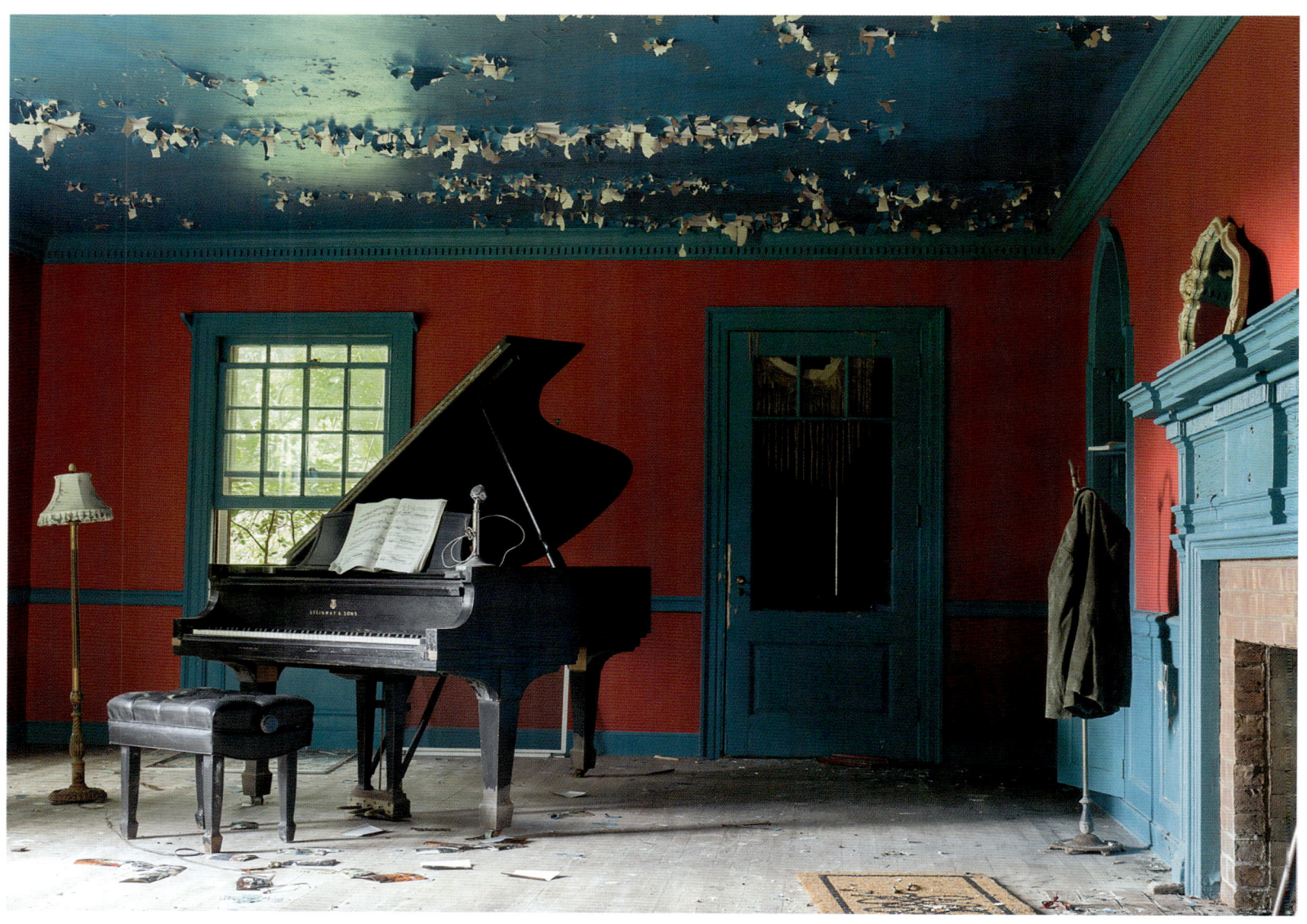

"THE STEINWAY"
Suffolk County, New York

This Steinway piano sits in a room with family photographs scattered around. The house had not been vacant for long, proving how quickly natural things like temperature can do damage.

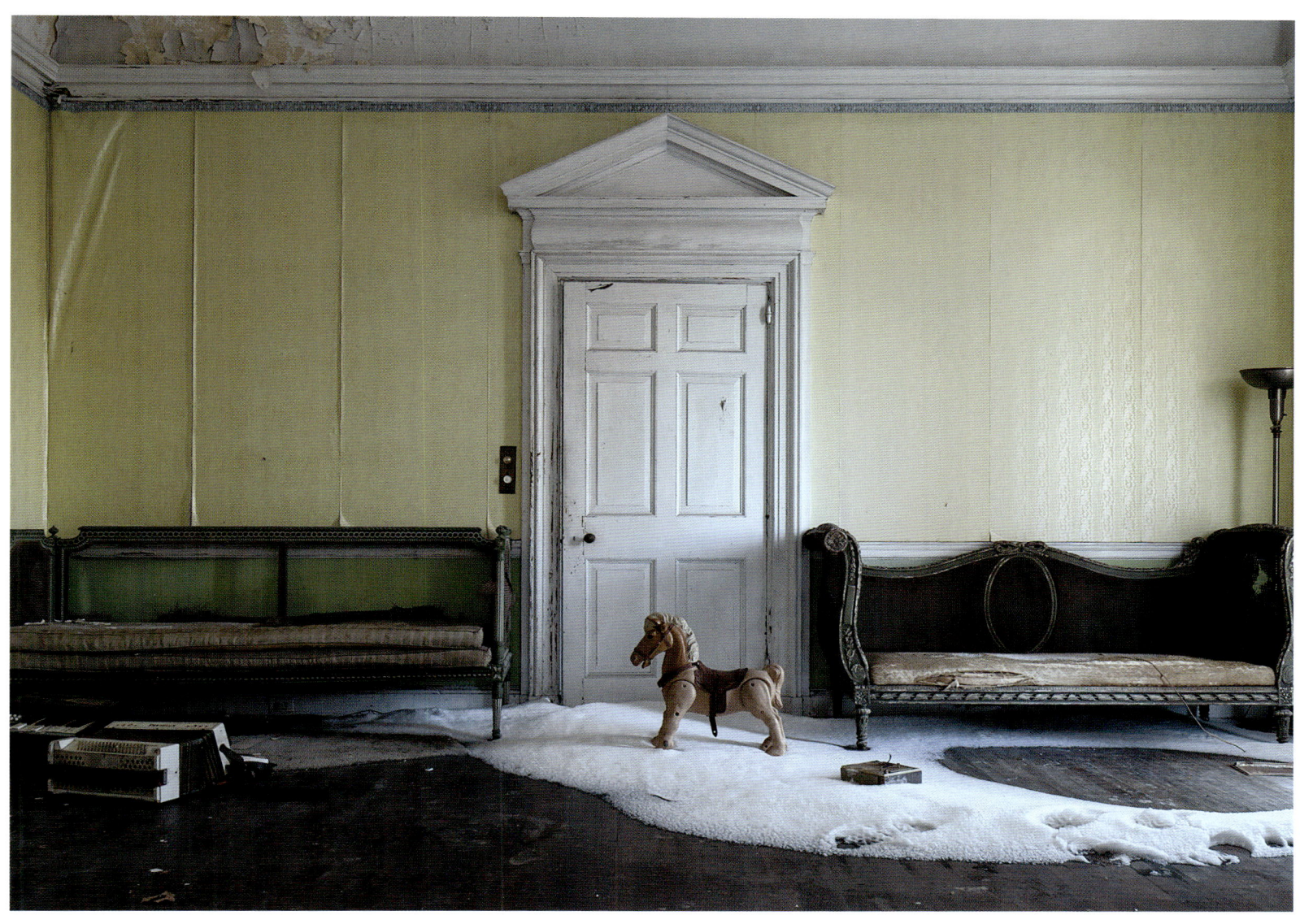

"FROZEN IN TIME"
Suffolk County, New York

In this mansion, the windows were blown out and the doors were wide open, leaving everything inside exposed to the elements. On this winter day, a snowstorm encroached into the living room.

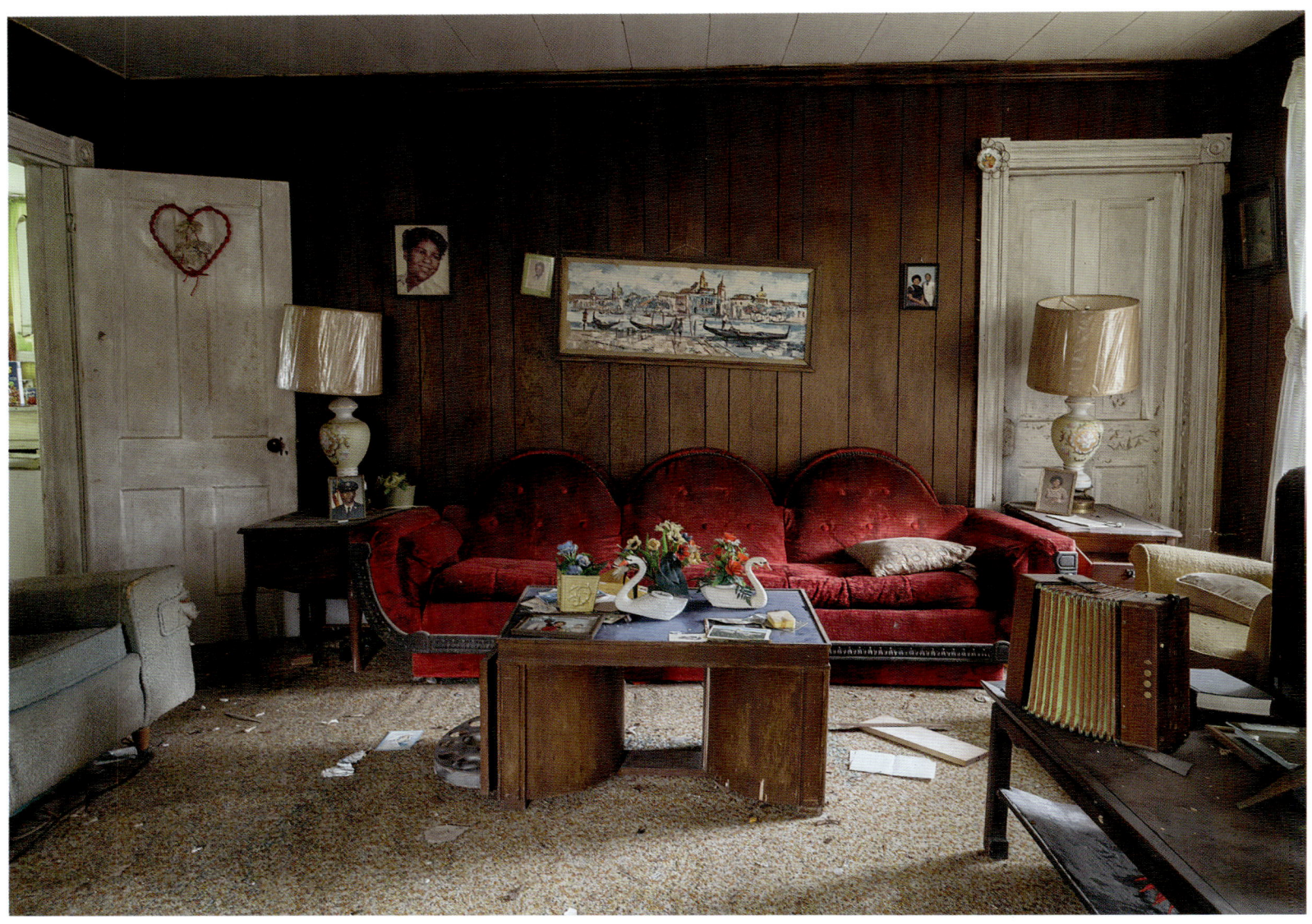

"THE LOVERS' DEN"
Kent County, Maryland

Hidden behind trees, this home prompted me to pull over. The front door lay on the ground and led me into a time capsule. Many of the items left behind were vintage, and they provided a glimpse into the life of the previous owners. Fun fact: The street this house was on was called "Lovers Lane."

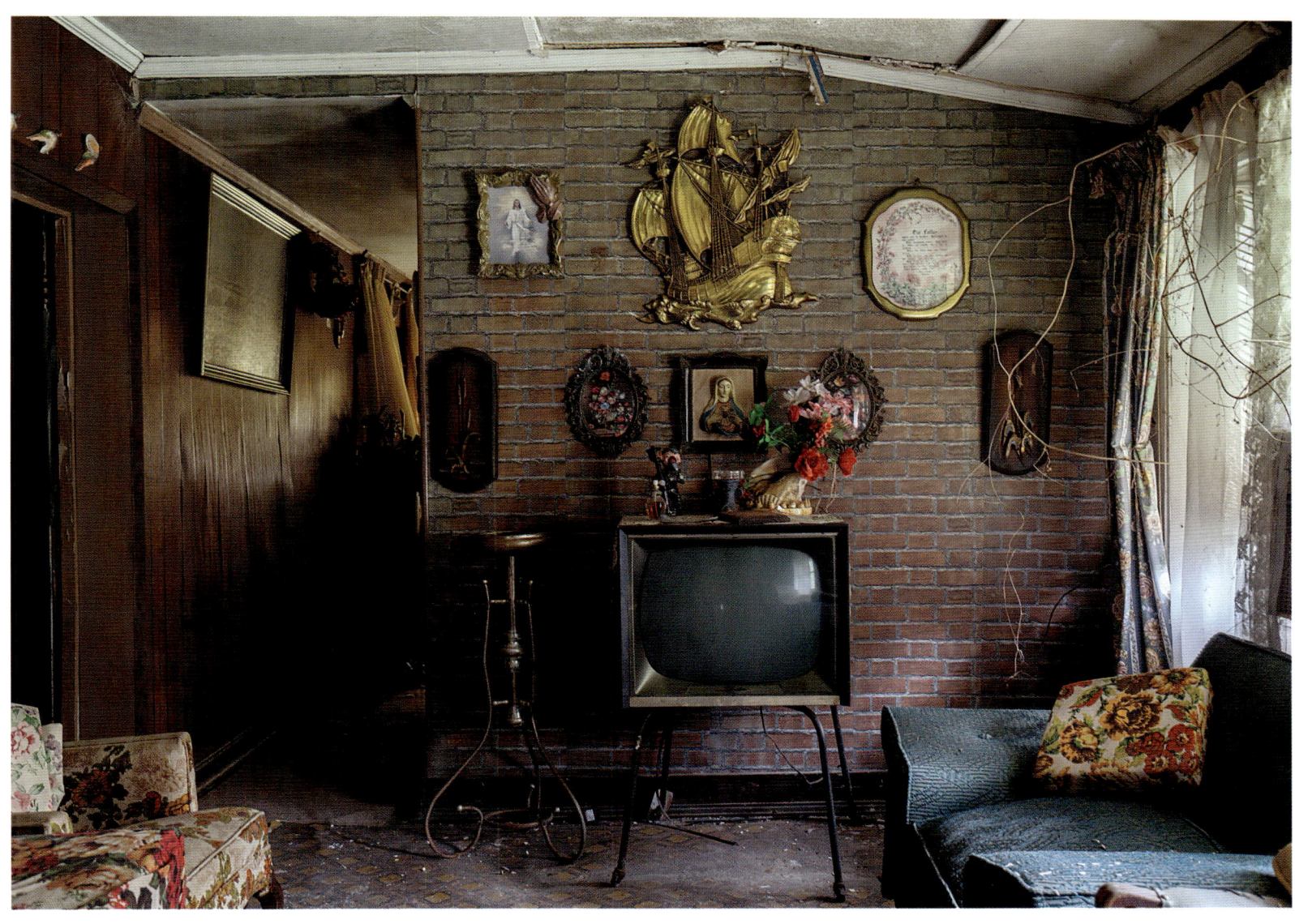

"THE GOLDEN SHIP"
Talbot County, Georgia

Every other room in this home was filled to the ceiling with mid-century antiques; this room was a mix of different time periods, along with religious artifacts. It's always fascinating to see what items people put together.

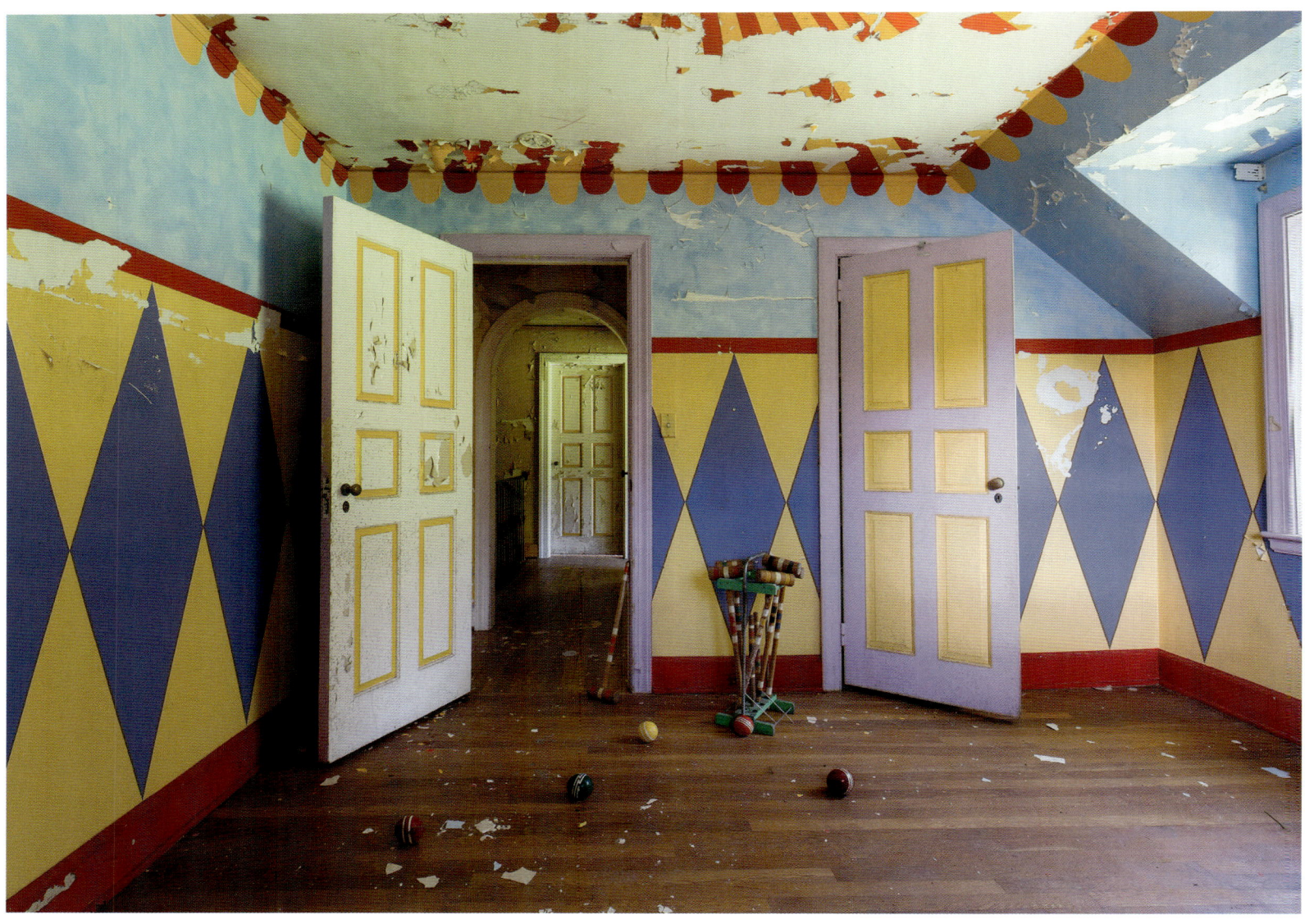

This room and stairway are located in an entirely circus-themed house. The peeling paint and vibrant colors inside made it one of the most eccentric places I've photographed, with a yellow foyer and staircase (seen on pages 48-49), a green living room, and a blue-and-orange bedroom. Even the bathroom was painted in red and white stripes.

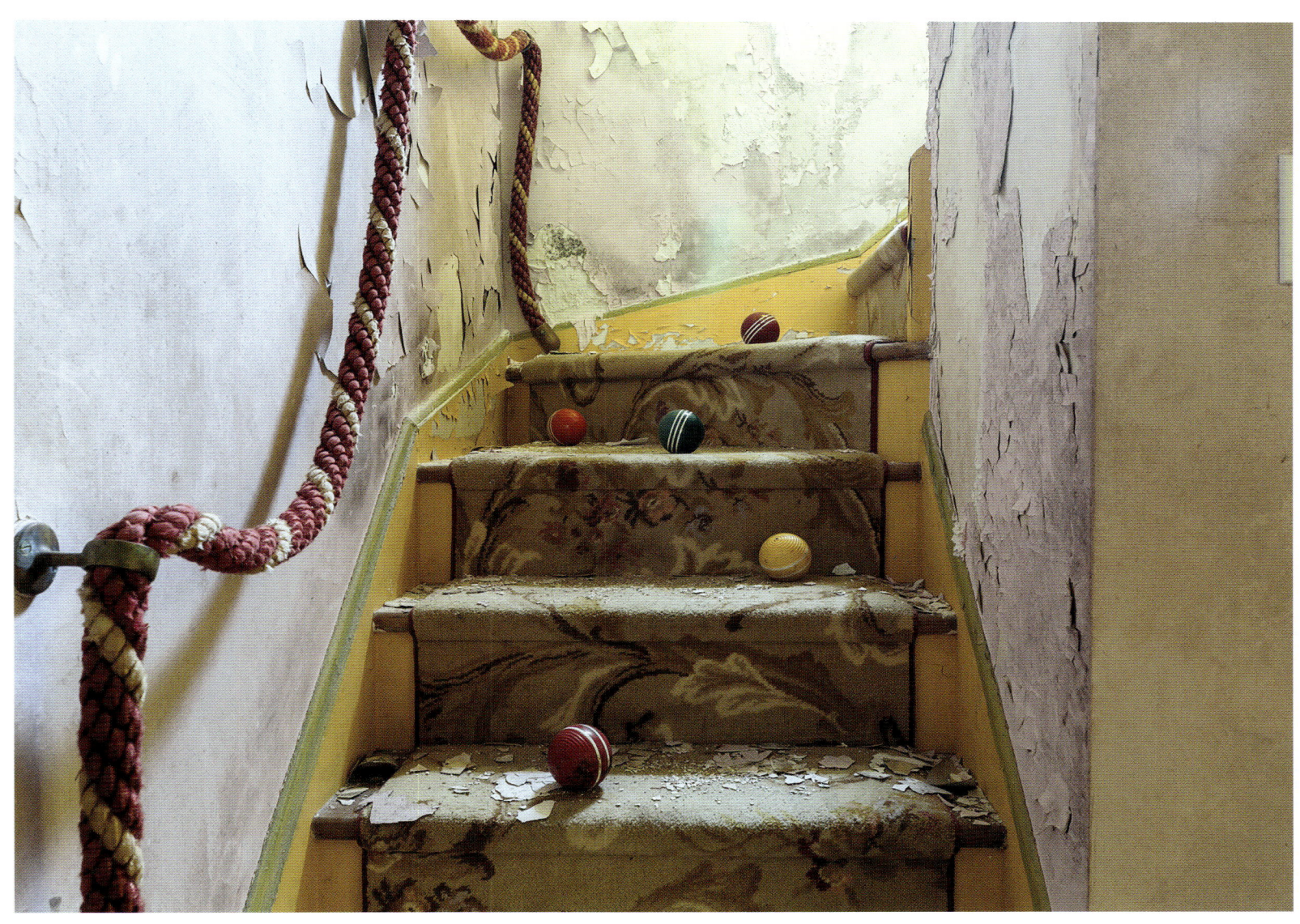

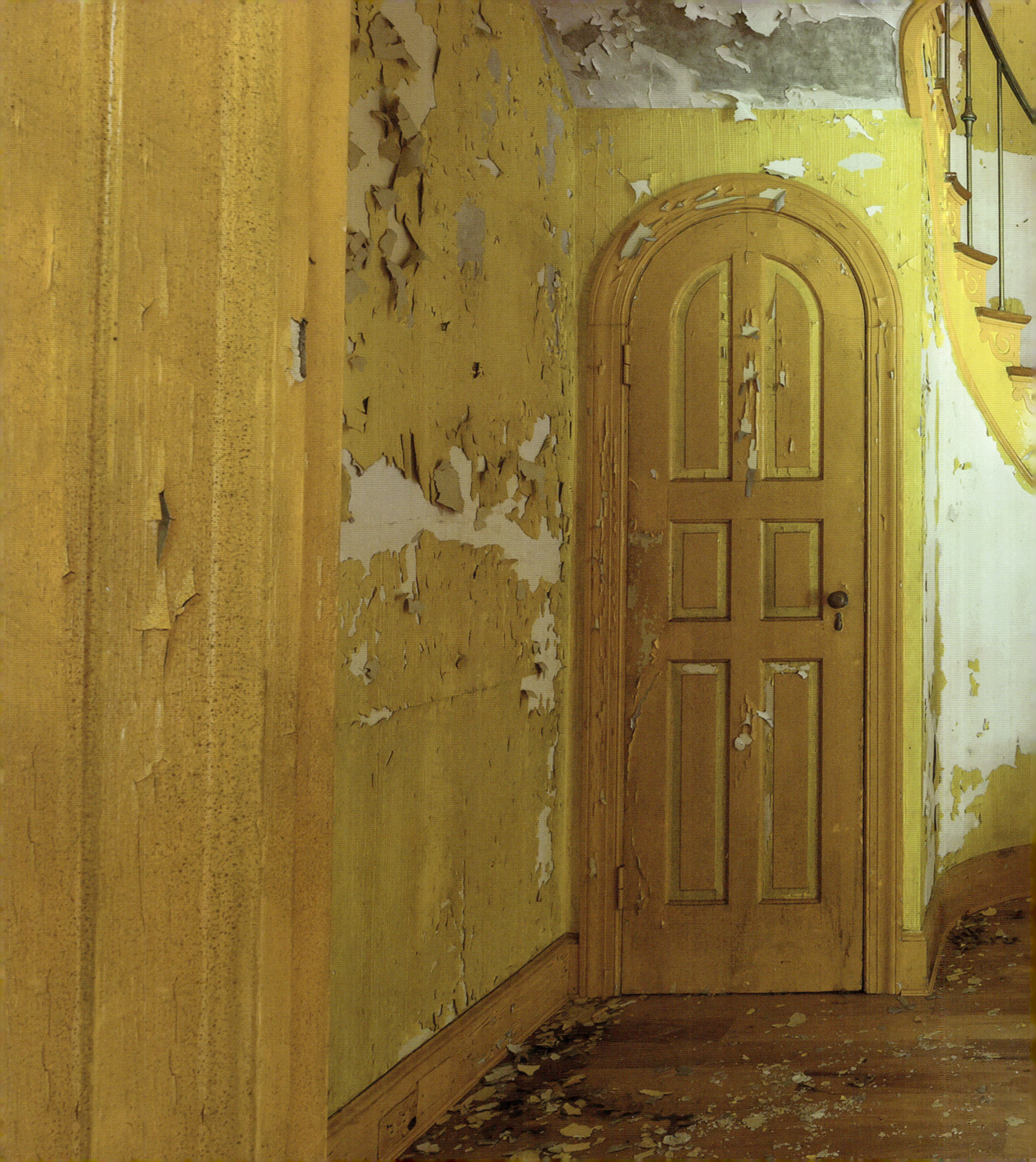

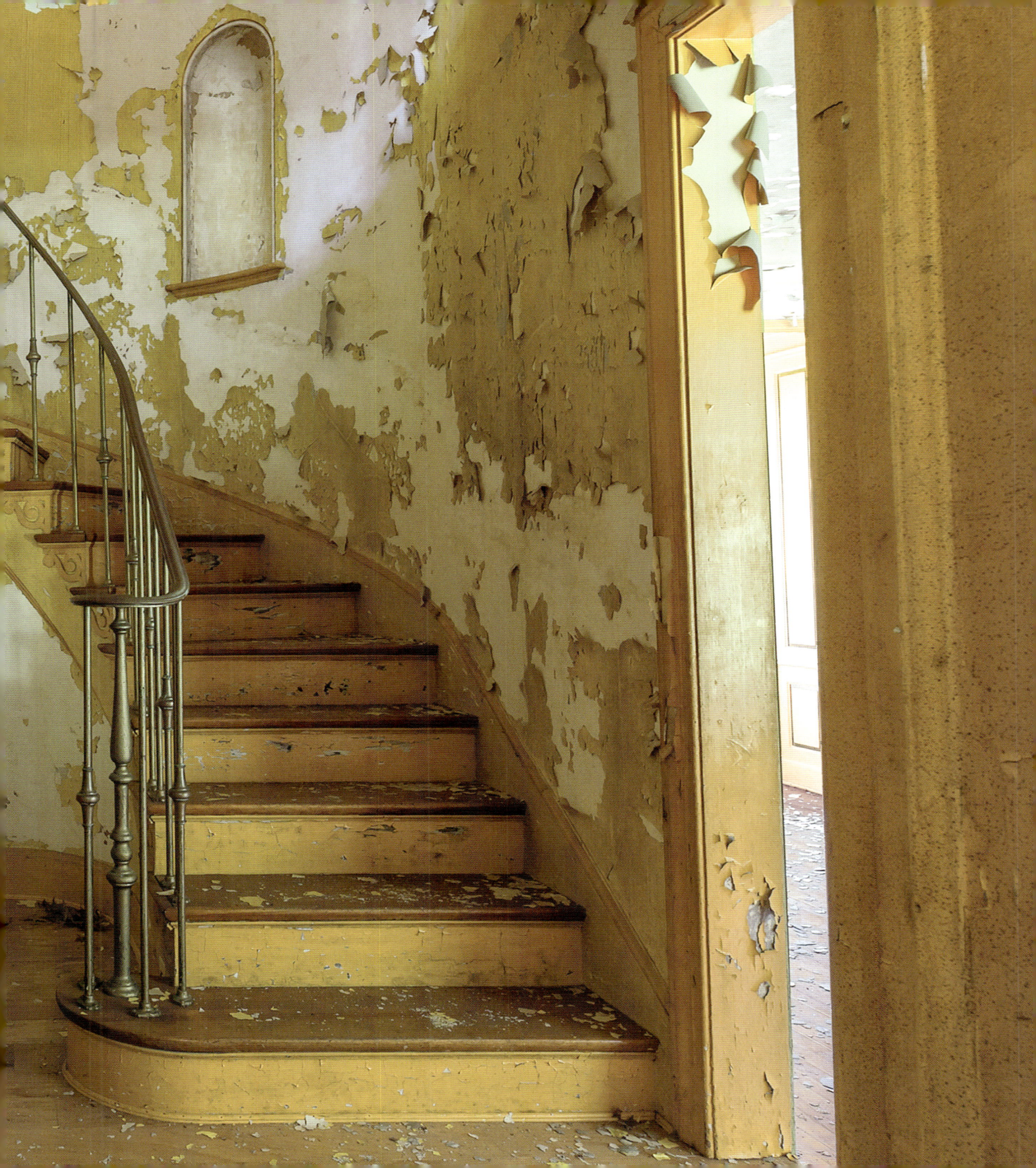

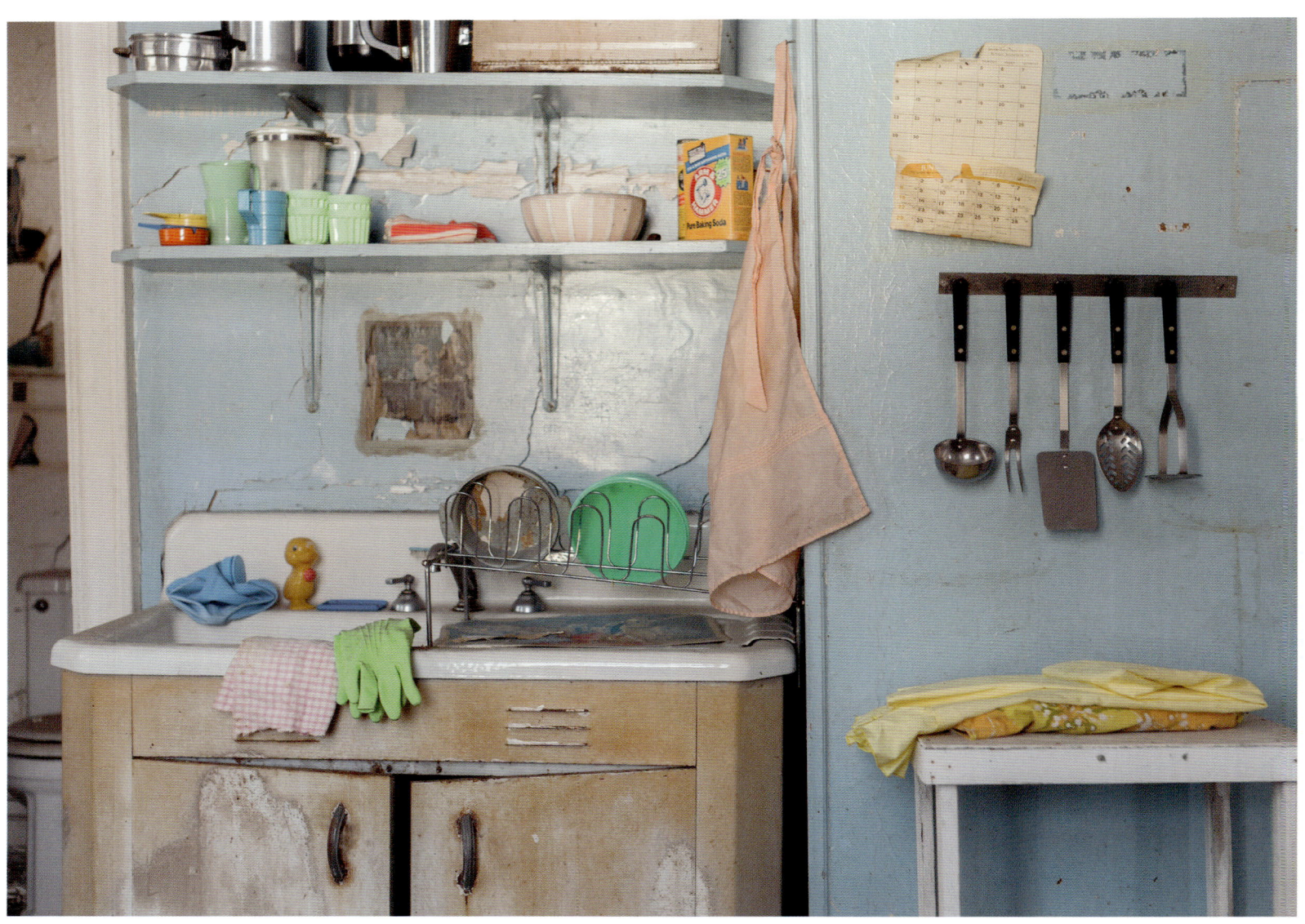

"ABOVE THE ABANDONED PHARMACY"
Sullivan County, New York

The kitchen in this apartment had a similar aesthetic to the pharmacy that operated underneath it, which had been preserved since the 1950s. A calendar on the wall suggests that the last inhabitants lived here around the same time.

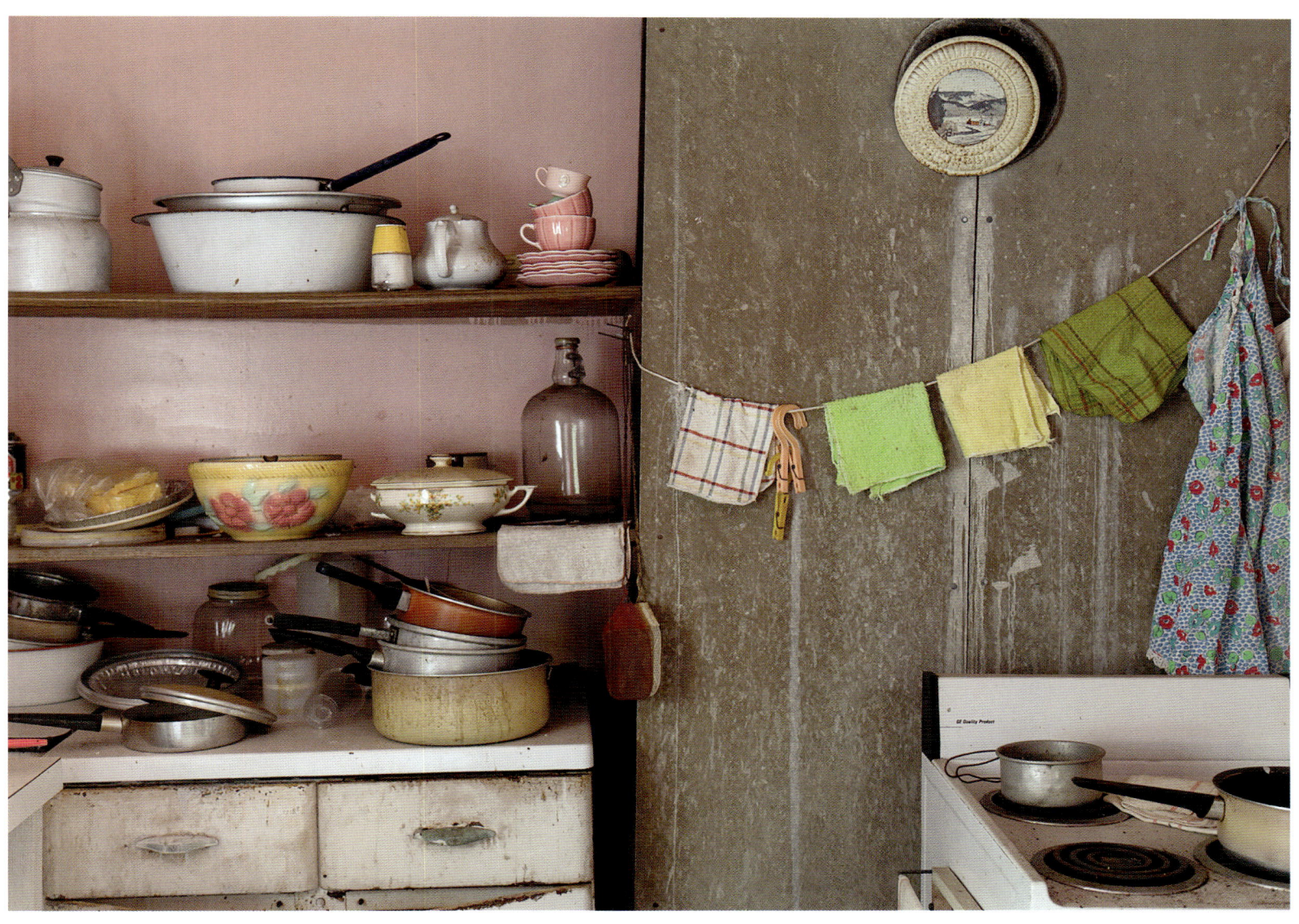

"A KITCHEN CLOTHESLINE"
Northcumberland County, Virginia

Across from a church and next to a cemetery sat this run-down house. It seemed to have been a place where many people lived, possibly a residential facility. There were several bedrooms upstairs.

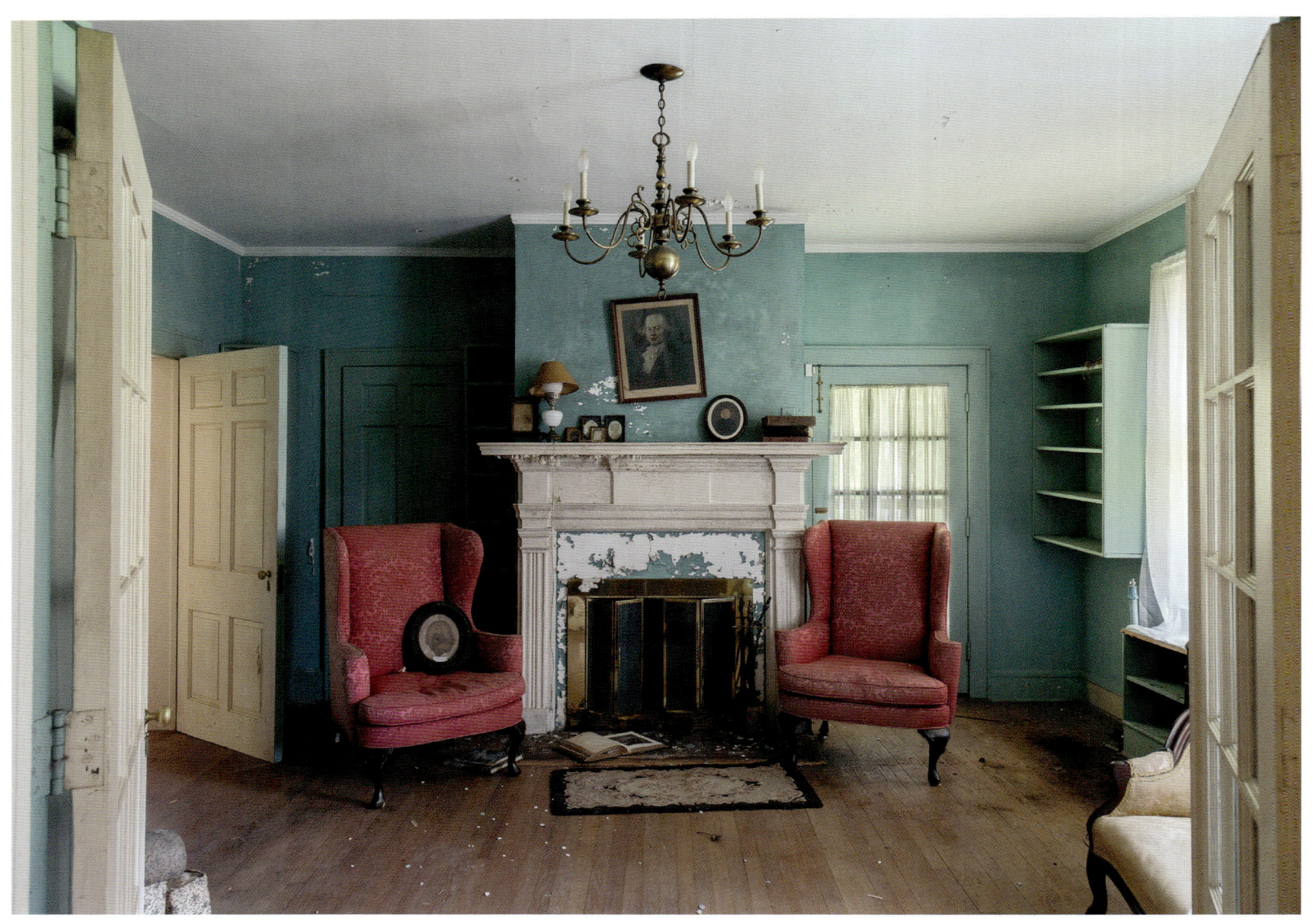

"AMERICAN DECAY"
Westmoreland County, Virginia

This house was filled with many historical pieces, including portraits of former presidents. It is possible that it once belonged to a lawyer, a politician, or a member of the clergy. This was one of the most colorful houses I've photographed and had some of the oldest items.

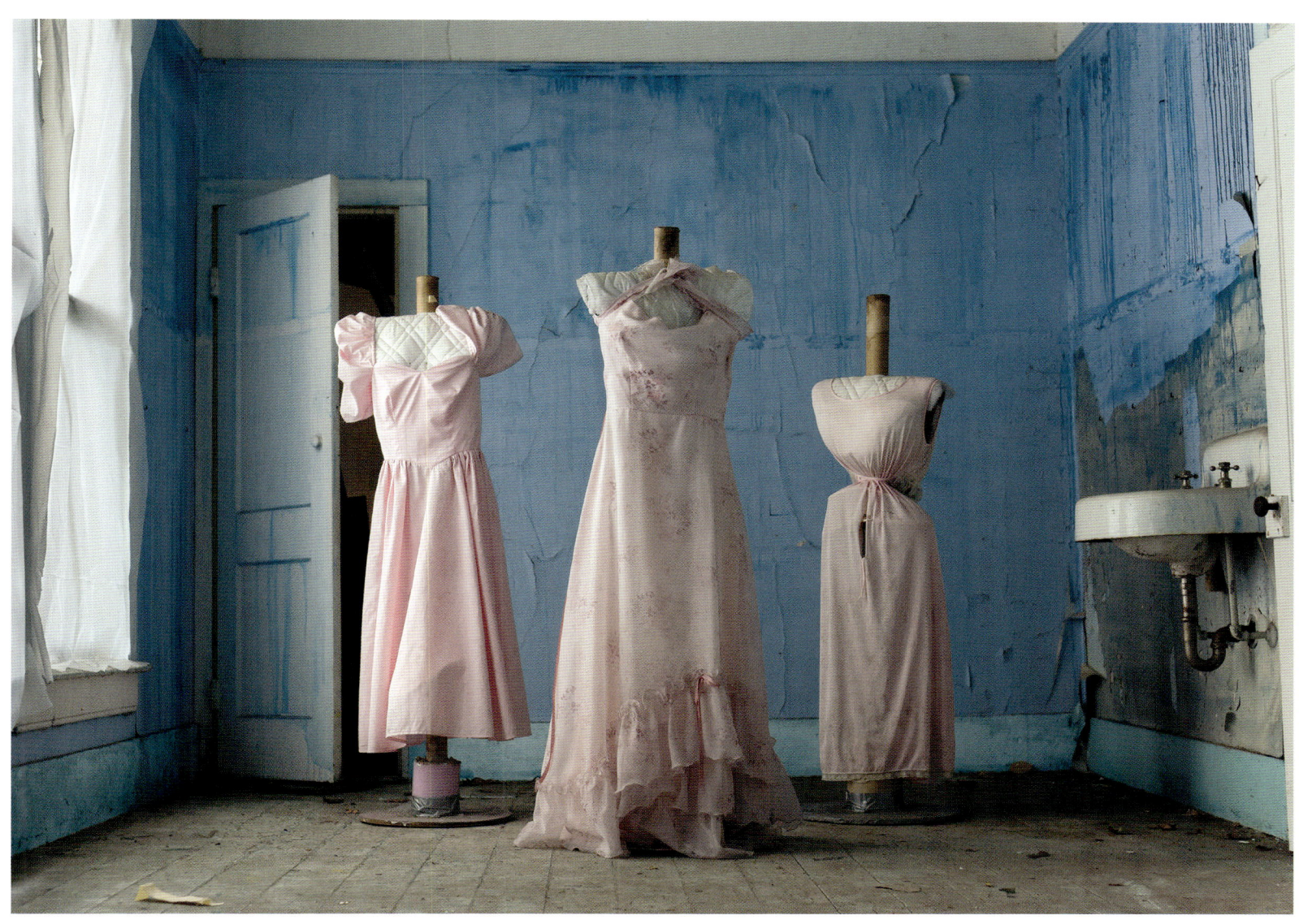

"THREE PINK DRESSES"
Greene County, New York

This mansion was once used as an art studio. Sitting on a corner near a bridge, it's impossible to miss. When I visited, it had been used last as an artist's space. Each room had different colors and props, and art installations were placed all around, including one room with floor-to-ceiling pink clothing. These dress forms made from mattresses were lined up like a scene from surreal fairytale.

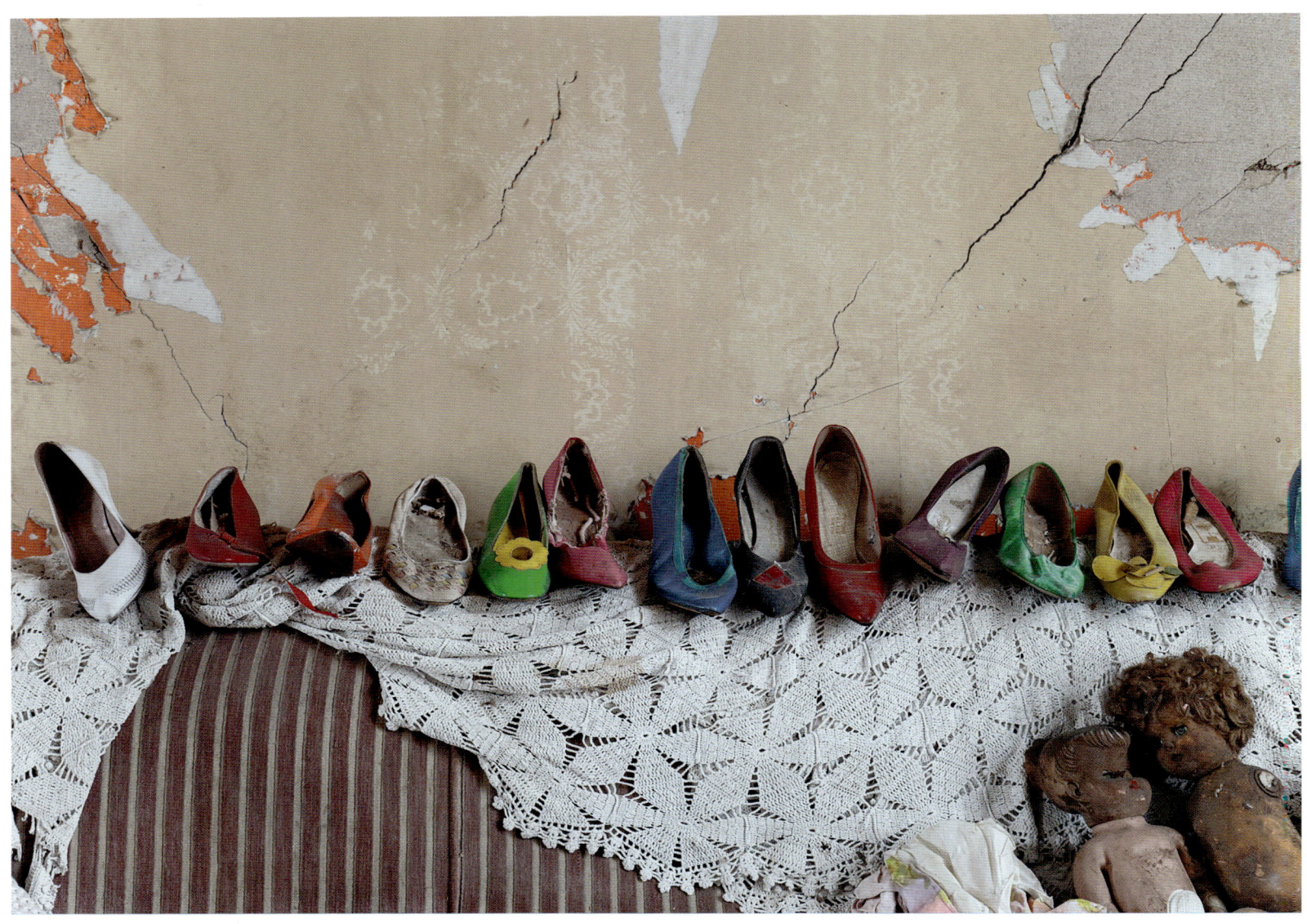

"THE FASHIONISTA'S SHOES"
DeKalb County, Illinois

Several abandoned houses in a row were filled with vintage clothing from the late 1800s through the 1980s. One house in particular was filled with shoes, colorful dresses, purses, and perfume bottles. This woman was a fashionista.

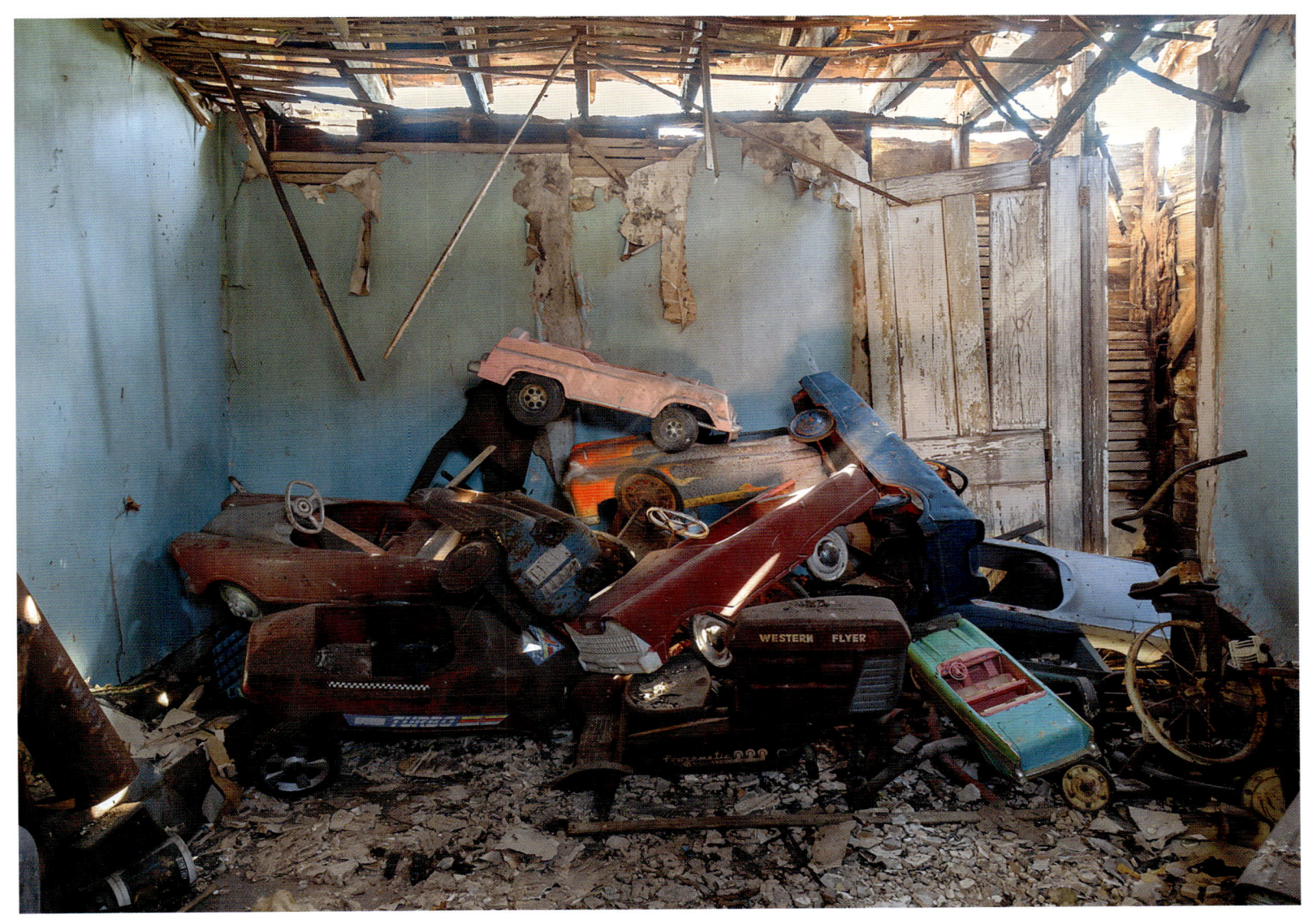

"THE TOY CAR JUNKYARD"
Smyth County, Virginia

This house contained more than a dozen metal die-cast pedal cars, most likely from the 1950s, thrown around in various rooms. This room appeared almost like a miniature junkyard.

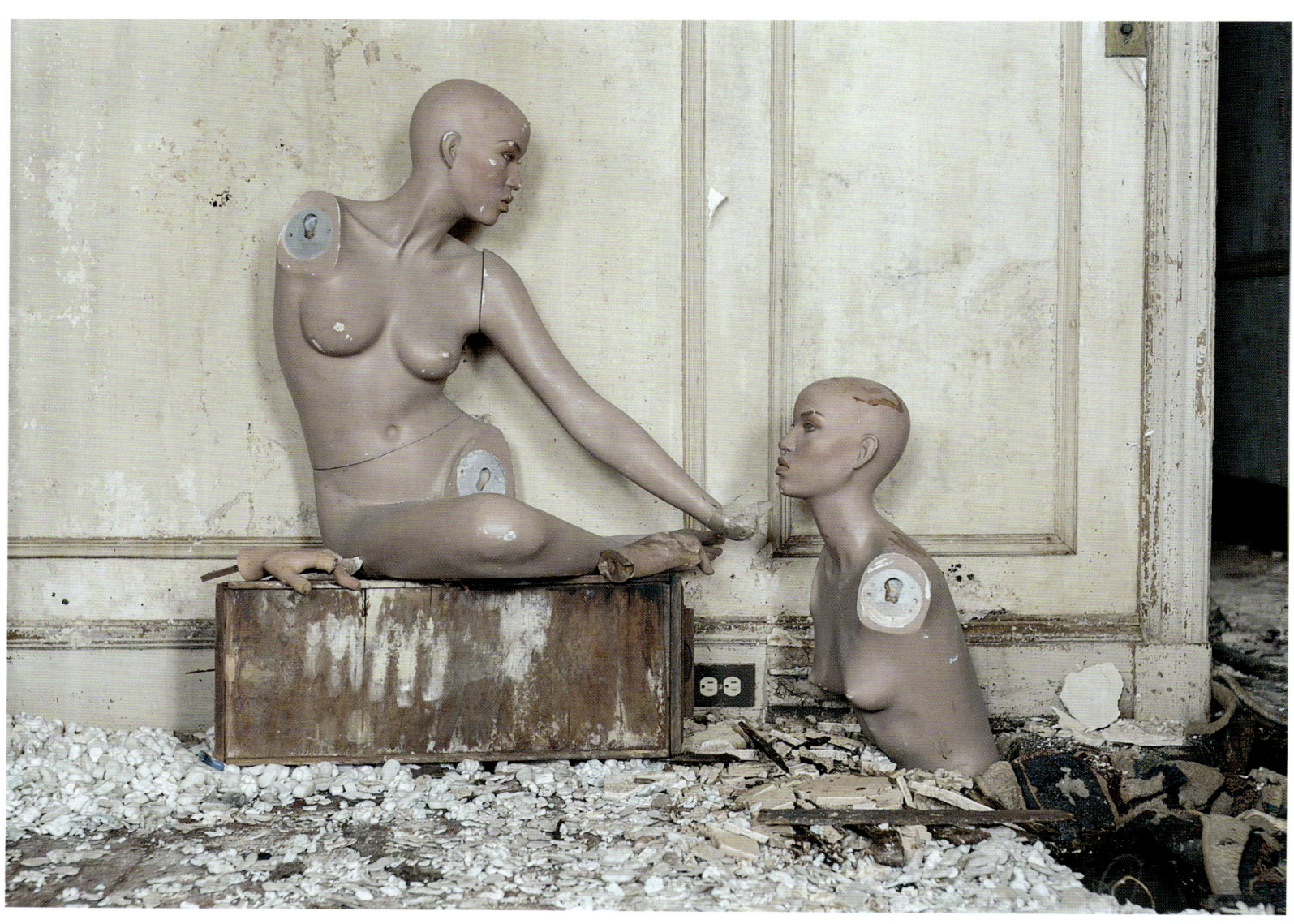

"THE MANNEQUIN COLLECTION"
Baltimore, Maryland

One of the most dangerous places I've explored, this home completely collapsed not long after I took this photograph. It was filled with hundreds of mannequins (also seen on pages 58-59), and it may have been used as a storage space for a local museum. Many of the mannequins had been thrown into the basement, and others were propped up on the stairs. One sat on a box, appearing to be in conversation with another mannequin that was sinking into the unstable floor of the third story.

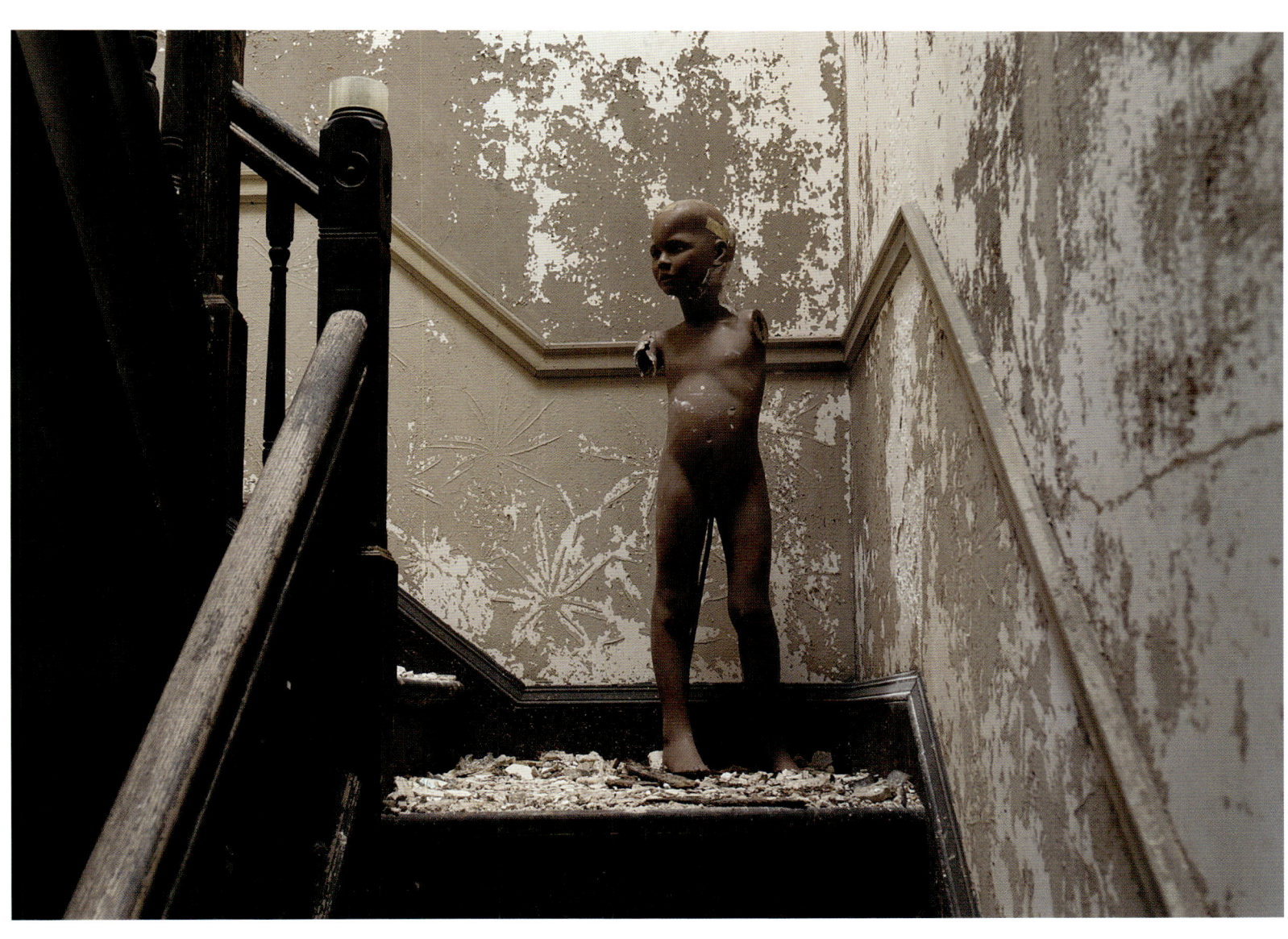

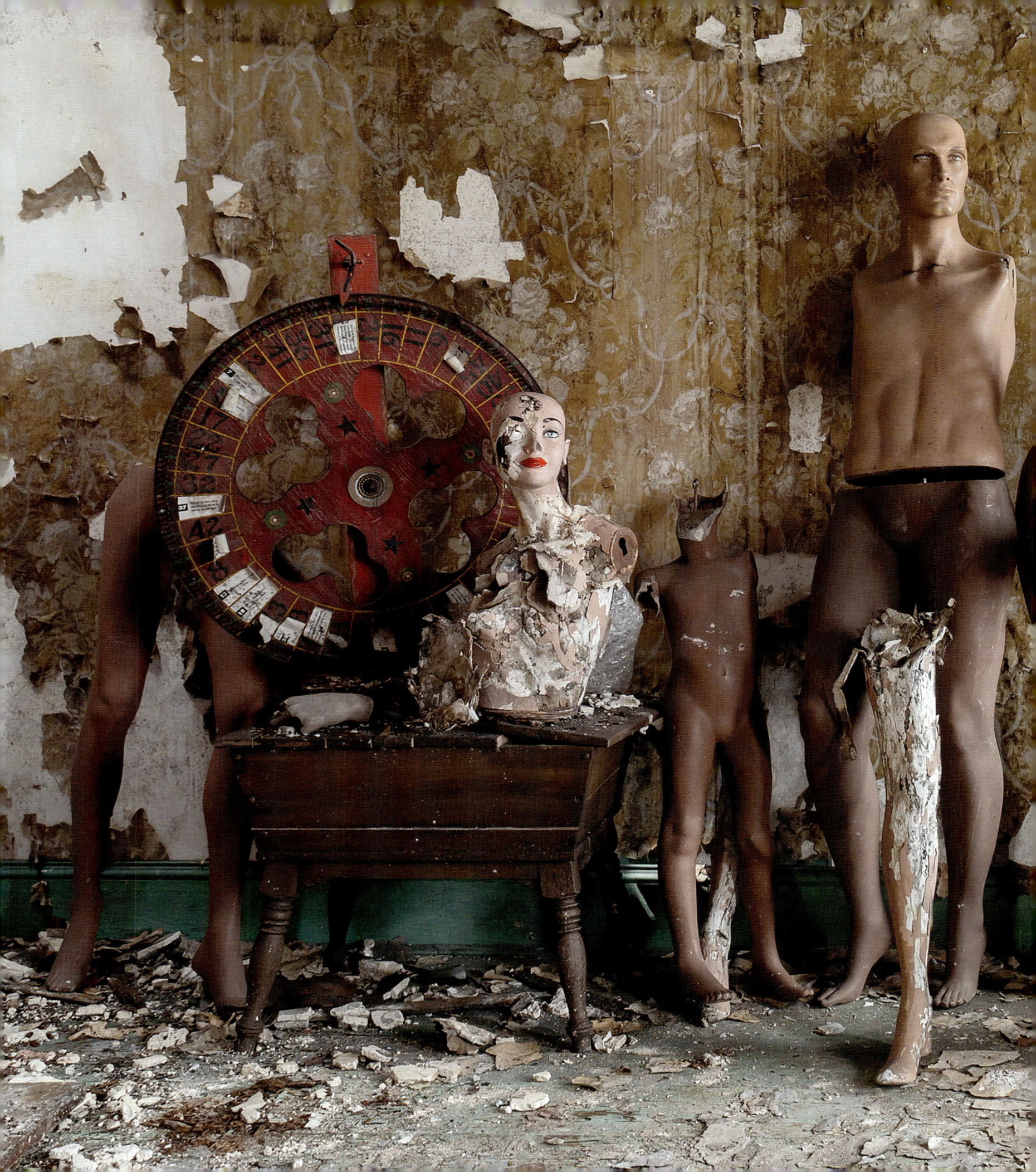

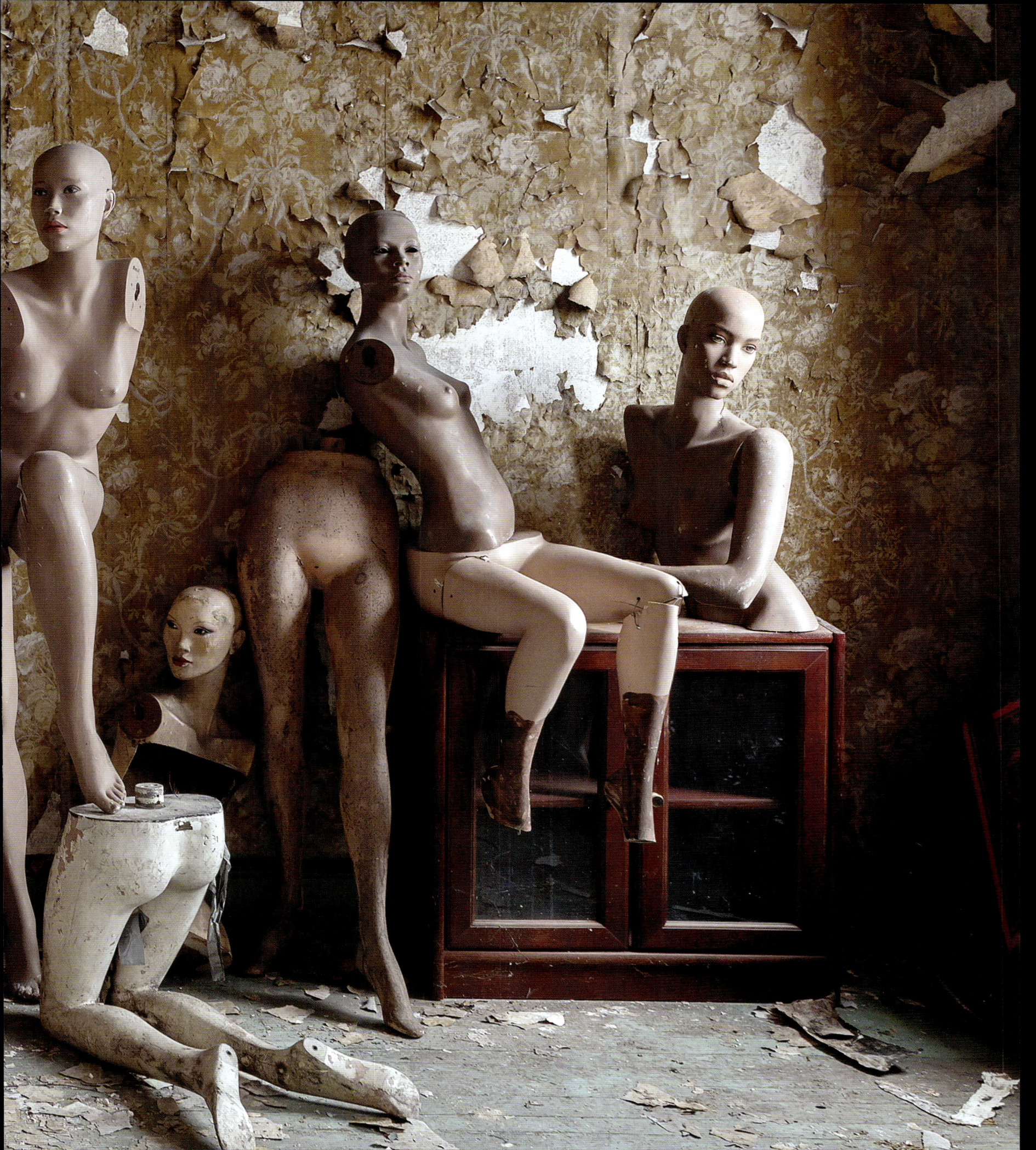

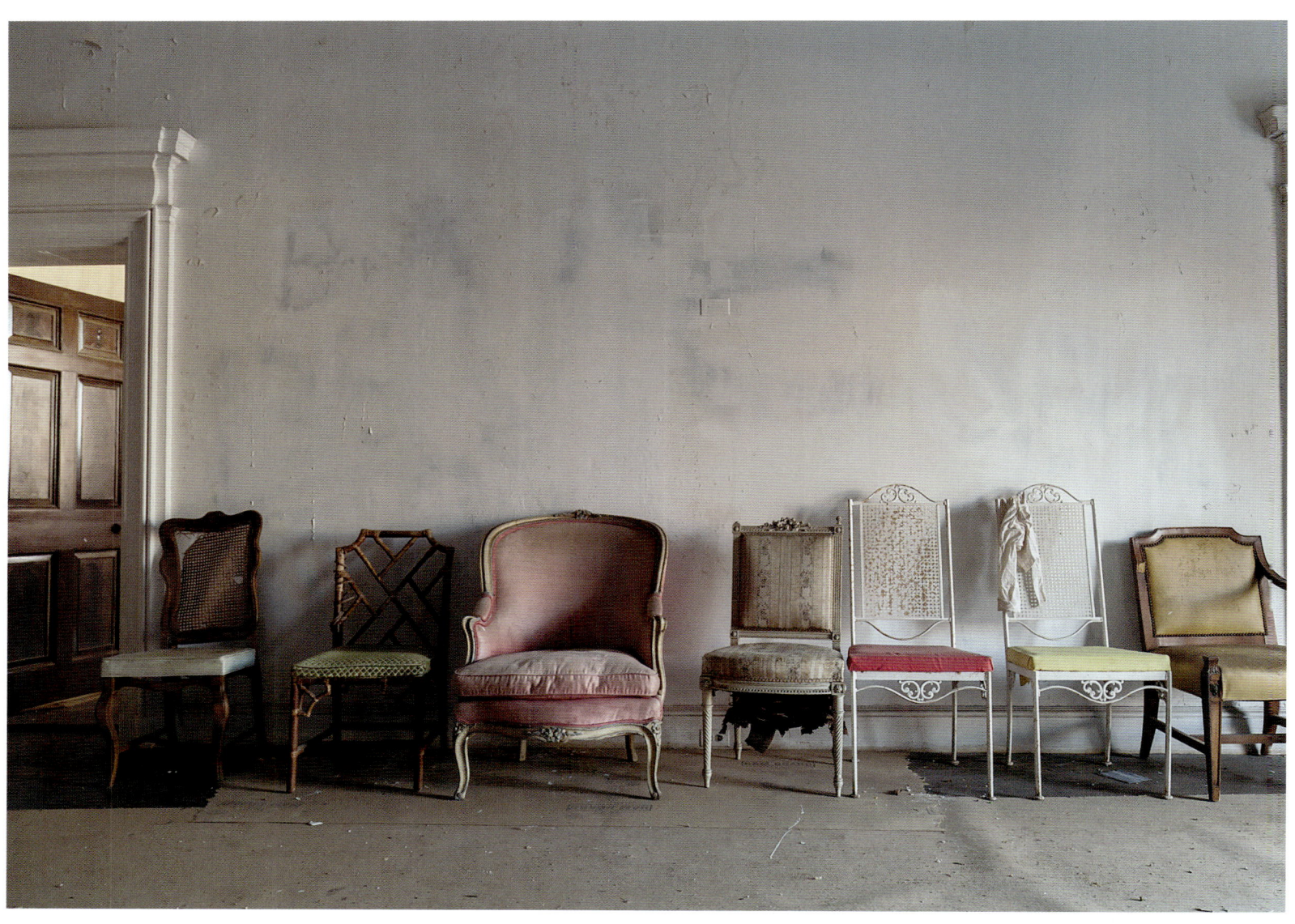

"THE CHAIRS"
Nassau County, New York

In a mansion on the Gold Coast, these chairs reflect the luxury and wealth that once existed in such a grand place.

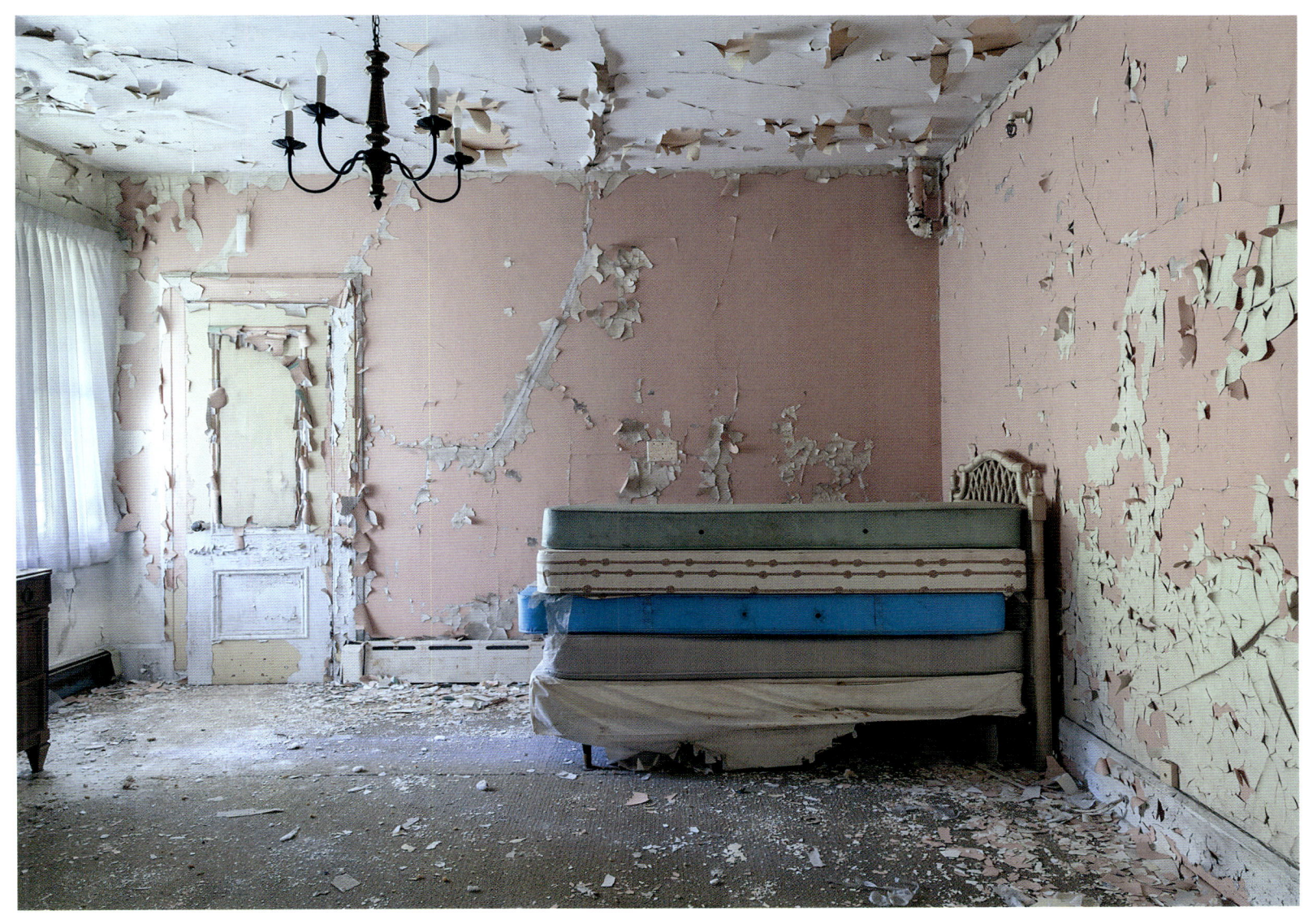

"THE PRINCESS AND THE PEA"
Westchester County, New York

In this large retirement home, there were many bedrooms filled with furniture, including several mattresses. Here, several are stacked on the bed, providing colorful contrast.

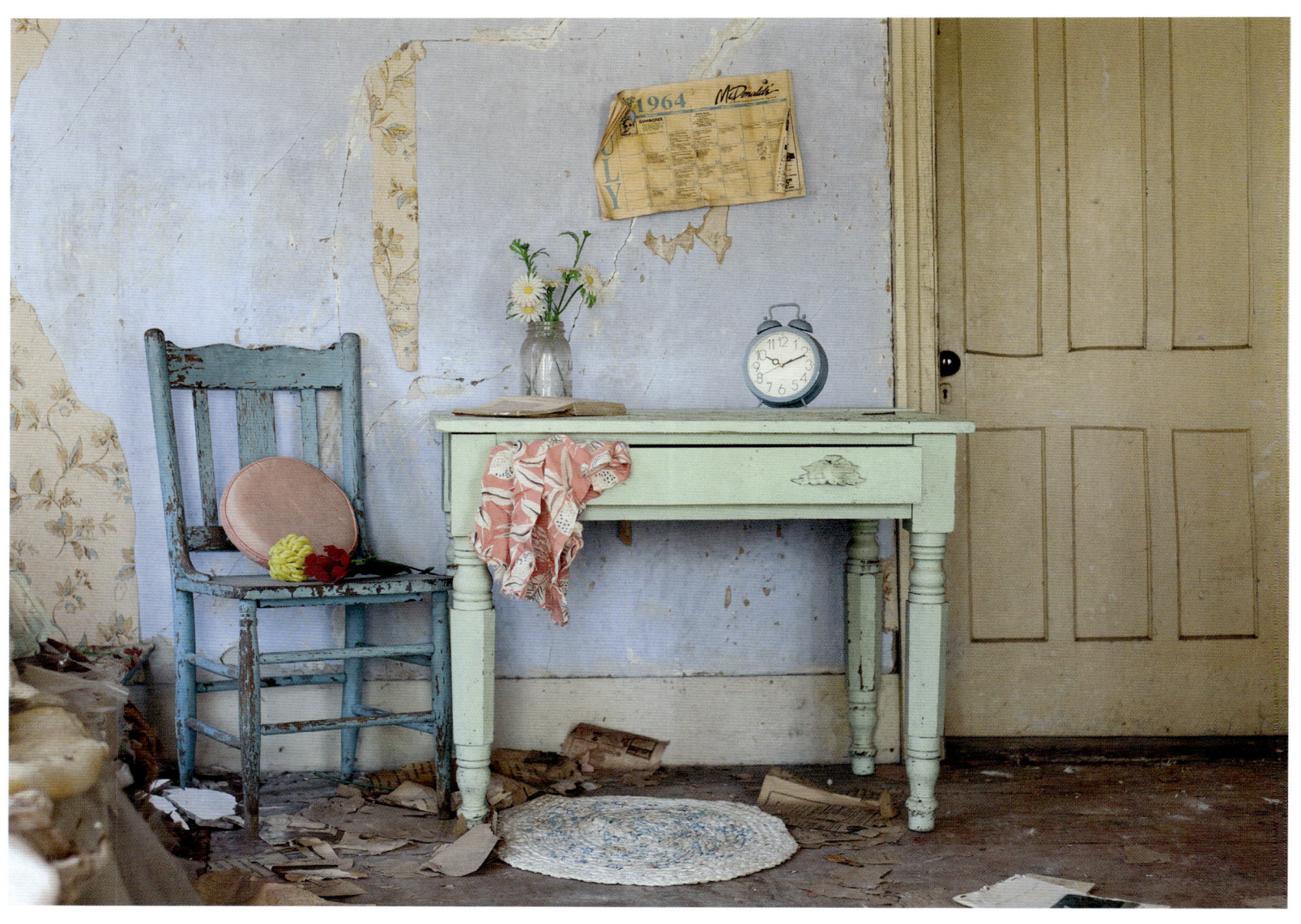

"1964"
Greene County, New York

This old boardinghouse was filled with colorful furniture. A clock and calendar were frozen in a moment from years past.

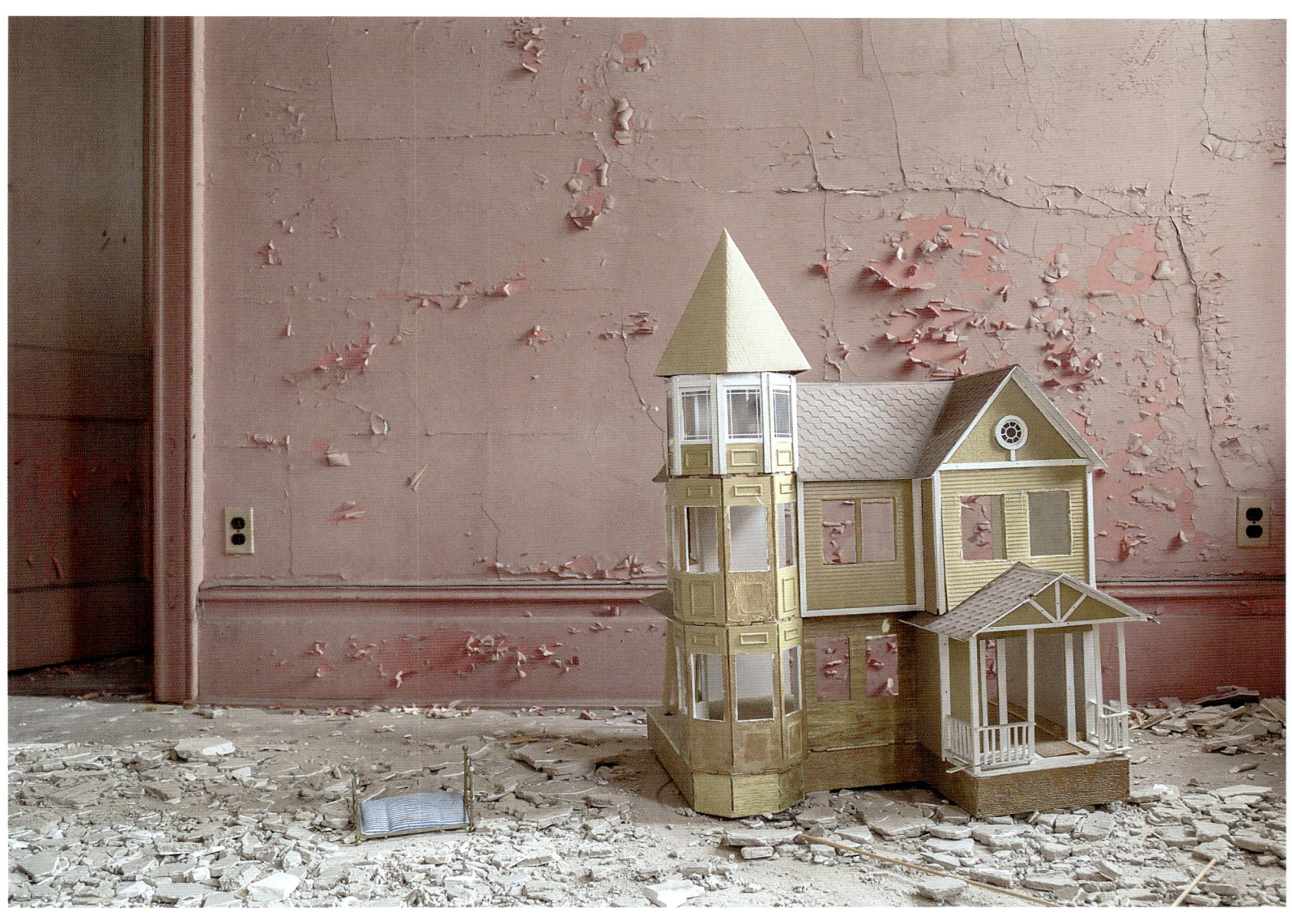

"THE ABANDONED DOLLHOUSE"
Sullivan County, New York

This dollhouse was in an apartment above an abandoned pharmacy. Among other objects and children's toys thrown around, this lone dollhouse stood out not only visually but metaphorically.

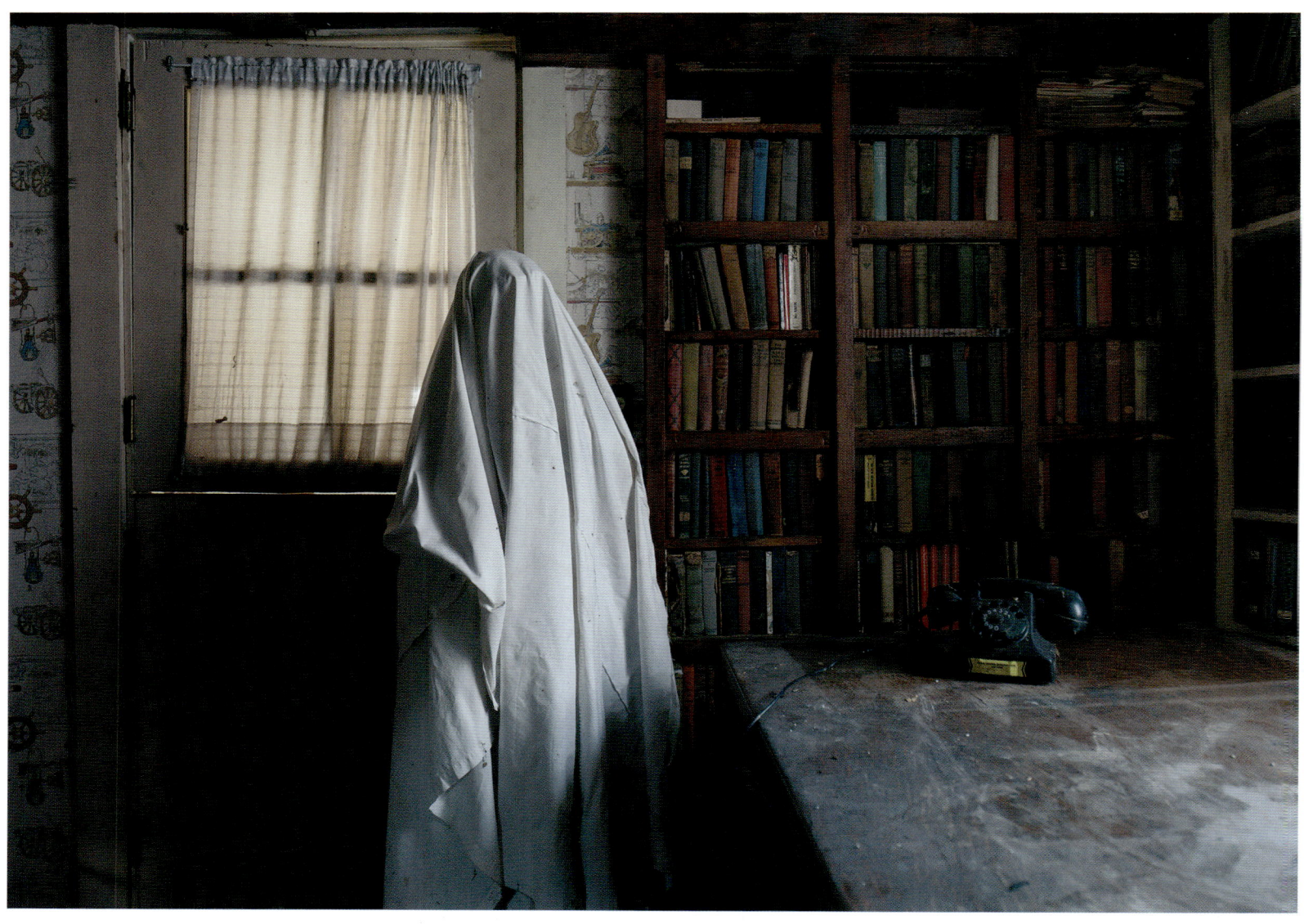

"THE GHOST OF MARY"
Orange County, New York

In a house across the street from a church, I found a life-size statue of Mary with human prosthetic eyes hidden under a sheet.

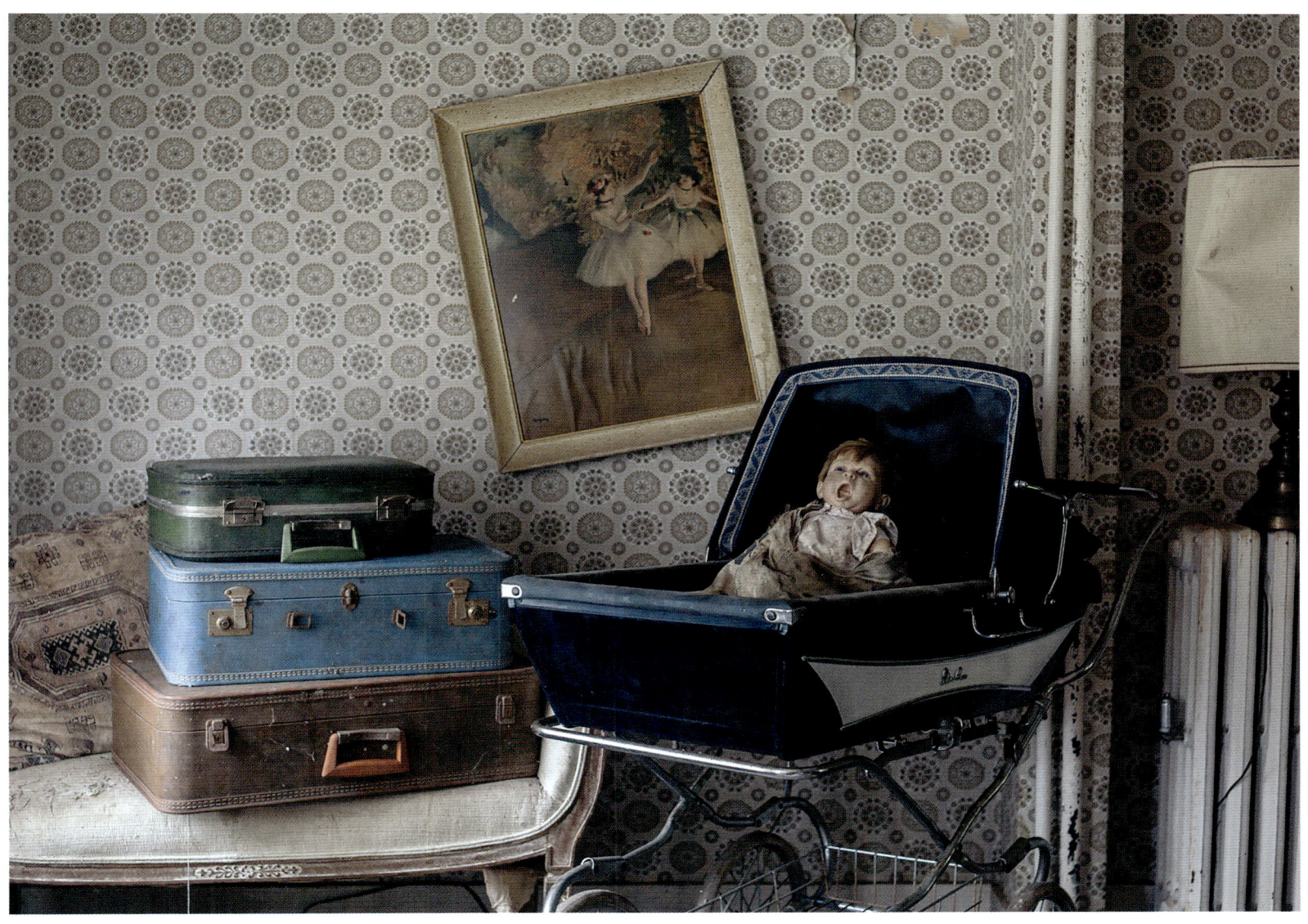

"THE SCREAMING CHILD"
Greene County, New York

In a downstairs room in what I believe to be a former boardinghouse was this lone doll carriage.

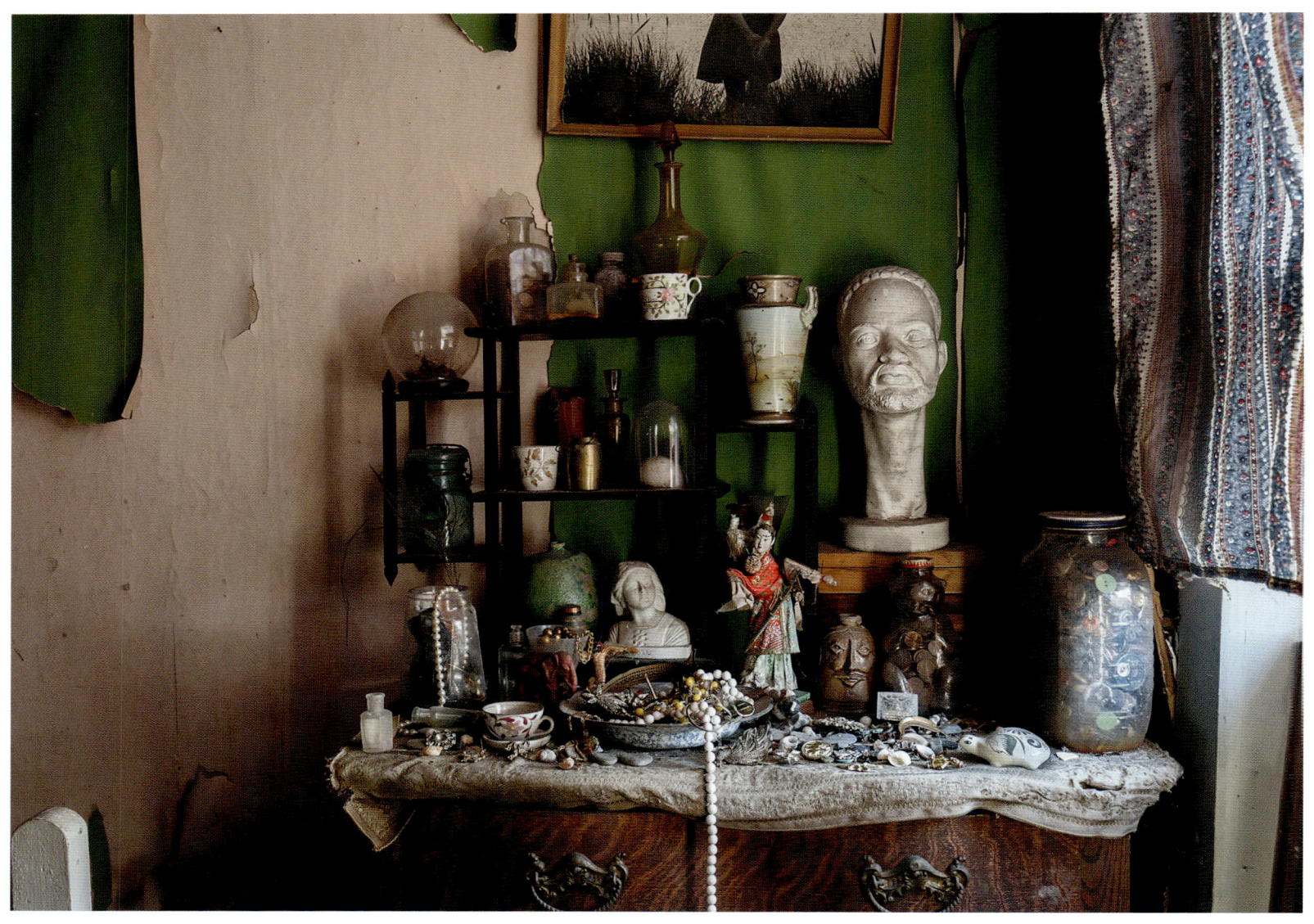

"A CURIOUS COLLECTION"
Delaware County, New York

I imagine that the objects on this dresser—jewelry, china, art, jars filled with buttons and coins—belonged to a well-traveled collector with many prized possessions that held distinct memories.

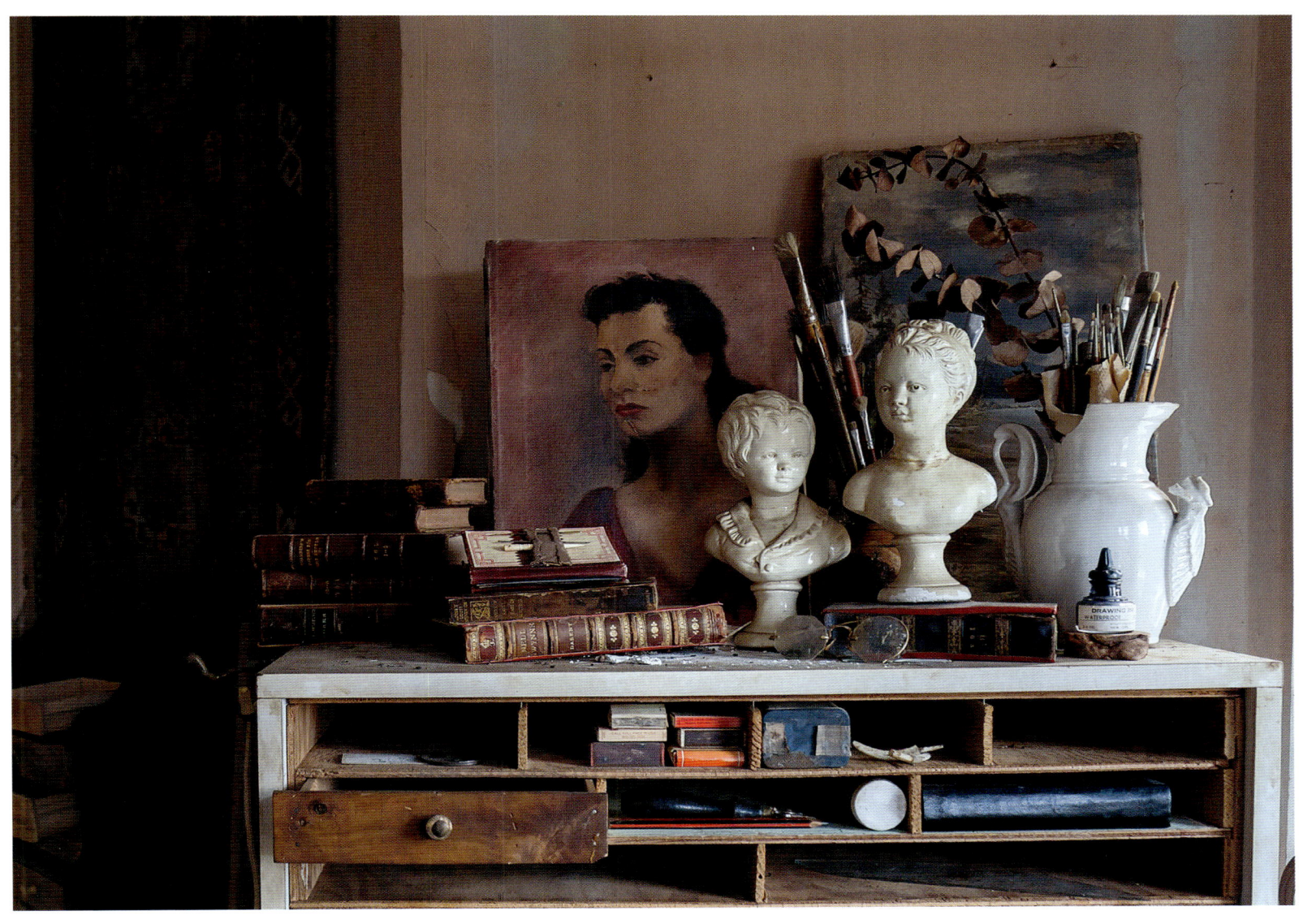

"THE ARTIST'S STUDIO"
Sullivan County, New York

In a dilapidated Victorian home, there were so many paintings in the attic that they were stacked to the ceiling. Sitting by the window was this desk with art supplies and a painting of a woman—maybe the artist herself?

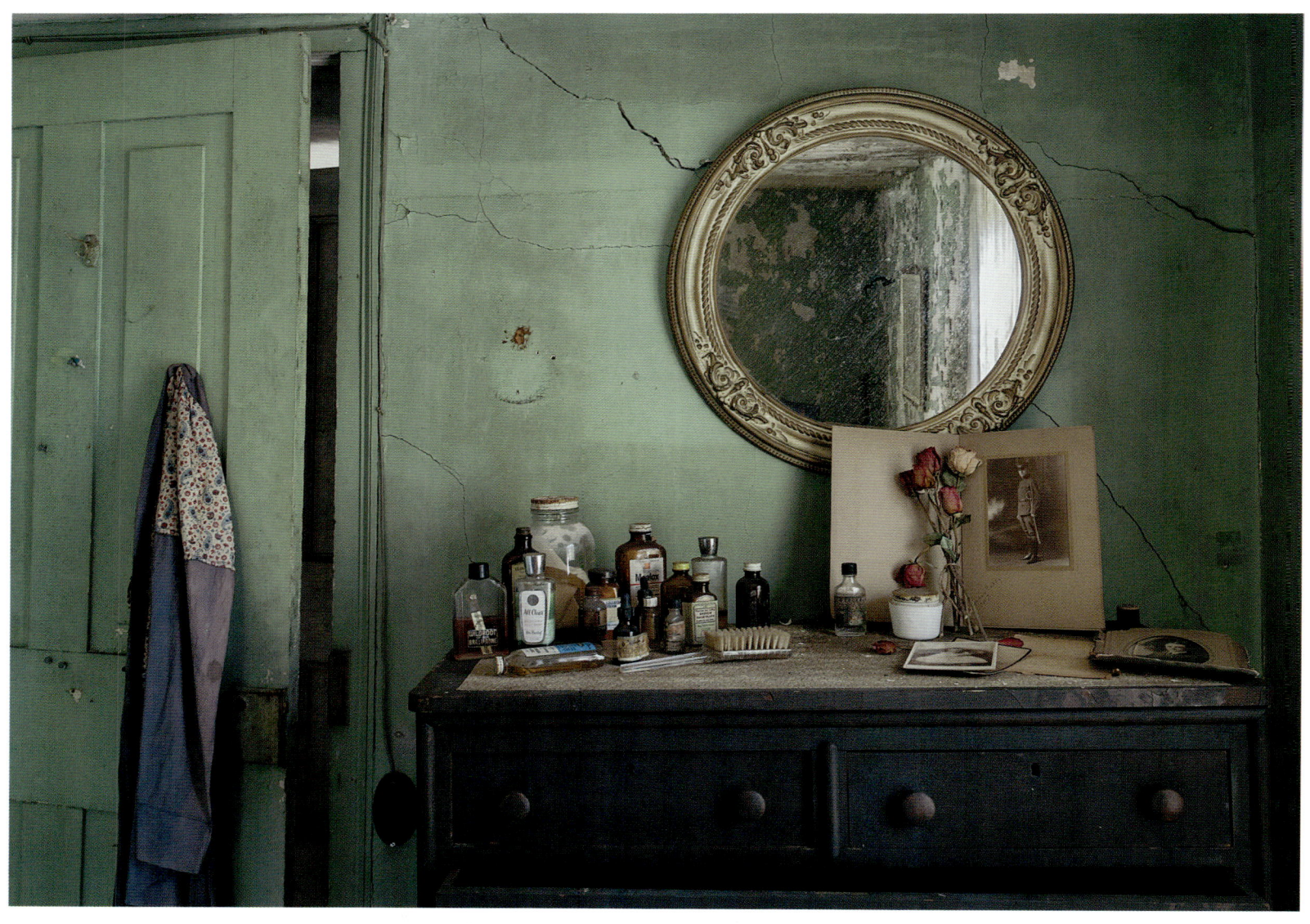

"THE MOURNER'S HOME"
Westchester County, New York

Tucked away in the woods sat this house from another time. In a tiny bedroom, the bureau may have belonged to a woman who lost her lover—and kept dried flowers and a photograph to remember him by.

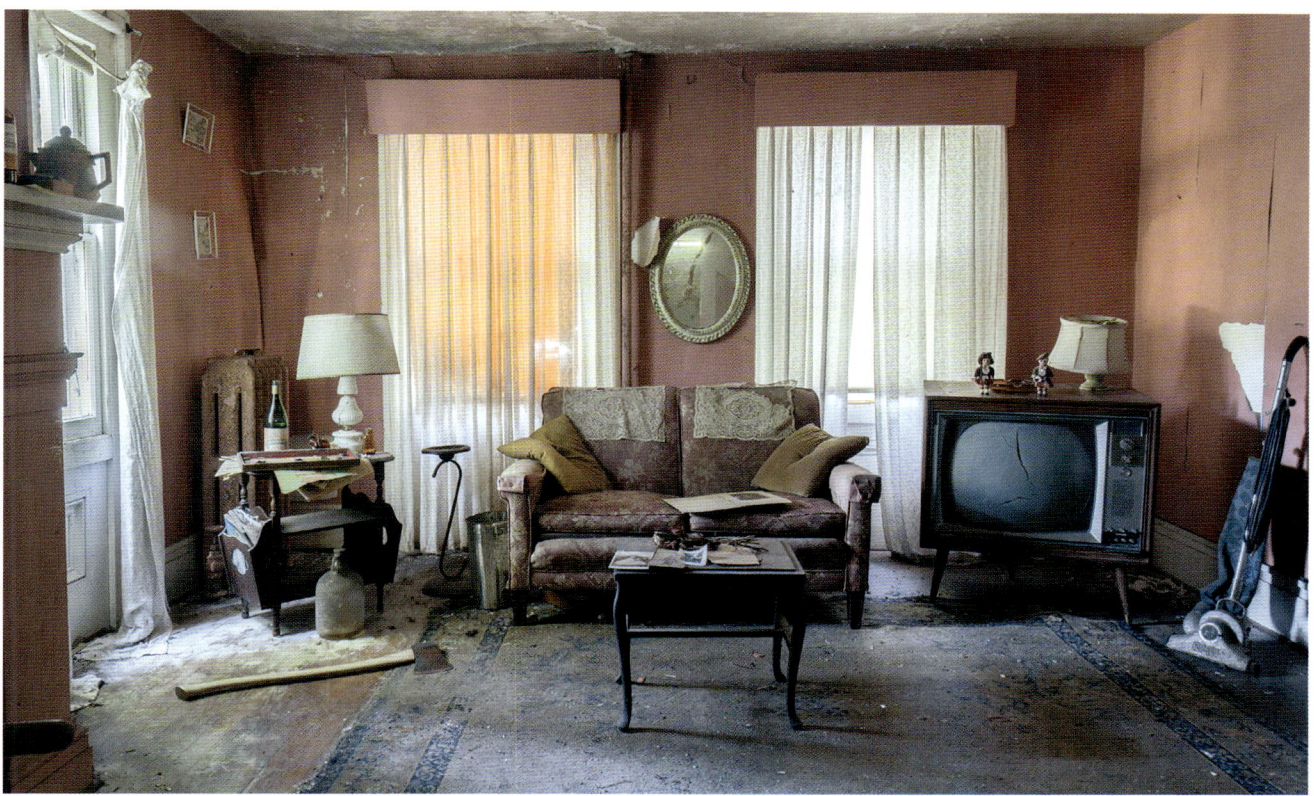

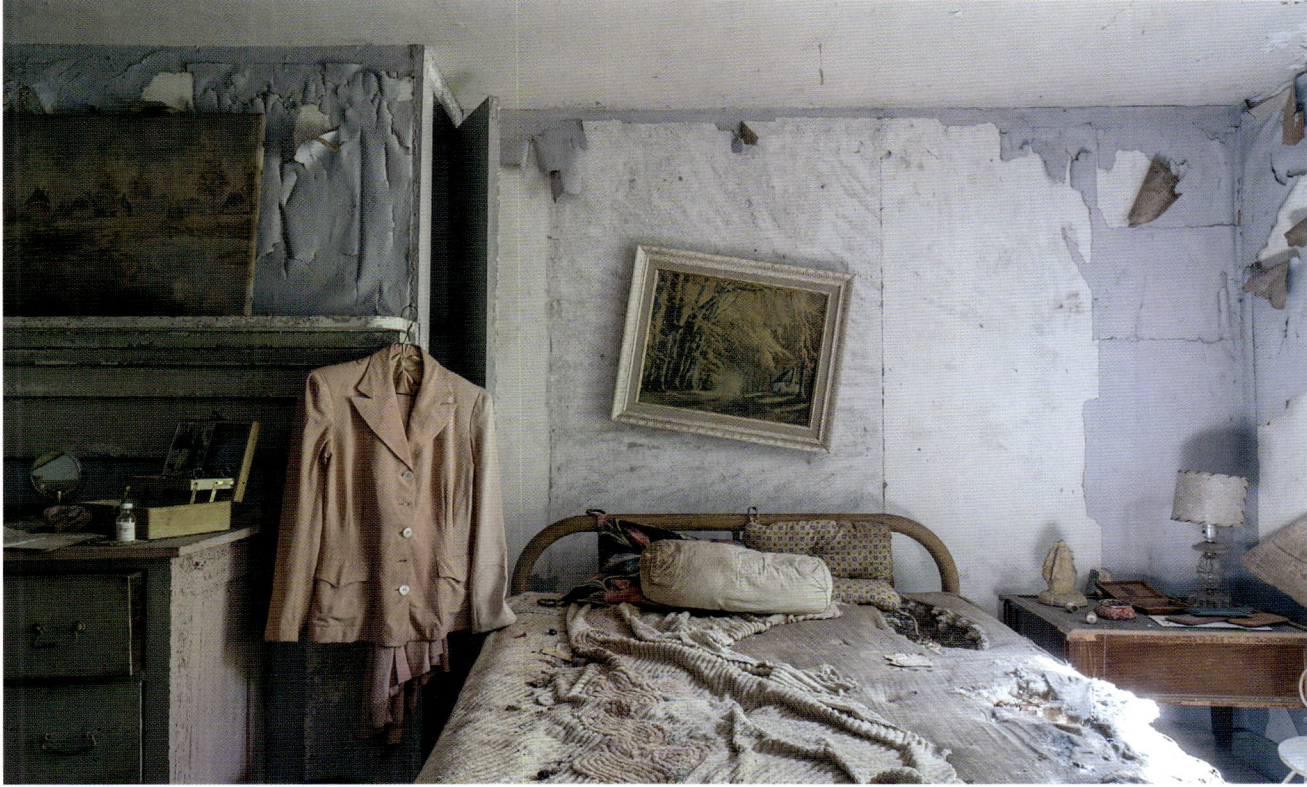

The bottom photo here shows the main bedroom in the same home. The paint was peeling off the walls, and the mattress was deteriorating. Next to the bed was a dresser holding a jewelry box filled with precious items, as well as perfumes and hygiene products. Shoes and clothing were left all around. Above is the living room, bright, with an ax lying on the floor.

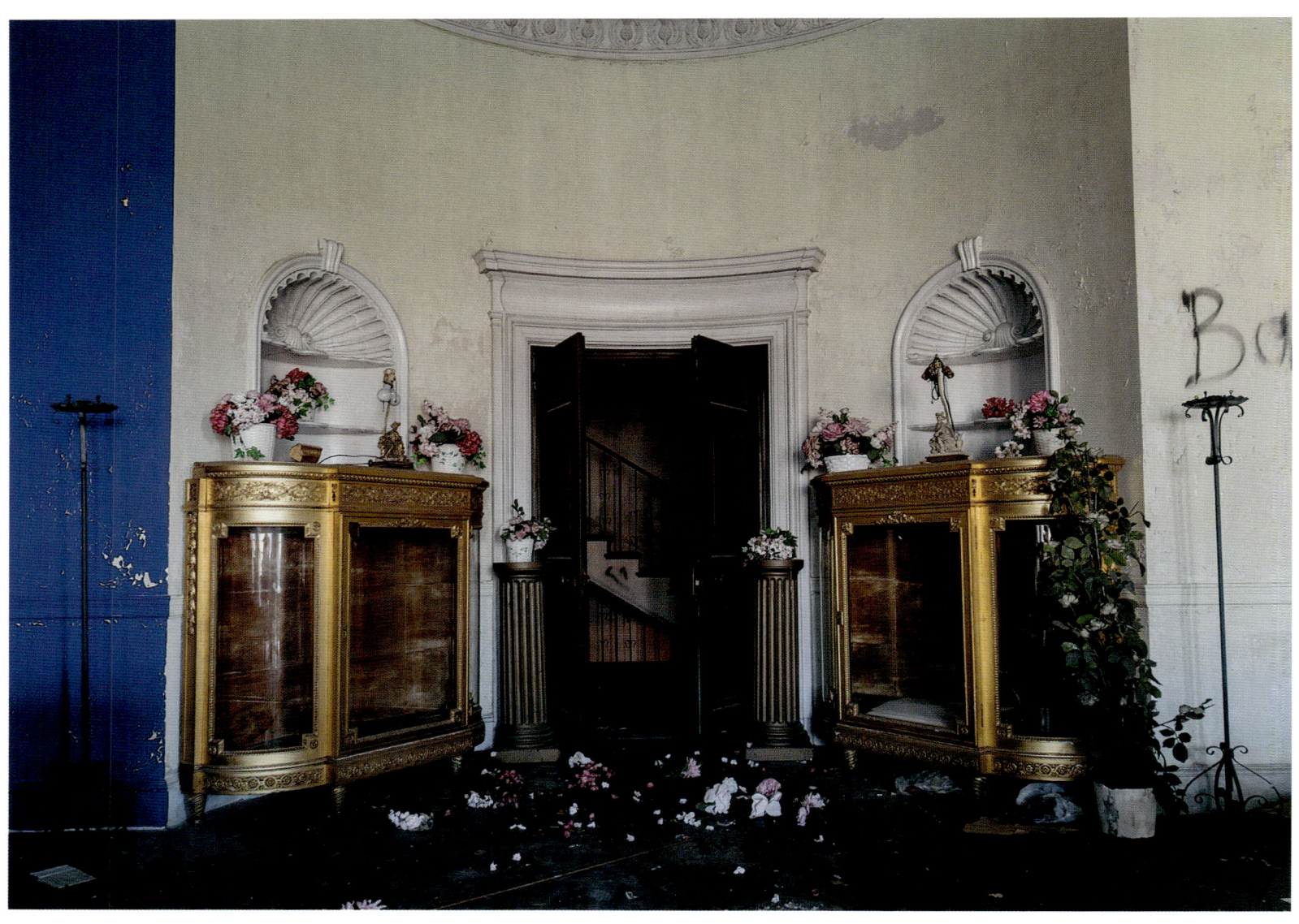

"THE GOLD CASES"
Nassau County, New York

This grand Gold Coast mansion was fully decorated, as it had been a show house in the 1980s. Each room was set up by a different designer before the house was abandoned. With the fake flowers, golden cabinets, and accent pedestals, the designer of this room was going for an opulent look.

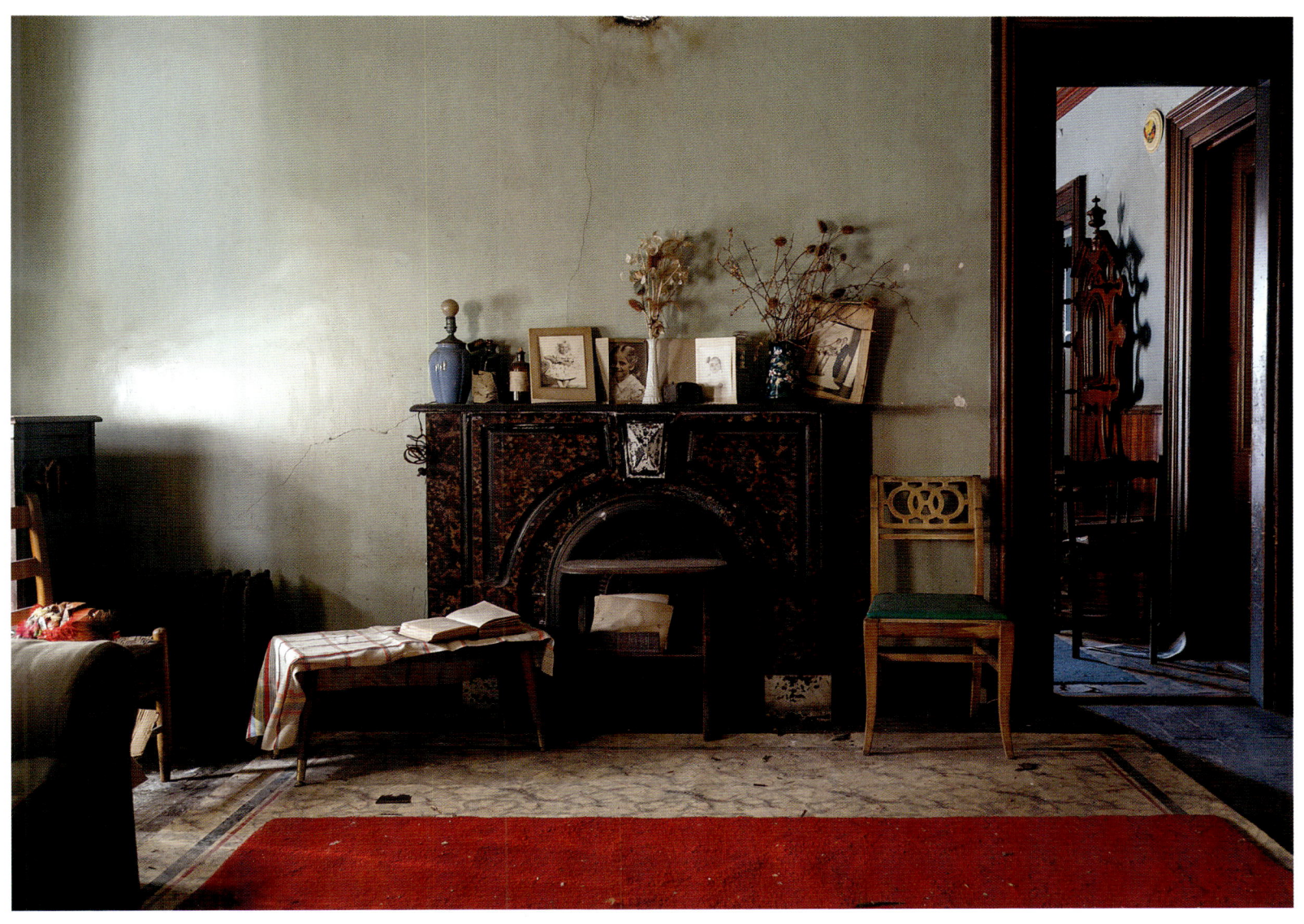

"THE RED RUG"
Orange County, New York

This particular house was one of my favorites to explore. It was filled with antique furniture, including a vanity and trunk in the attic. Though each room had a different aesthetic, all were styled in a beautiful way.

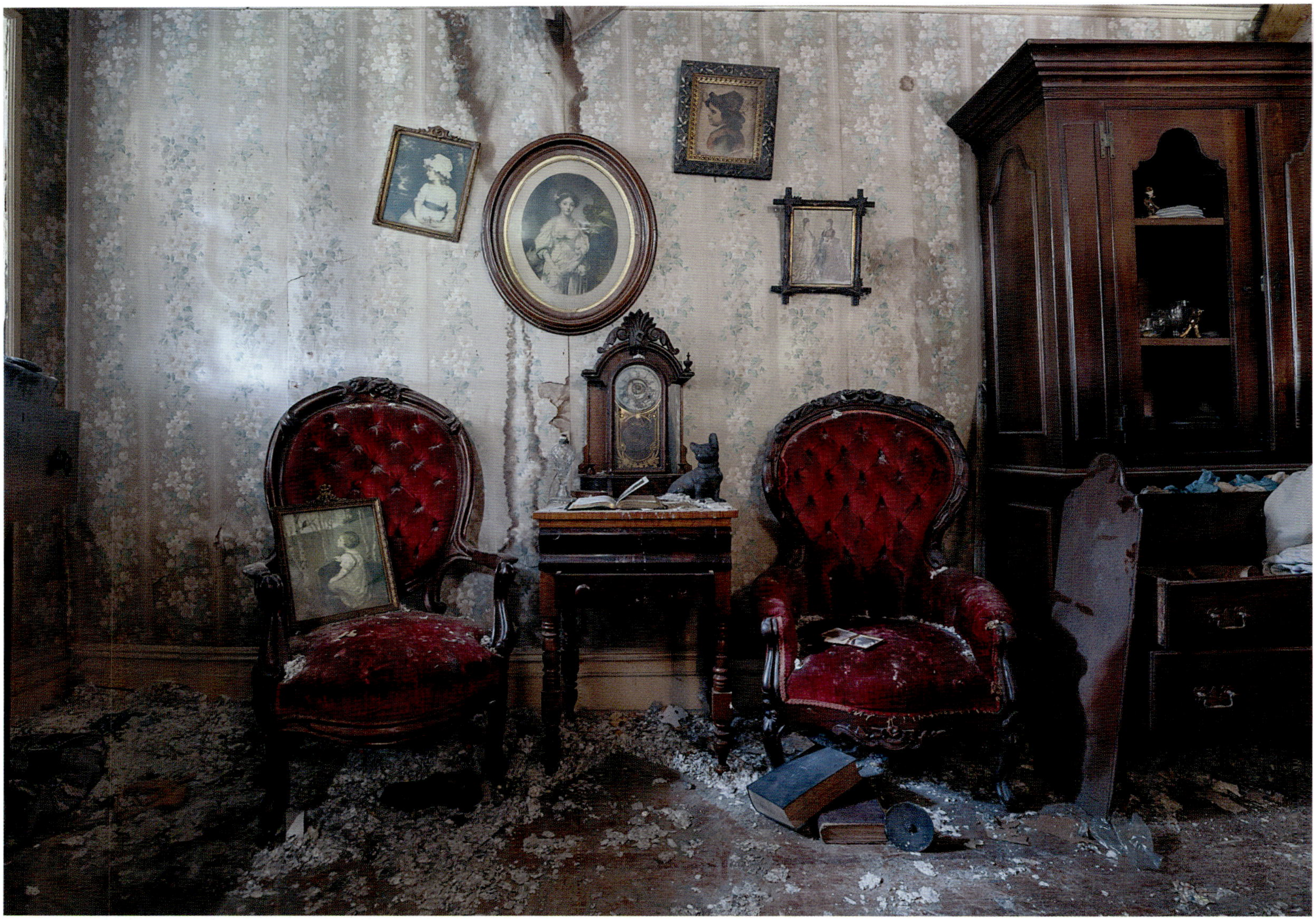

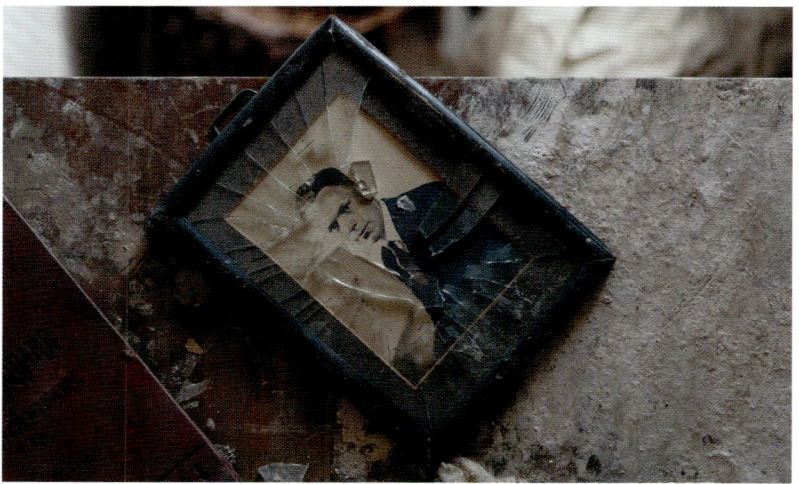

This is one of my favorite houses I've photographed. Each room was tiny yet filled with Victorian-era antiques, including clocks, paintings, and a piano. The man in this photograph might have been a relative of the owners, or maybe even a previous owner of the house himself. The way he's peering through the shattered glass, it seems as if he's asking to be remembered.

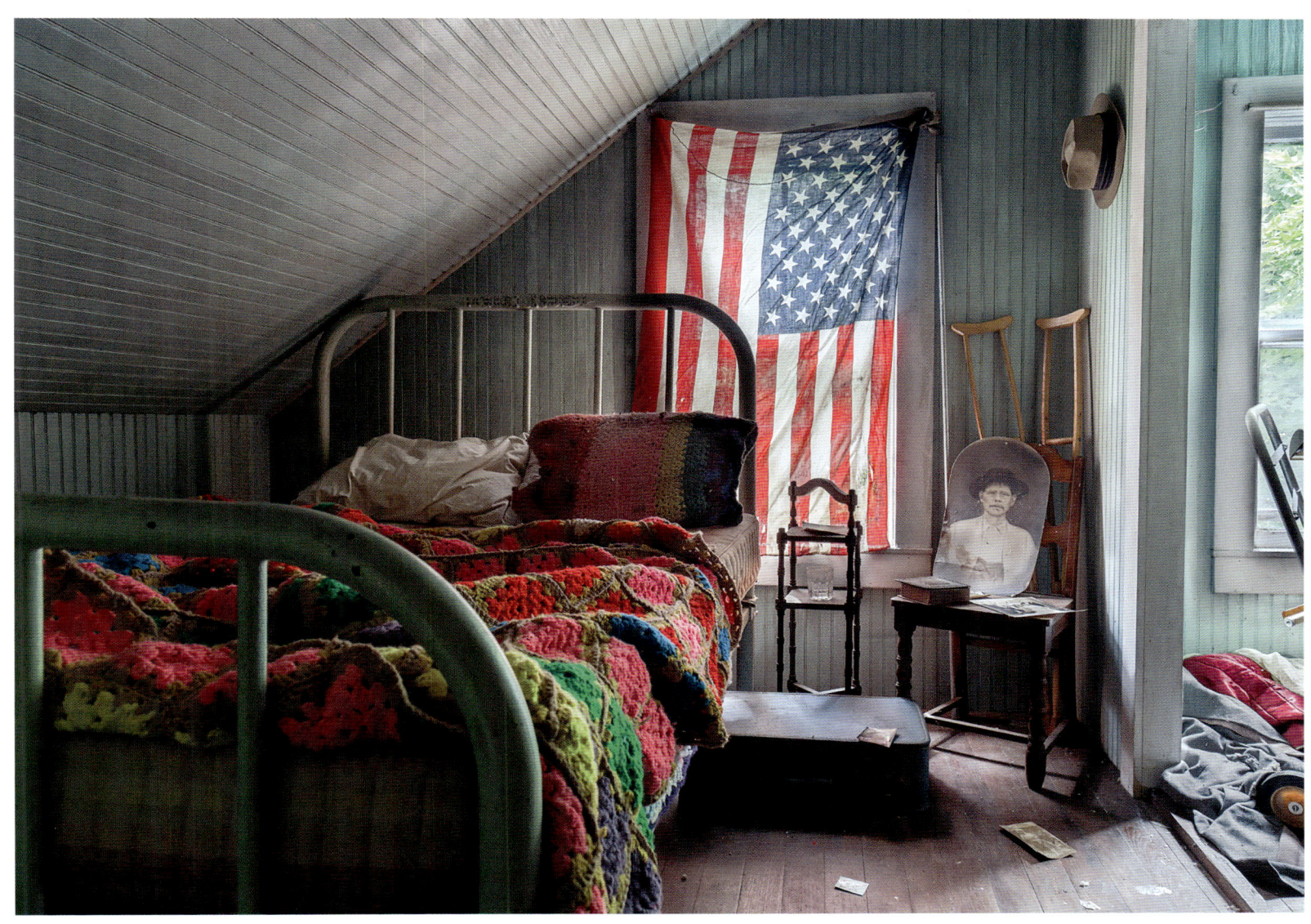

"OLD GLORY IN THE WINDOW"
Middlesex County, Connecticut

Near this colorful bed sit a pair of crutches and a portrait of an old man—a relative of someone who lived here? Based on the many photographs found in this house, I believe it once belonged to a veteran.

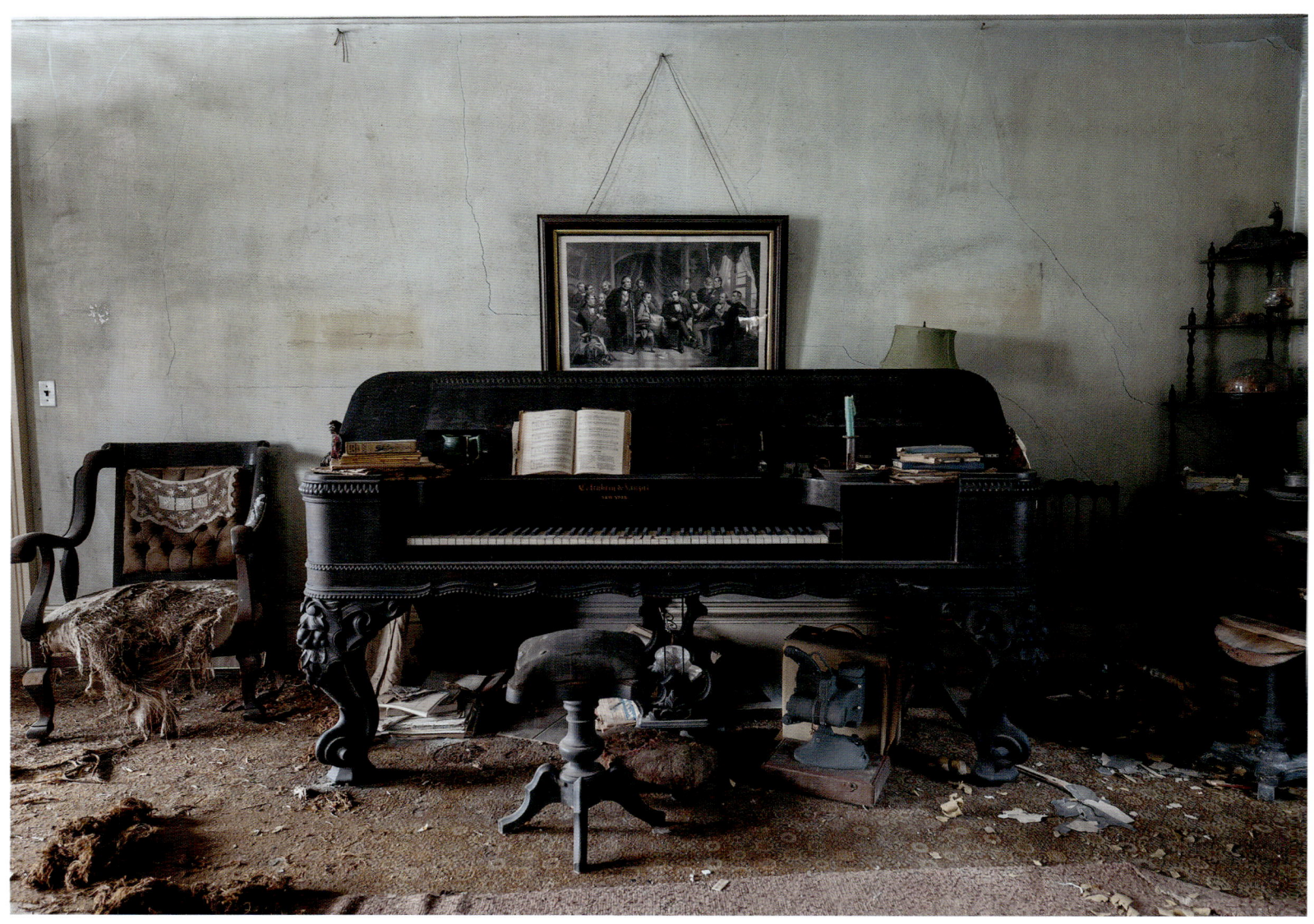

"THE PIANO IN THE PARLOR"
Suffolk County, New York

This antique Calenberg & Vaupel piano dates back to the 1860s. The chair on its left is stuffed with horsehair, which was common in America in the Victorian era, up until the early 1900s.

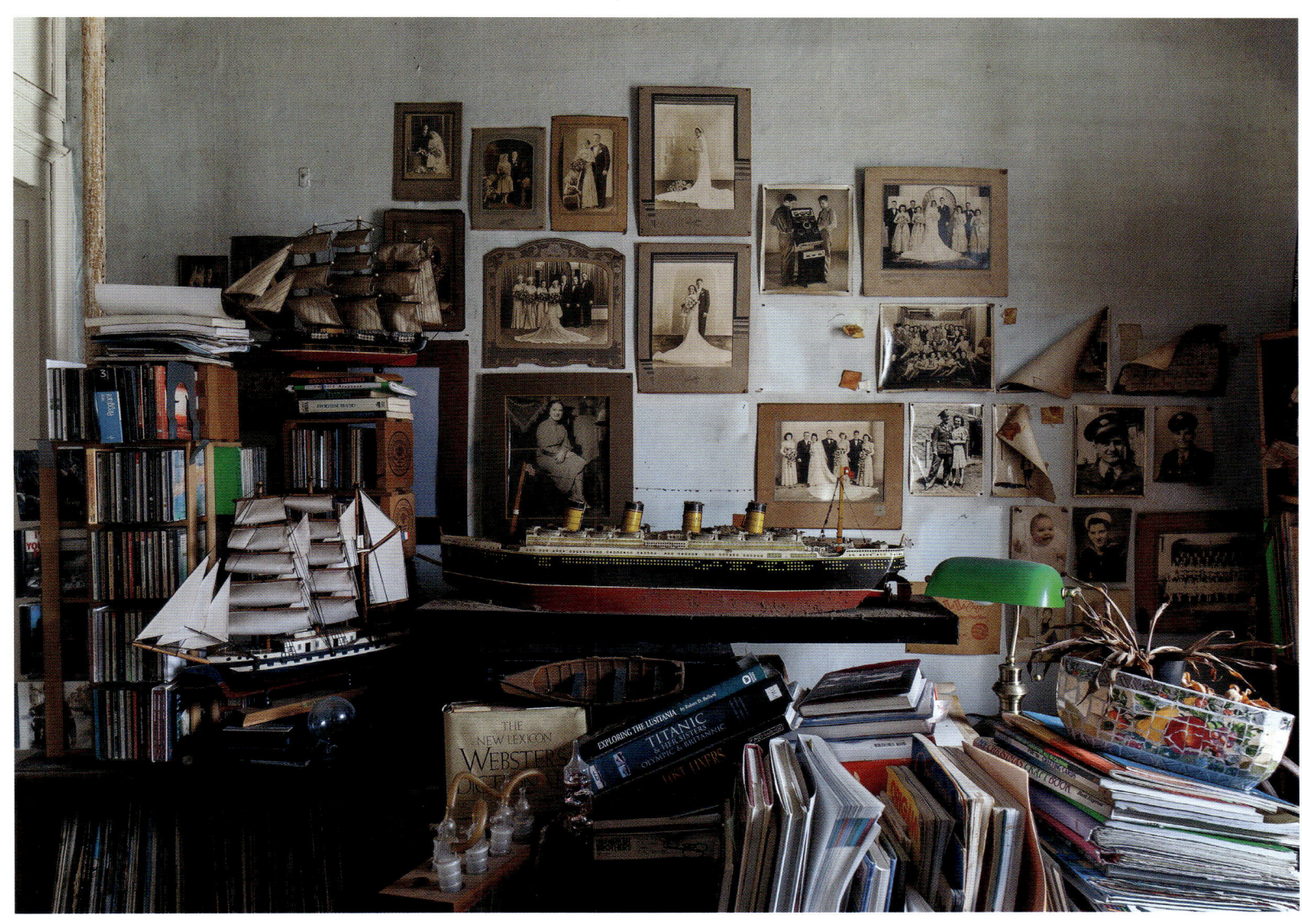

"HYMN TO THE SEA"
Tolland County, Connecticut

An elderly woman lived in this house filled with ocean-related items, including ship models, maps, nautical instruments, books, and various *Titanic*-related memorabilia. Family portraits hung from the wall behind the model ship. She clearly loved the sea and maybe was even a relative of someone on the *Titanic*.

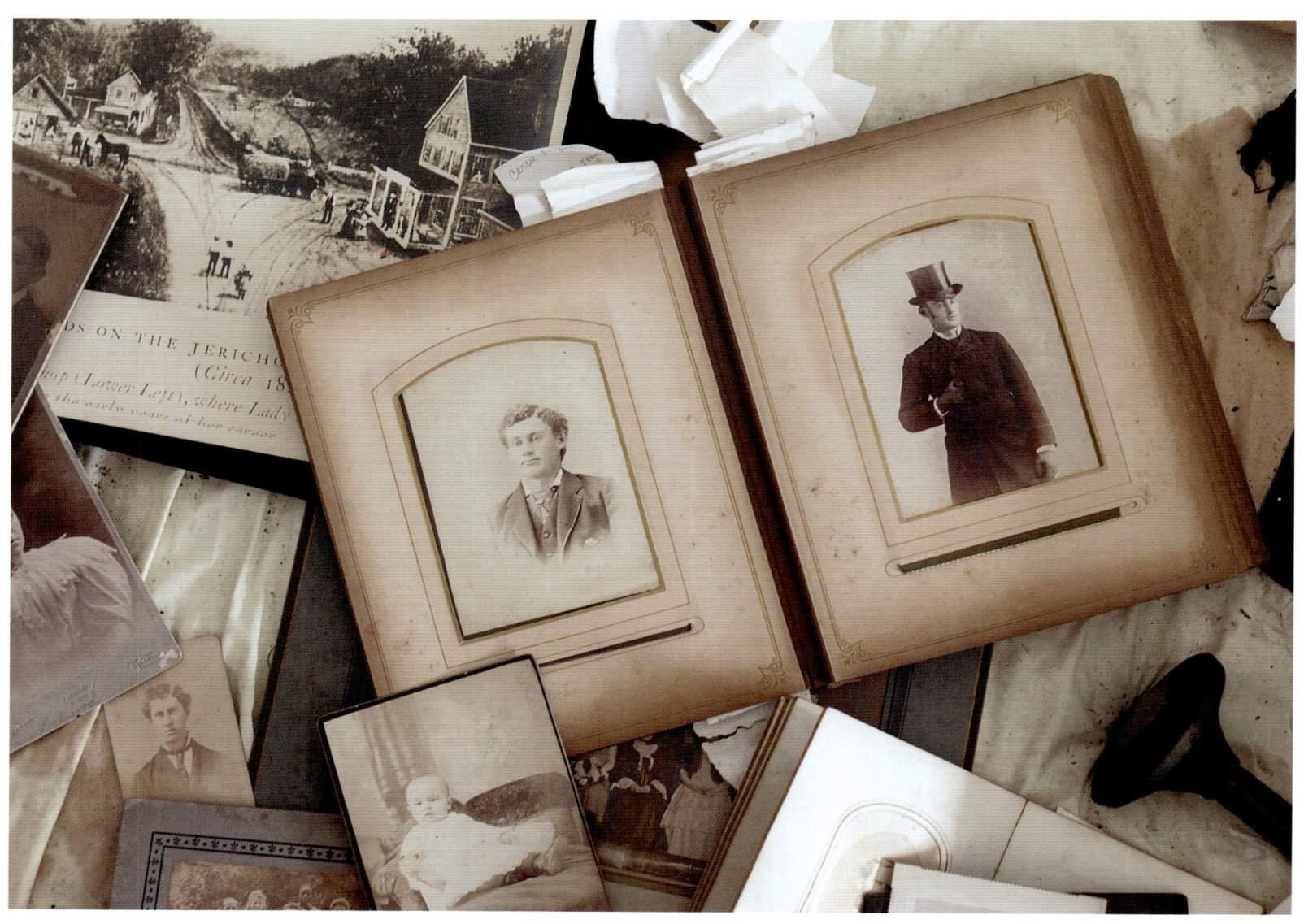

"PORTRAITS OF A FAMILY"
Suffolk County, New York

This collection of photographs showed generations of a family going back to the nineteenth century.

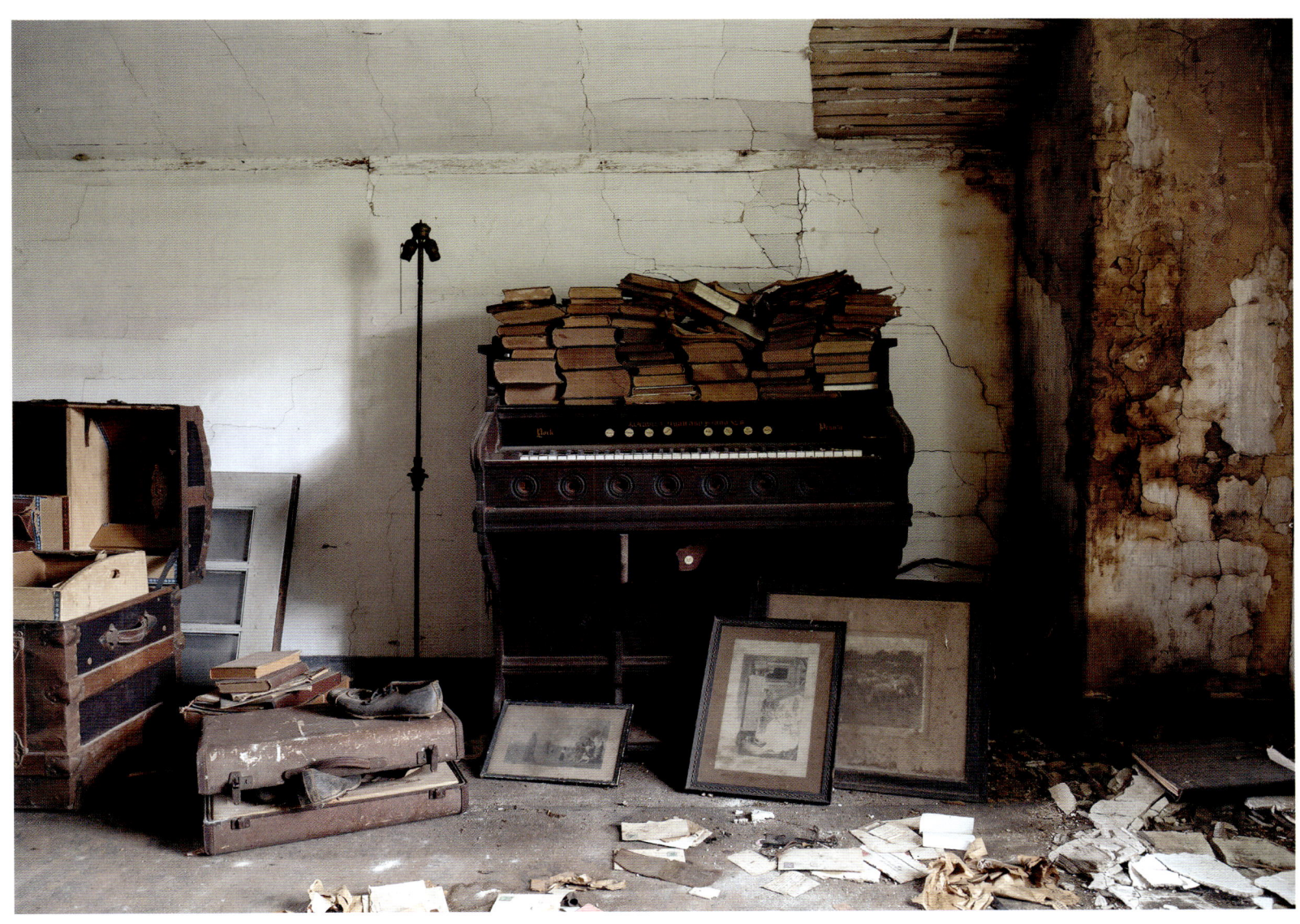

"THE ORGAN IN THE ATTIC"
Richmond County, Virginia

This colonial-style house previously belonged to a war veteran. Outside was a family cemetery, and in the attic were an organ, pictures, and books scattered about.

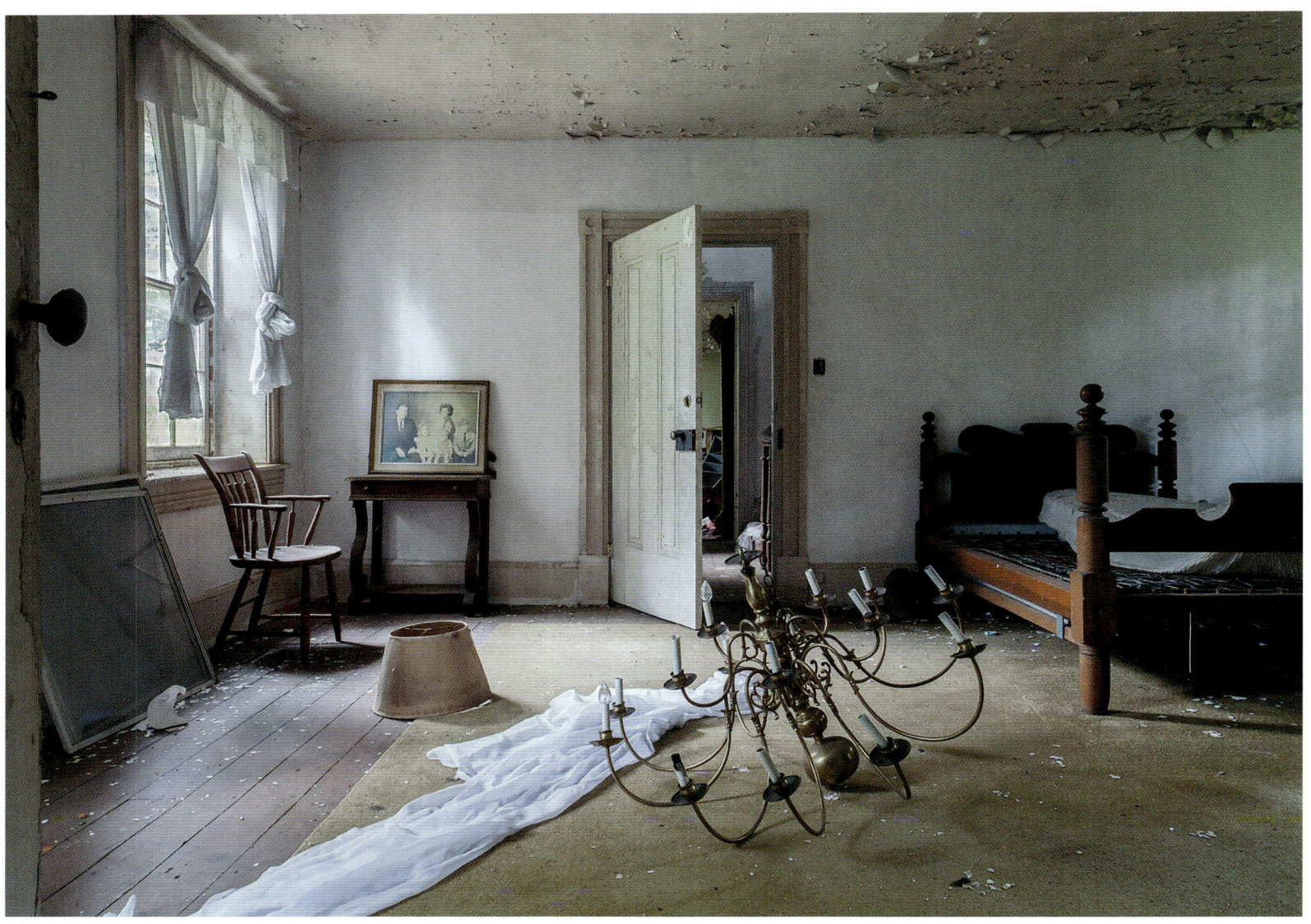

"THE CONGRESSMAN'S HOME"
New Castle County, Delaware

Upon entering this heavily graffitied home, I noticed pictures of many notable political figures, including many posing with the homeowner, who was a politician himself. In a back room were campaign signs and posters from when the politician had run for office. These photos are from an upstairs bedroom.

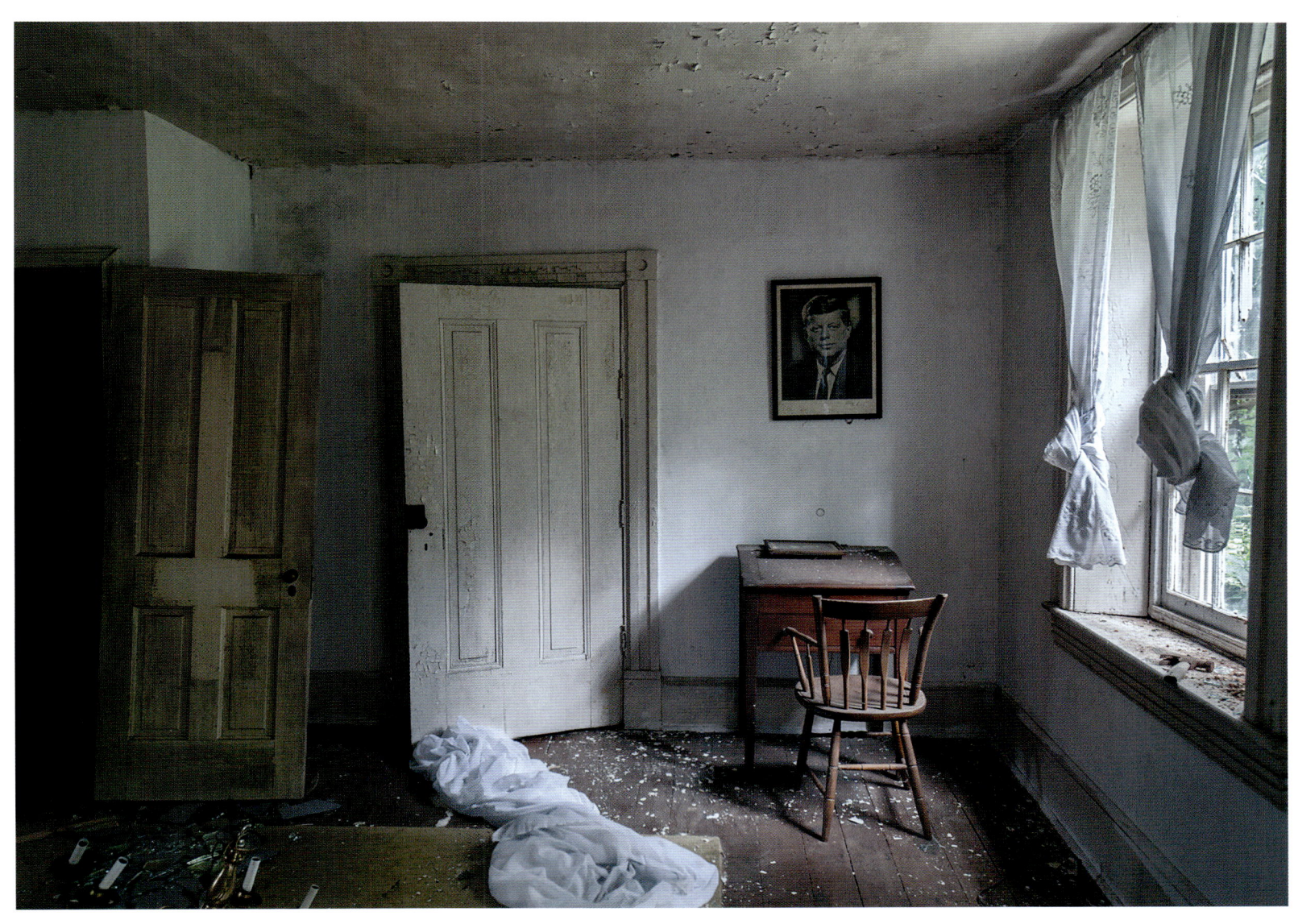

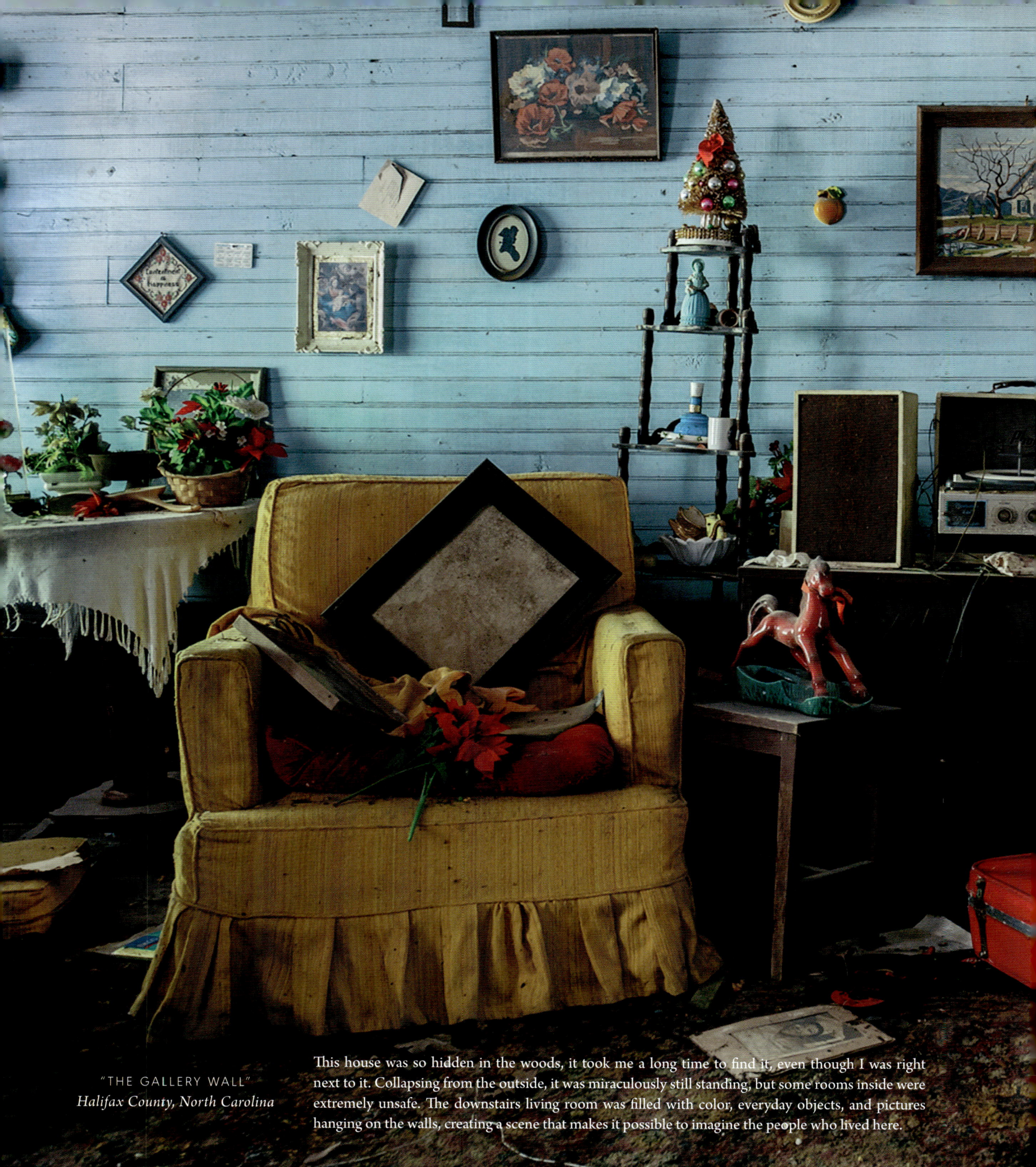

"THE GALLERY WALL"
Halifax County, North Carolina

This house was so hidden in the woods, it took me a long time to find it, even though I was right next to it. Collapsing from the outside, it was miraculously still standing, but some rooms inside were extremely unsafe. The downstairs living room was filled with color, everyday objects, and pictures hanging on the walls, creating a scene that makes it possible to imagine the people who lived here.

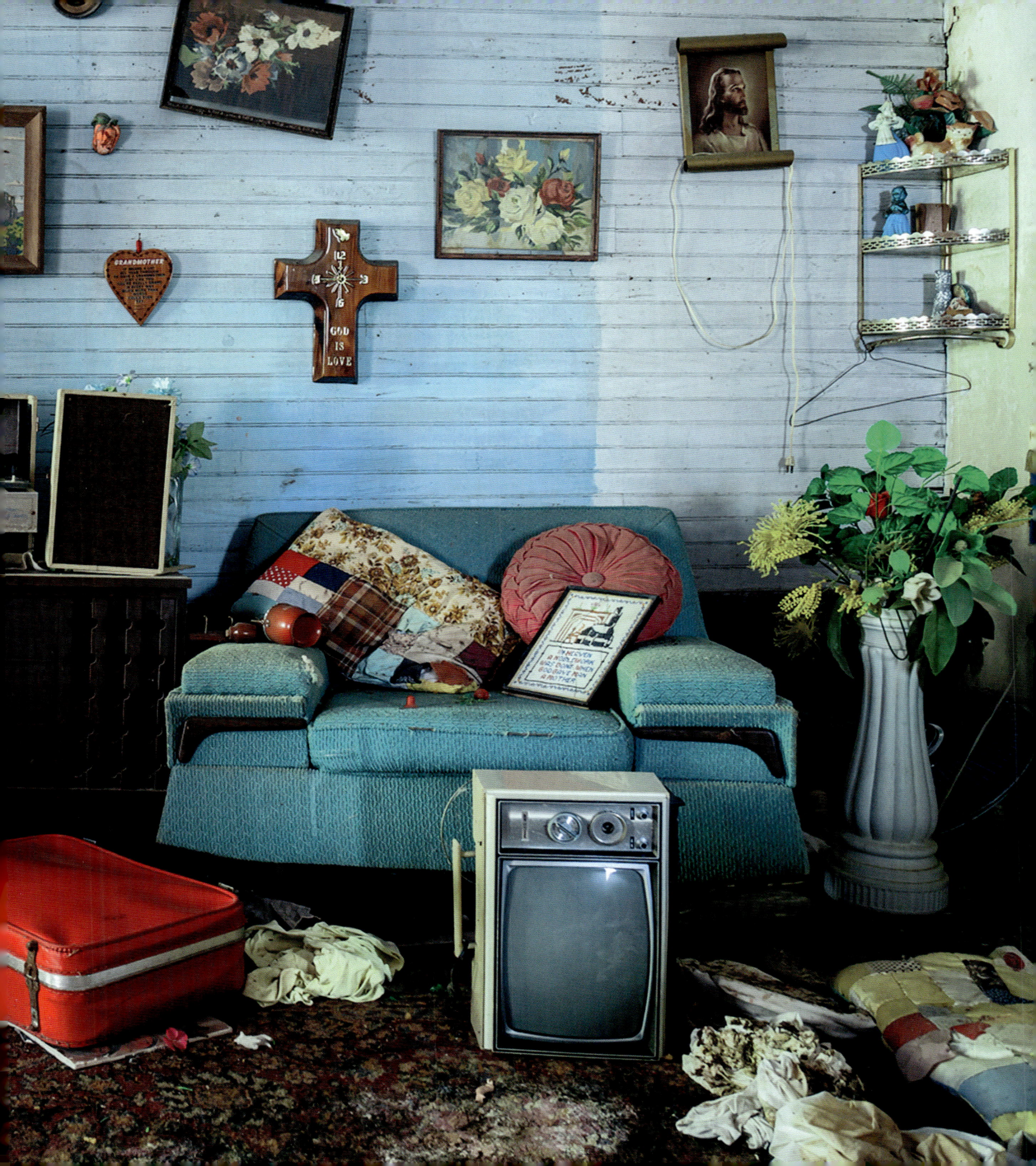

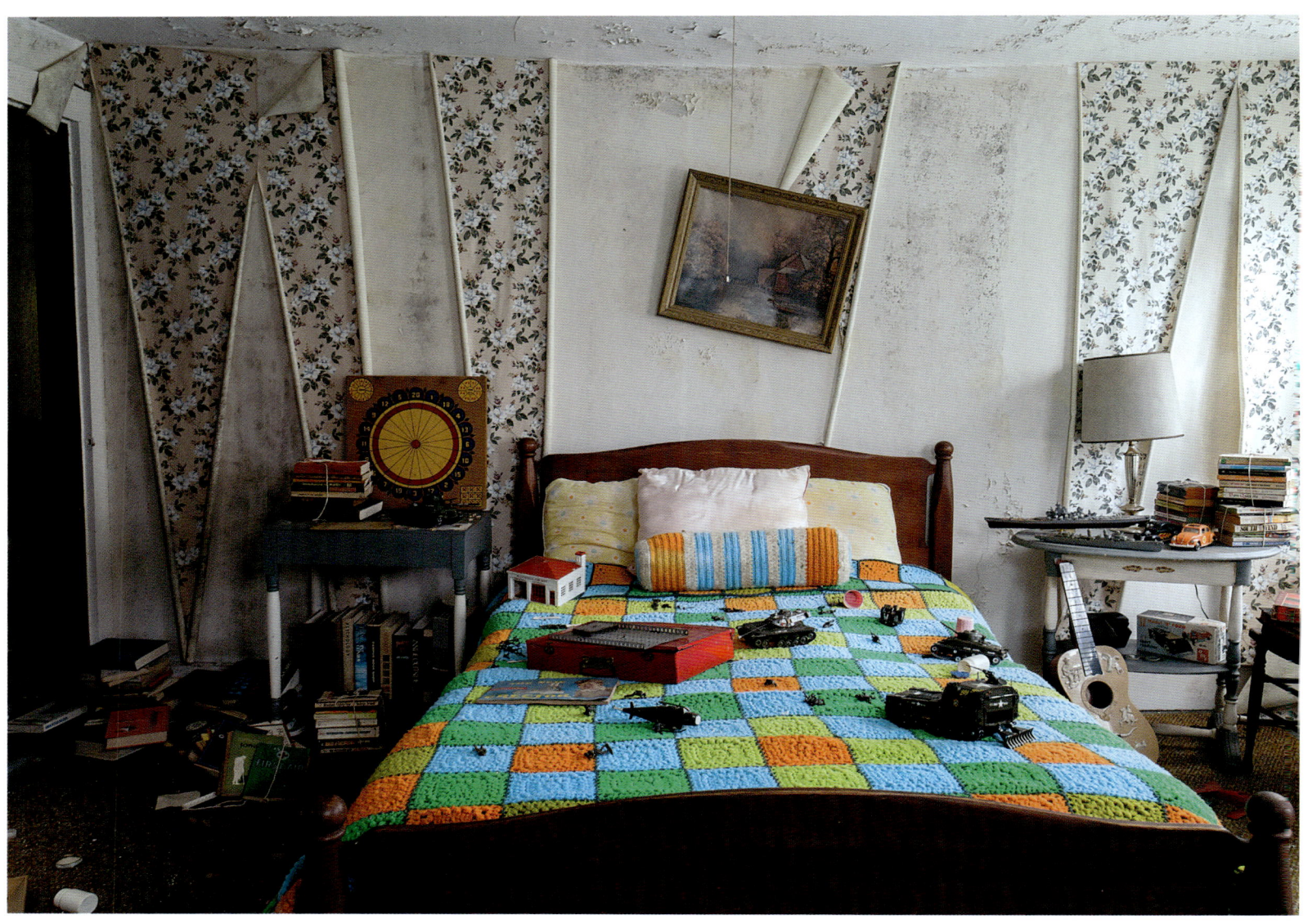

"THE TOY SOLDIERS"
Windham County, Connecticut

Entering this room felt like stepping back in time to a 1950s childhood. Surrounded by toy soldiers, books, and musical instruments, I could practically hear the sound of a child playing. This was a particularly challenging picture to take because the room was small but had a large dresser, where I placed my camera.

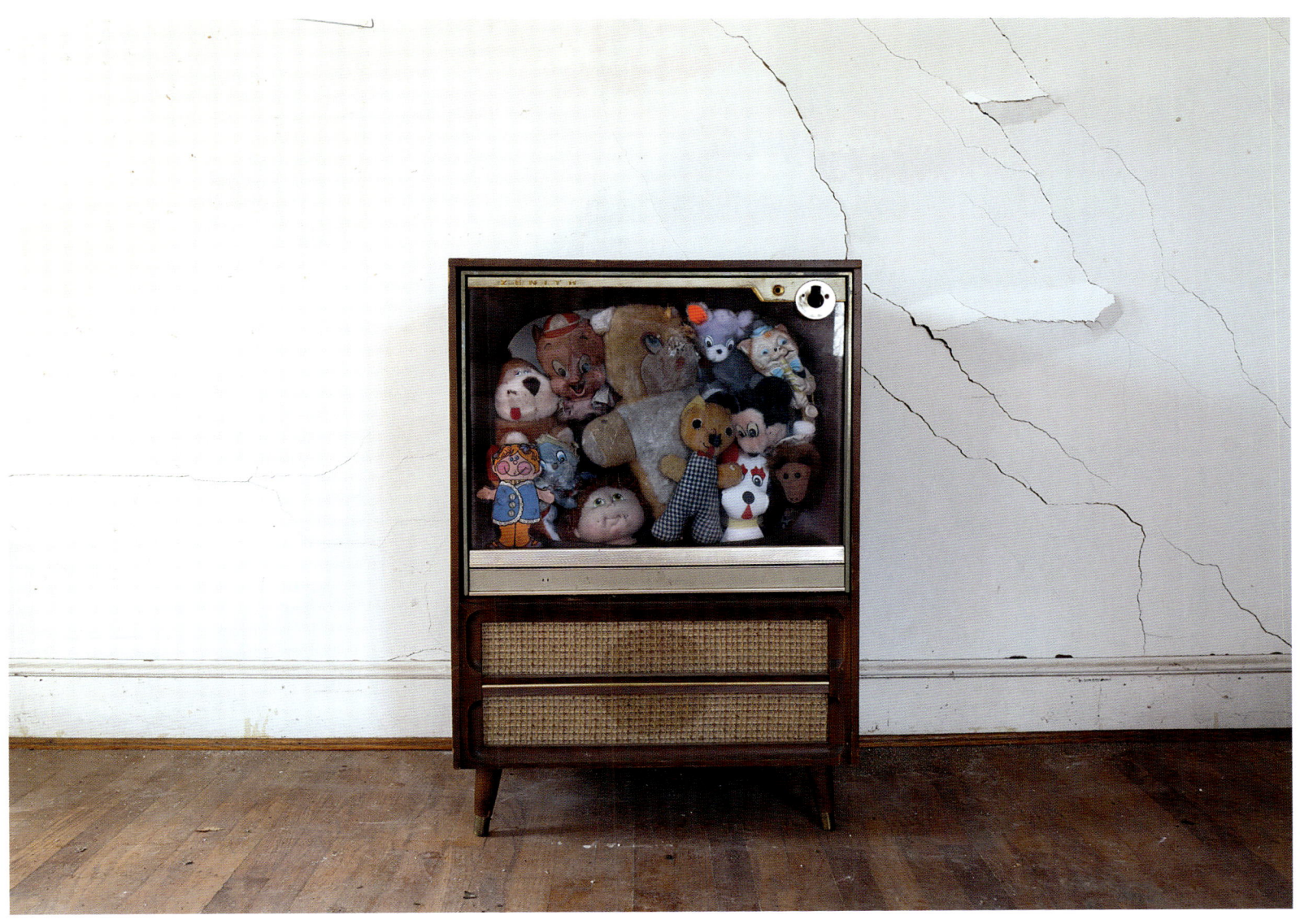

"TOONS ON TELEVISION"
Northumberland County, Virginia

This house was filled with items from many decades, but it was the stuffed animals left around, even in the back of an old television, that I found most striking.

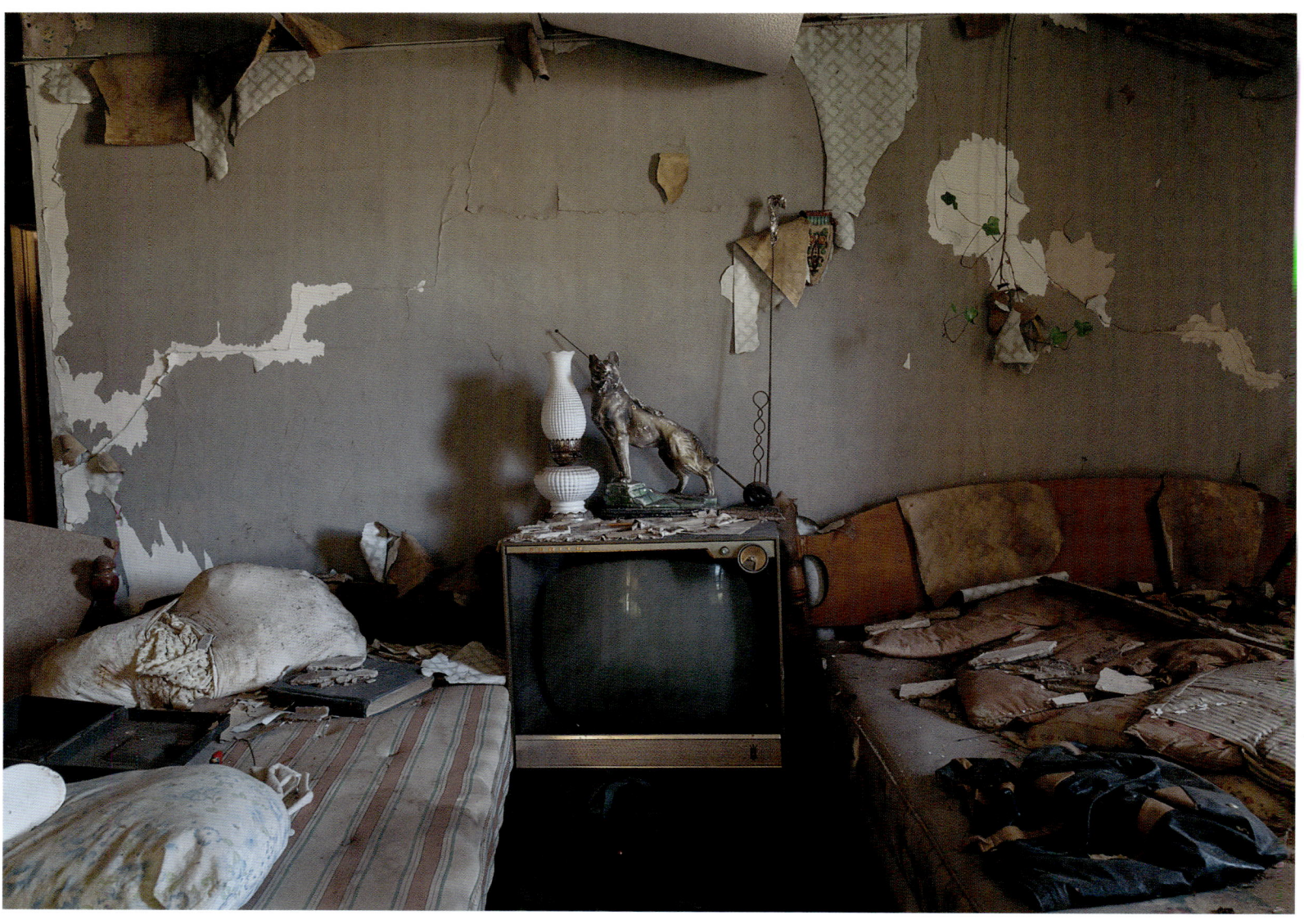

"THE LONELY DOG"
Kent County, Maryland

I discovered this house while driving through Maryland. It was hidden by thick bushes, and the front door had been knocked down and had growth on top of it. The interior was from a completely different time. In this upstairs bedroom, two beds, a TV, and a dog statue created an arresting composition with the light coming in from the windows behind me.

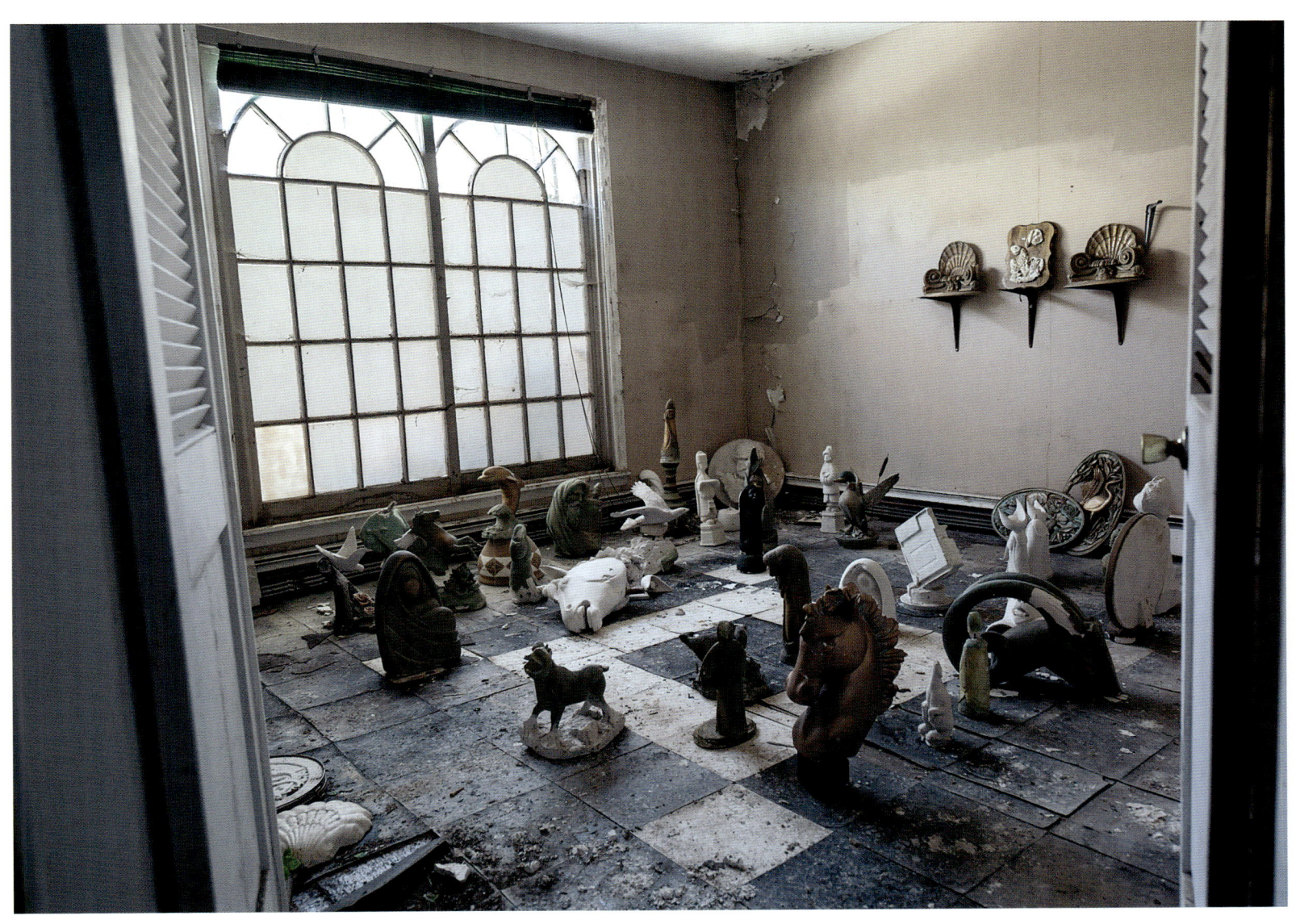

"THE CHESSBOARD"
Sullivan County, New York

This is one of the most unusual rooms I've seen, with garden statues and art laid out on a tiled floor in a manner resembling a giant chessboard. I assume this arrangement was created by another photographer.

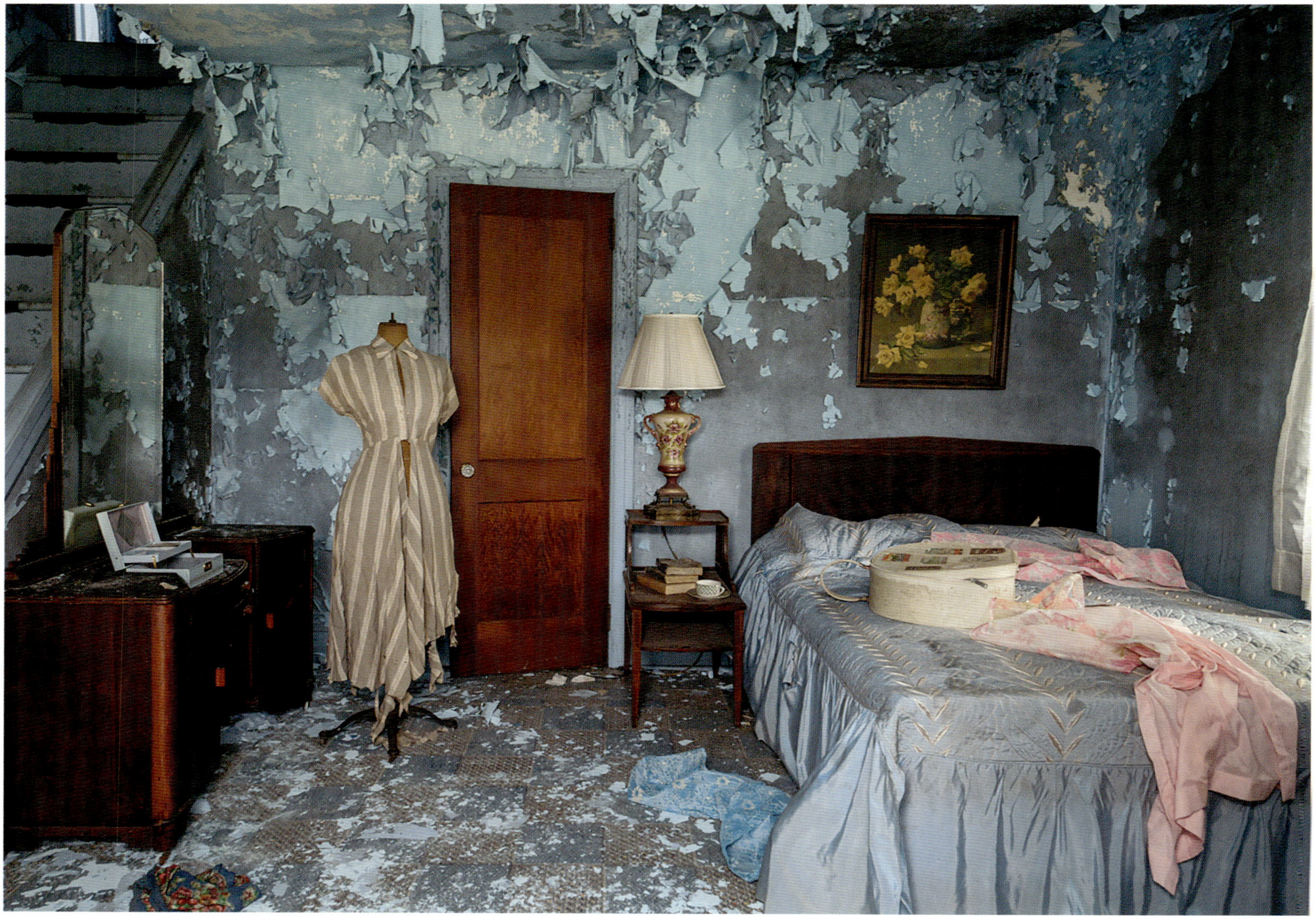

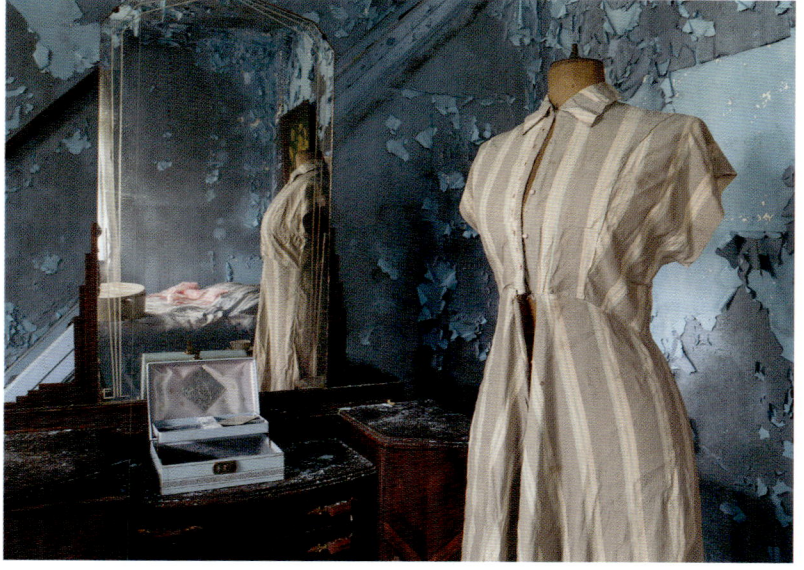

"THE SEAMSTRESS'S HOME"
Somerset County, New Jersey

With such an abundance of sewing materials, including this vintage dress form, this house was owned by a seamstress. It was full of many other vintage pieces, including an art deco–style dresser and mid-century furniture, lamps, and kitchenware.

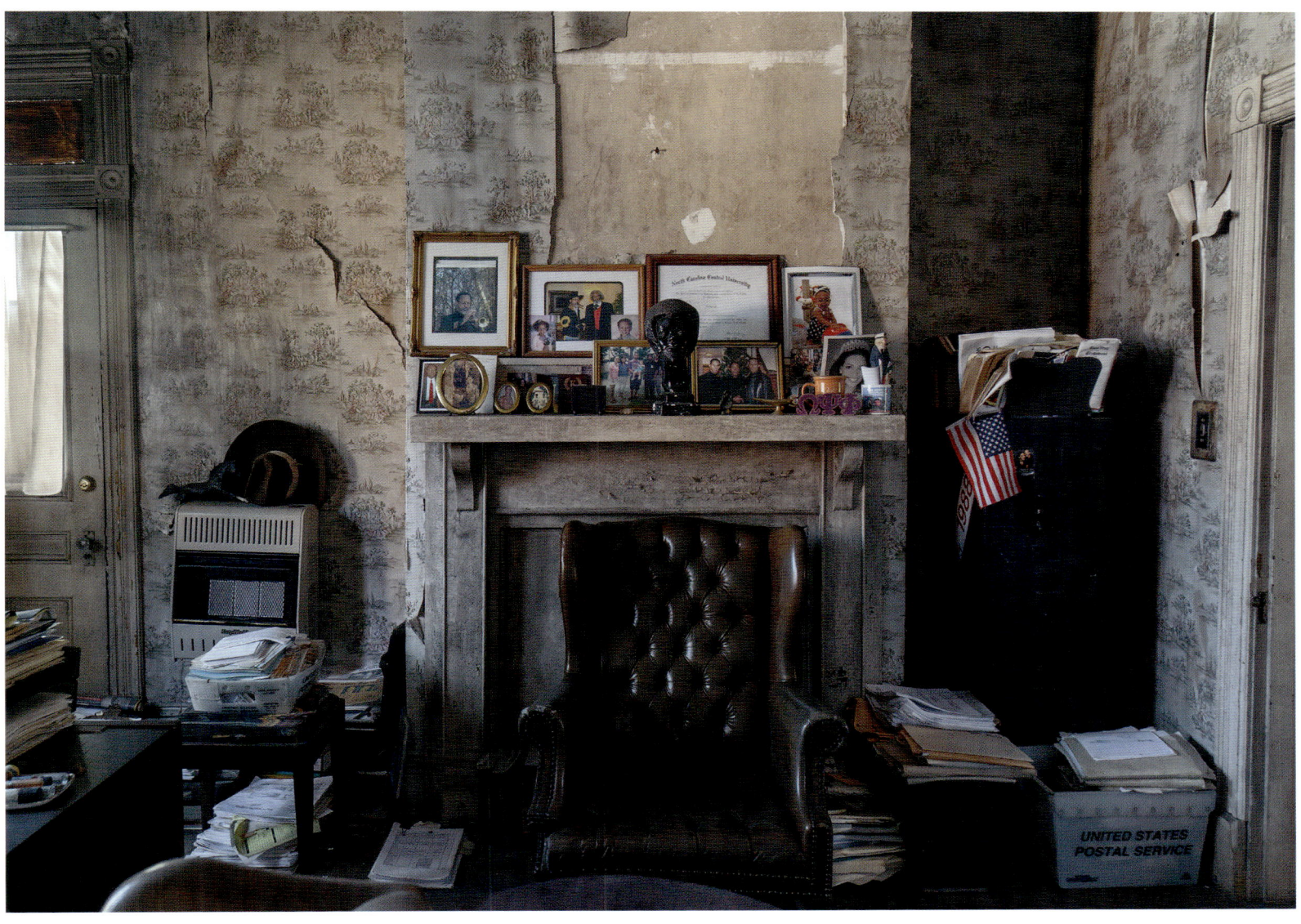

"A FAMILY'S LEGACY"
Lenoir County, North Carolina

In this house, filled with African American history and historical items, a single leather chair sat by a fireplace. Portraits and family pictures covered the mantel.

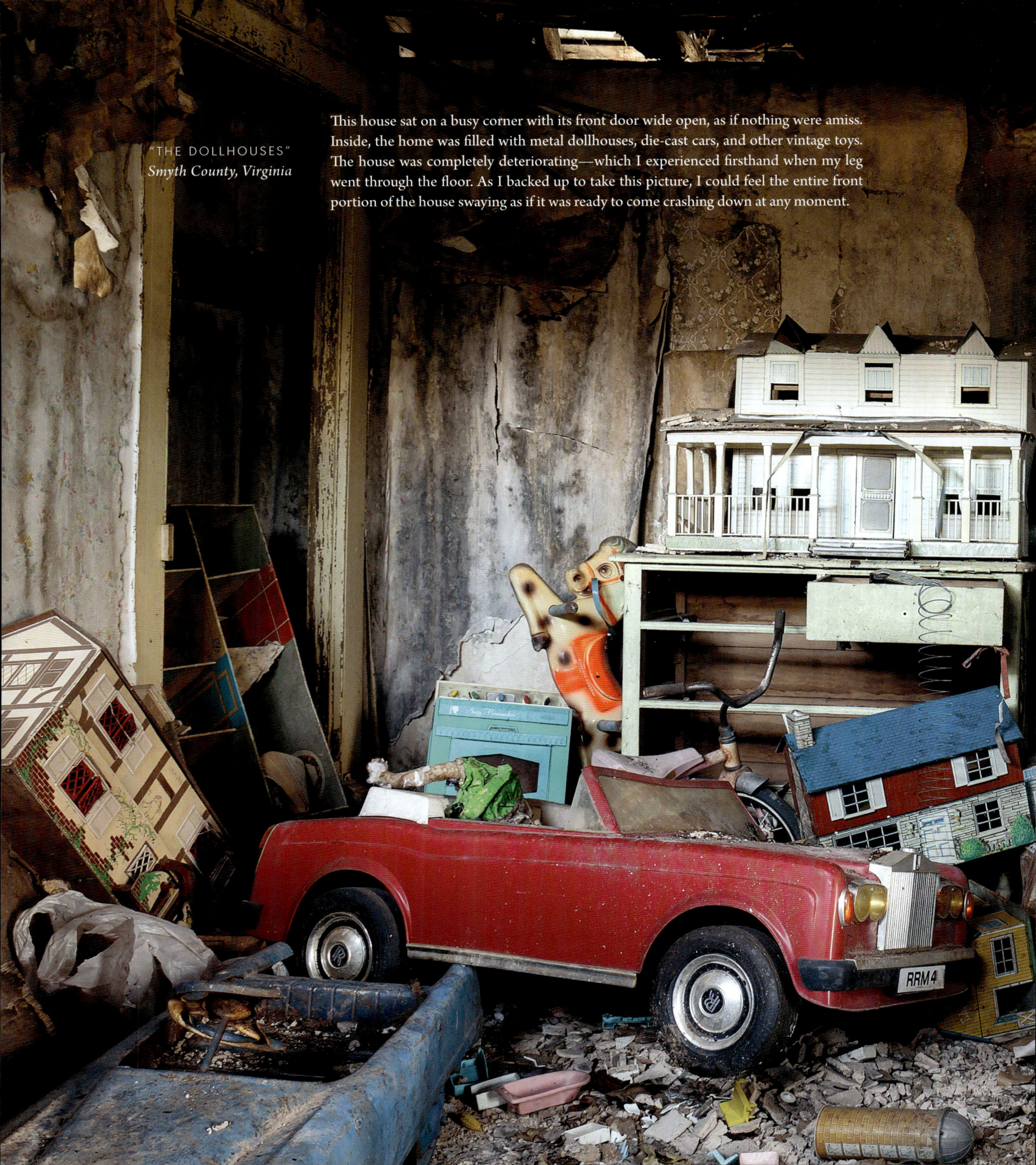

"THE DOLLHOUSES"
Smyth County, Virginia

This house sat on a busy corner with its front door wide open, as if nothing were amiss. Inside, the home was filled with metal dollhouses, die-cast cars, and other vintage toys. The house was completely deteriorating—which I experienced firsthand when my leg went through the floor. As I backed up to take this picture, I could feel the entire front portion of the house swaying as if it was ready to come crashing down at any moment.

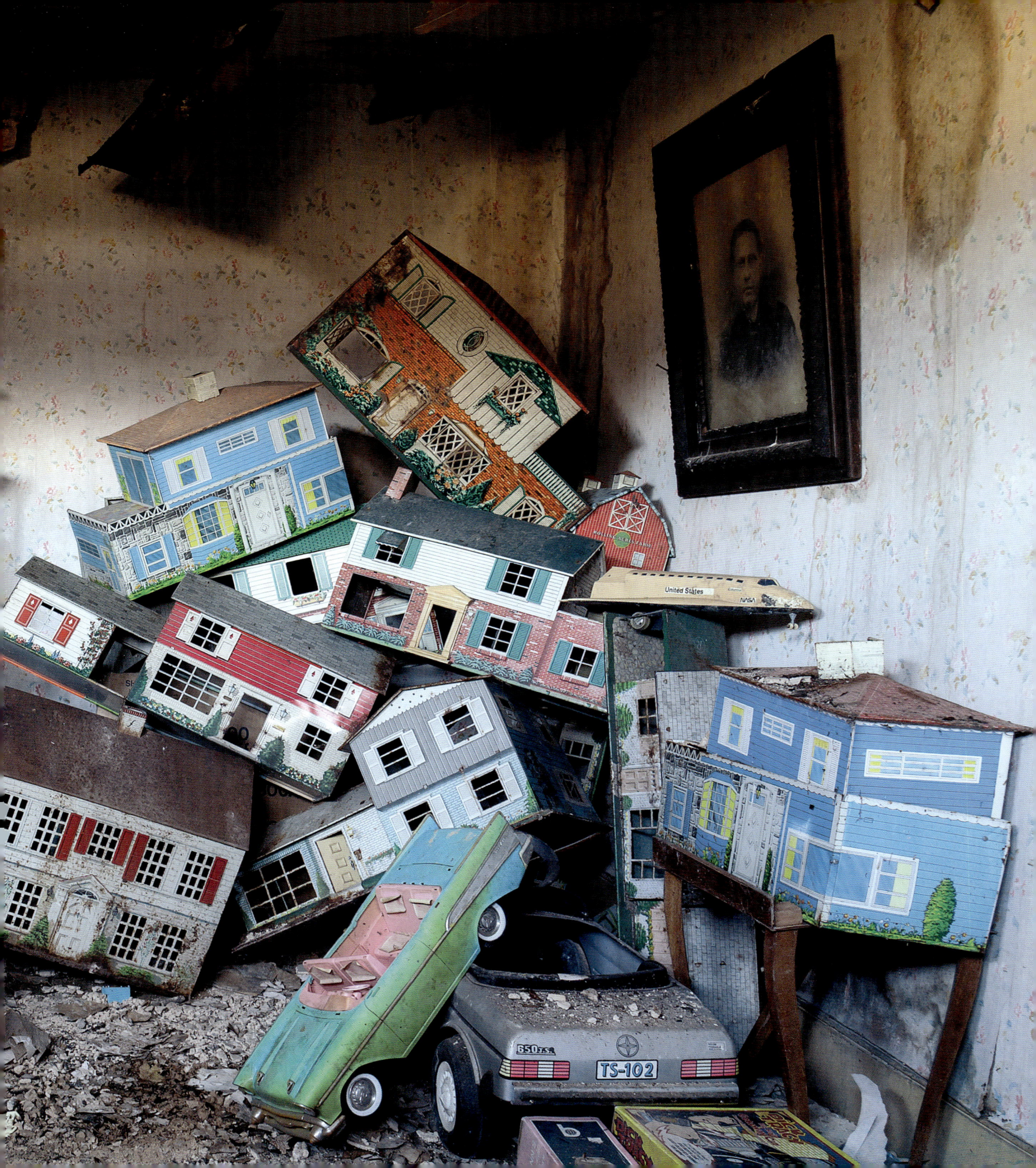

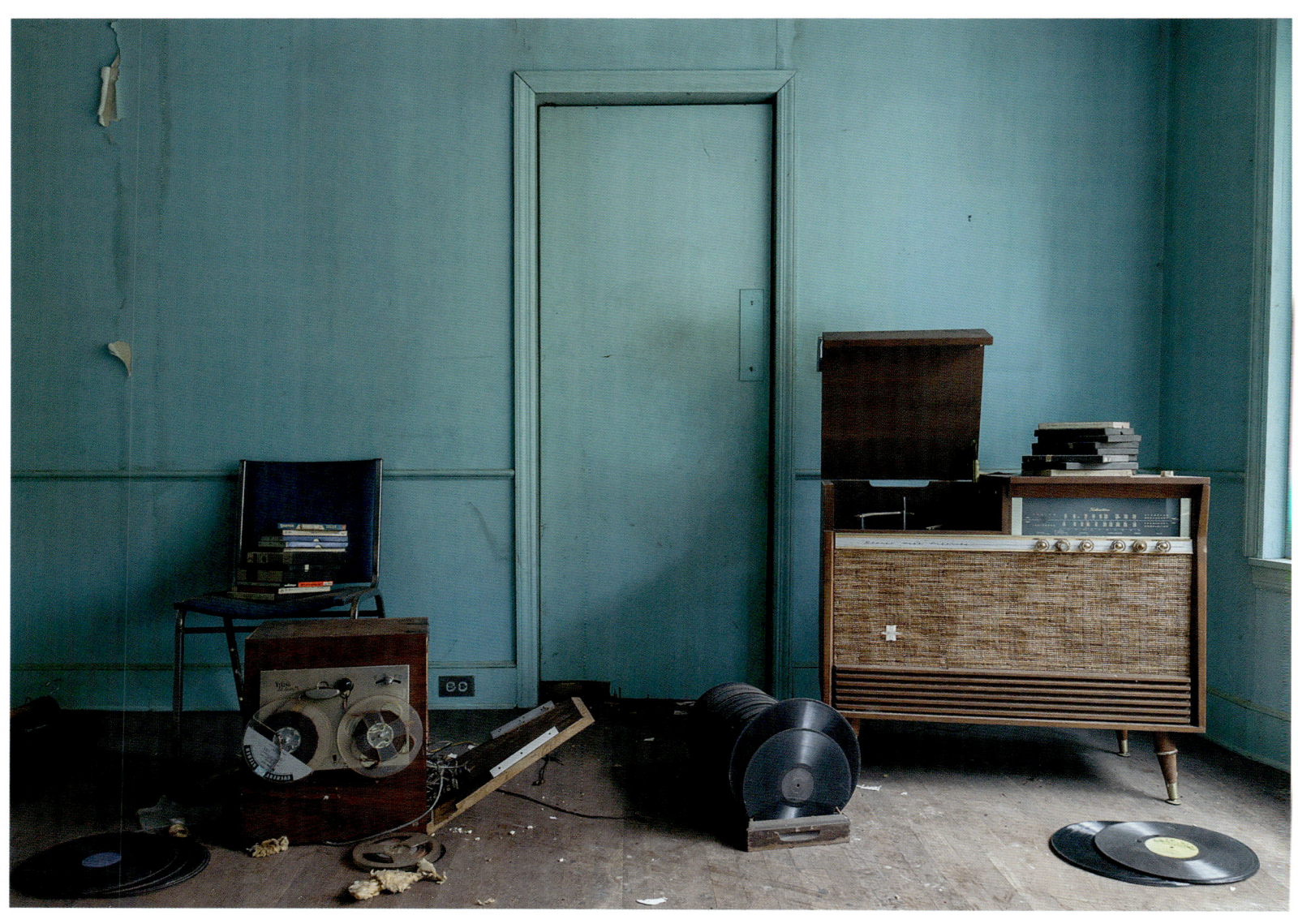

"THE MUSIC LOVER'S ROOM"
Nassau County, New York

On the property of one "Gold Coast" estate, I found this guesthouse. The inside walls were bright, and records sat on the floor near a mid-century record player.

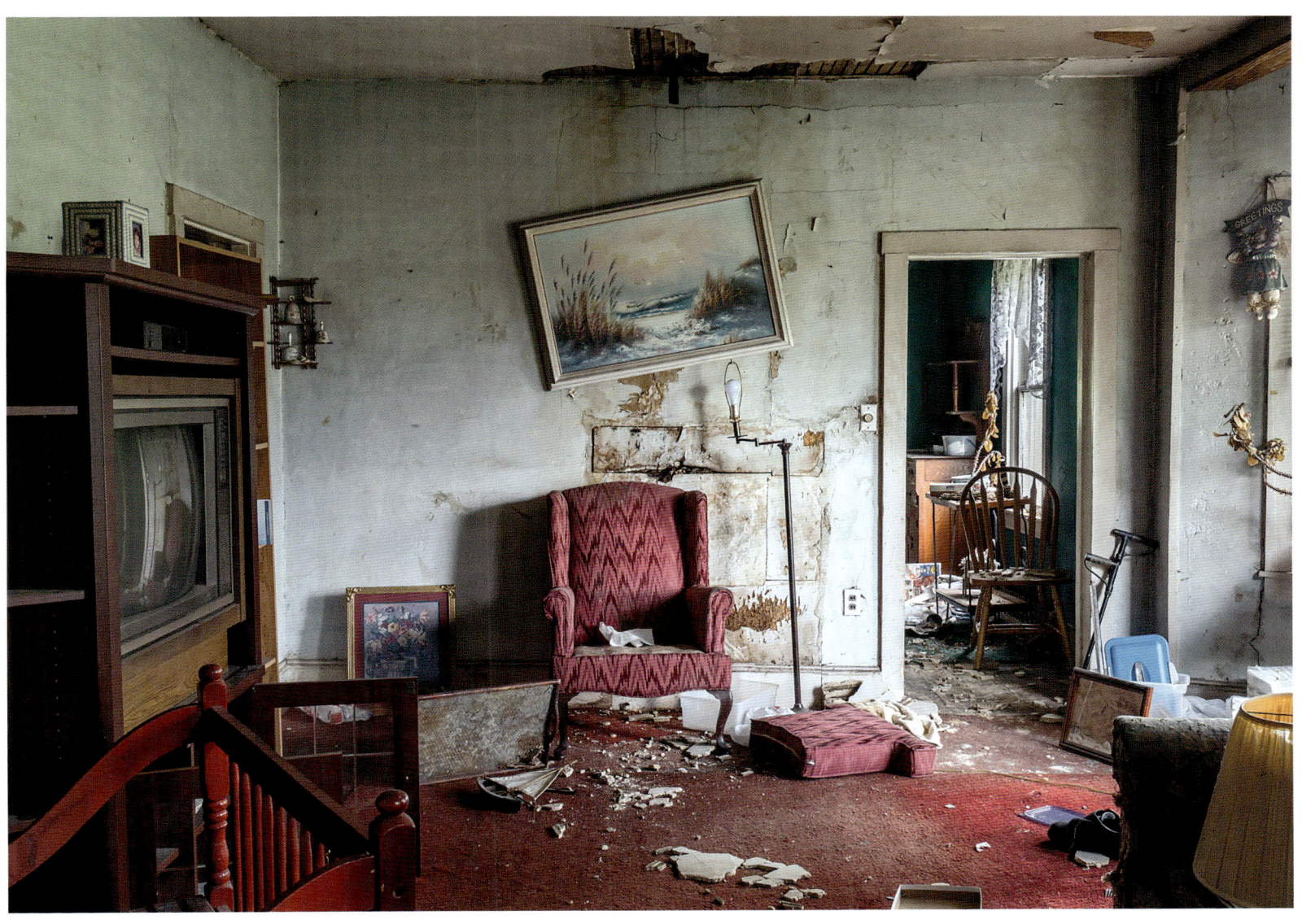

"GRANDMA'S GONE"
New Castle County, Delaware

Driving down a busy highway in Maryland, I noticed several small, overgrown, and abandoned houses slightly set back from the road. One had belonged to an elderly woman and was painted in many vibrant colors. This photo shows one side of her living room. On the other side, a poster reading "For Grandma" hung on the wall amid photographs.

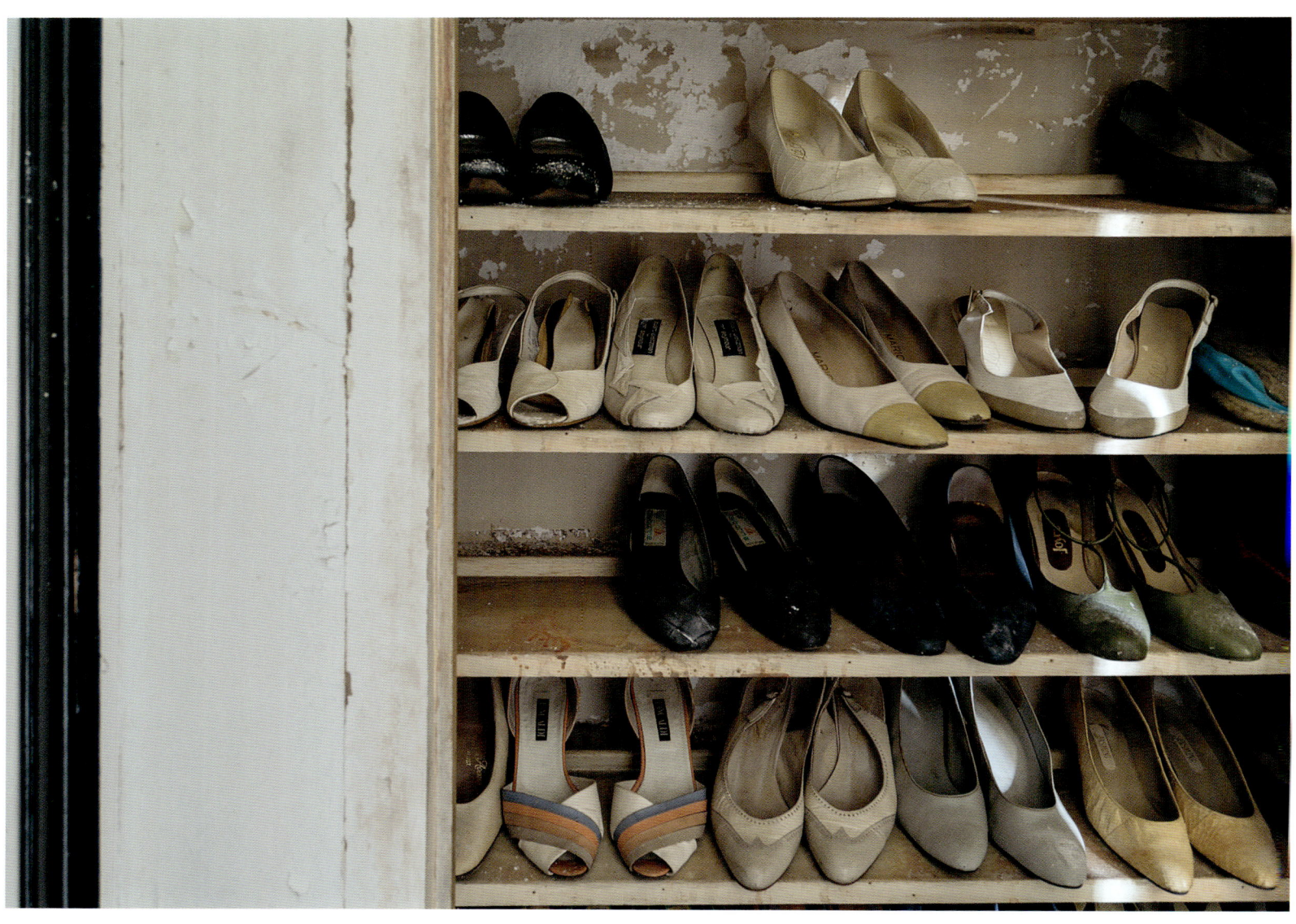

"THE SHOE CLOSET"
Nassau County, New York

It's not surprising to find a shoe closet in a luxurious mansion. However, it is strange to find one filled with shoes in a mansion that is abandoned. Who was the woman who lived such a lavish lifestyle, and when was the last time she walked in these shoes?

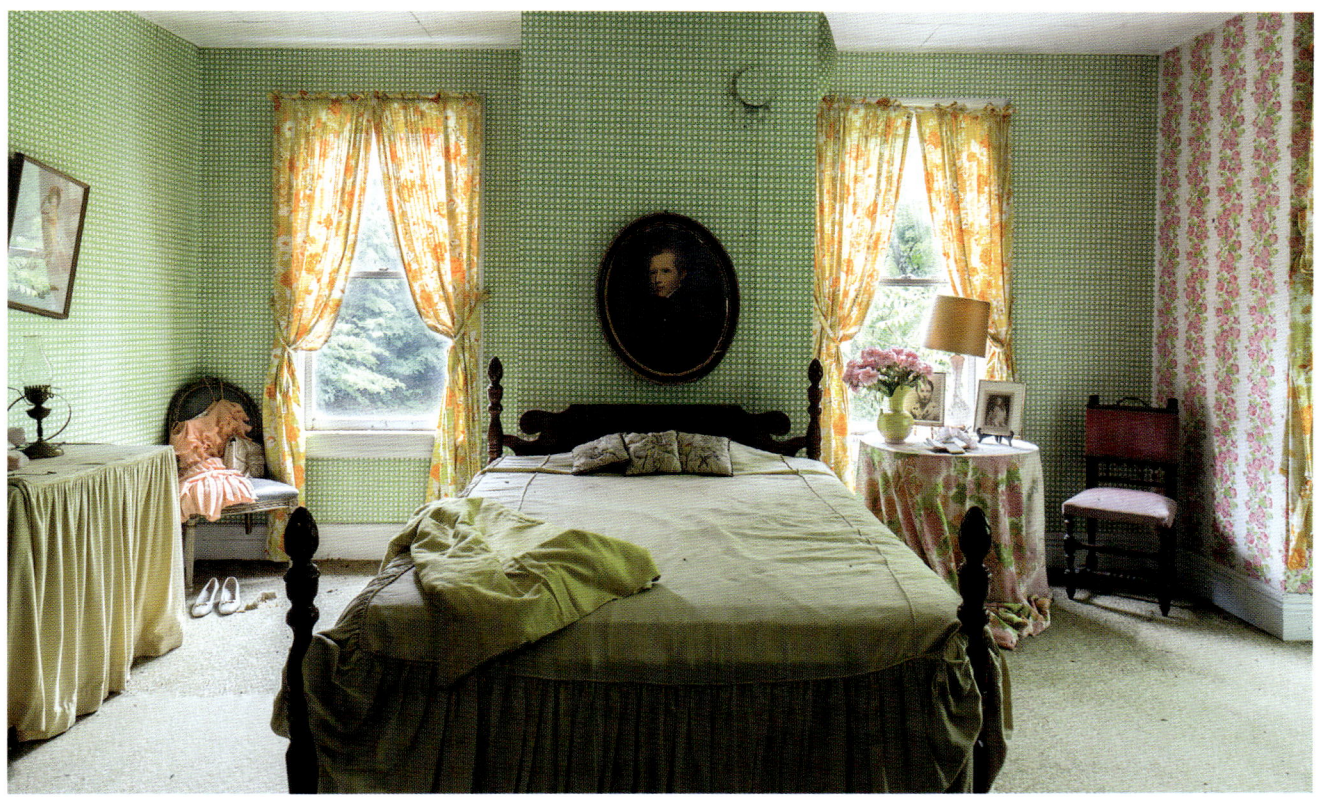

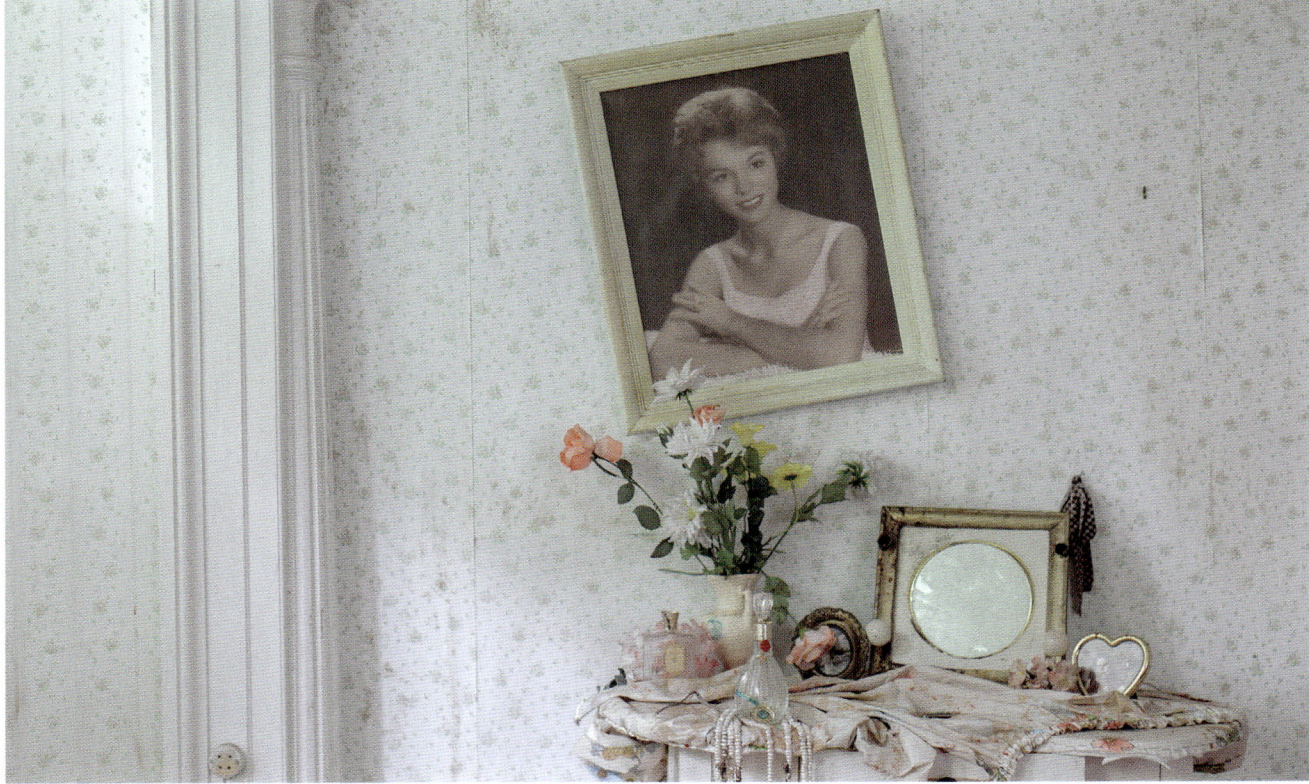

"THE MODEL'S HOUSE"
Dutchess County, New York

It has been said that this house belonged to a famous fashion model. It was filled with clothing, and above a vanity in the main bedroom hung a portrait of an unknown woman. Objects on the vanity included perfume, pearls, and a photo of a woman in a heart-shaped frame.

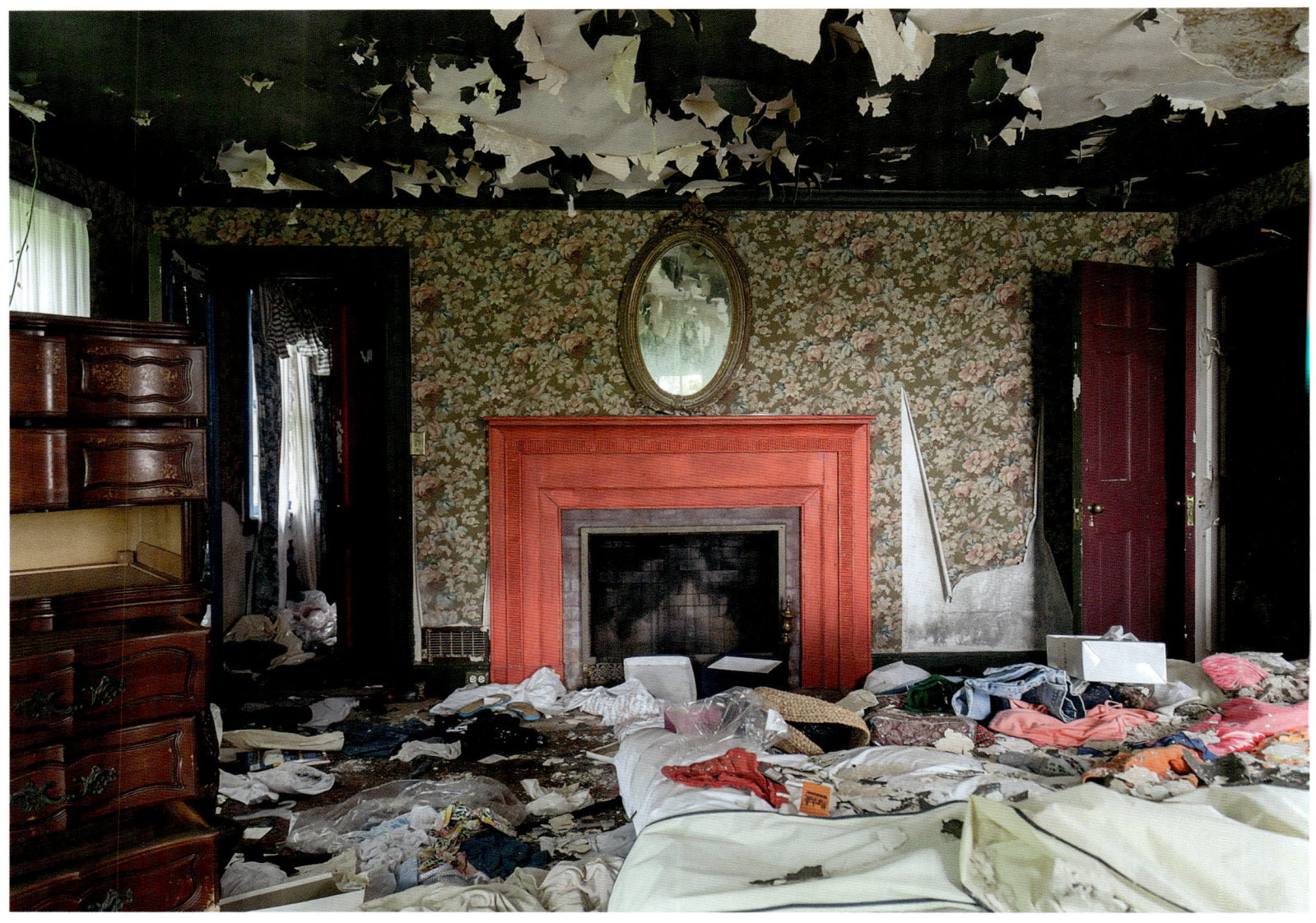

"THE PINK FIREPLACE"
Suffolk County, New York

The woman who lived with her partner in this master bedroom had an obsession with color. She made unusual, bright, and out-of-place color choices.

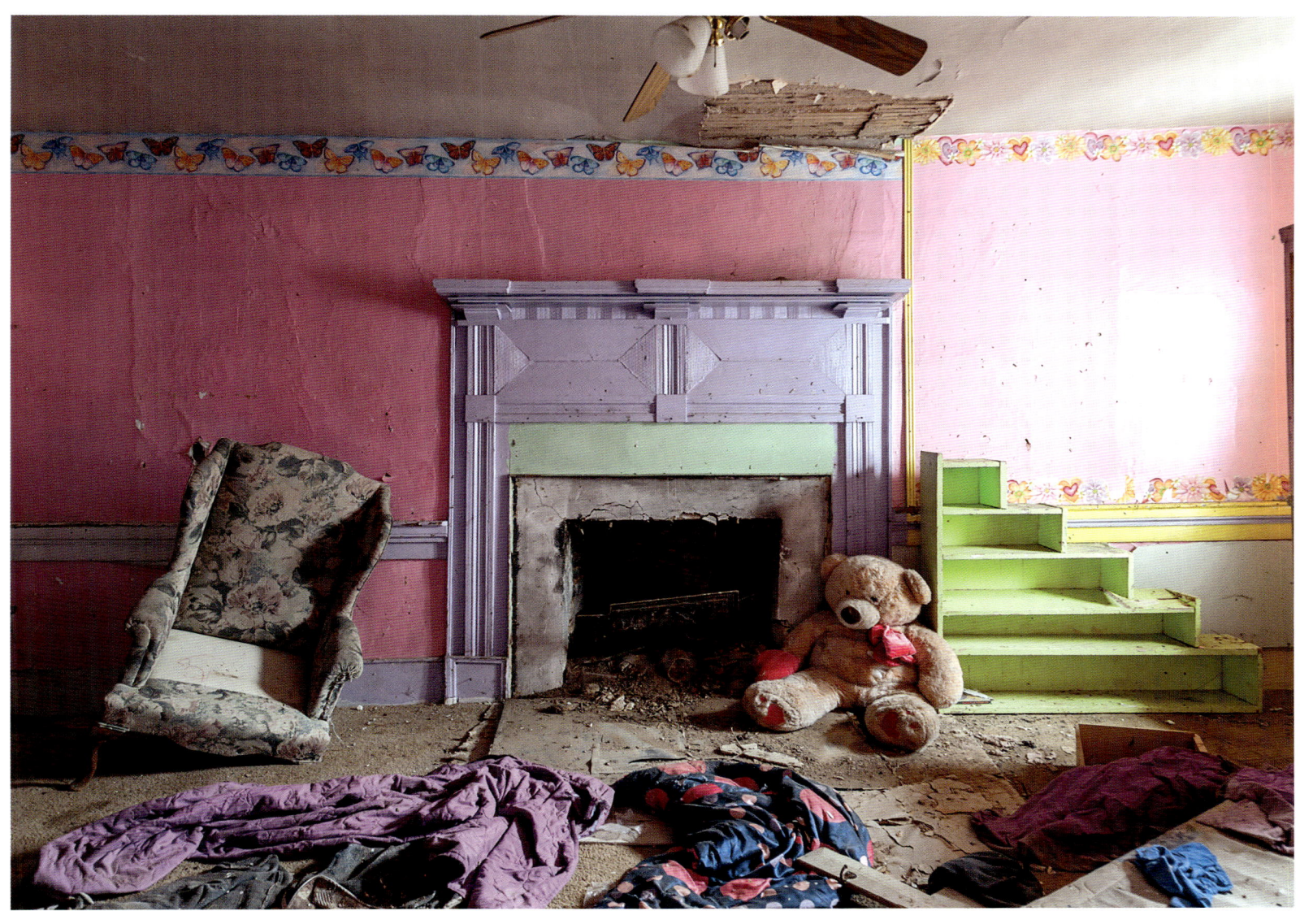

It's not uncommon to find colorful paint in abandoned homes, but this room in an old white farmhouse stood out: although it was the downstairs living room, it looked like a child's bedroom.

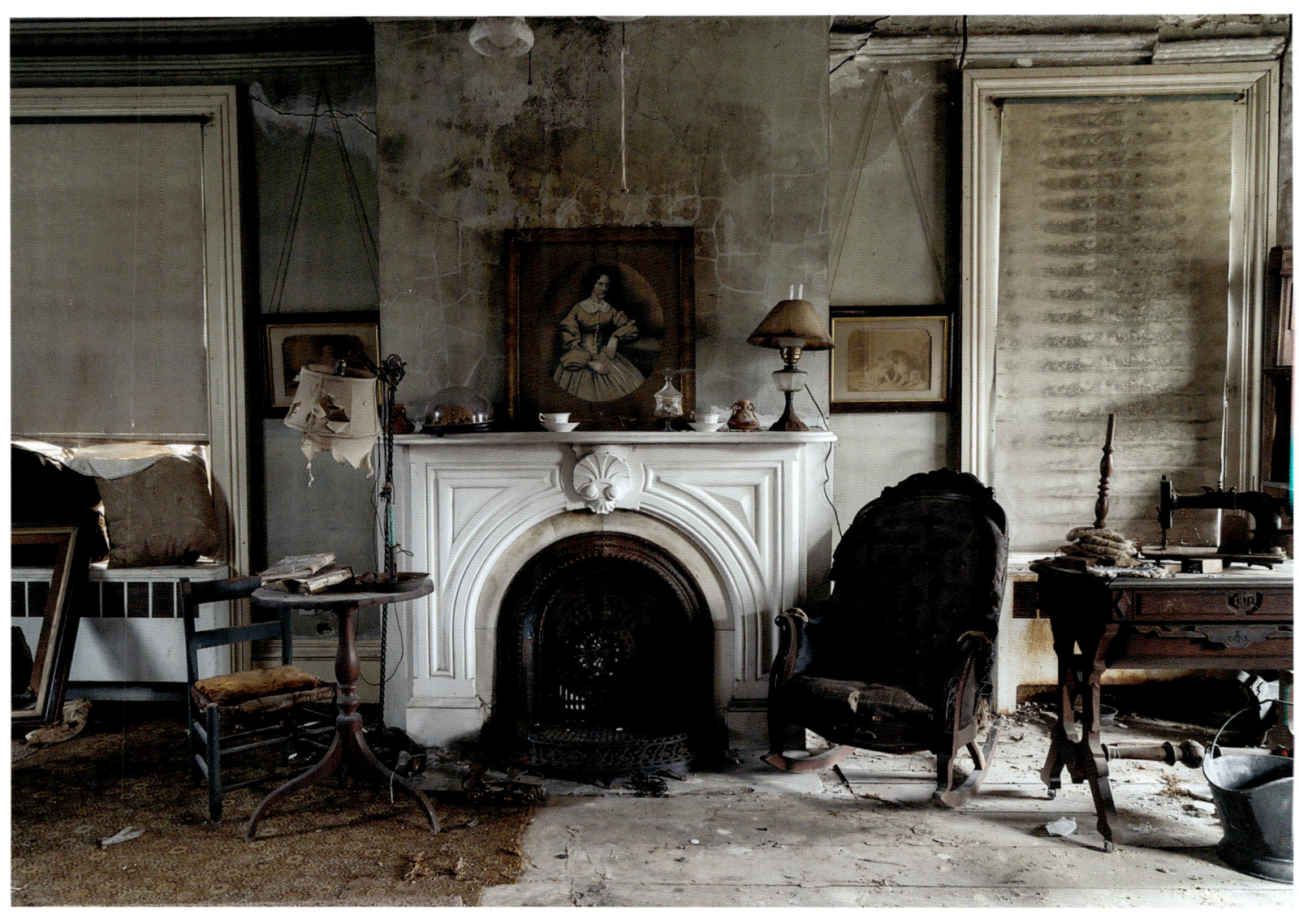

"MARION CARLL FARM"
Suffolk County, New York

Built in 1860, this historic house (above and opposite) has a long family history, and most of the objects inside date to the nineteenth century or earlier. The owner, Marion Carll, was well-known and beloved in the local community, but after her passing, the estate sat abandoned for more than forty years due to a legal battle, and the elements of time have deteriorated the outside and much of the inside. The lady in the painting above the fireplace was most likely a relative of Marion's, or perhaps Marion herself as a young woman.

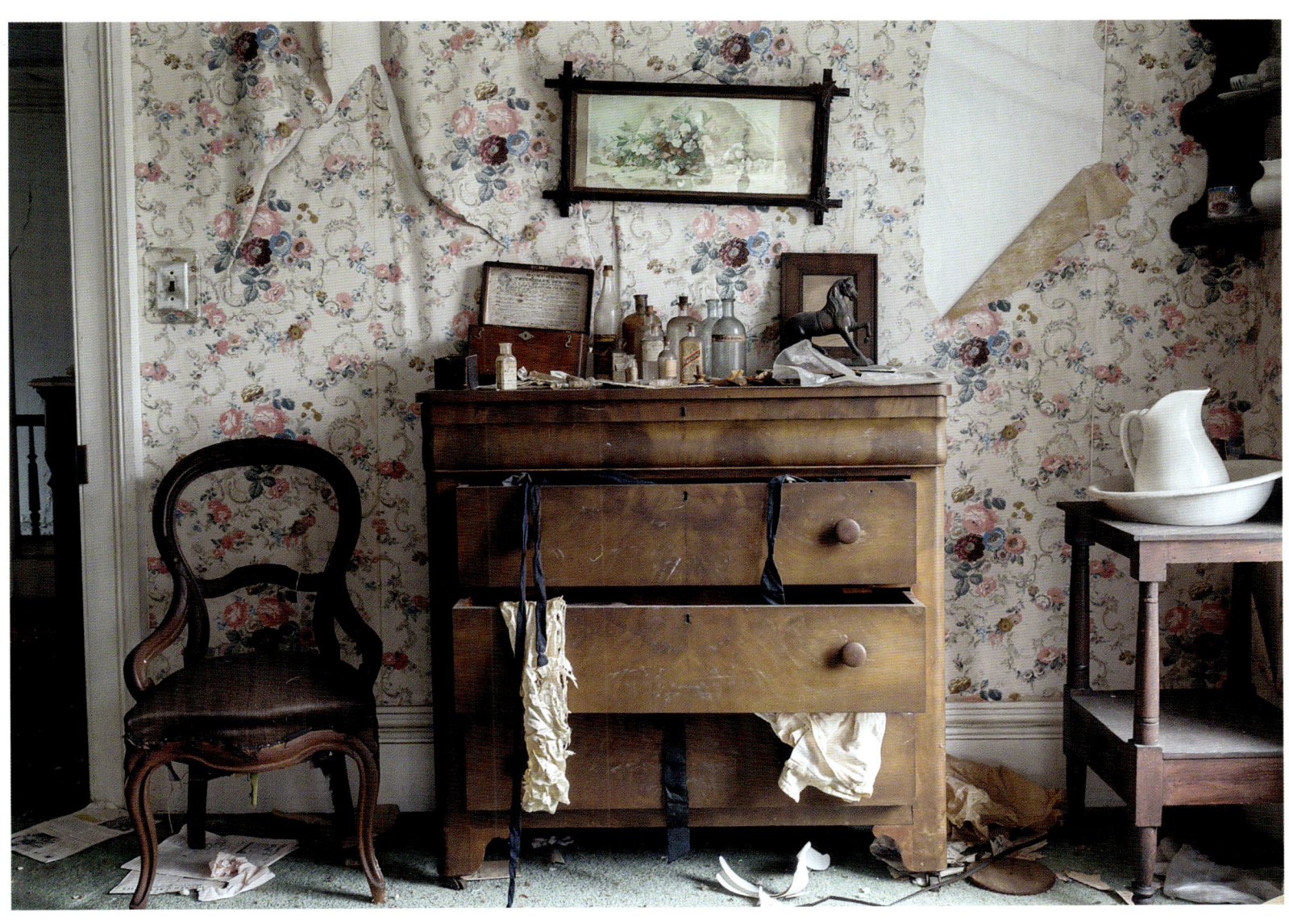

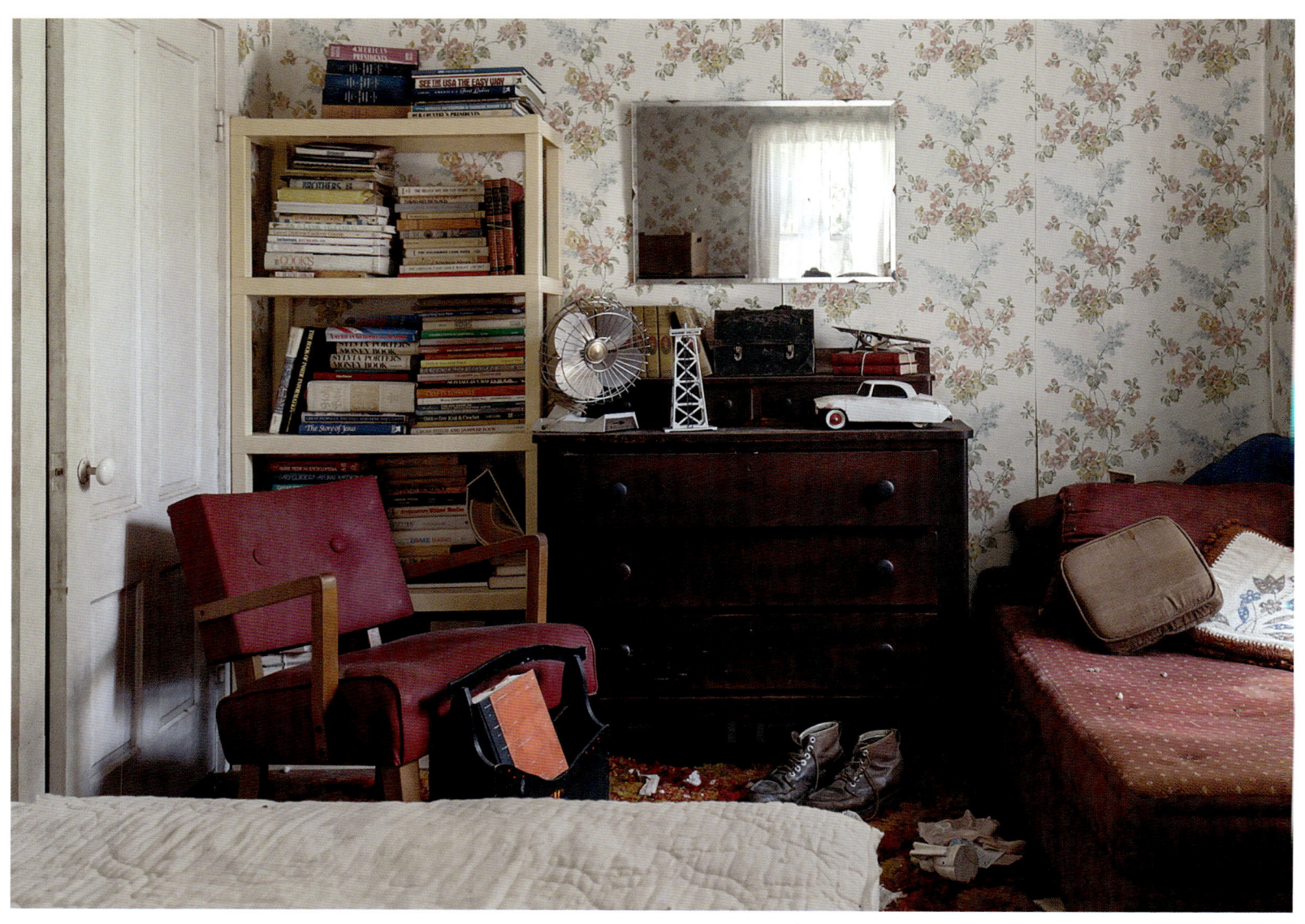

"THE READER'S CORNER"
Windham County, Connecticut

Almost everything left in this house was from around the 1950s. This room, like the upstairs child's bedroom, holds books, toys, and shoes. The subjects of the books range from cooking to American history to embroidery.

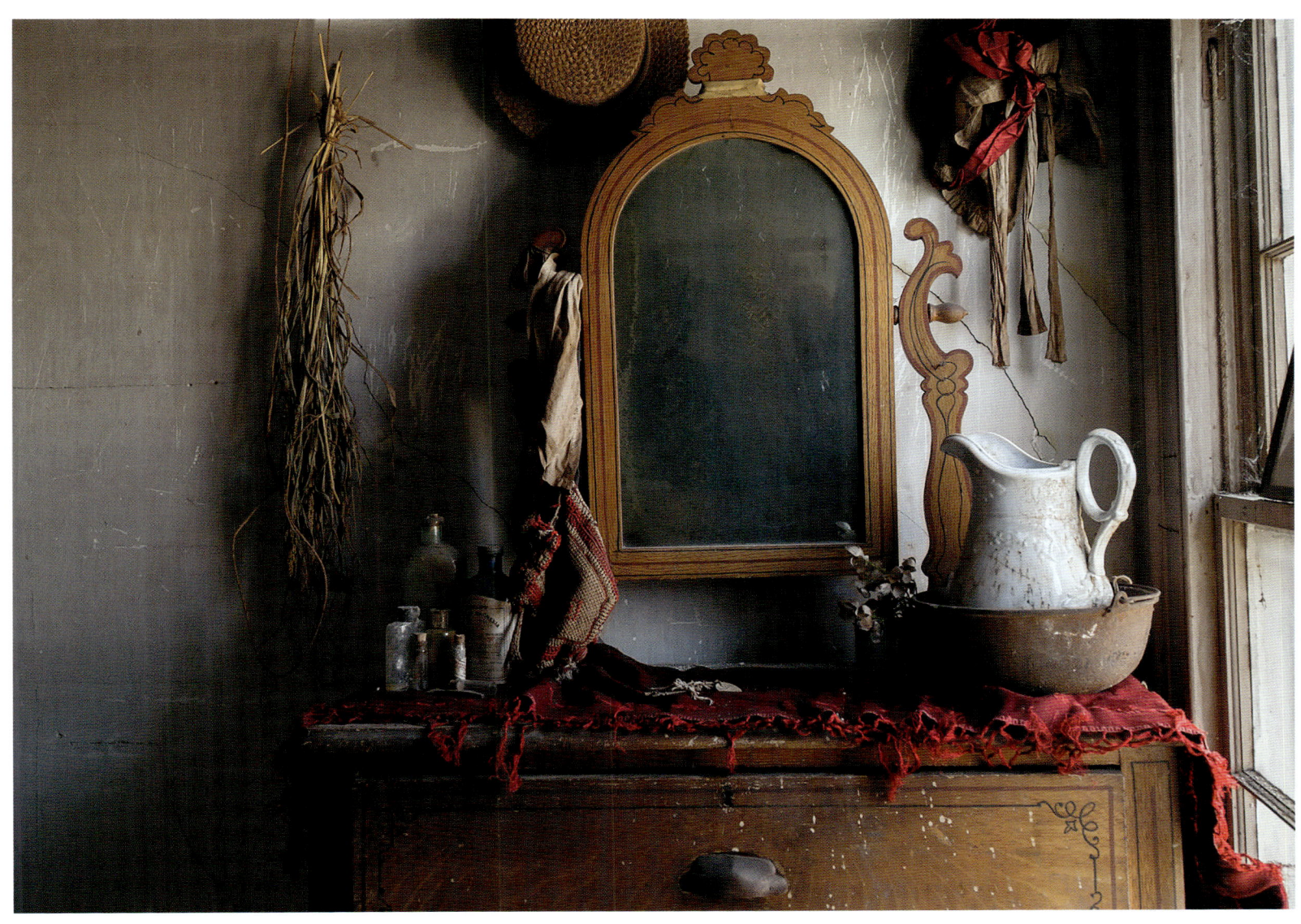

"THE DRESSING TABLE"
Suffolk County, New York

This house was extremely well hidden, and inside it I found many pictures, clothes, and personal items left behind. I don't believe that the home was abandoned long ago but rather that the owner kept and used older things.

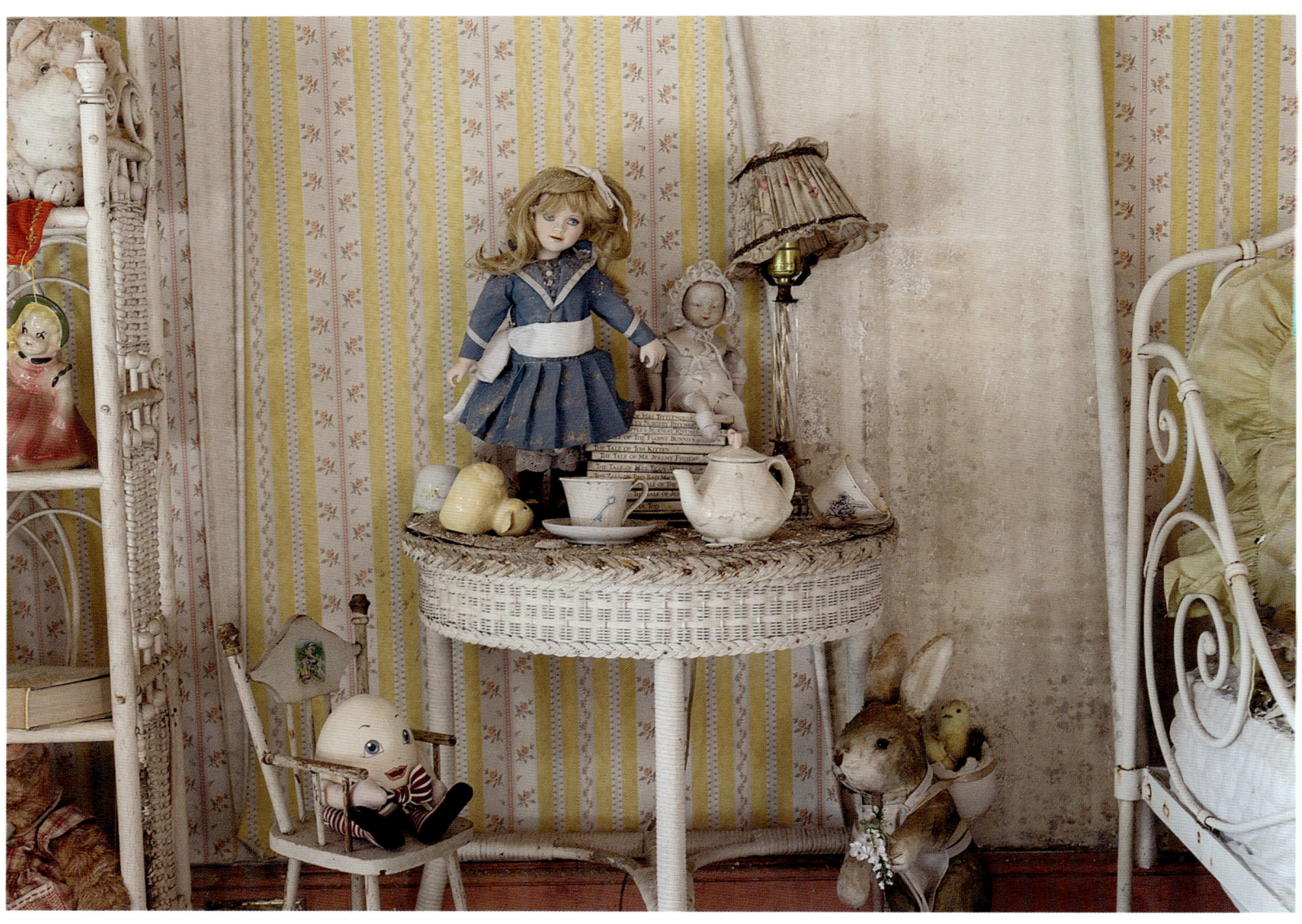

"ALICE'S TEA PARTY"
Suffolk County, New York

Dolls, books, and china sit on a table, a play scene from a child who must have loved this room. Now, with peeling wallpaper and scattered debris, it shows a reminder of what once was, and its ultimate and inevitable demise.

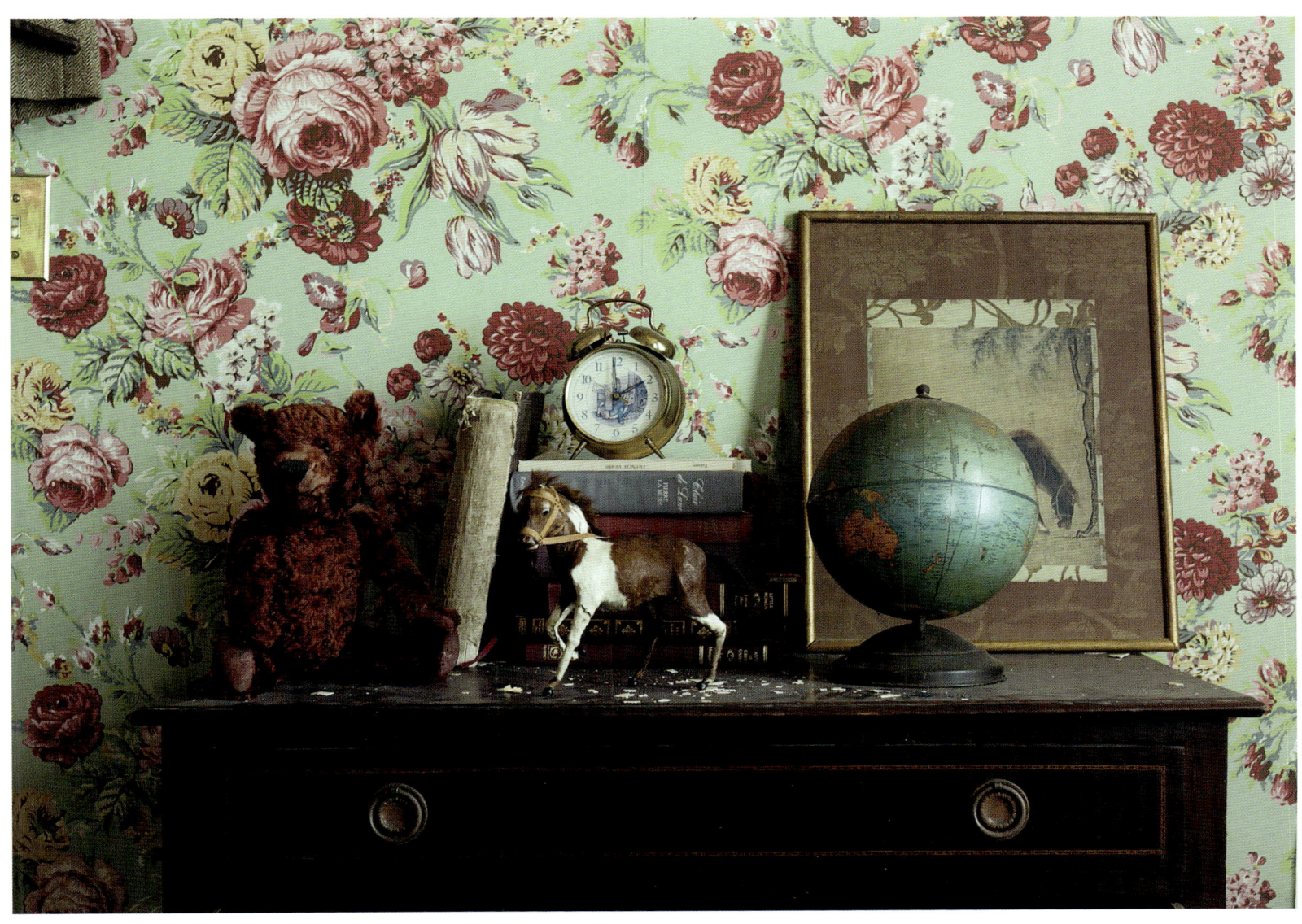

"STORYTIME"
Suffolk County, New York

This house is in my hometown, and I would always drive by and see it set back from the road across a field. When I discovered it was abandoned, I was shocked to find these childhood objects inside such a creepy-looking house.

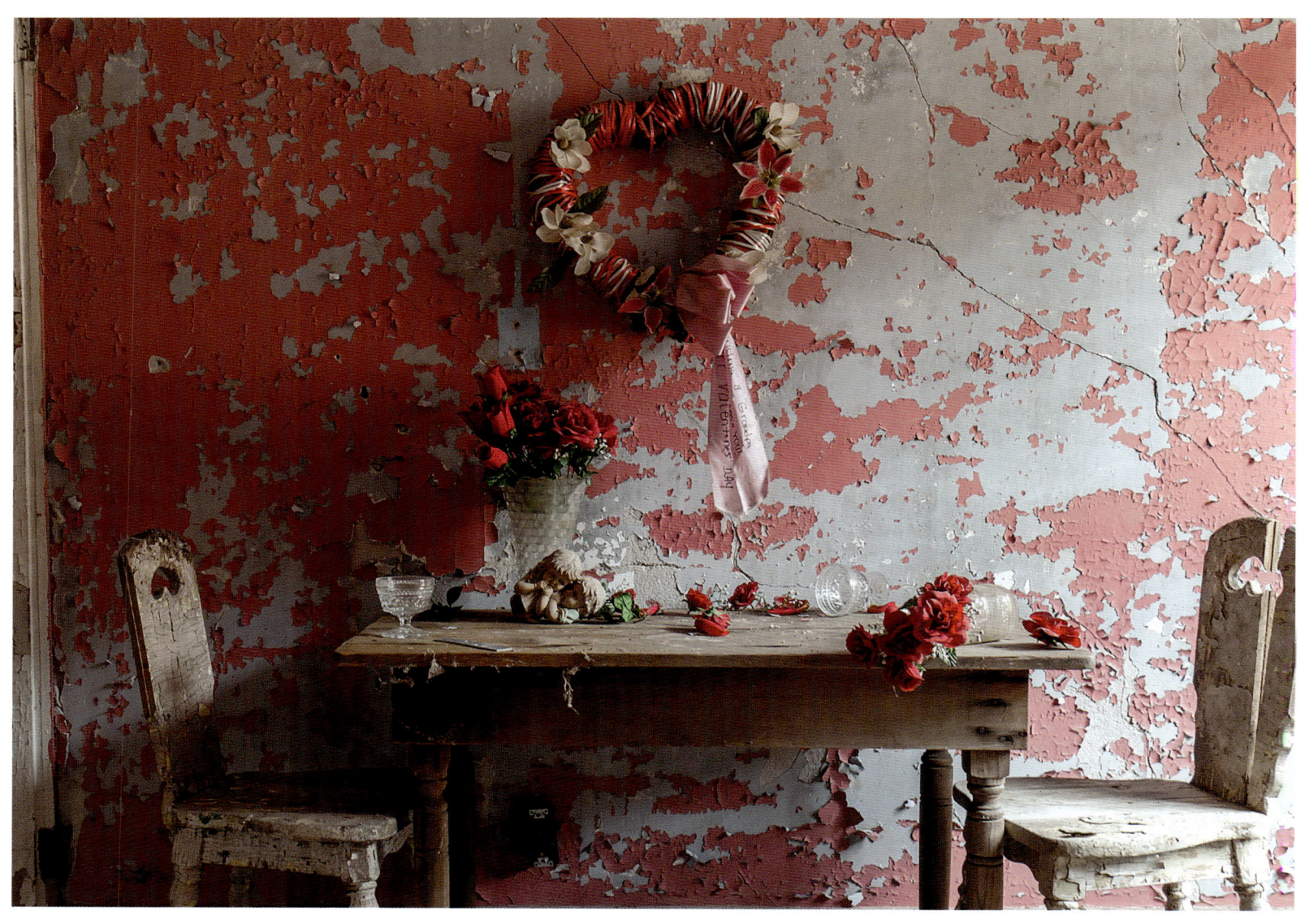

"A LONELY VALENTINE"
Sullivan County, New York

I imagine that this house belonged to an elderly couple. The bow on the hanging wreath read "Happy Valentine's Day, Grandma and Grandpa."

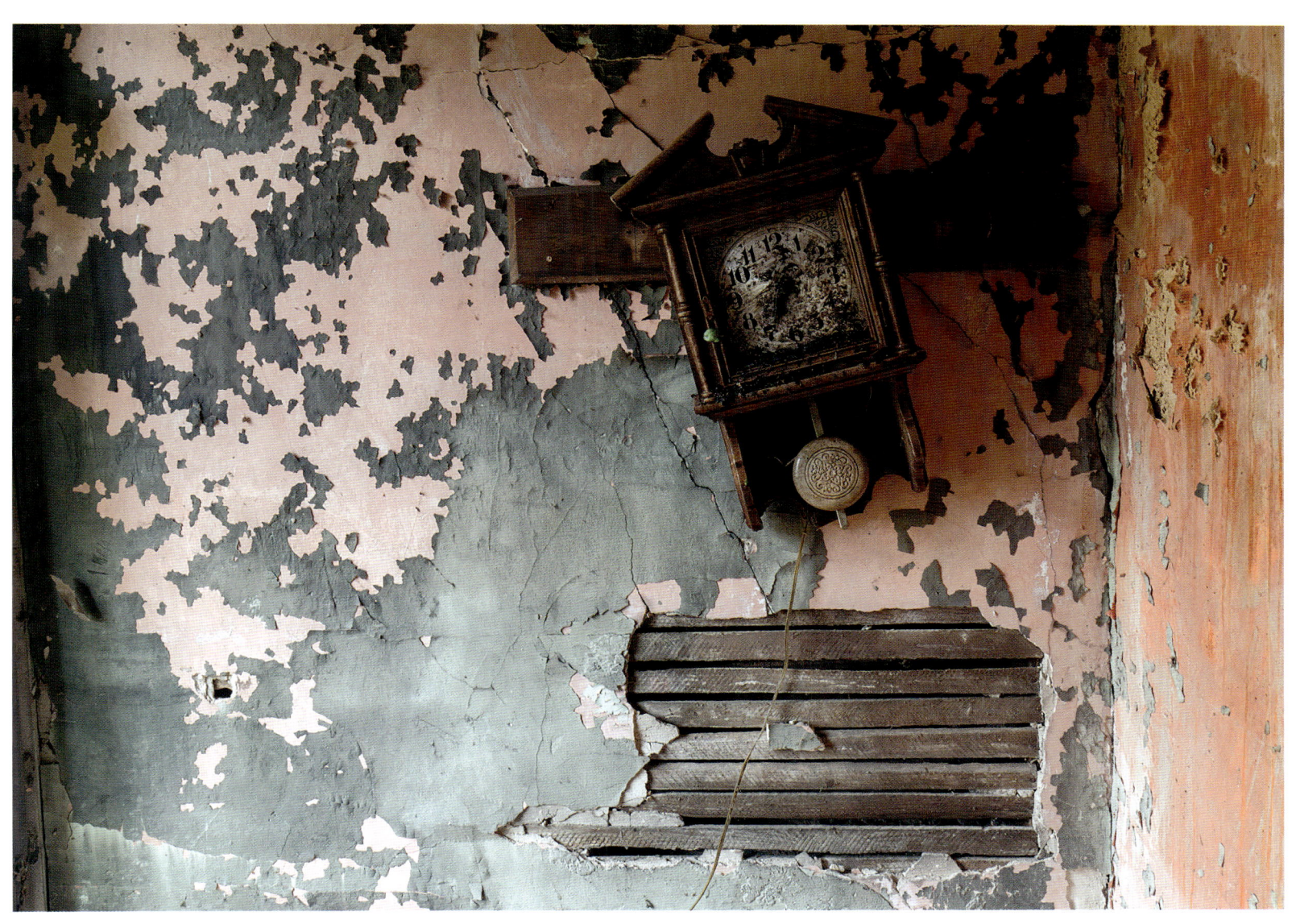

"THE TILTED CLOCK"
Cumberland County, Virginia

A stopped clock in an abandoned house always speaks volumes. When did the clock last tell time? Was it long after people were living there, or had it stopped before they left?

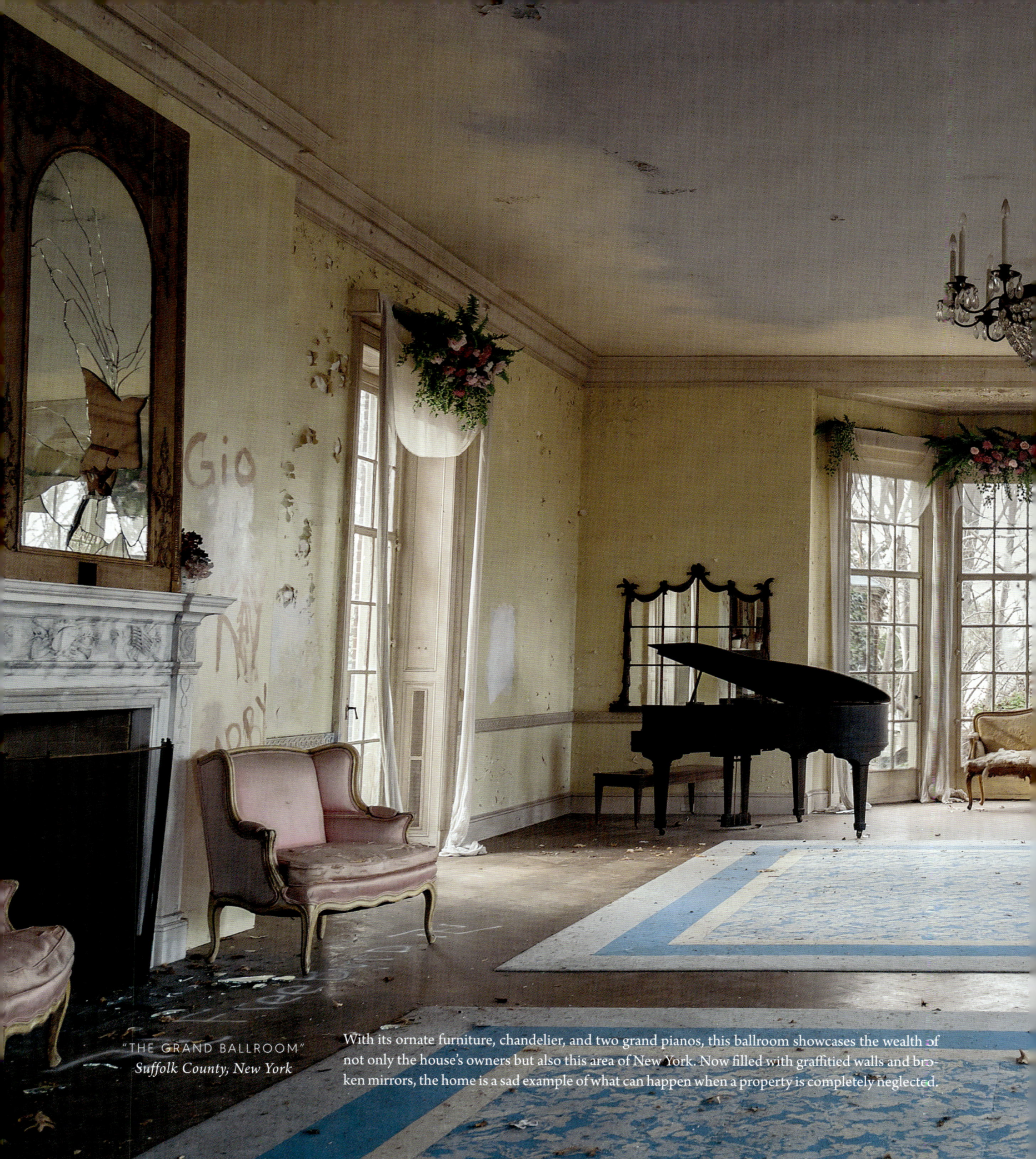

"THE GRAND BALLROOM"
Suffolk County, New York

With its ornate furniture, chandelier, and two grand pianos, this ballroom showcases the wealth of not only the house's owners but also this area of New York. Now filled with graffitied walls and broken mirrors, the home is a sad example of what can happen when a property is completely neglected.

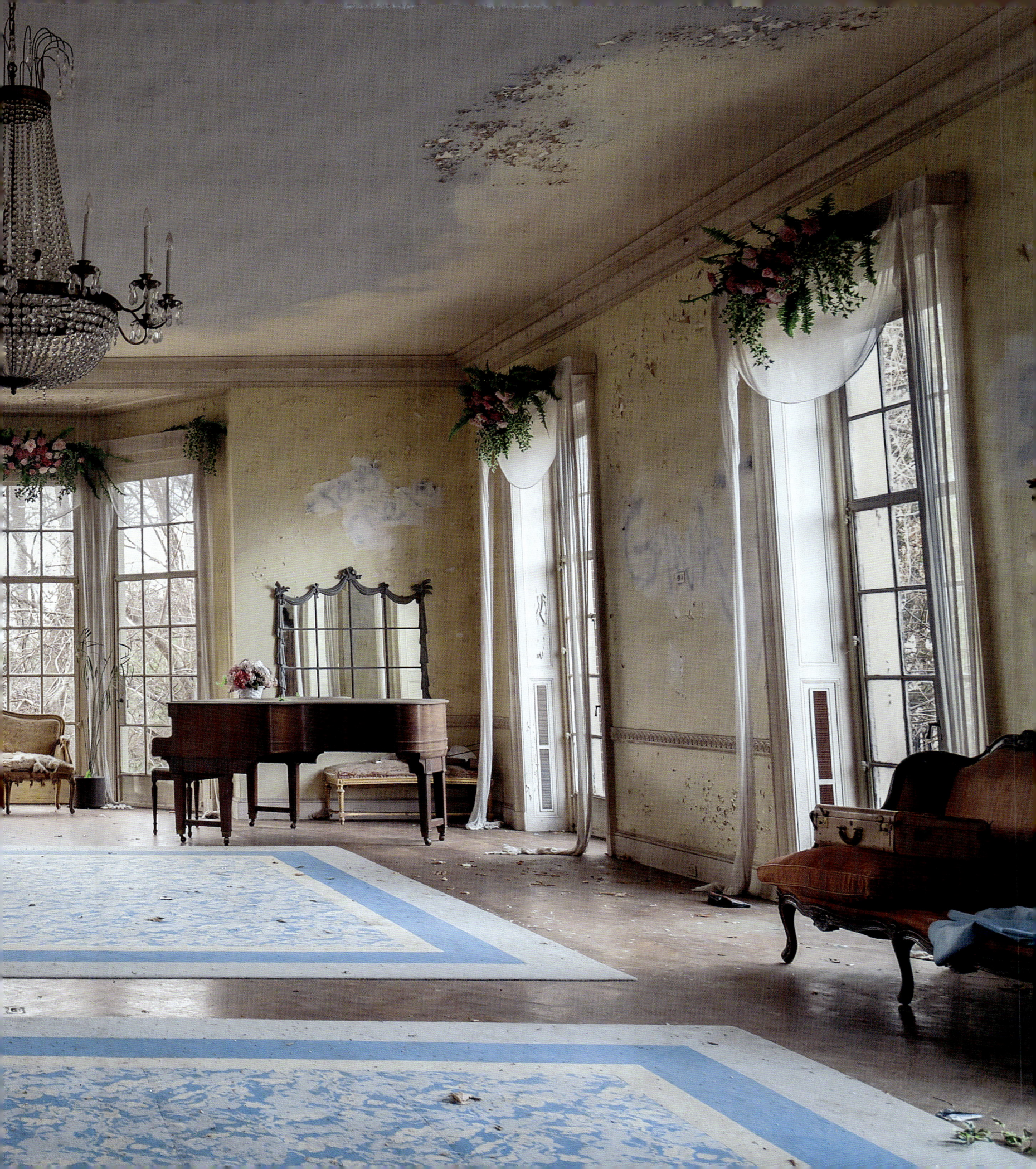

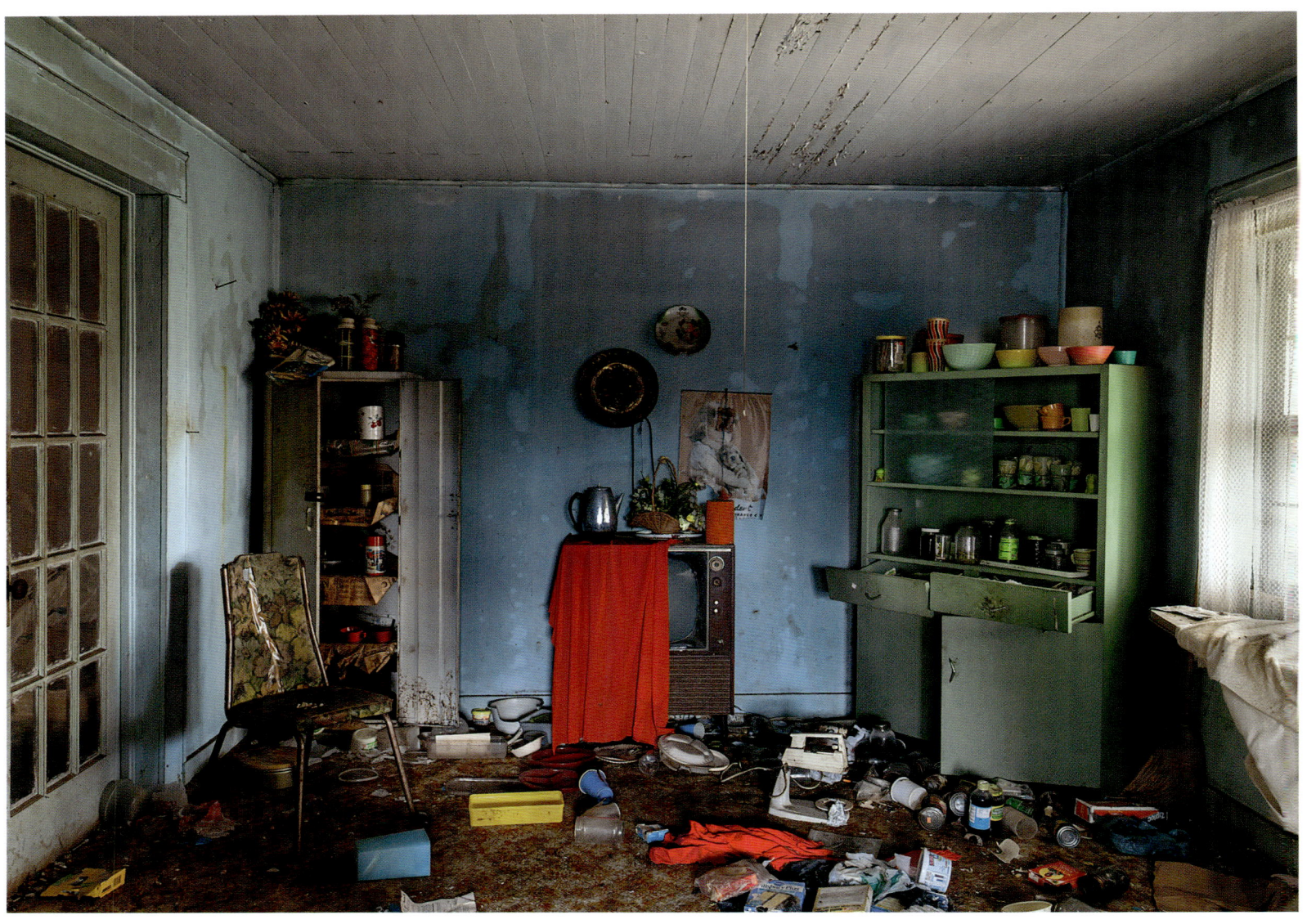

"THE TV TABLE"
Terrell County, Georgia

This room may be one of my favorites that I have photographed. It was filled with such a wide assortment of objects, as if the owners had used the room for everything. Nothing went together, yet all the colors fit perfectly.

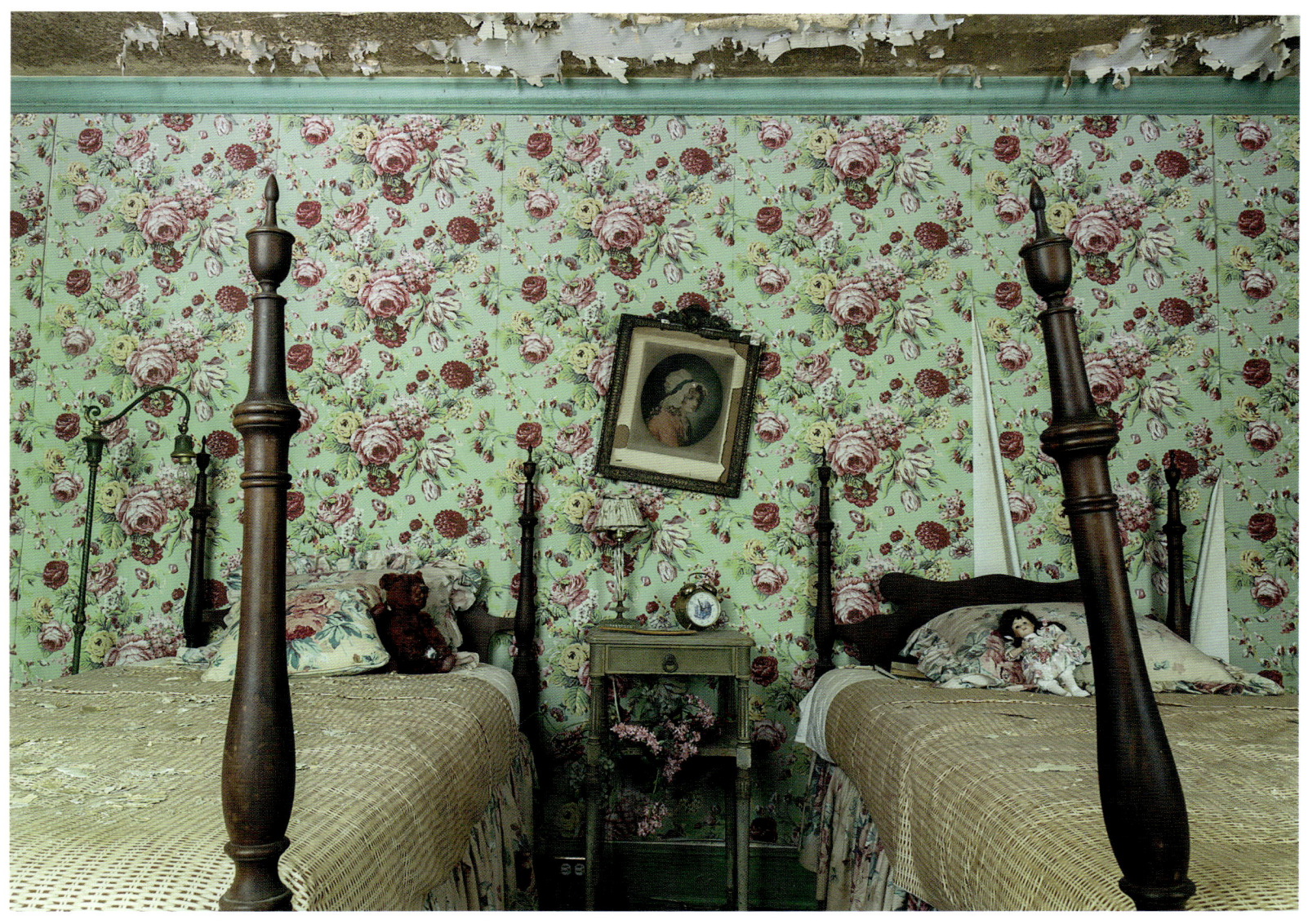

"THE TWIN BEDS"
Suffolk County, New York

This is the upstairs bedroom in a house you would never know had been filled with tragedy. Above the two beds and toys left behind, the ceiling paint peels from extreme temperatures.

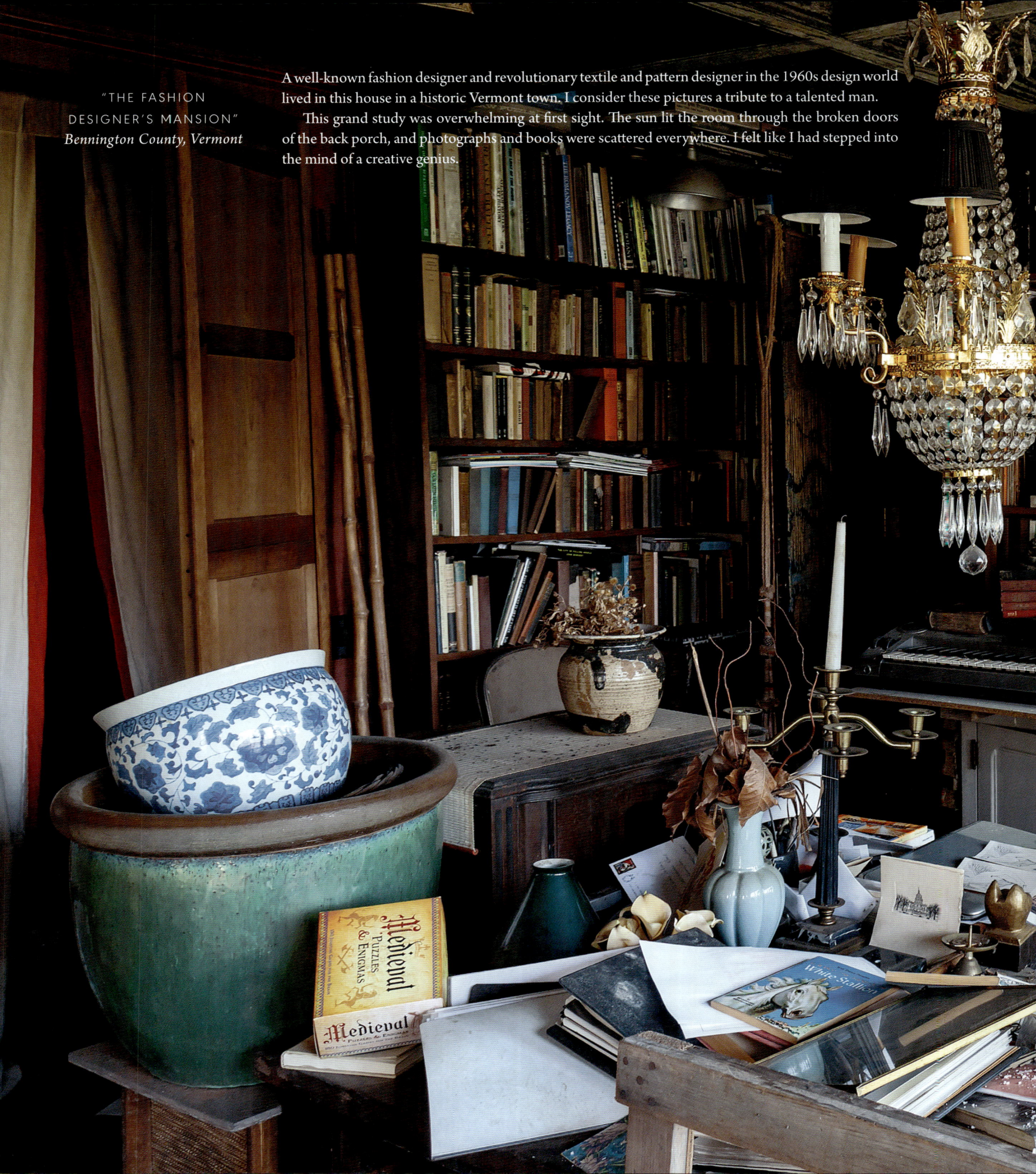

"THE FASHION
DESIGNER'S MANSION"
Bennington County, Vermont

A well-known fashion designer and revolutionary textile and pattern designer in the 1960s design world lived in this house in a historic Vermont town. I consider these pictures a tribute to a talented man.

This grand study was overwhelming at first sight. The sun lit the room through the broken doors of the back porch, and photographs and books were scattered everywhere. I felt like I had stepped into the mind of a creative genius.

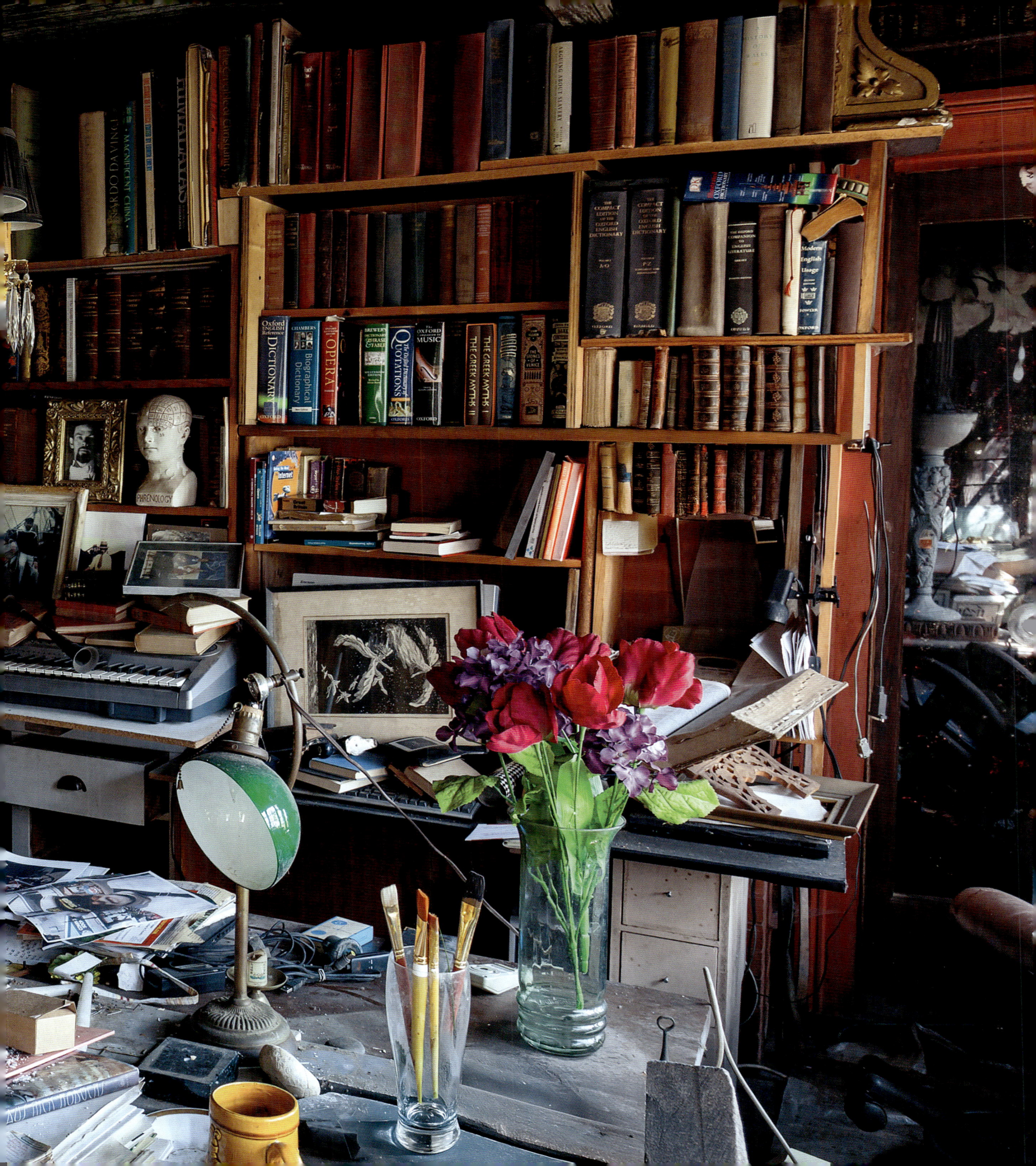

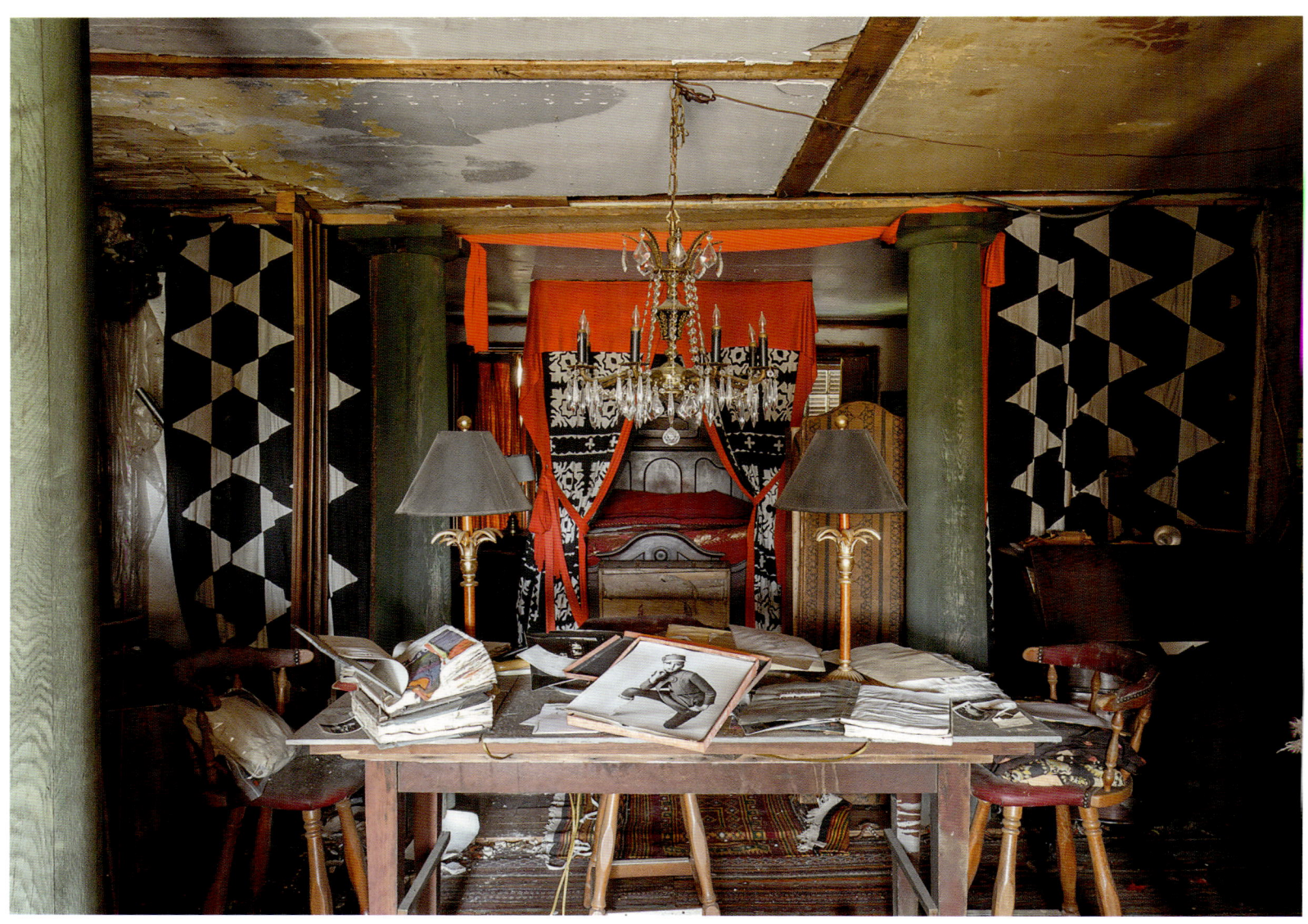

This photo is a peek inside a room containing hanging designer fabrics, a book of fabric samples from the 1960s, and photographs of models wearing the man's designs. His life's work was scattered throughout a dark, damp, and decaying living room. Beyond the table, a bedroom with draped curtains and a bed can be seen.

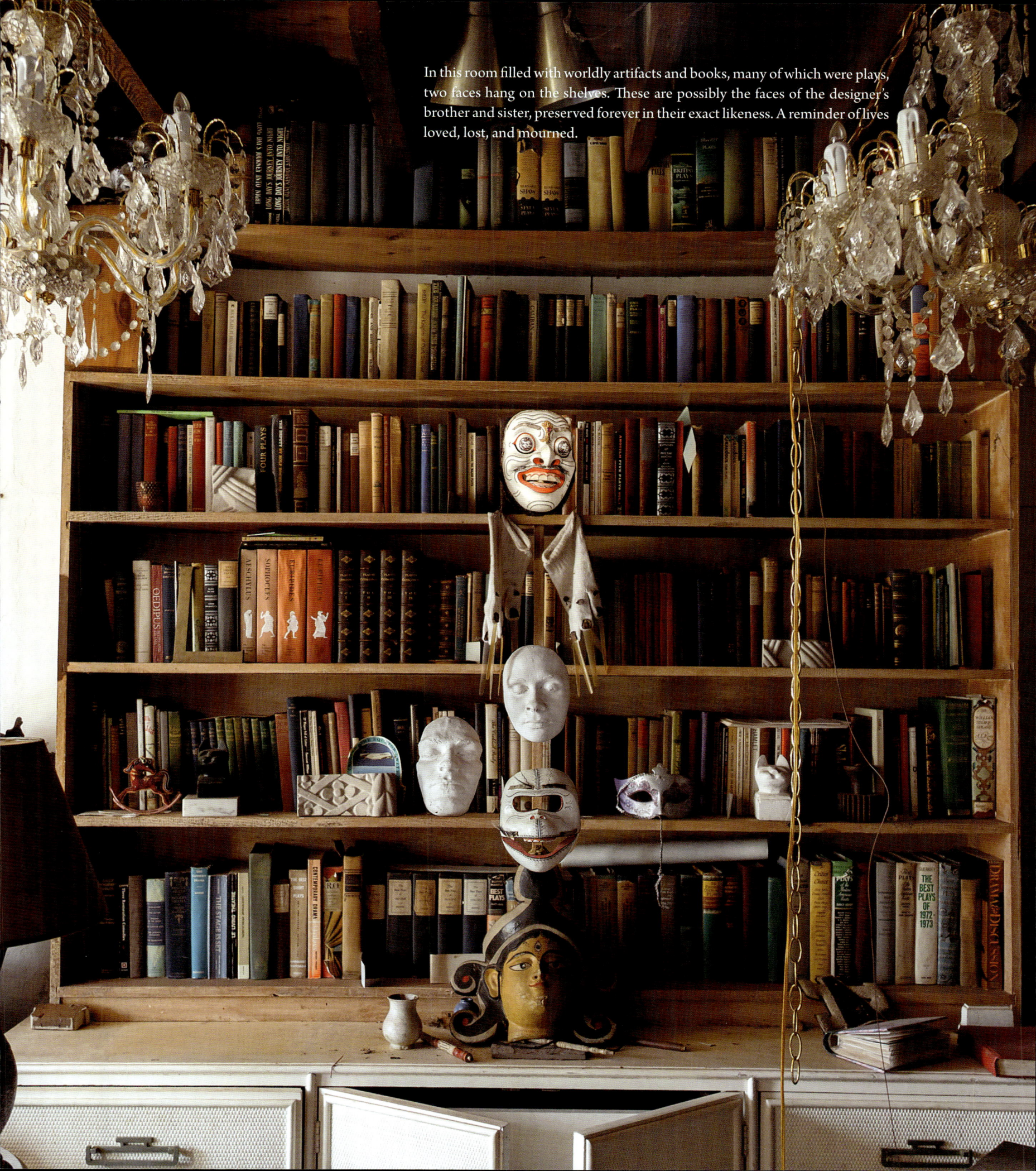

In this room filled with worldly artifacts and books, many of which were plays, two faces hang on the shelves. These are possibly the faces of the designer's brother and sister, preserved forever in their exact likeness. A reminder of lives loved, lost, and mourned.

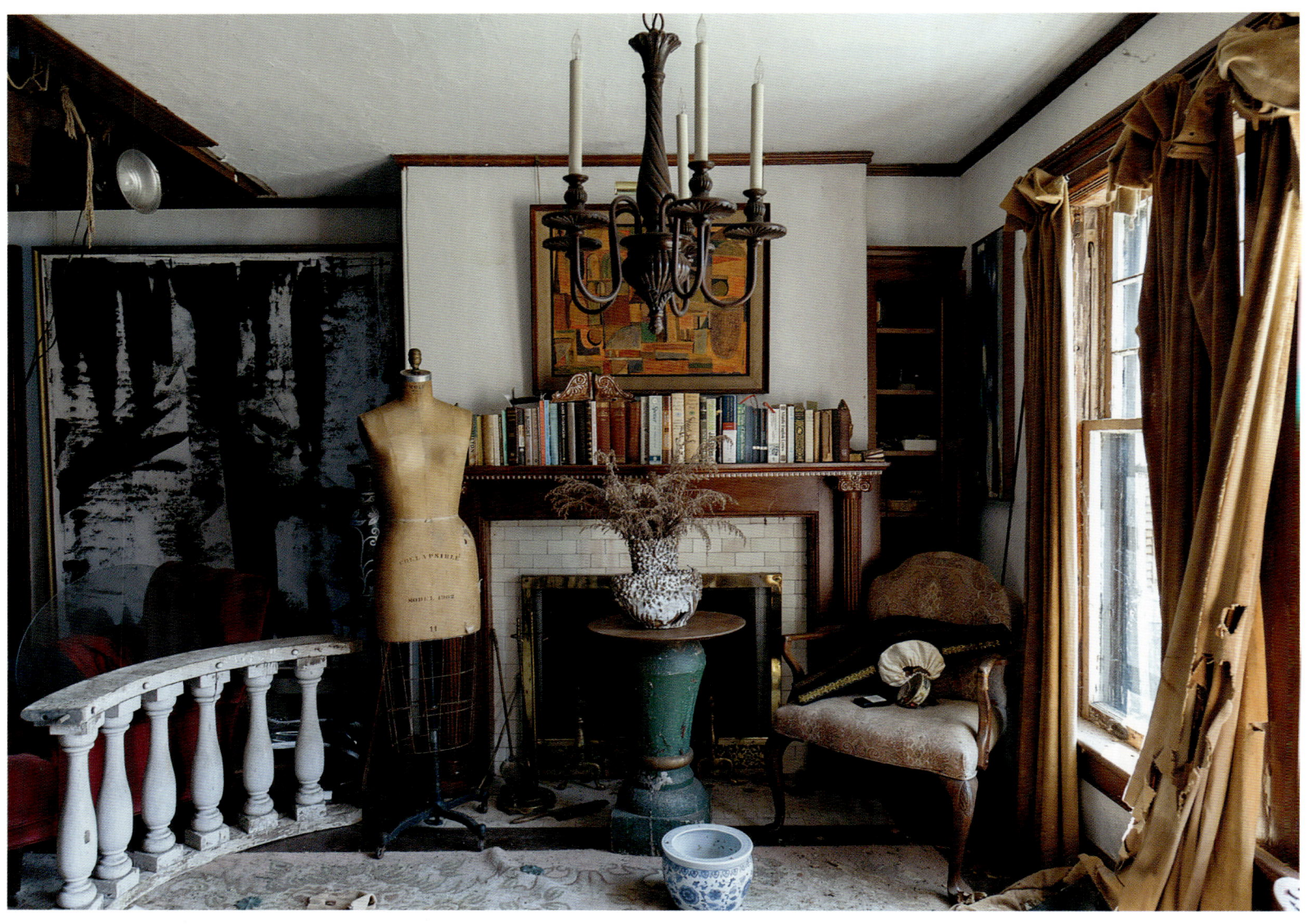

A cold breeze came in through the blown-out windows in this room. Above the dress form hung a work, possibly original, by the artist Paul Klee.

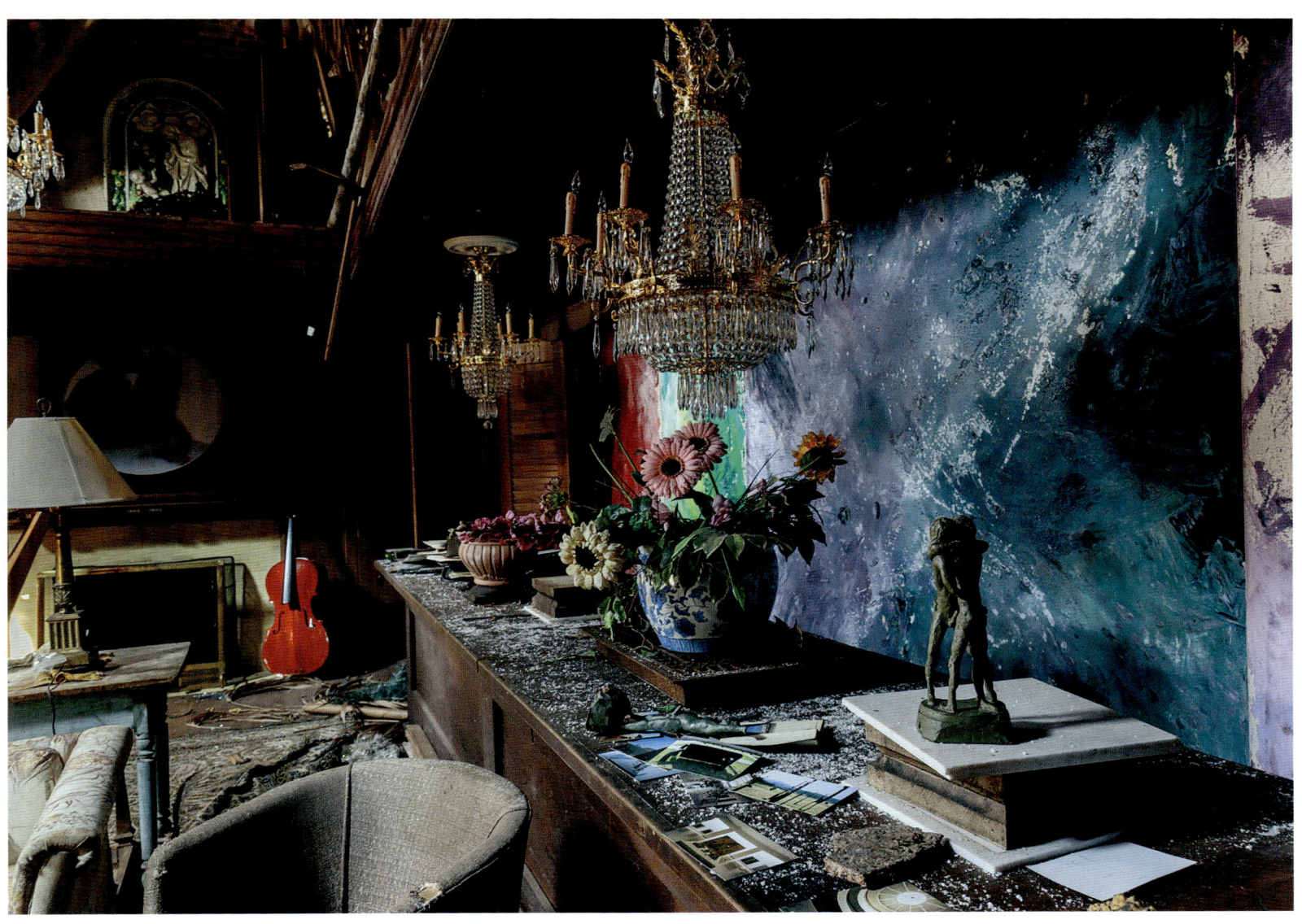

In the foreground of this picture, a statue of two figures embracing stood, with photographs and fashion magazines scattered around them.

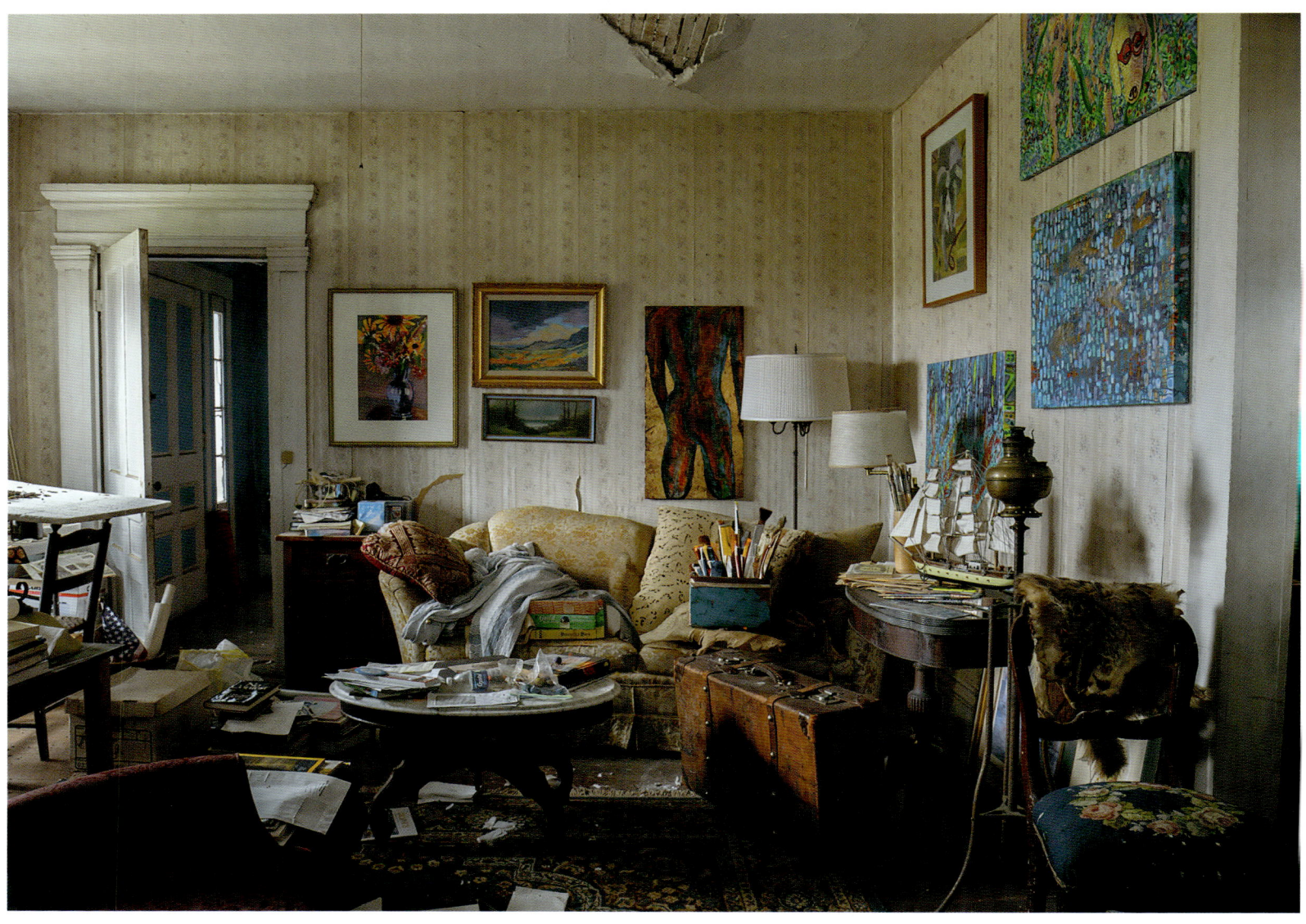

"THE ARTIST'S FARMHOUSE"
Grand Isle County, Vermont

The artist who lived in this farmhouse (above and opposite) left behind hundreds of her paintings, as well as nautical items and antiques. On a dresser, a wooden model ship sat in front of a map of Vermont.

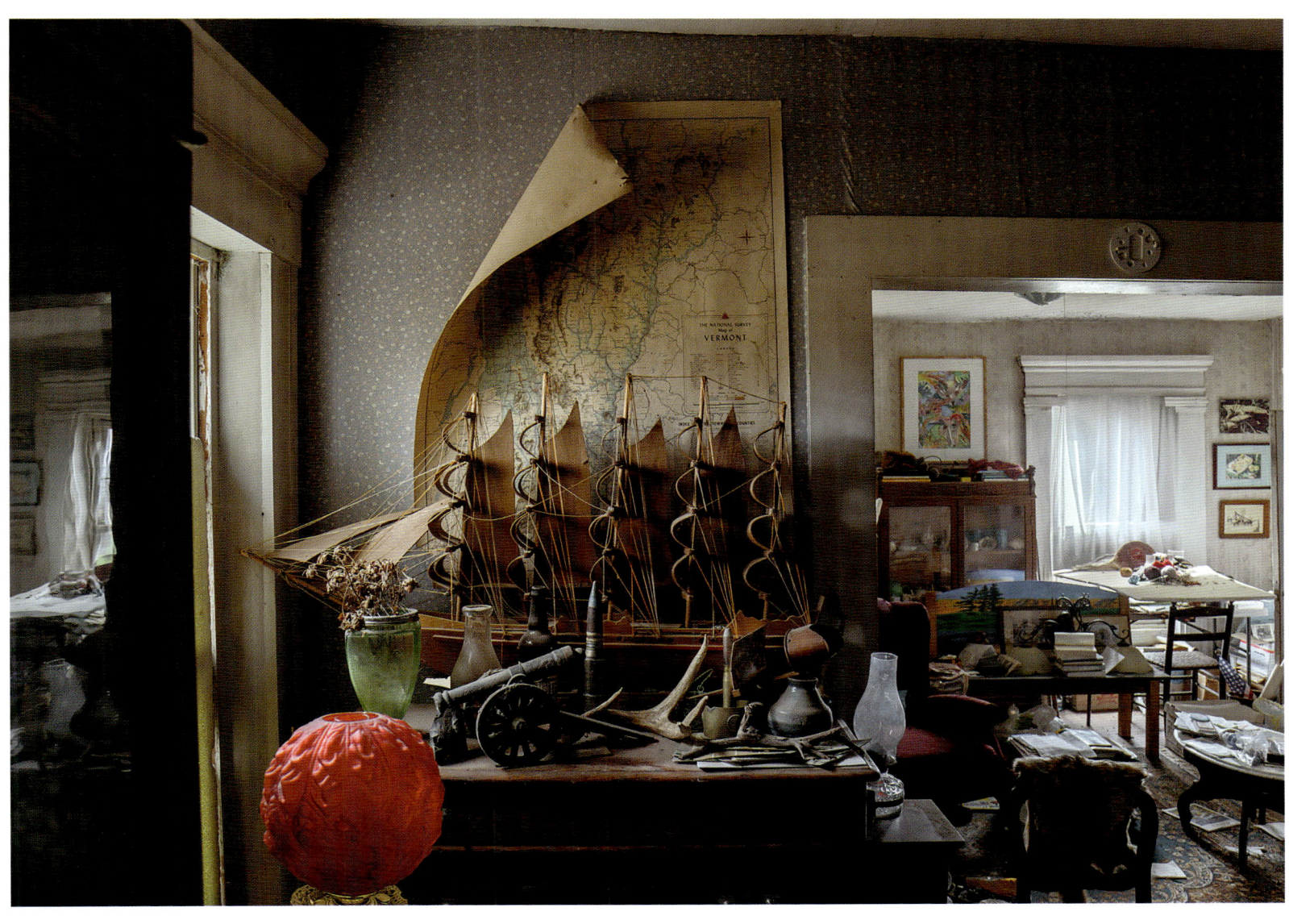

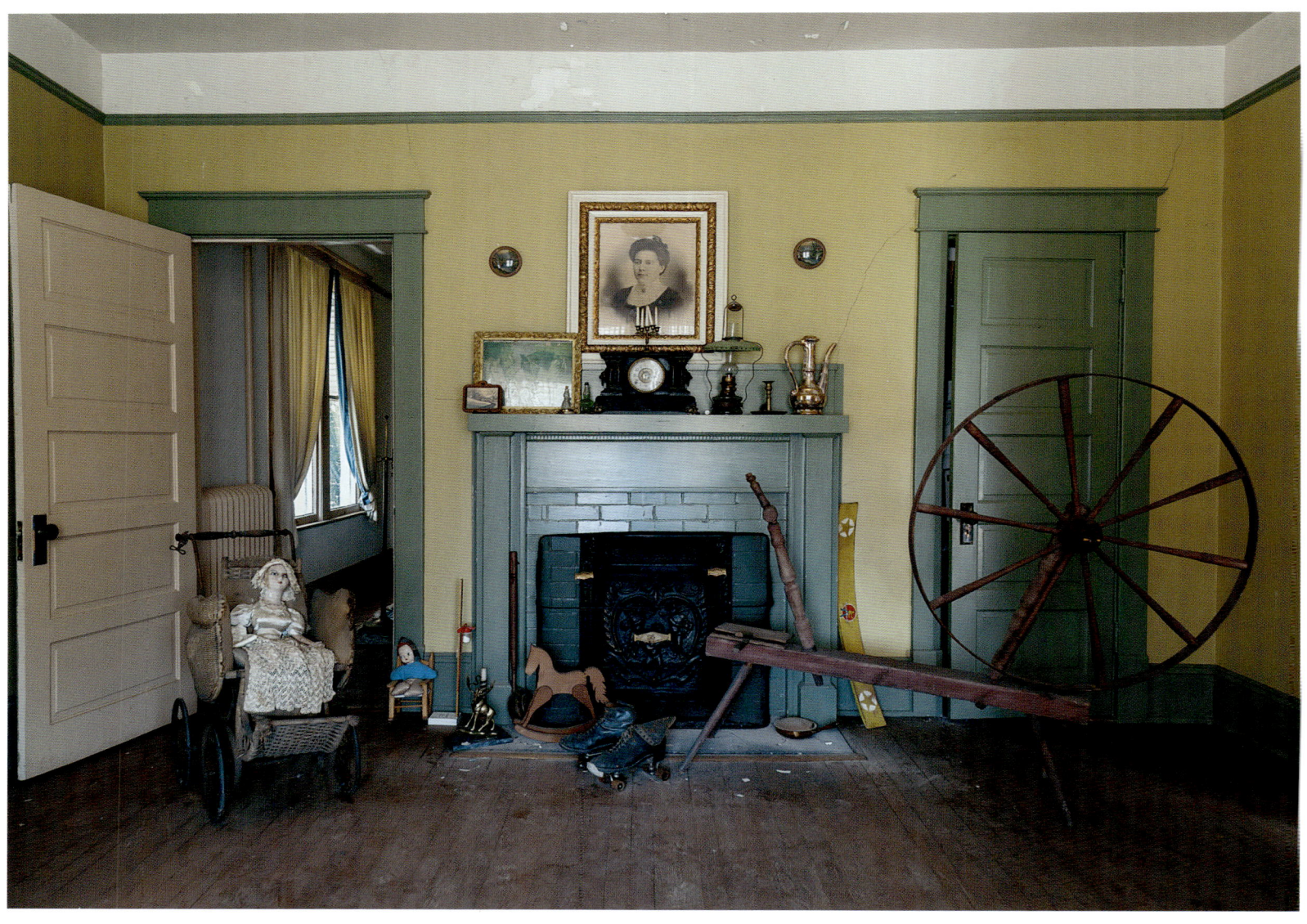

"THE SPINNING WHEEL"
Nash County, North Carolina

This large house is in a rural town that was once wealthy but has experienced an economic downturn. The town is scattered with homes that are boarded up and run-down. The inside of this one provides a glimpse into how the family may have lived when the town was booming. These antiques would have been pricey back in the day.

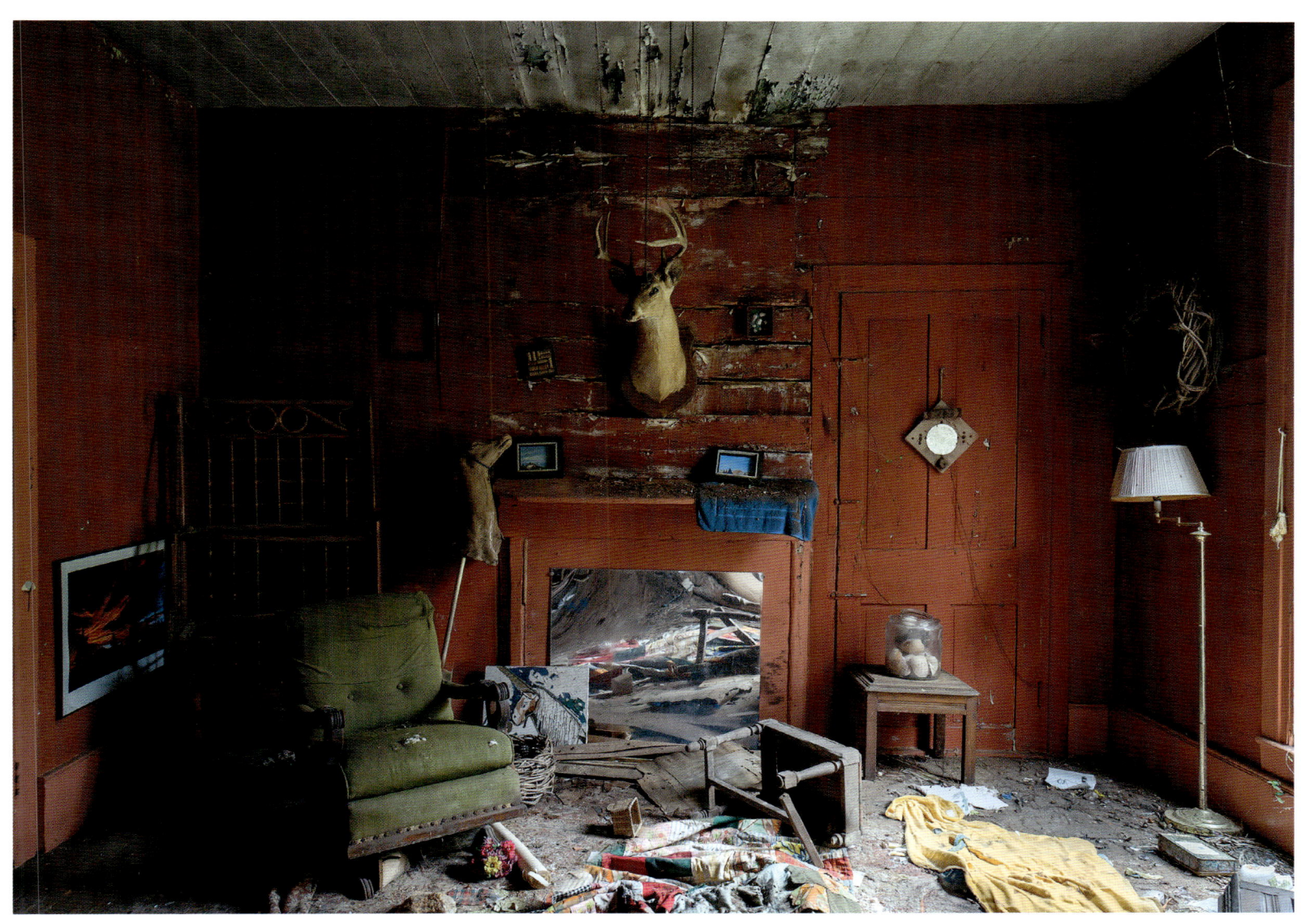

"THE STAG"
Troup County, Georgia

This is the first room I saw when I went inside this incredible large house that once belonged to an artist and sculptor. The rustic aesthetic evokes the feeling of a cozy cabin, yet it couldn't be more different from the other rooms of the house.

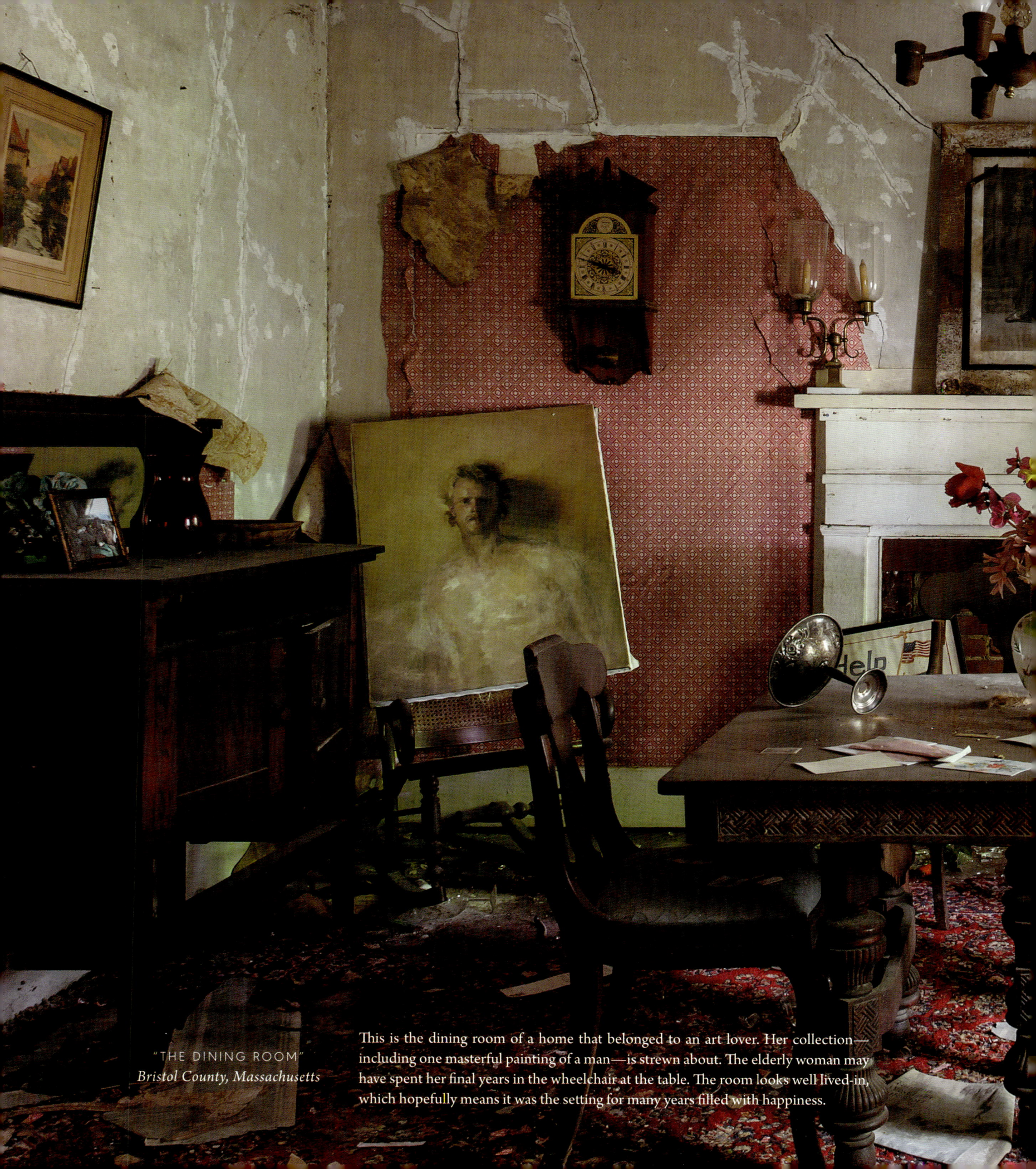

"THE DINING ROOM"
Bristol County, Massachusetts

This is the dining room of a home that belonged to an art lover. Her collection—including one masterful painting of a man—is strewn about. The elderly woman may have spent her final years in the wheelchair at the table. The room looks well lived-in, which hopefully means it was the setting for many years filled with happiness.

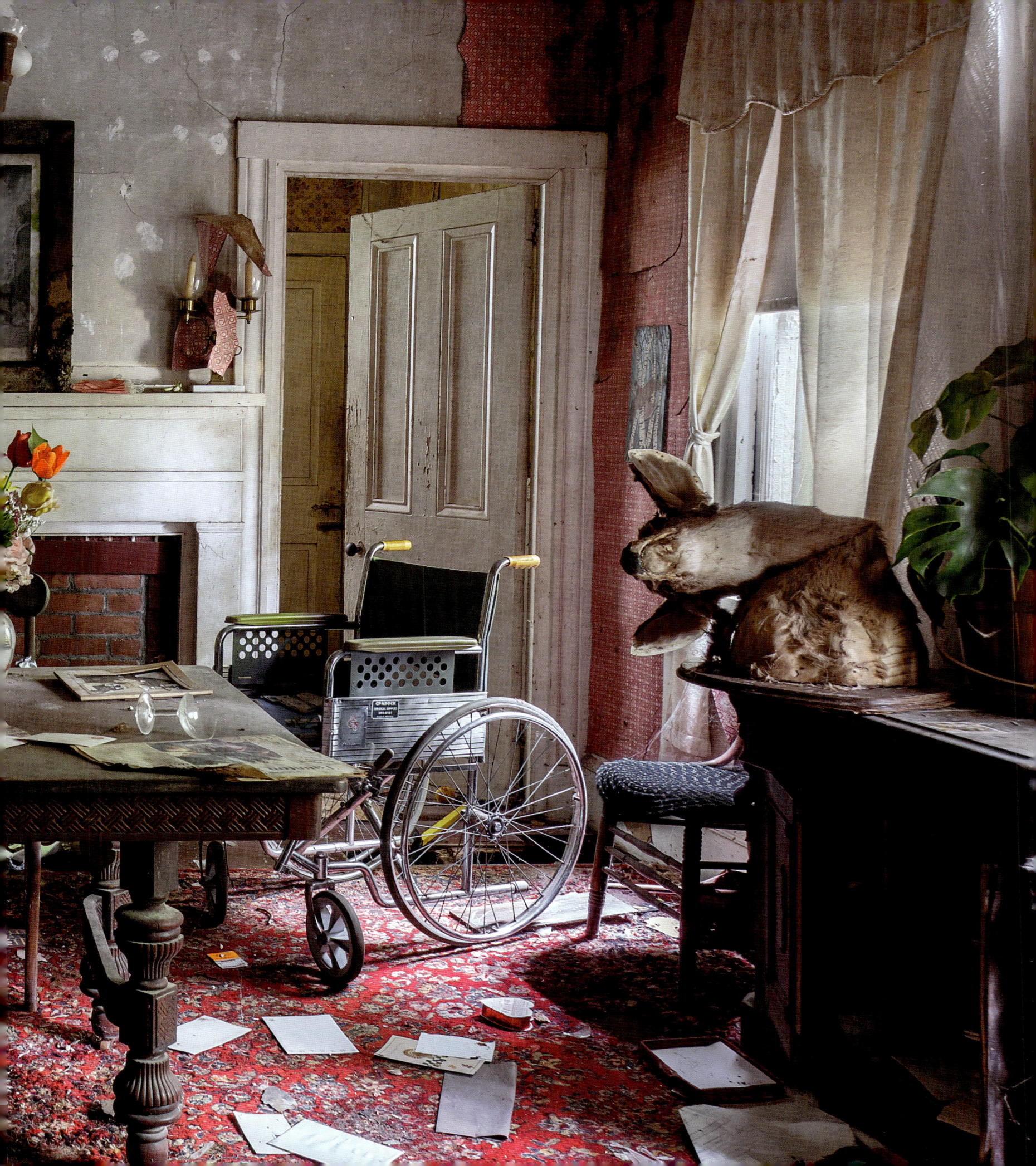

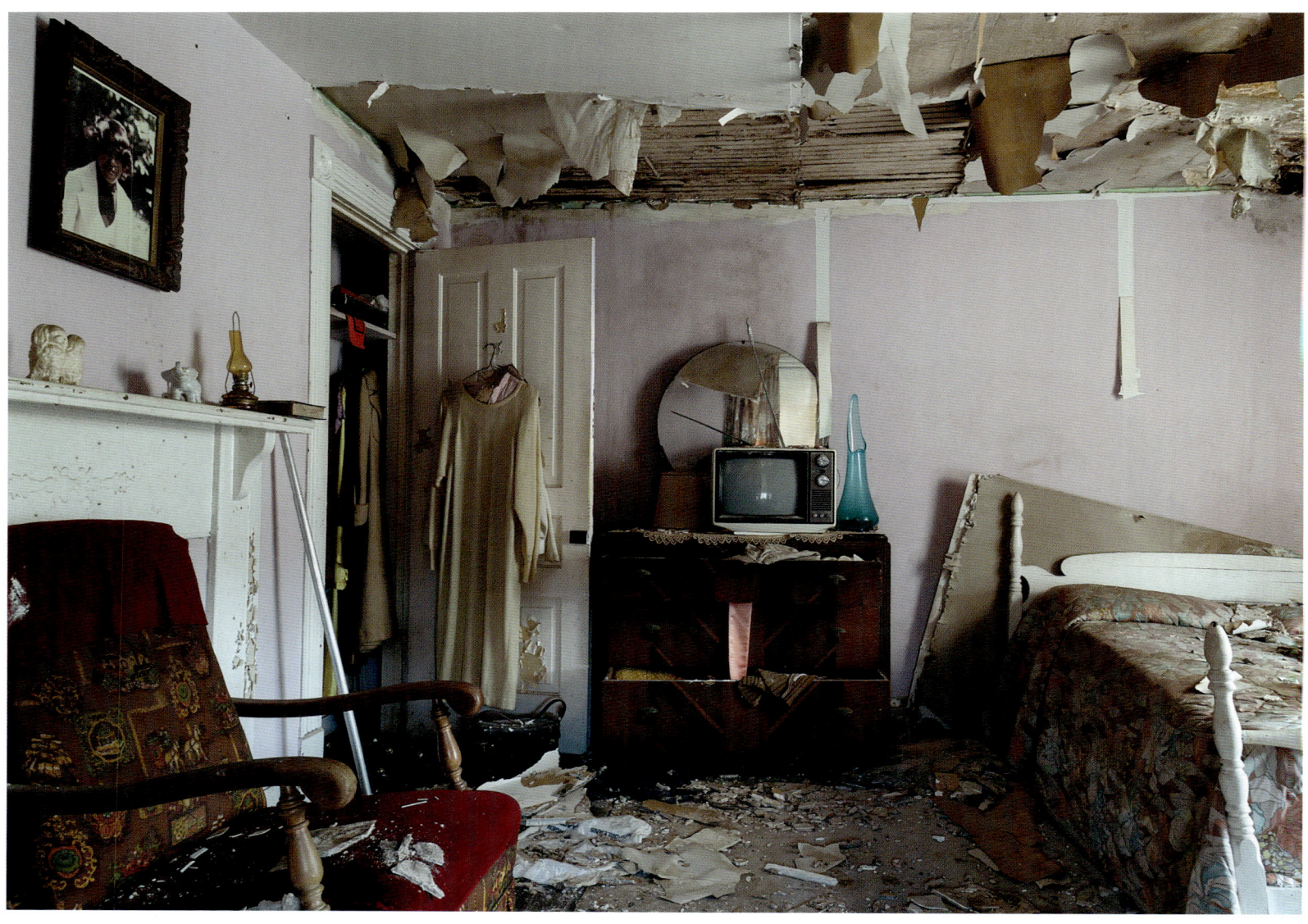

"THE LAVENDER BEDROOM"
Culpeper County, Virginia

The rooms in this house were filled with rustic items. Many were collectibles and have most likely been lost, as the condition of the house suggested it wouldn't be standing for much longer.

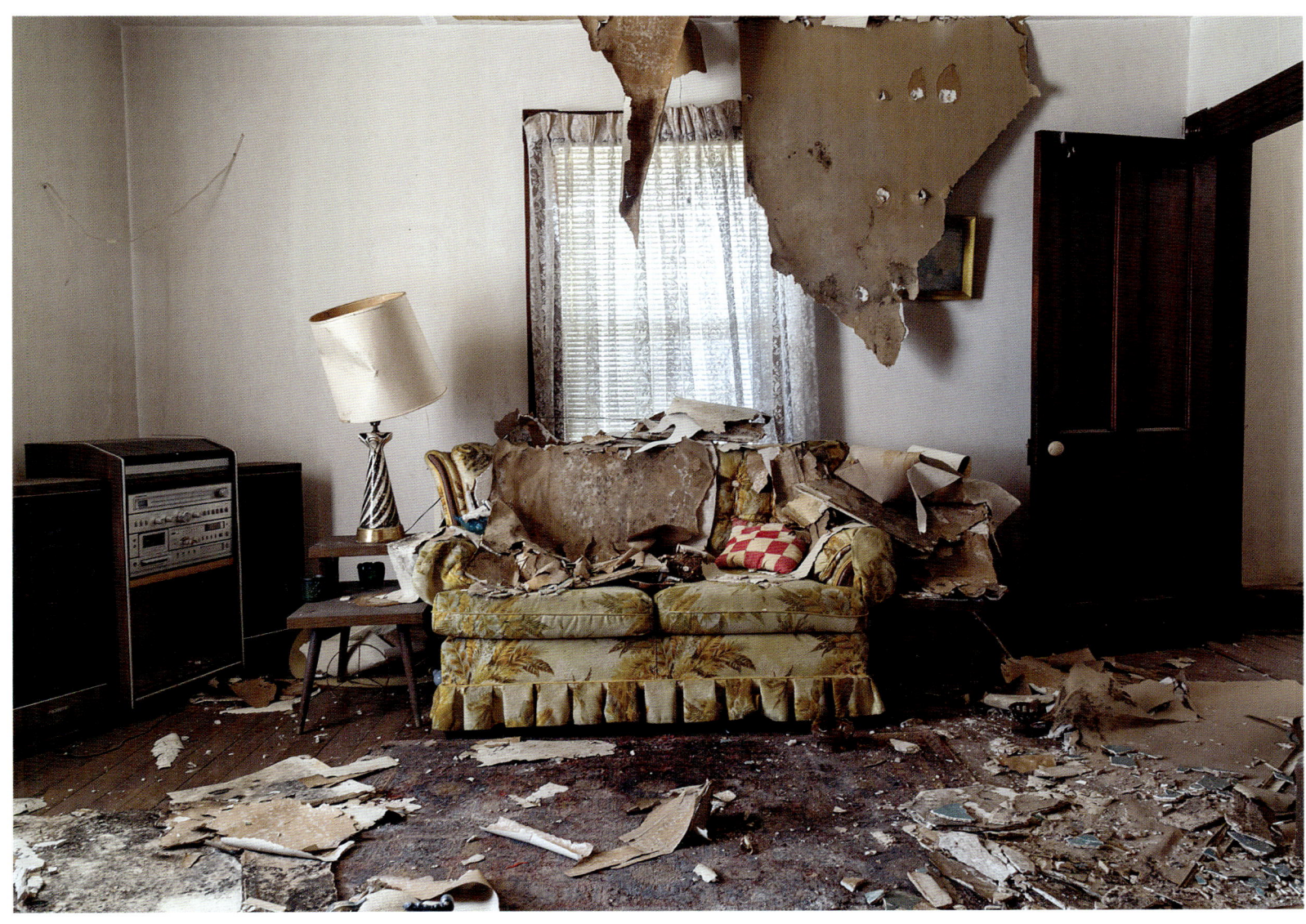

"THE GREEN COUCH"
Culpeper County, Virginia

This home was filled with mid-century décor that had been heavily affected by water damage, which was sad to see.

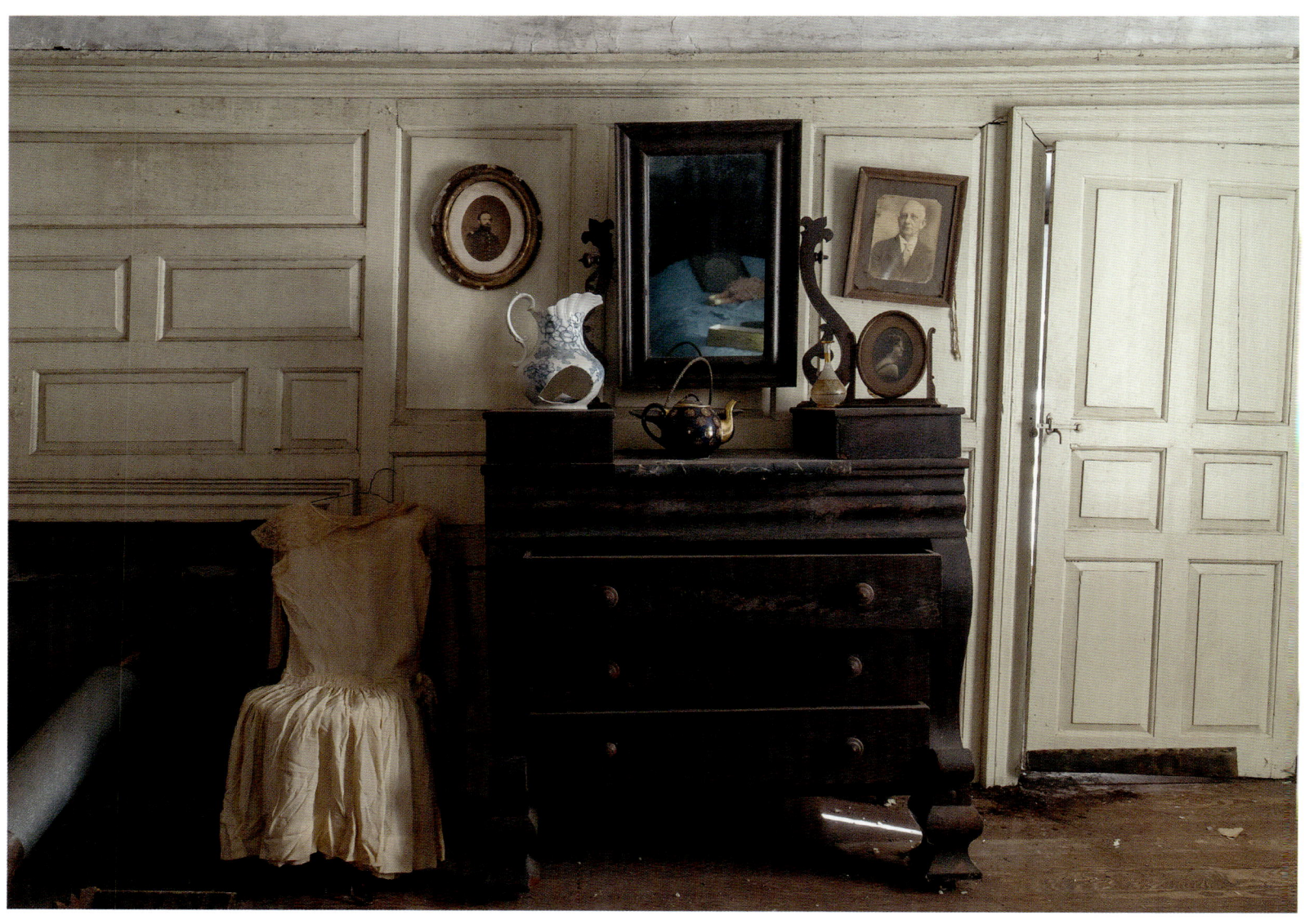

"THE DRESS ON THE CHAIR"
Fairfield County, Connecticut

This house is close to the road yet barely noticeable. Dating to the mid-nineteenth century, it was full of antiques, with some even spilling out into the yard.

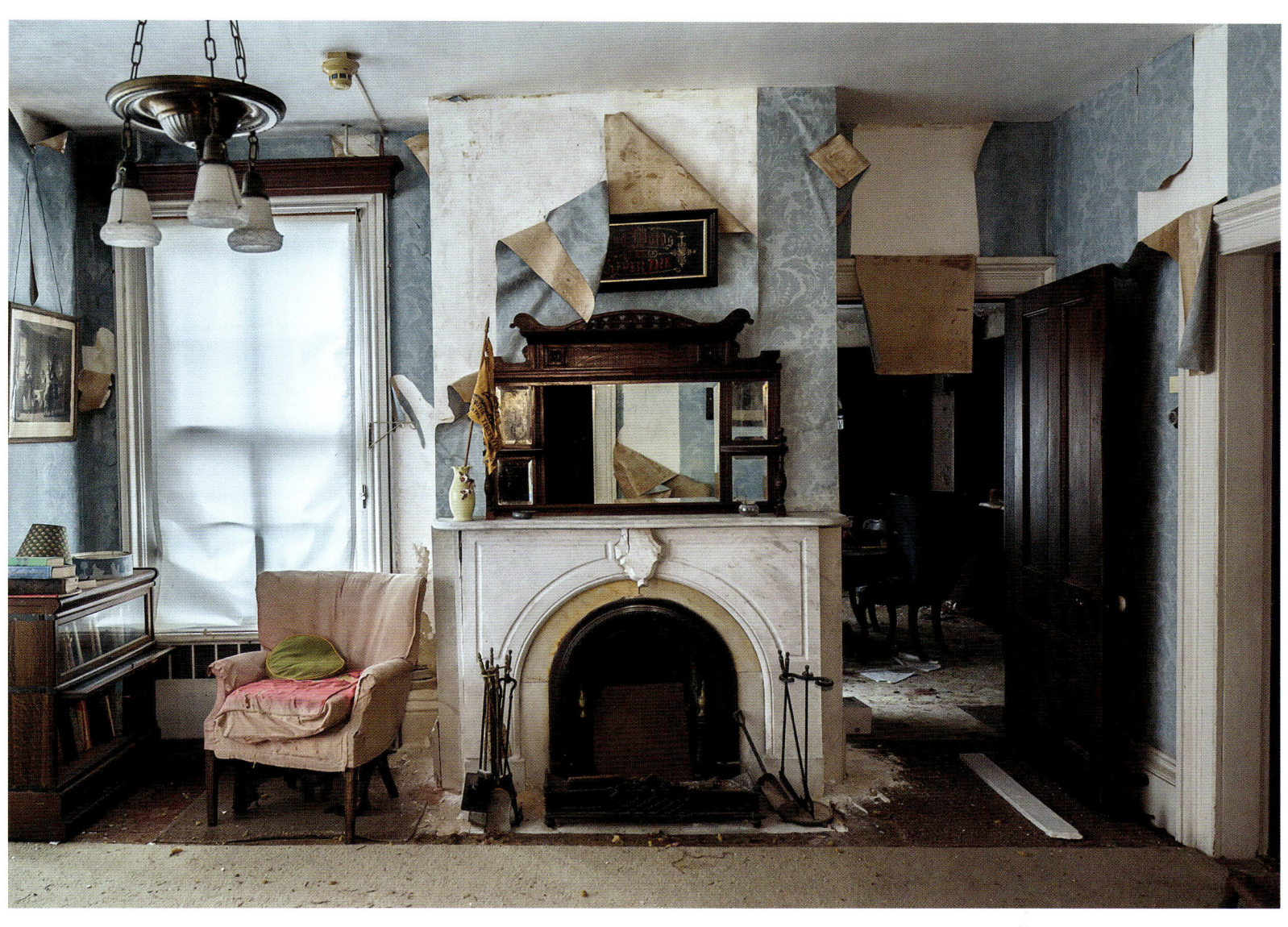

"A REGAL LIVING ROOM"
Suffolk County, New York

In the living room of this historic house, I found books, furniture, and peeling wallpaper. I feel that this picture really captures what happens when a house is neglected over time.

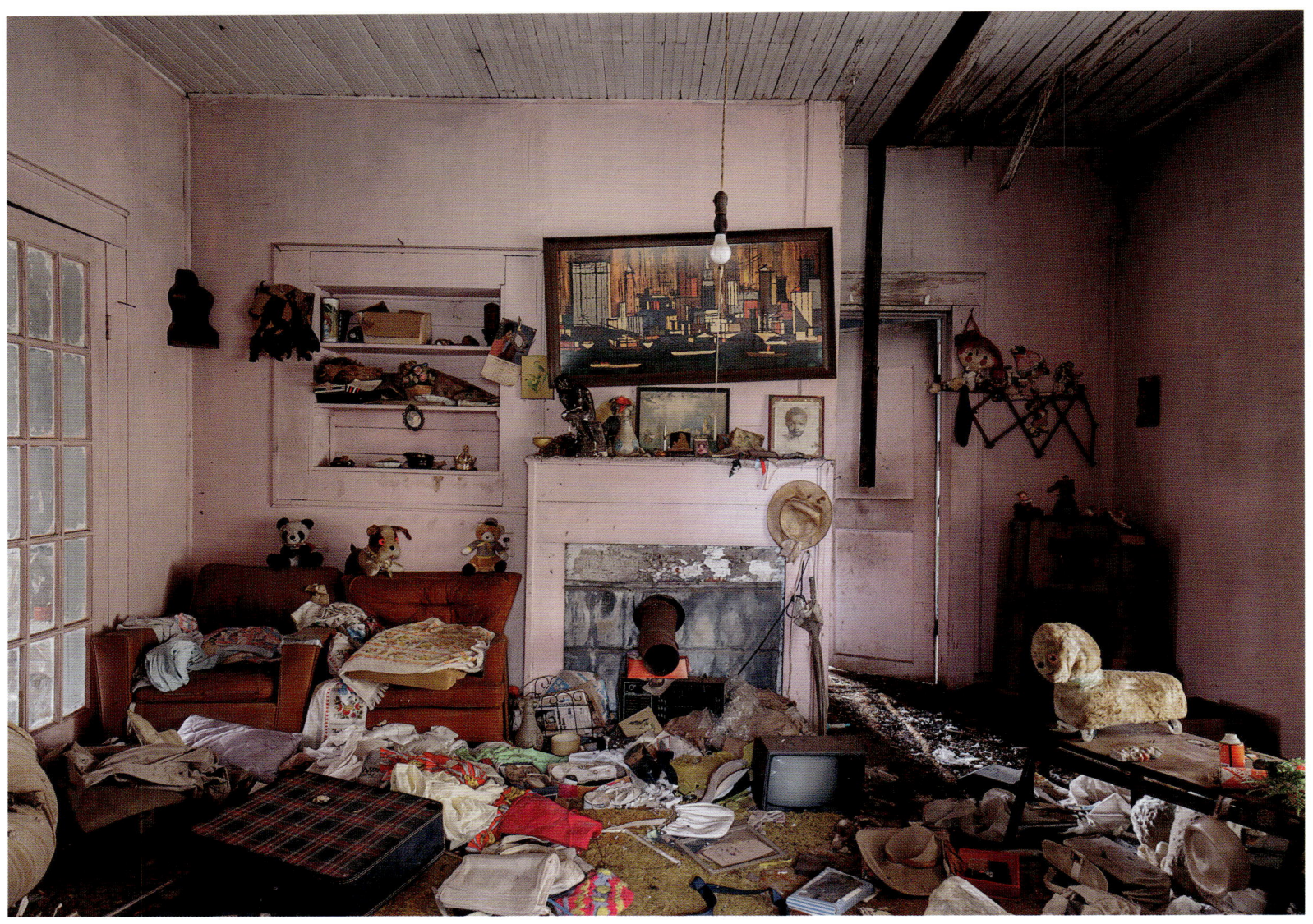

"THE PINK FAMILY ROOM"
Lee County, Georgia

This room was a hoard of clothing, shoes, photographs, Christmas decorations, and so much more. Every piece tells a story, but I found the photographs on the mantel of the woman and the young boy the most compelling.

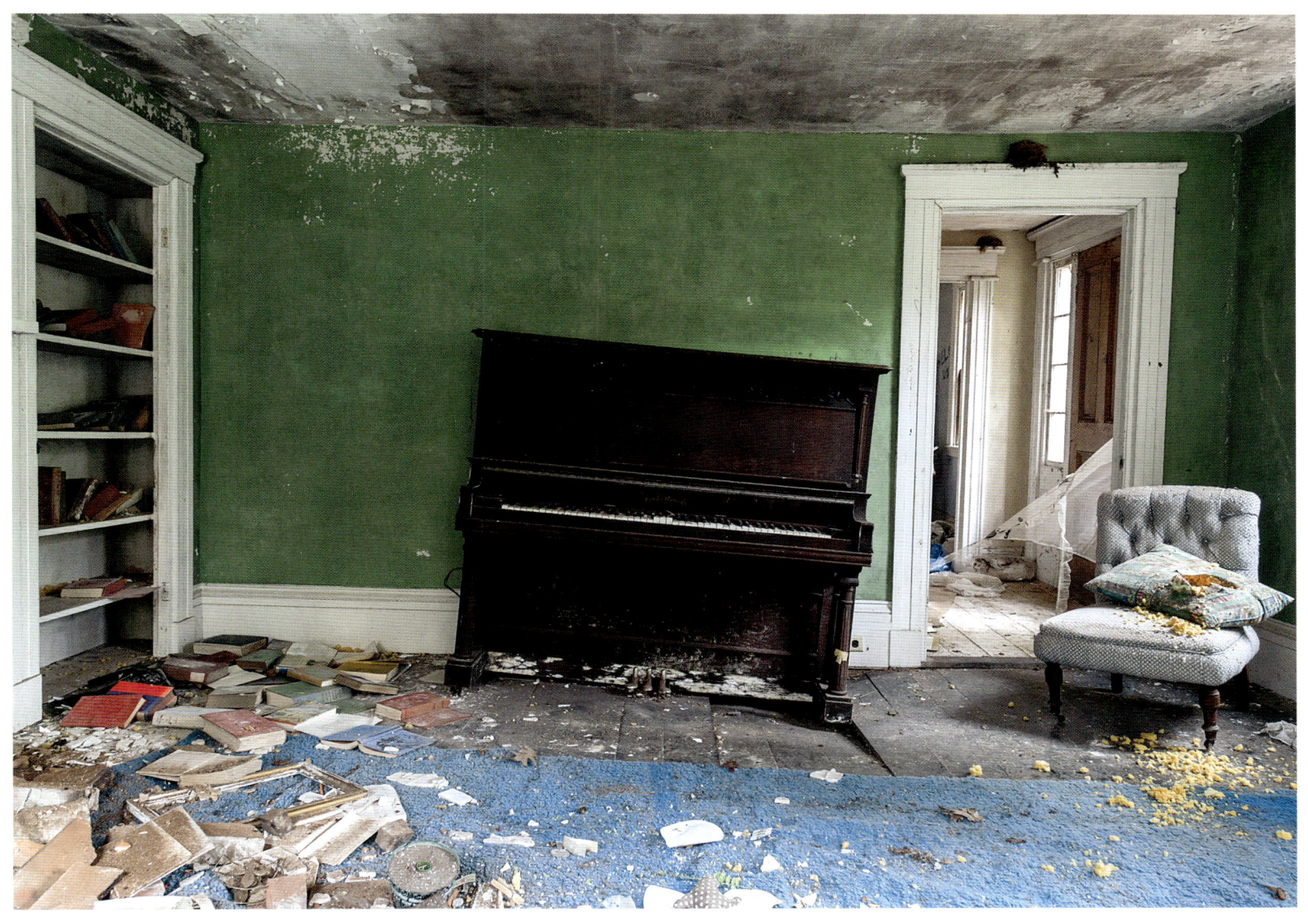

"THE LEANING PIANO"
Aroostook County, Maine

Inside this house, I found a room with a slanted floor. Books were falling off the shelves, and the piano was leaning to the right.

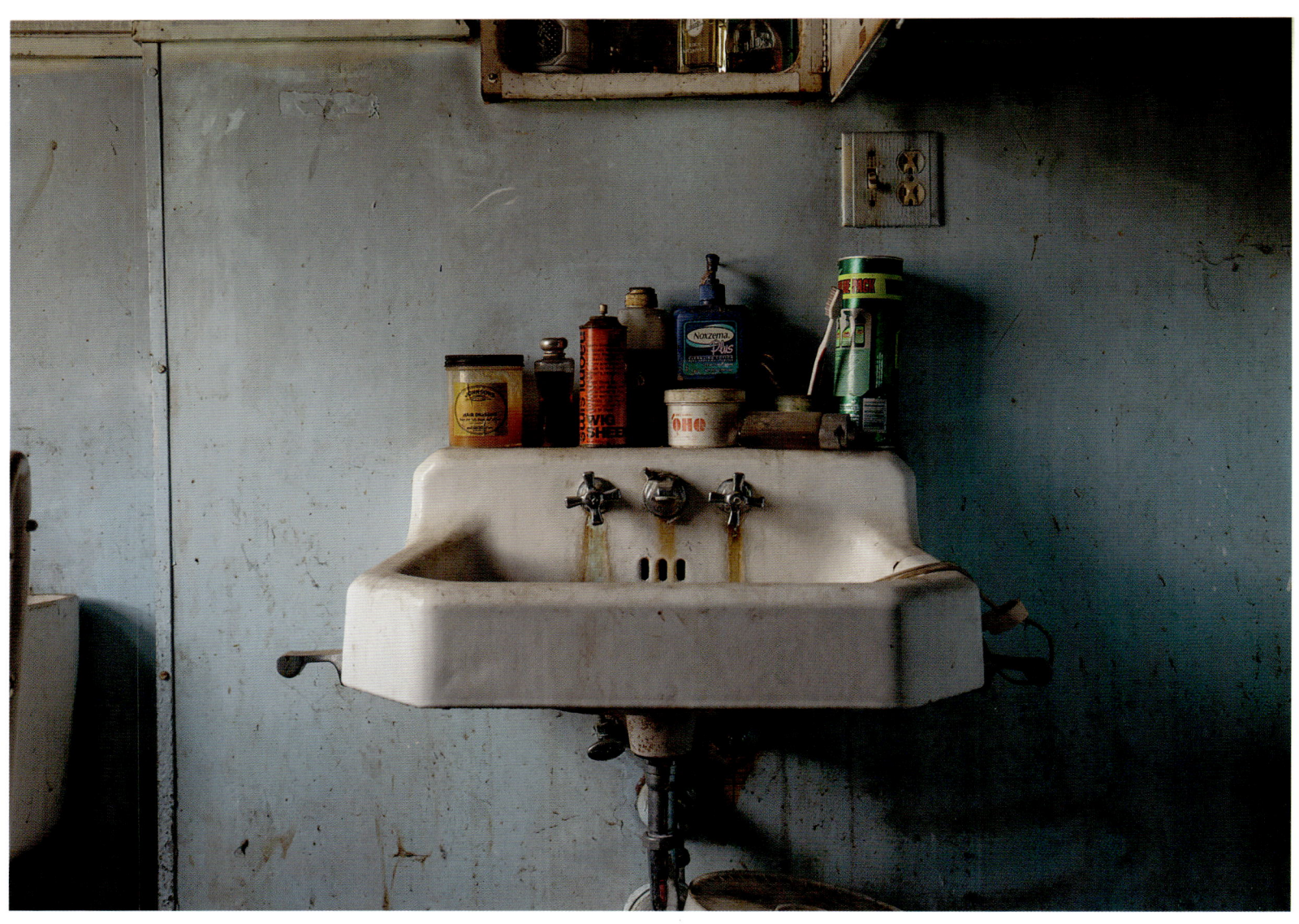

"THE SINK"
Frederick County, Virginia

Inside the bathroom of an artist's house was this sink lined with colorful products. Toiletries, medications, and beauty supplies always give an intimate glimpse into the lives of the people who left them behind.

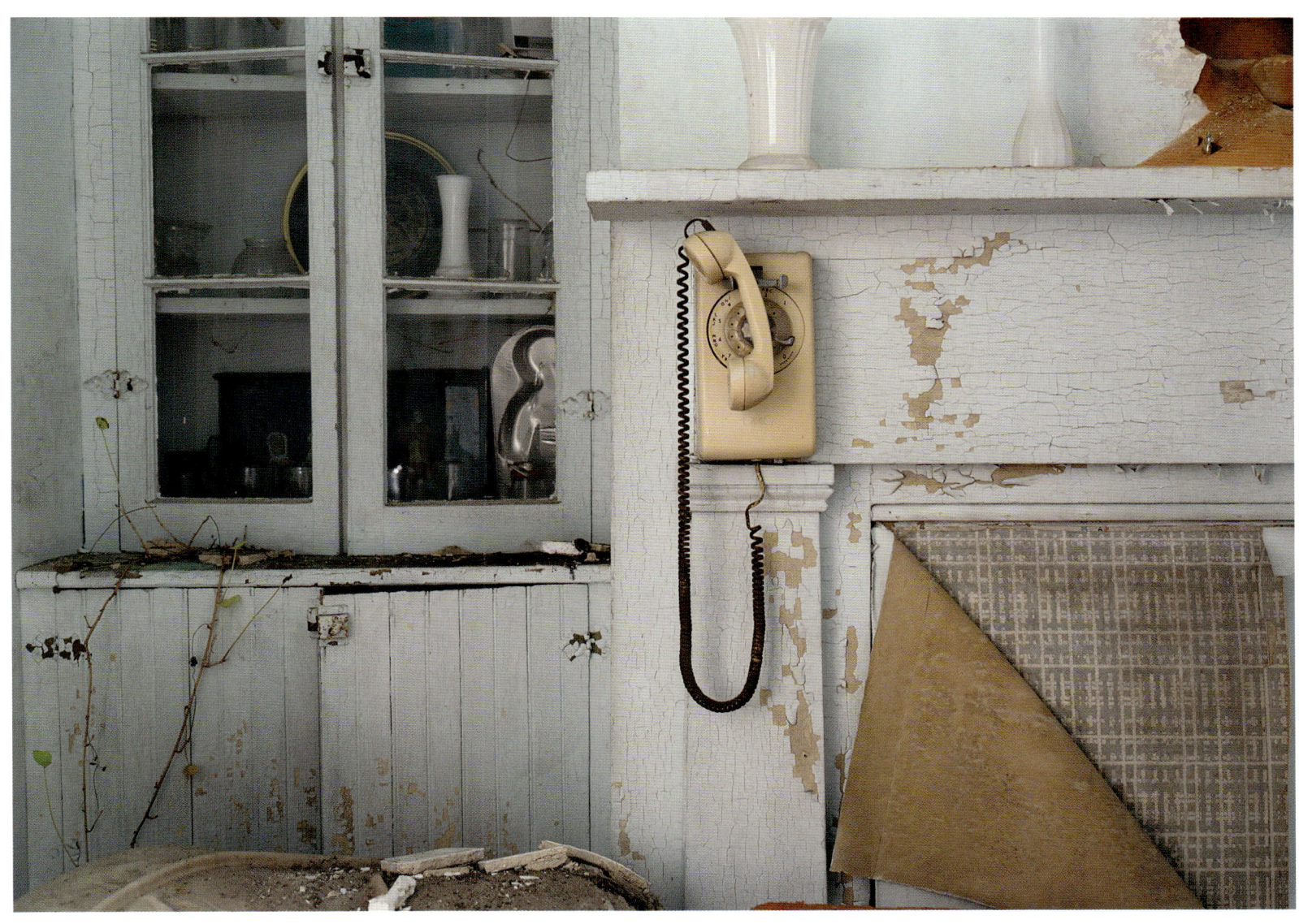

"THE ROTARY PHONE"
Richmond County, Virginia

This house had so much history and so many antiques in each room that trying to photograph it was a challenge. I found something beautiful in the simplicity of this rotary phone on the mantel and the plants growing in from the outside.

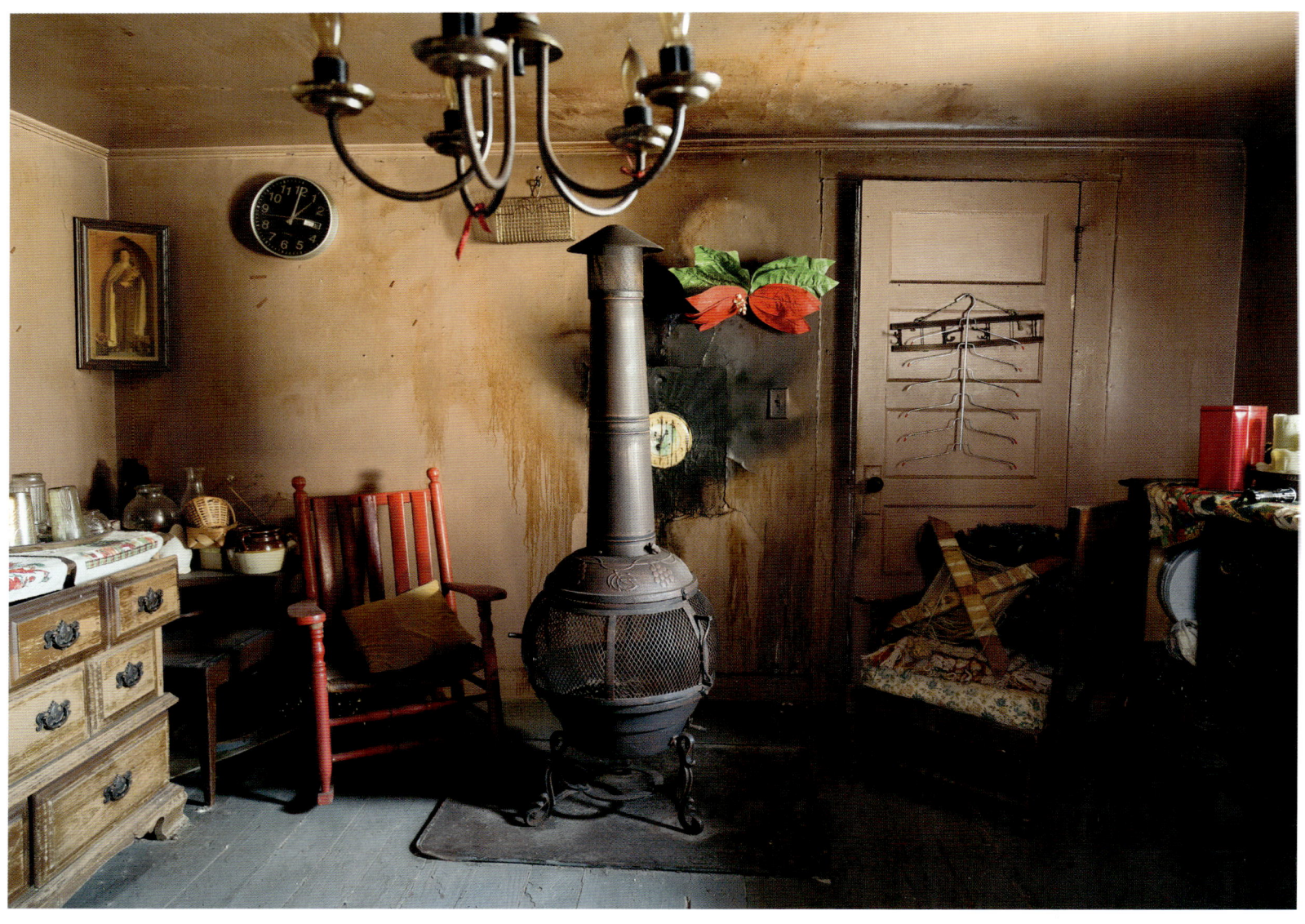

"AROUND THE FIRE"
Westmoreland County, Virginia

This room was filled with religious symbolism and objects. The light was dim, and it was extremely difficult to shoot.

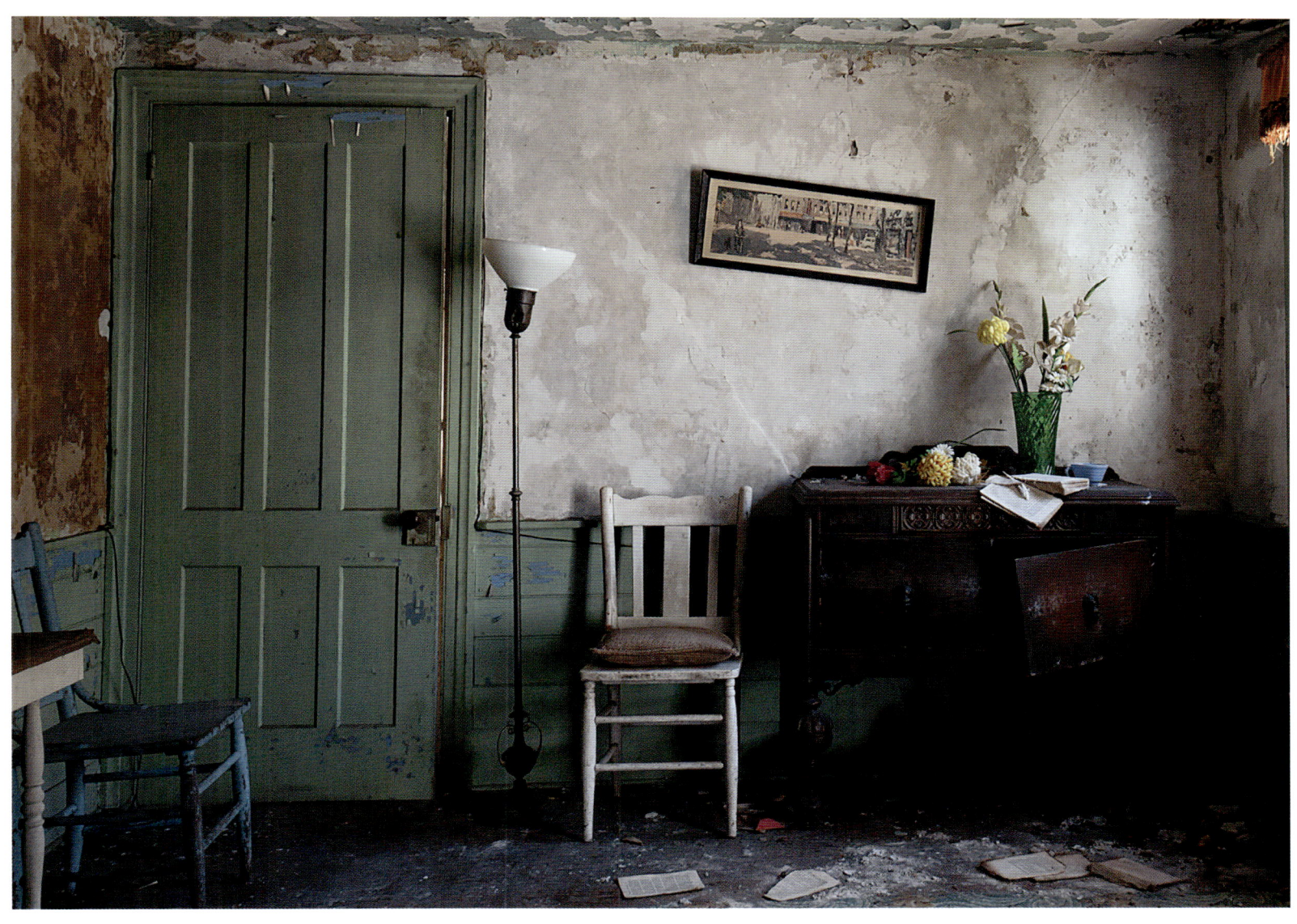

"THE FOYER"
Greene County, New York

I believe this house was once a retirement home. It was filled with colorful painted furniture, and books and fake flowers were scattered throughout. This is the main room at the entrance.

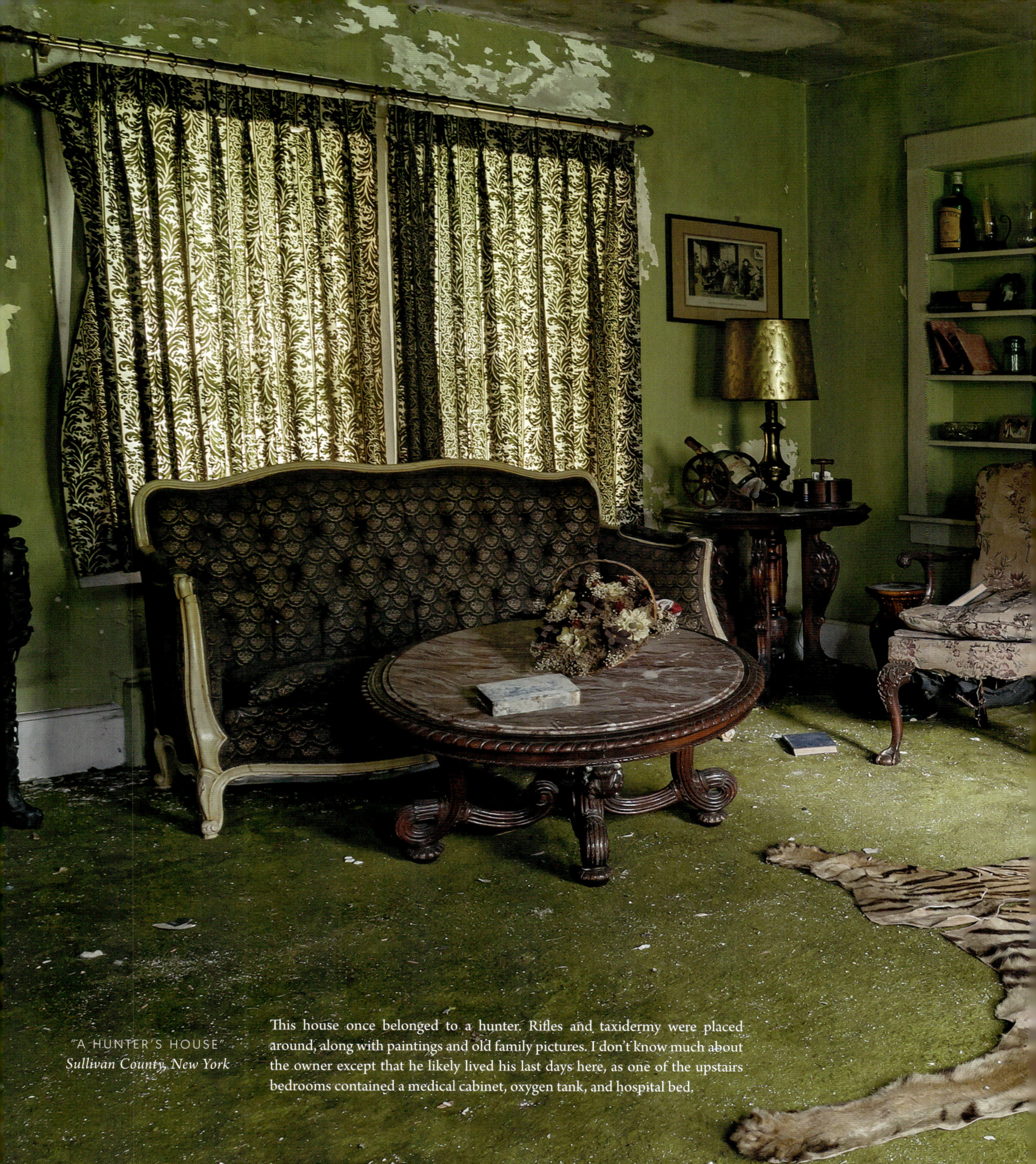

"A HUNTER'S HOUSE"
Sullivan County, New York

This house once belonged to a hunter. Rifles and taxidermy were placed around, along with paintings and old family pictures. I don't know much about the owner except that he likely lived his last days here, as one of the upstairs bedrooms contained a medical cabinet, oxygen tank, and hospital bed.

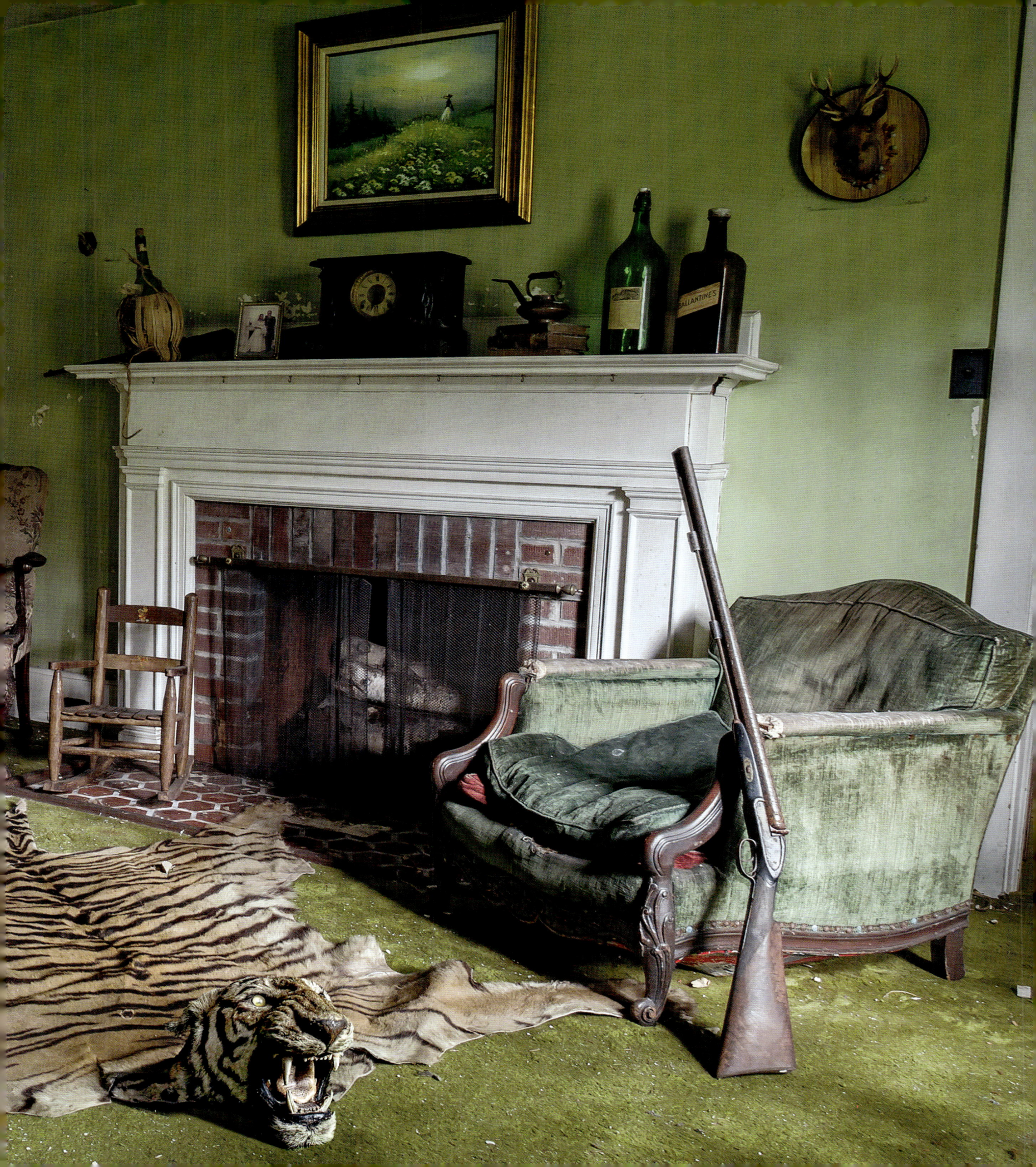

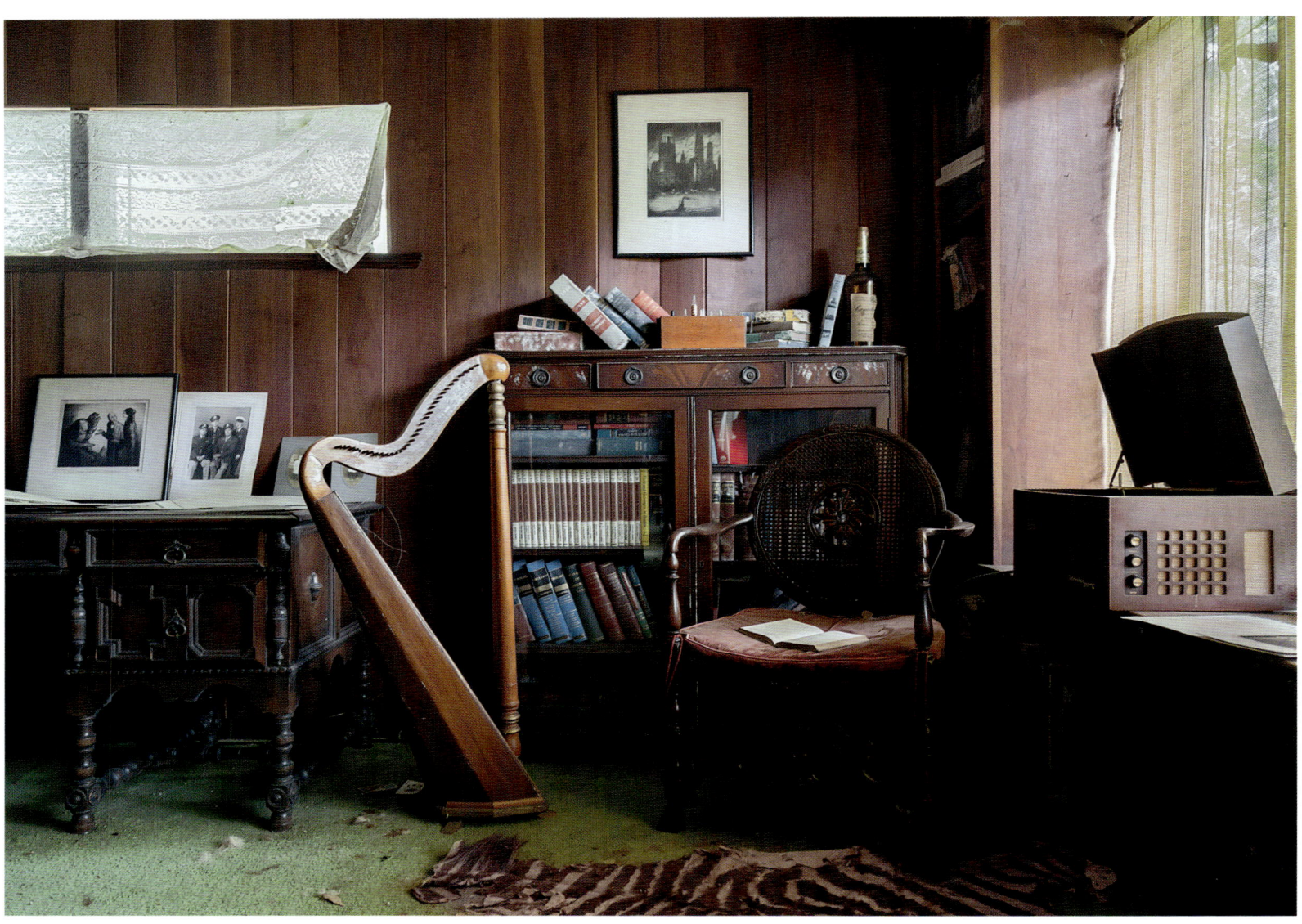

In another room of the hunter's house, a harp stood in front of a bookcase filled with medical tomes.

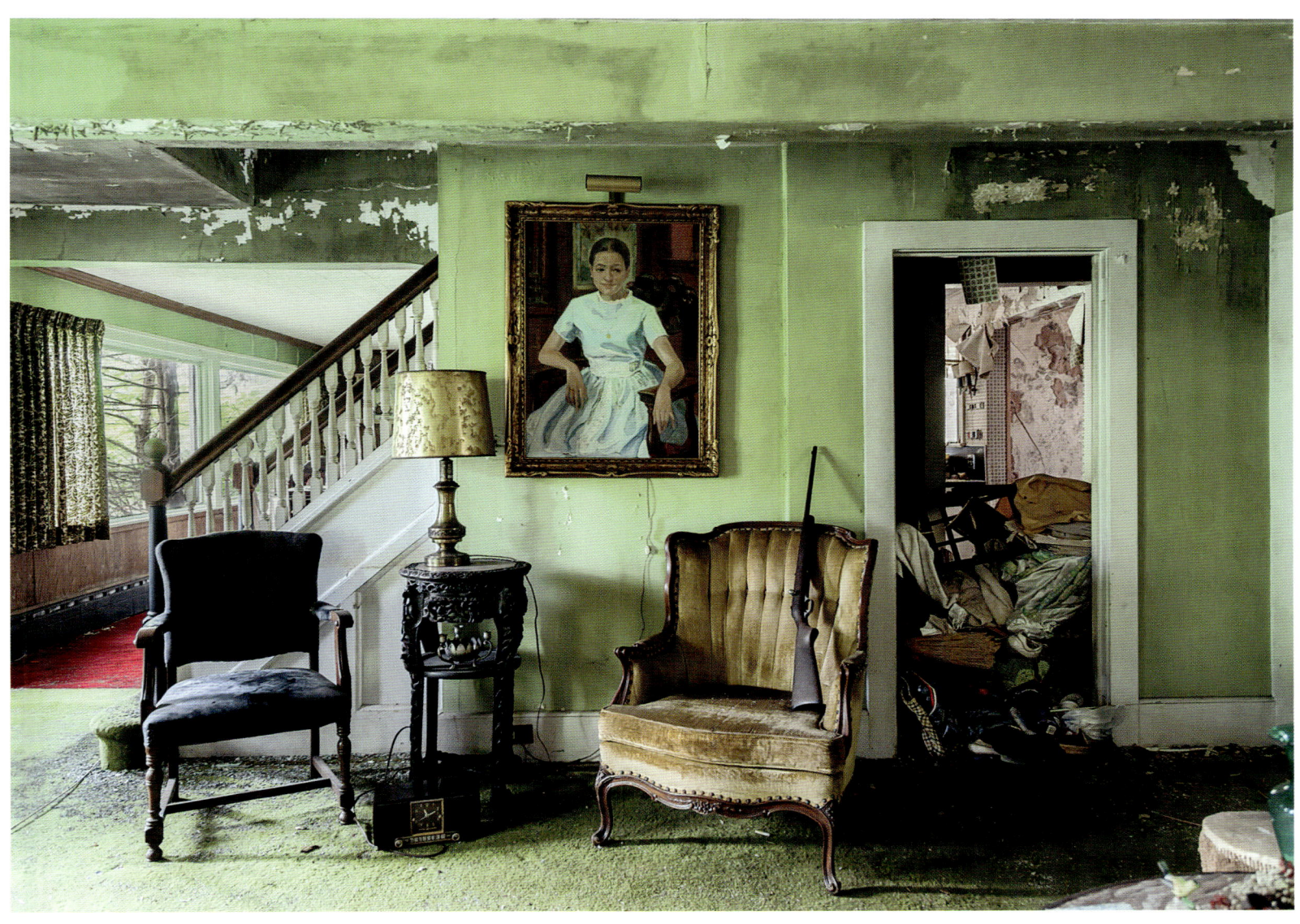

A woman in a painting looked back as if only she knew the secrets behind the walls of this house.

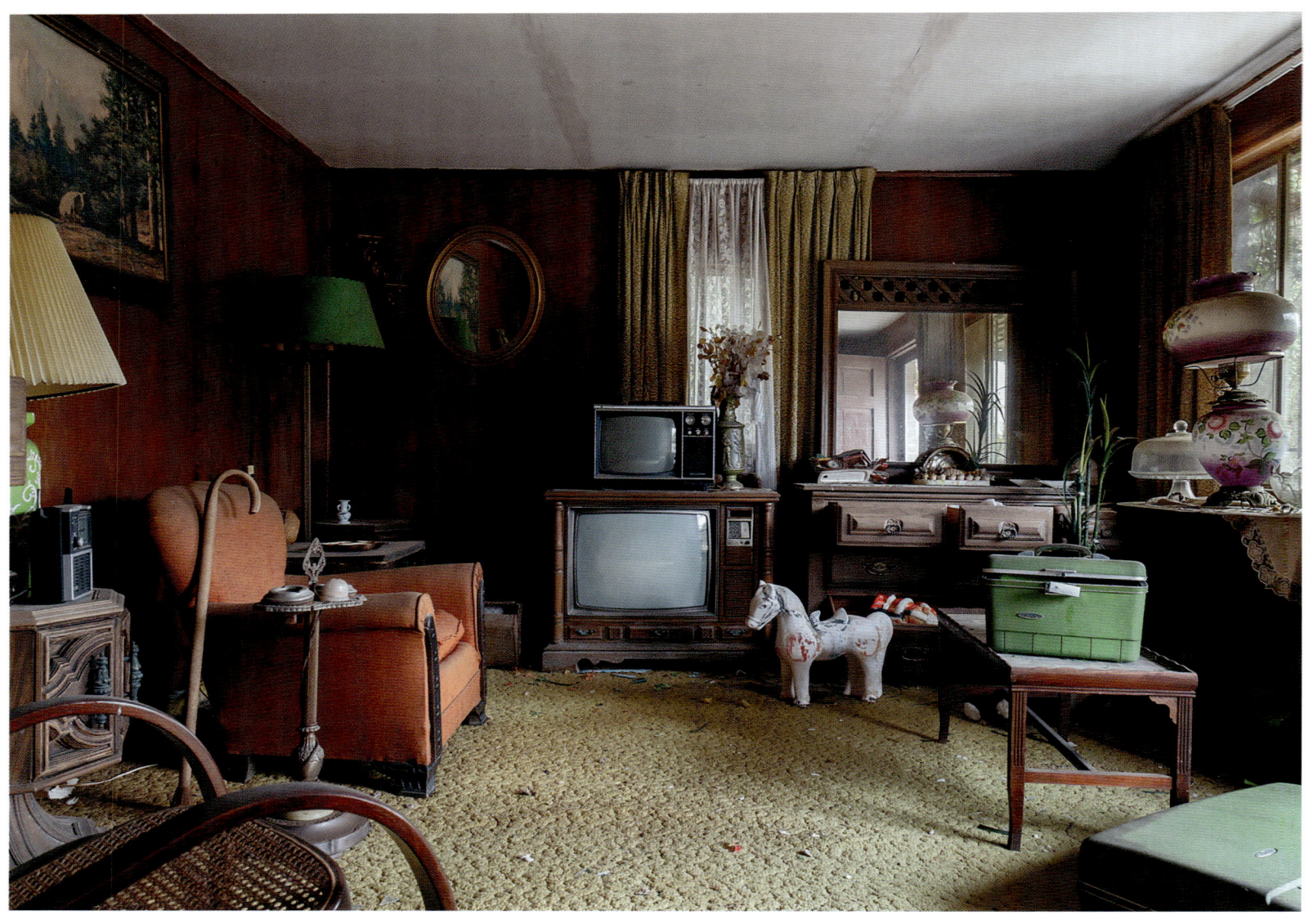

"THE TWO TVS"
Talbot County, Georgia

Besides the different colors in this home, there are many objects that have stories to tell, from the luggage and cane next to the chair to the stacked old televisions and family photos under the glass of a table.

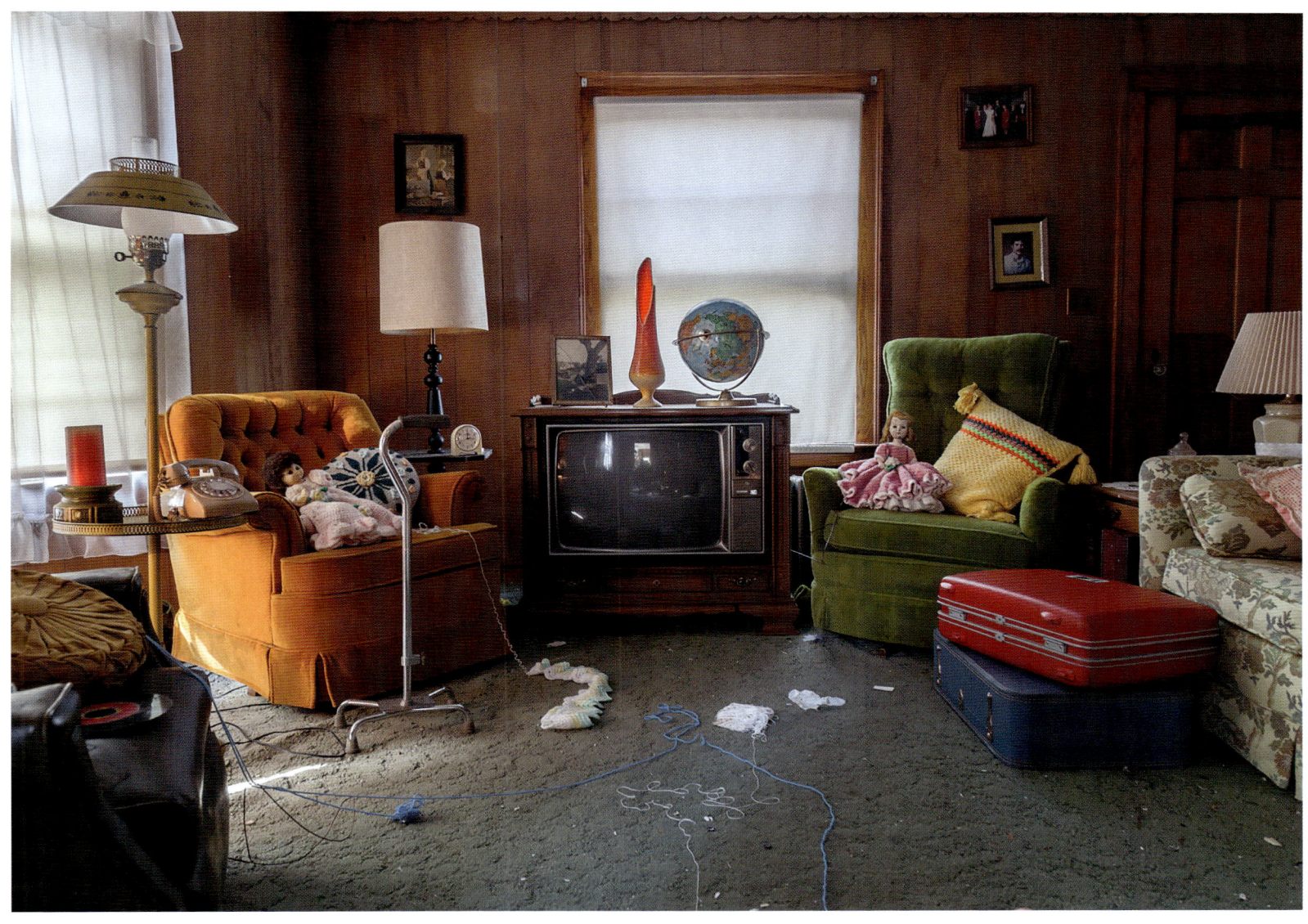

"GRANDMA'S HOUSE"
New London County, Connecticut

Known as Grandma's House, this home is full of mostly small rooms filled with all kinds of belongings. It is obvious that an older woman once lived here, and I imagine that she had grandchildren and led a happy life.

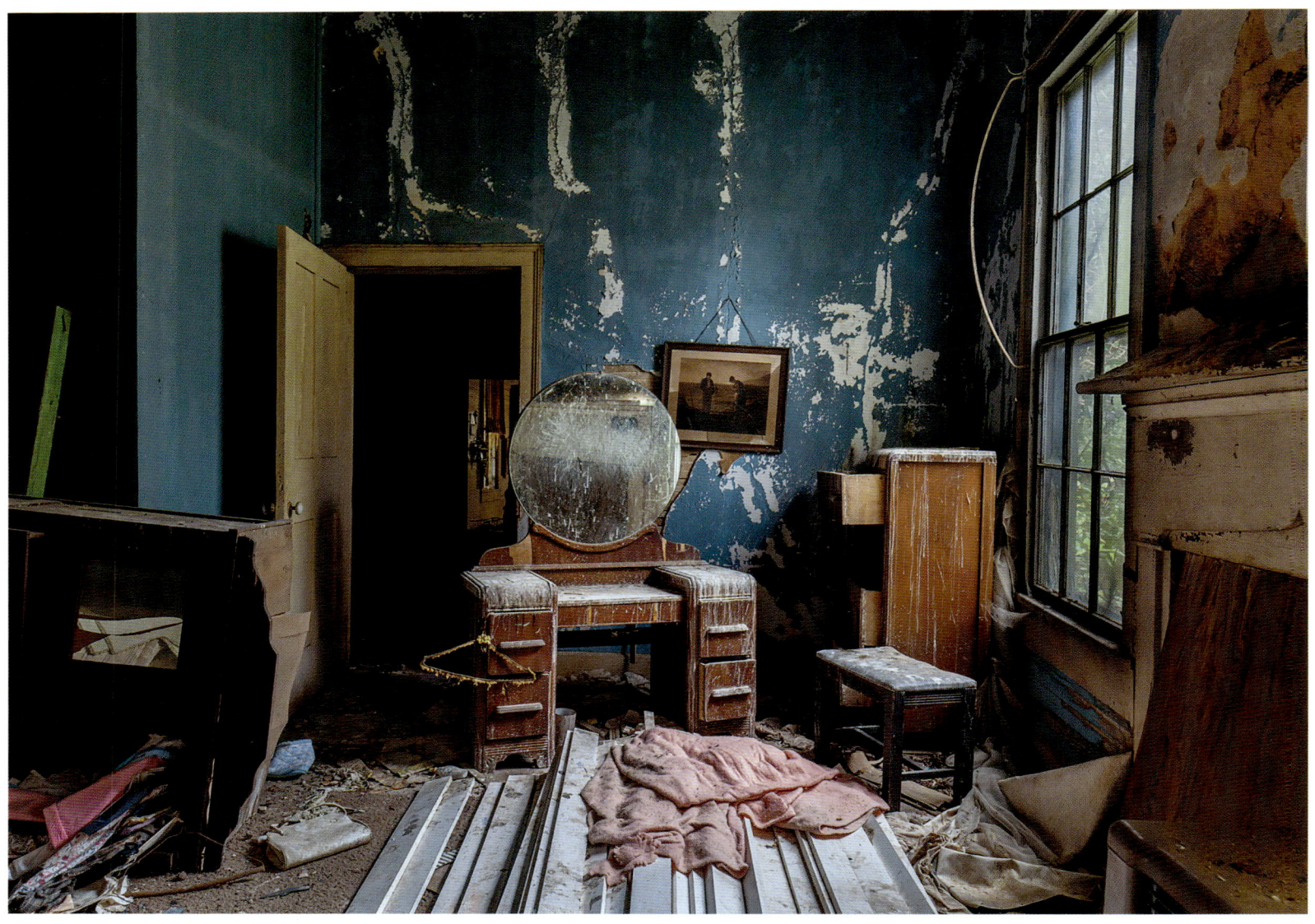

"THE PAINT-SPLATTERED VANITY"
Lee County, Alabama

This house was hidden so deep in the woods and so well preserved that it took a long time to actually find it. The search was worth it, as each room had colorful peeling paint and vintage furniture.

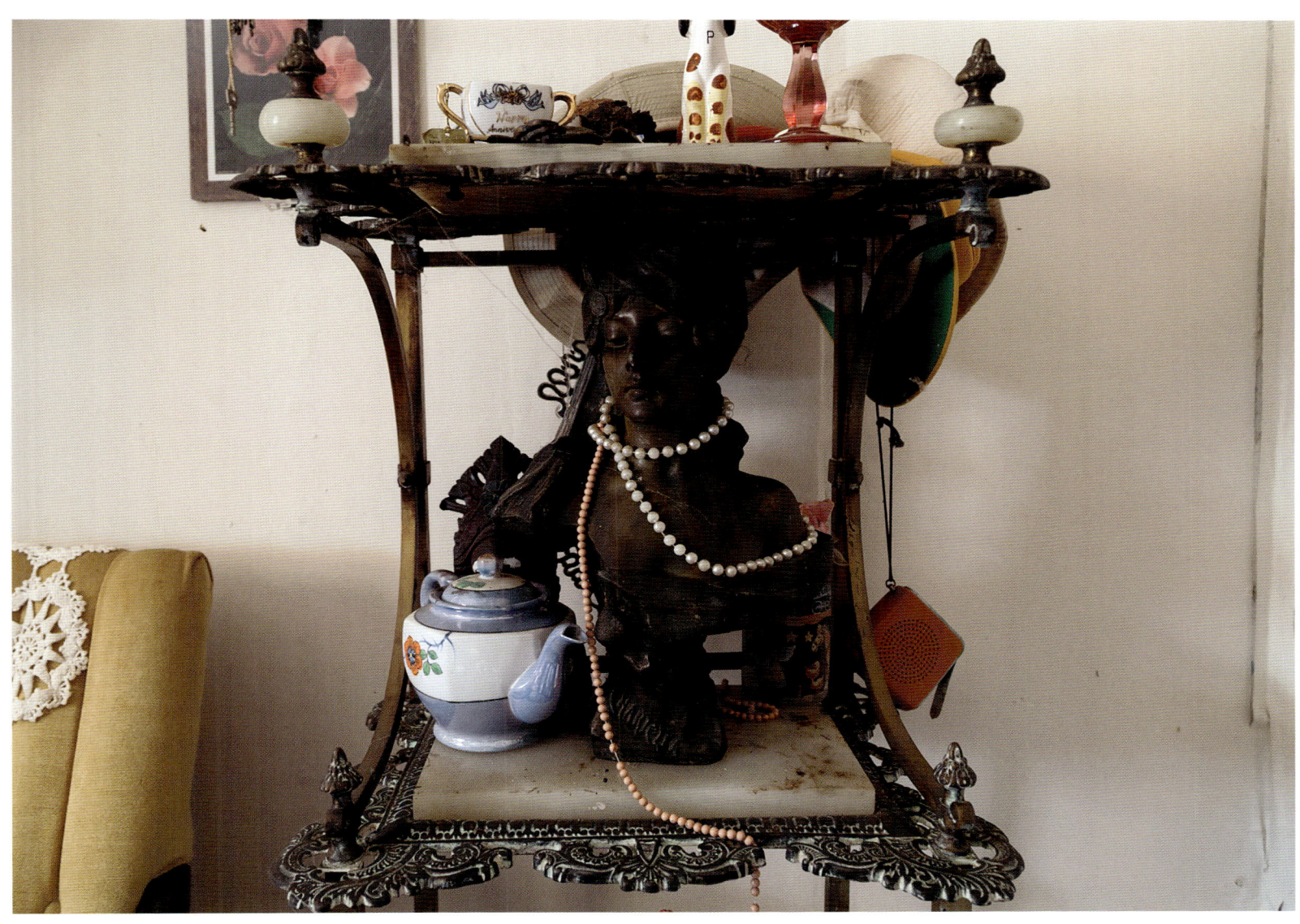

"THE LADY IN PEARLS"
Northumberland County, Virginia

The inside of this house was like a museum with all sorts of treasures. This bronze sculpture captured my attention with her melancholic look and her neck draped in pearls.

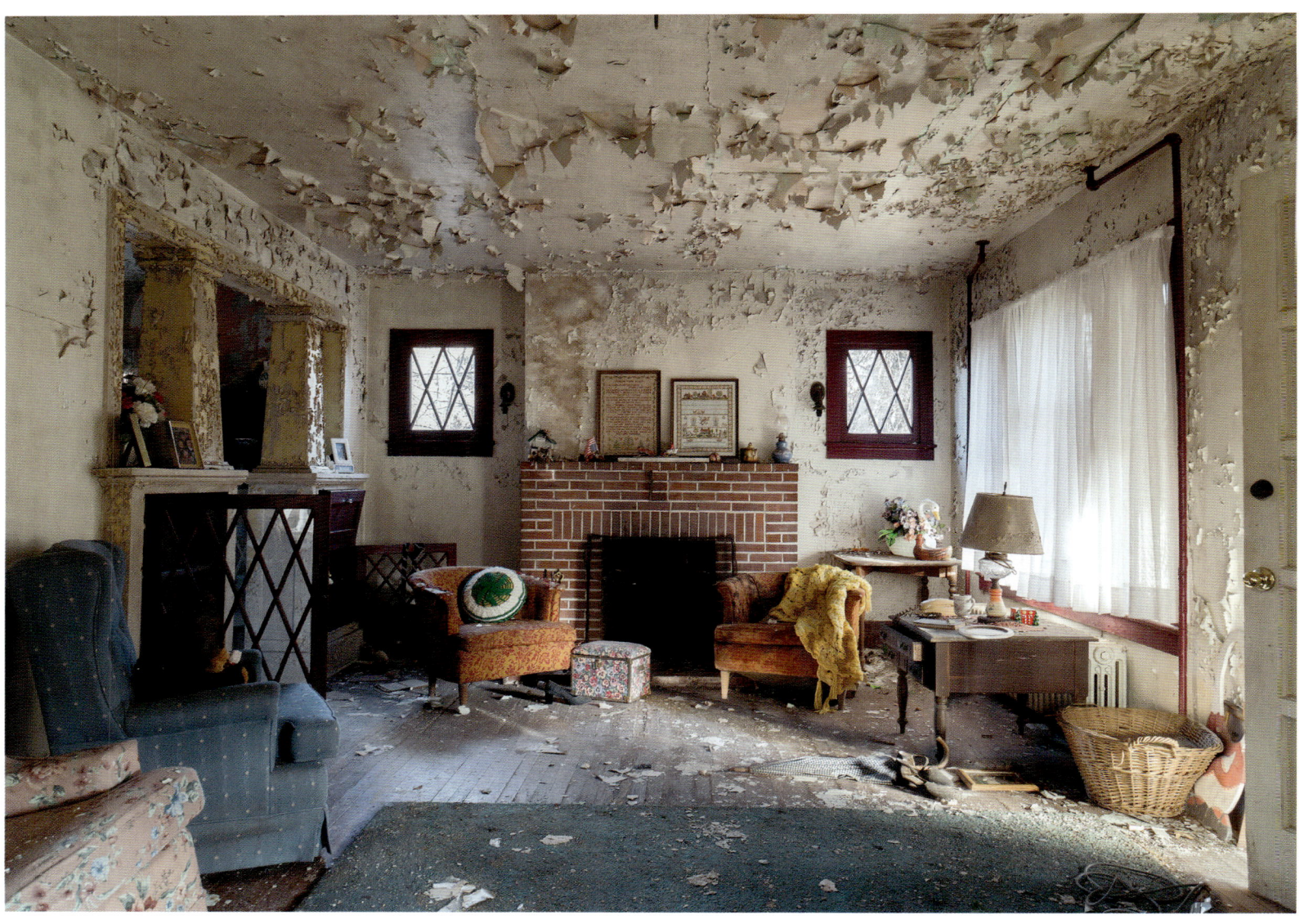

"HOME SWEET HOME"
New Castle County, Delaware

Walking up the driveway to this house, you can see a 1950 Dodge sedan that looks like it's been sitting there for decades. The interior, with its cracked walls, flaking paint, and vintage items, suggests that many decades have passed since this once-loved home has been occupied.

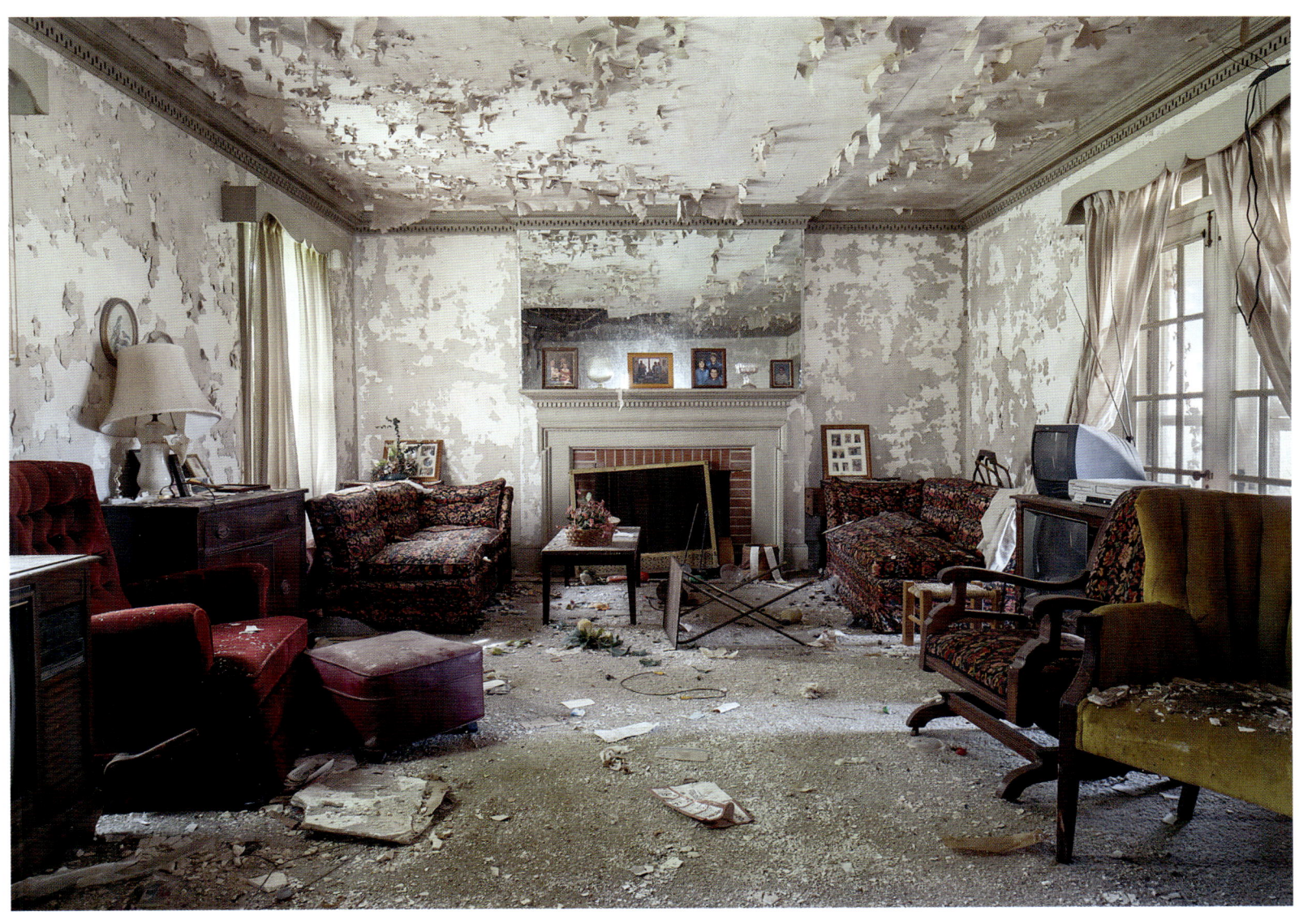

"A GENERATIONAL HOME"
Caroline County, Maryland

In this amazingly colorful house in Maryland, this family room stood out. It was filled with mid-century furniture, including chairs and TVs, and photographs that told the history of the house. These included photos of the family and family members' gravestones as well as photos of the house when it was first built. The peeling walls and ceiling shows how severe the decay is, suggesting the house may not stand for much longer.

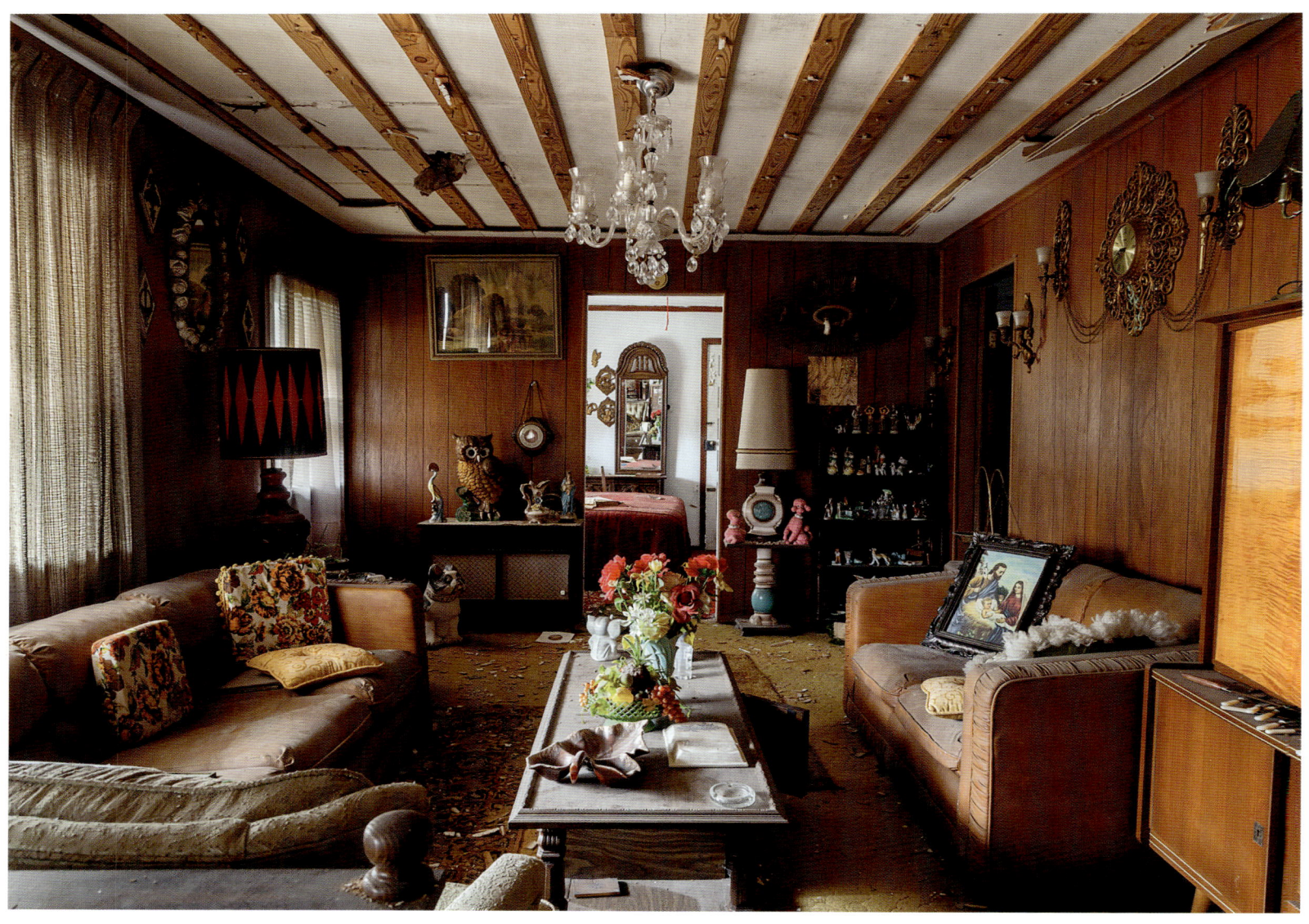

"THE PINK POODLES"
Talbot County, Georgia

This house has one of the most distinct looks I've seen in an abandoned home, with wood-beamed ceilings, mid-century furniture, and statement lamps. Every room was from a different era.

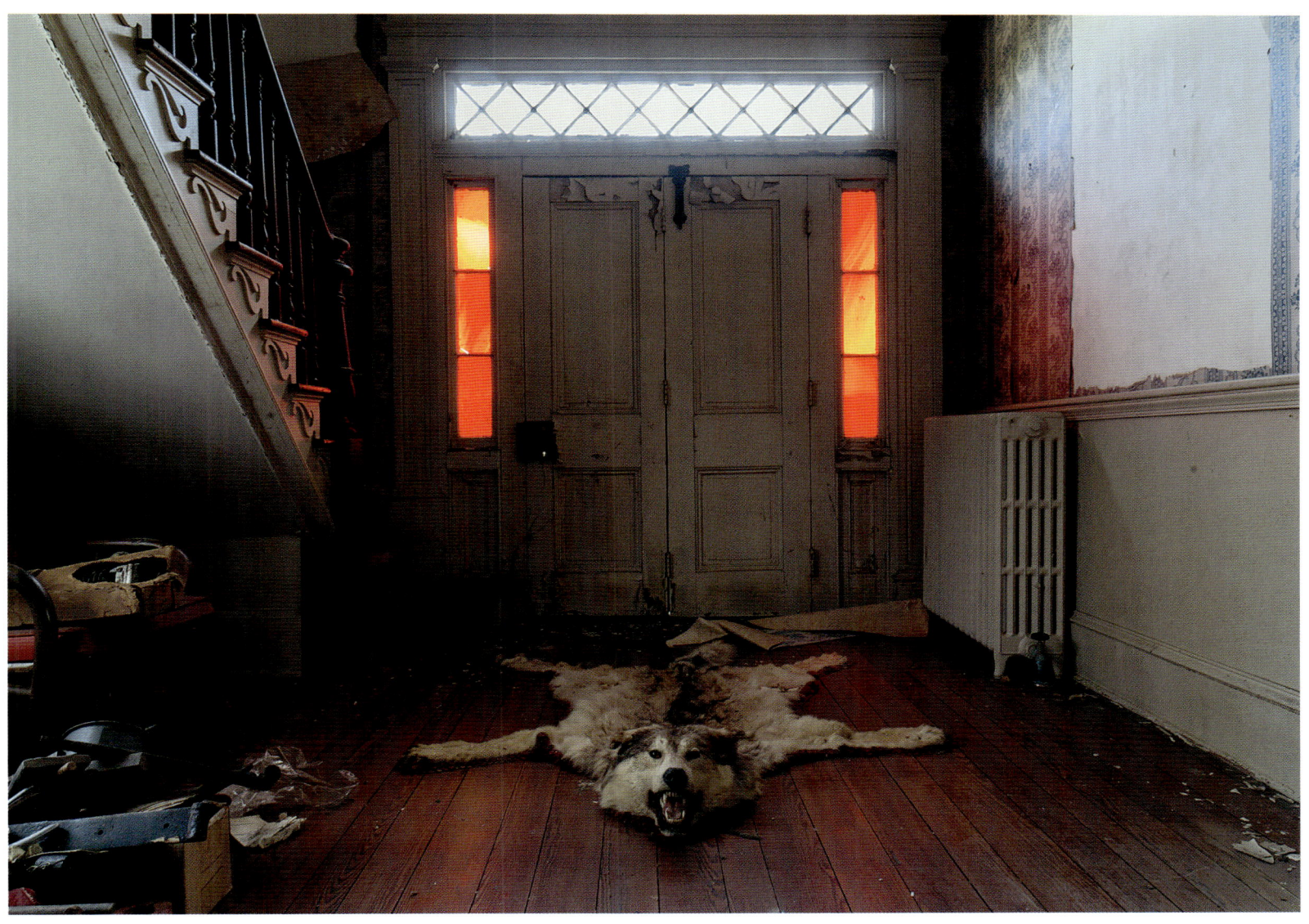

"A WOLF AT THE DOOR"
Westmoreland County, Virginia

This county is full of historic mansions. In this one, a taxidermy wolf rug, one of two in the house, guards the front door.

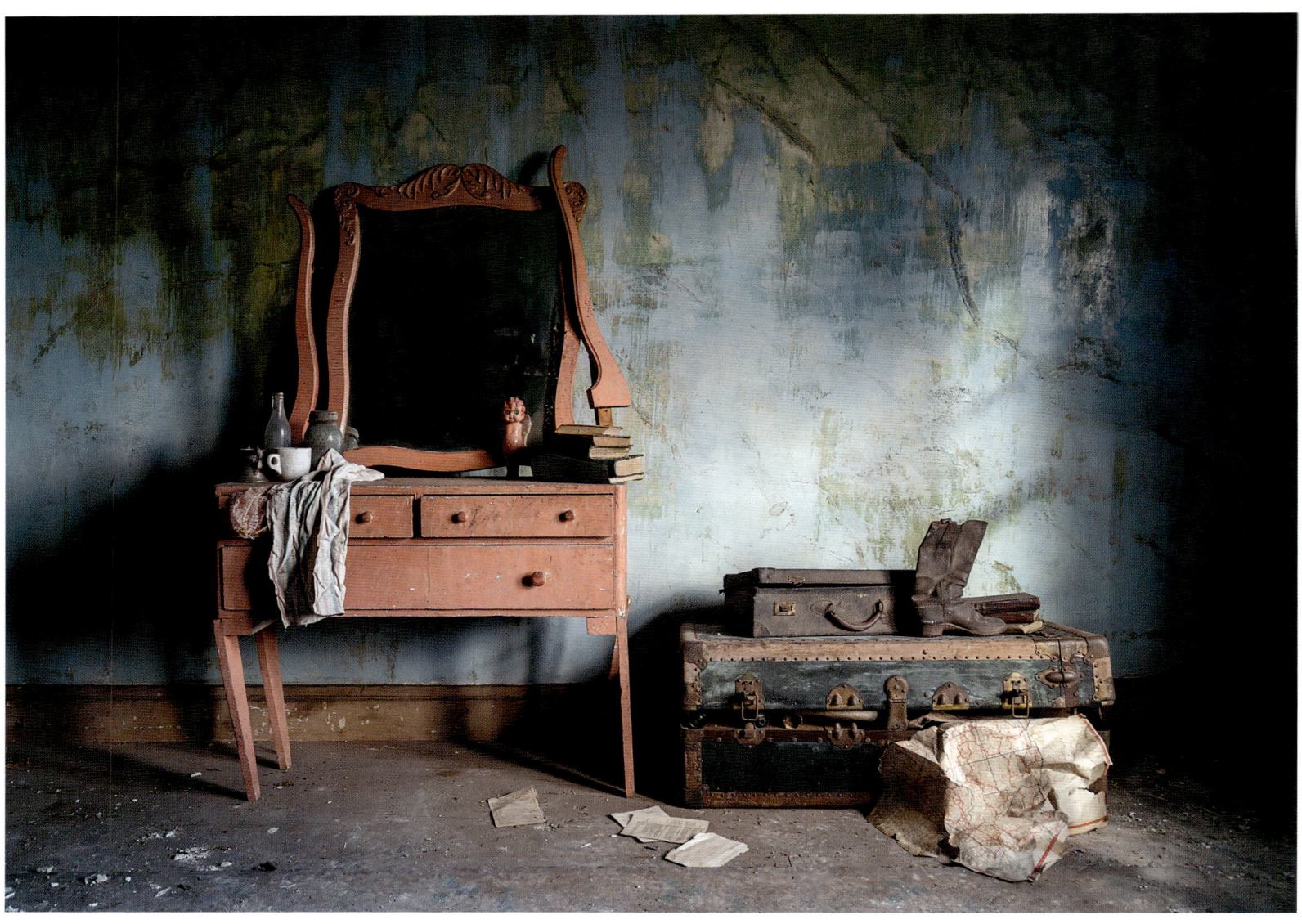

"THE LEANING VANITY"
Orange County, New York

I found this vanity in the attic of one of my favorite homes. There were many rooms that were more grand, but sometimes it's the simplicity that makes for a striking photograph.

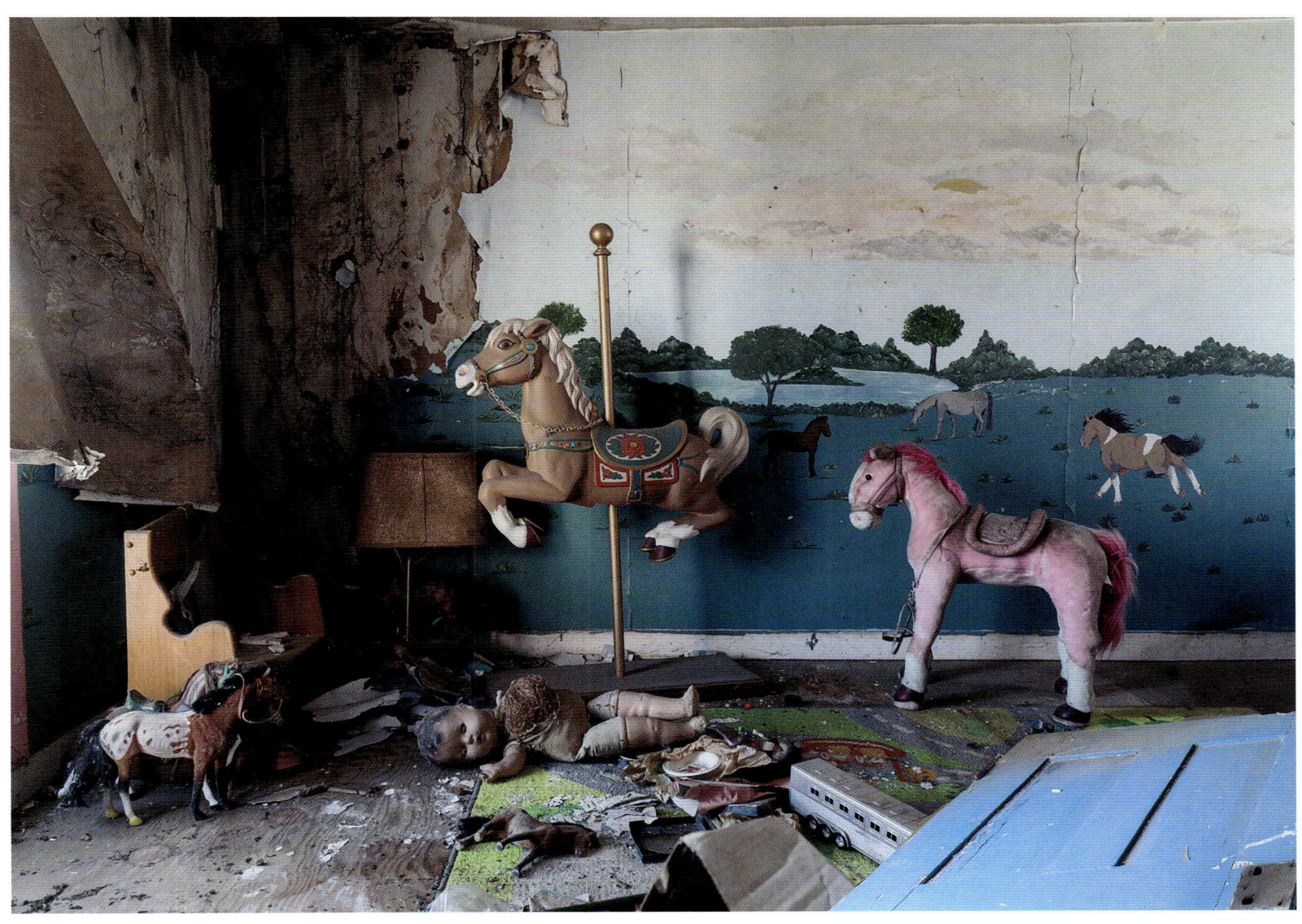

"THE CAROUSEL HORSES"
Cecil County, Maryland

This picture may be one of the most poignant in this book. The home has a turbulent backstory, but upstairs, these toys, a carousel horse, and a mural of wild horses remain. The exterior of the house shows signs that it will likely be demolished soon, and I hope some of these items, and even some positive memories, can be salvaged.

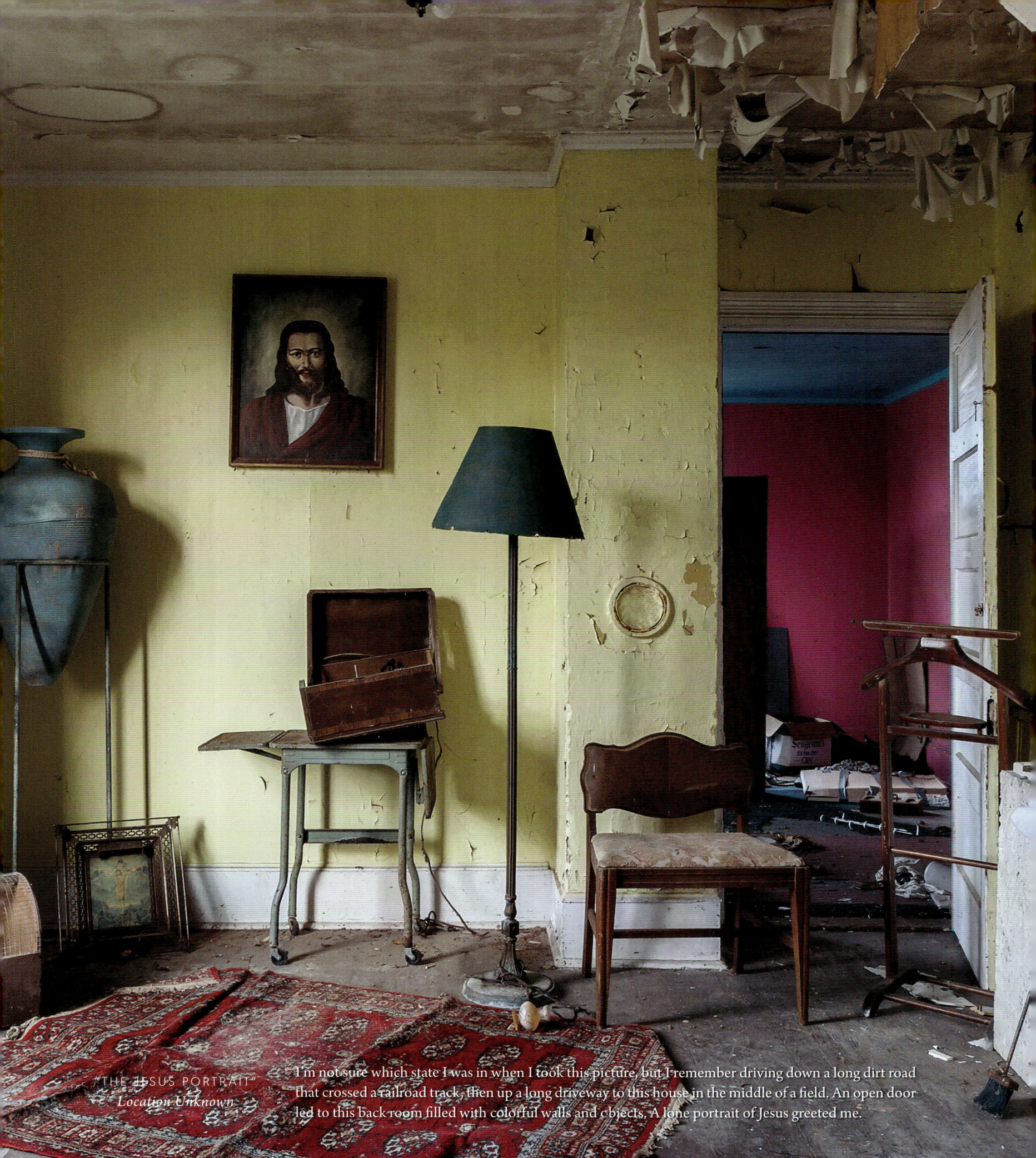

"THE JESUS PORTRAIT"
Location Unknown

I'm not sure which state I was in when I took this picture, but I remember driving down a long dirt road that crossed a railroad track, then up a long driveway to this house in the middle of a field. An open door led to this back room filled with colorful walls and objects. A lone portrait of Jesus greeted me.

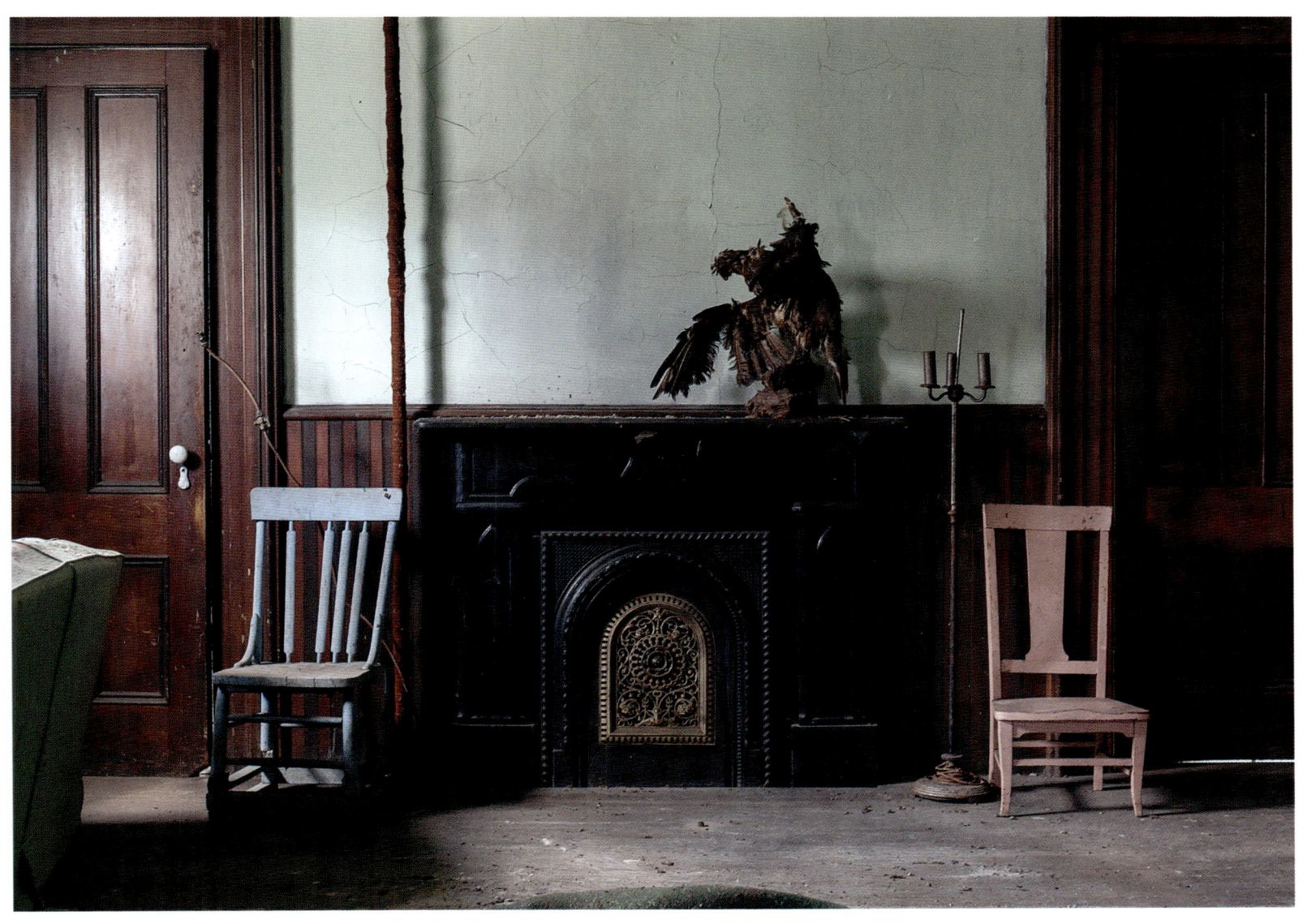

"THE BIRD ON THE MANTEL"
Orange County, New York

This taxidermy bird was missing feathers yet strikingly positioned. Juxtaposed with the two small chairs, it made for an interesting shot.

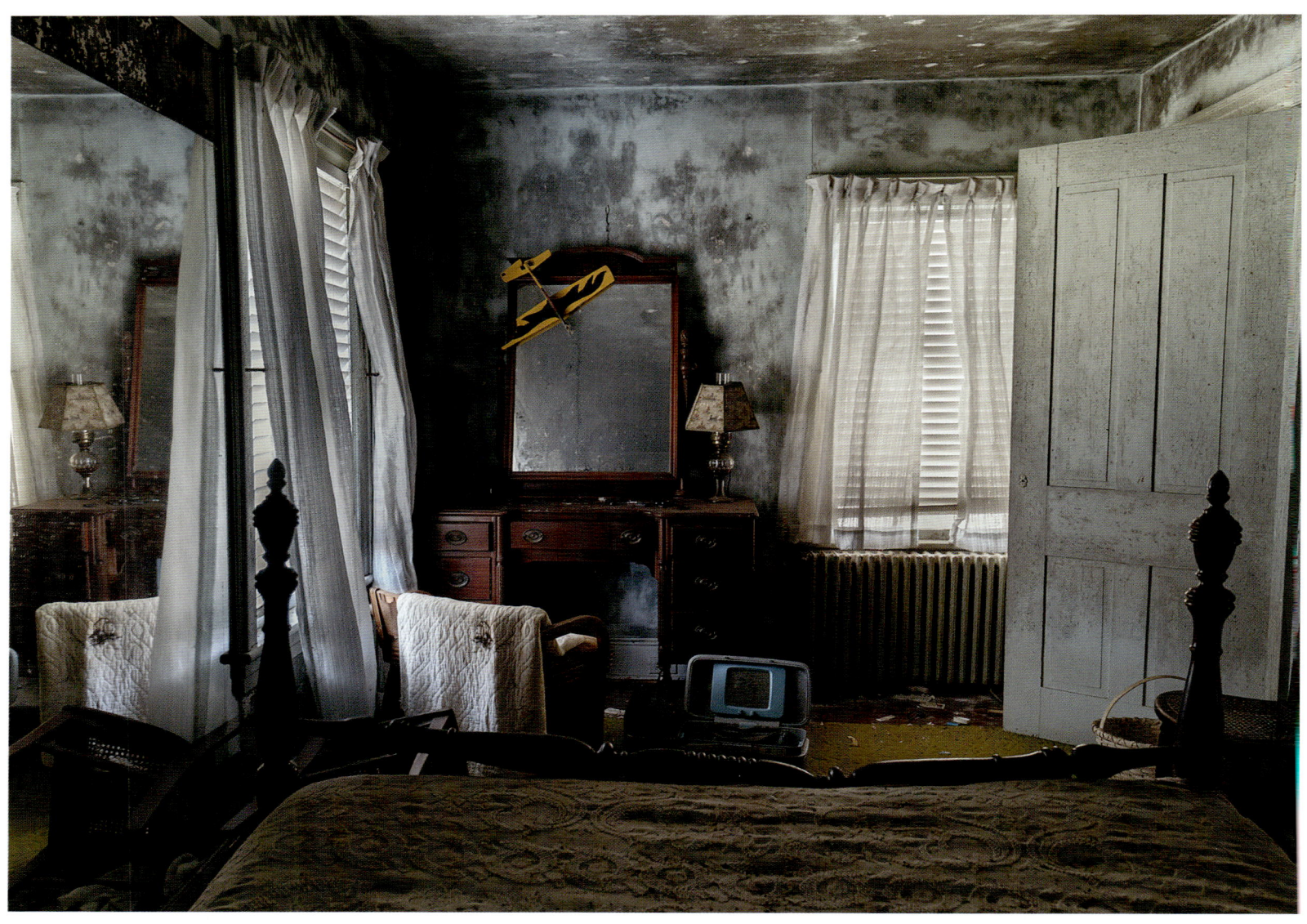

"THE TOY AIRPLANE"
Caroline County, Maryland

In this abandoned farmhouse, a toy plane hung on a child's dresser mirror. Another mirror reflected the entire room, creating the illusion that it was much bigger than it really was.

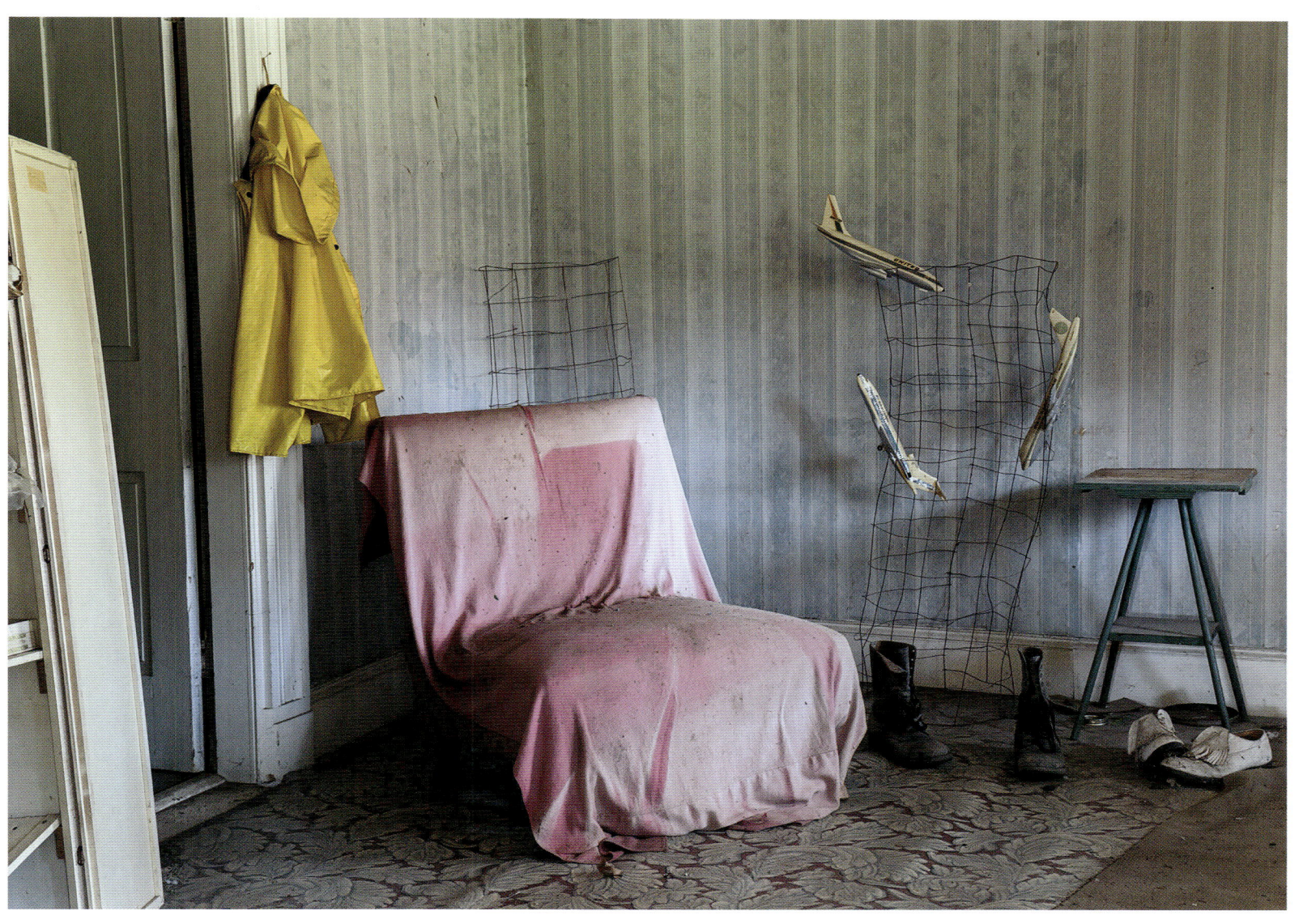

"THE CIRCLING PLANES"
Berks County, Pennsylvania

Once an old general store, this home was filled with unique items. The simple color of the sheet and coat stood out to me, as well as the model airplanes.

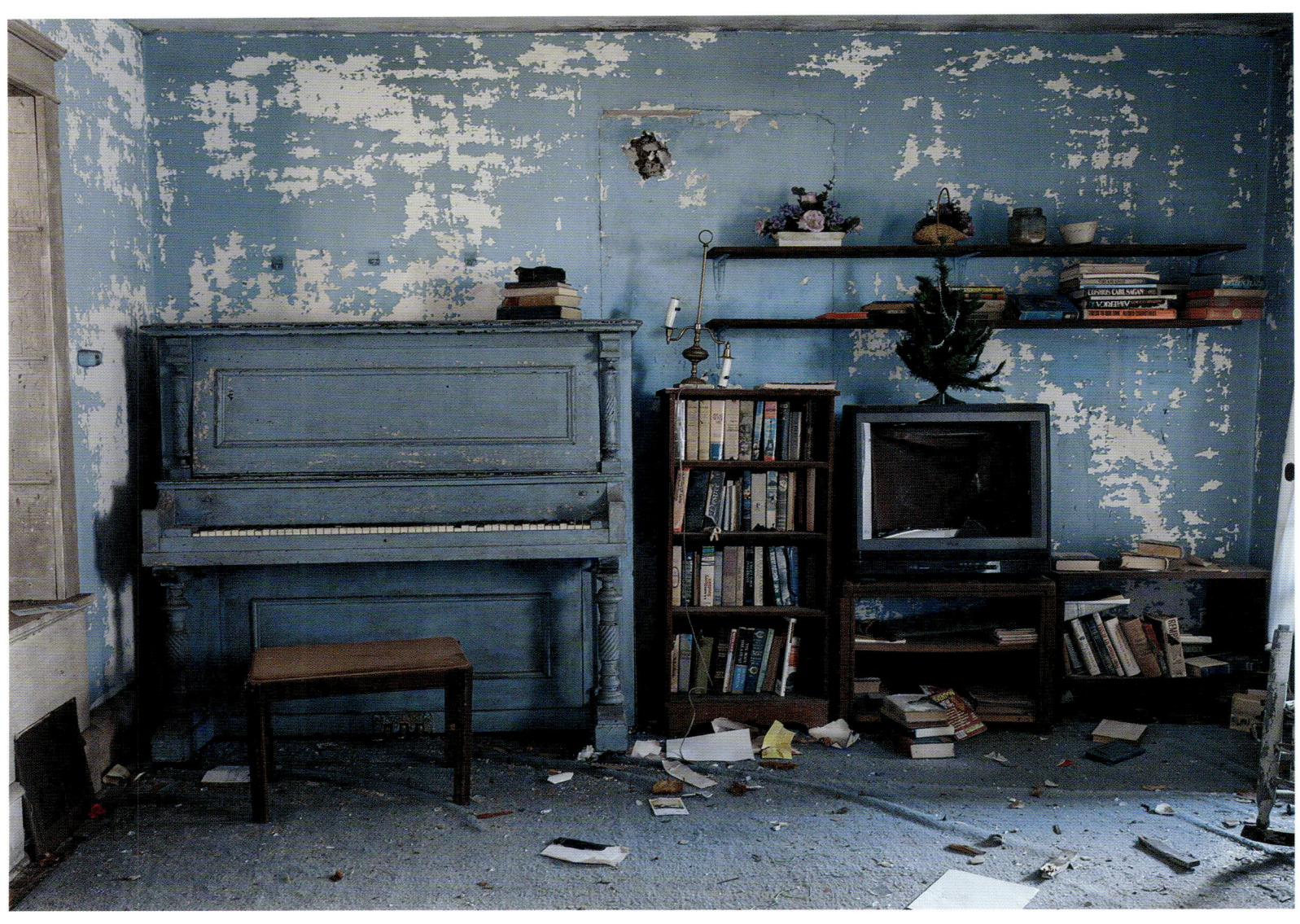

"THE BLUE PIANO"
Luzerne County, Pennsylvania

This house was filled with bold color choices, including this blue living room with a matching piano.

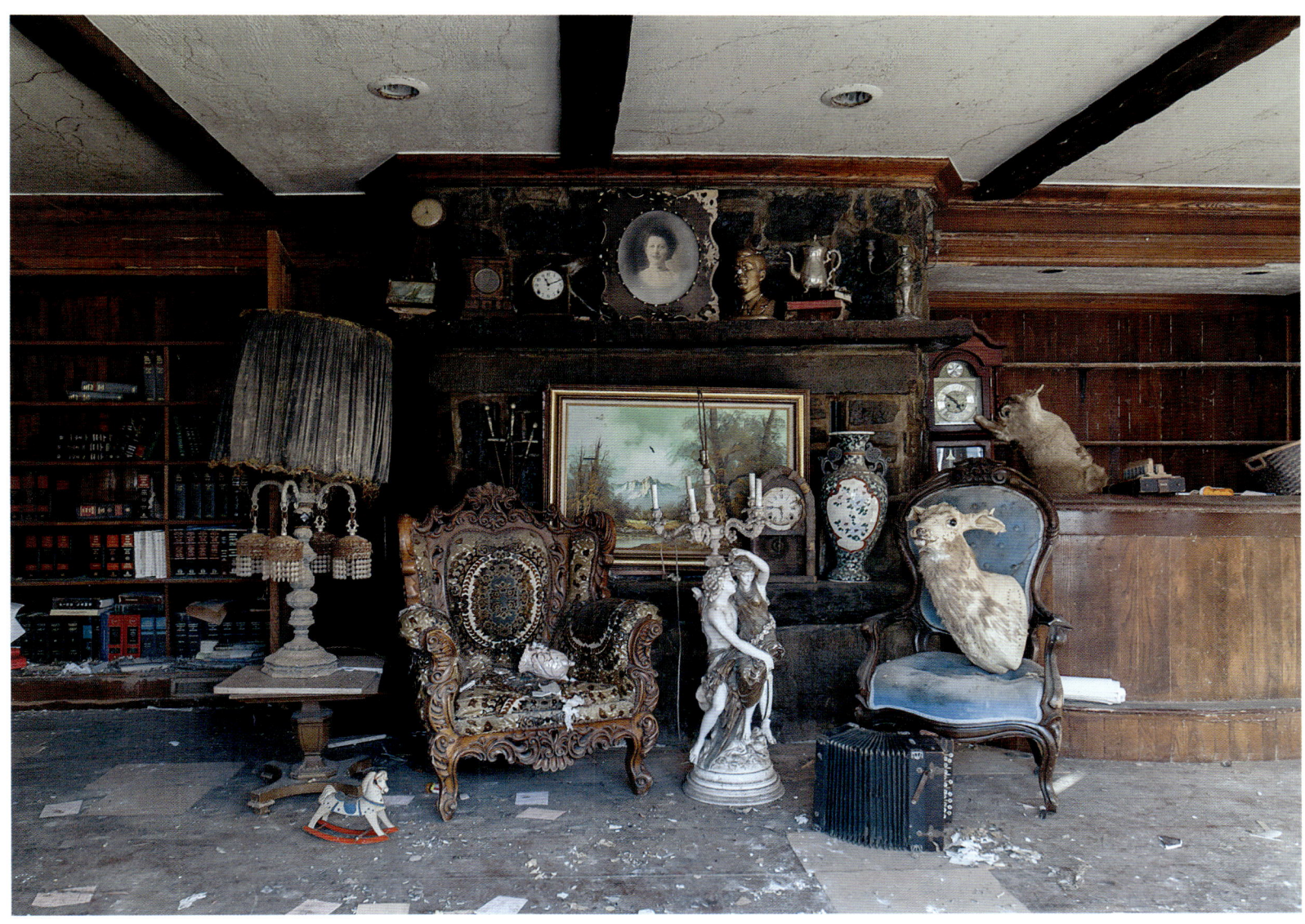

"AN ANTIQUE COLLECTION"
Ulster County, New York

This large house filled with antiques had been manipulated by many photographers before me, who had placed these items near the fireplace. Each object is a clue to who the owner was.

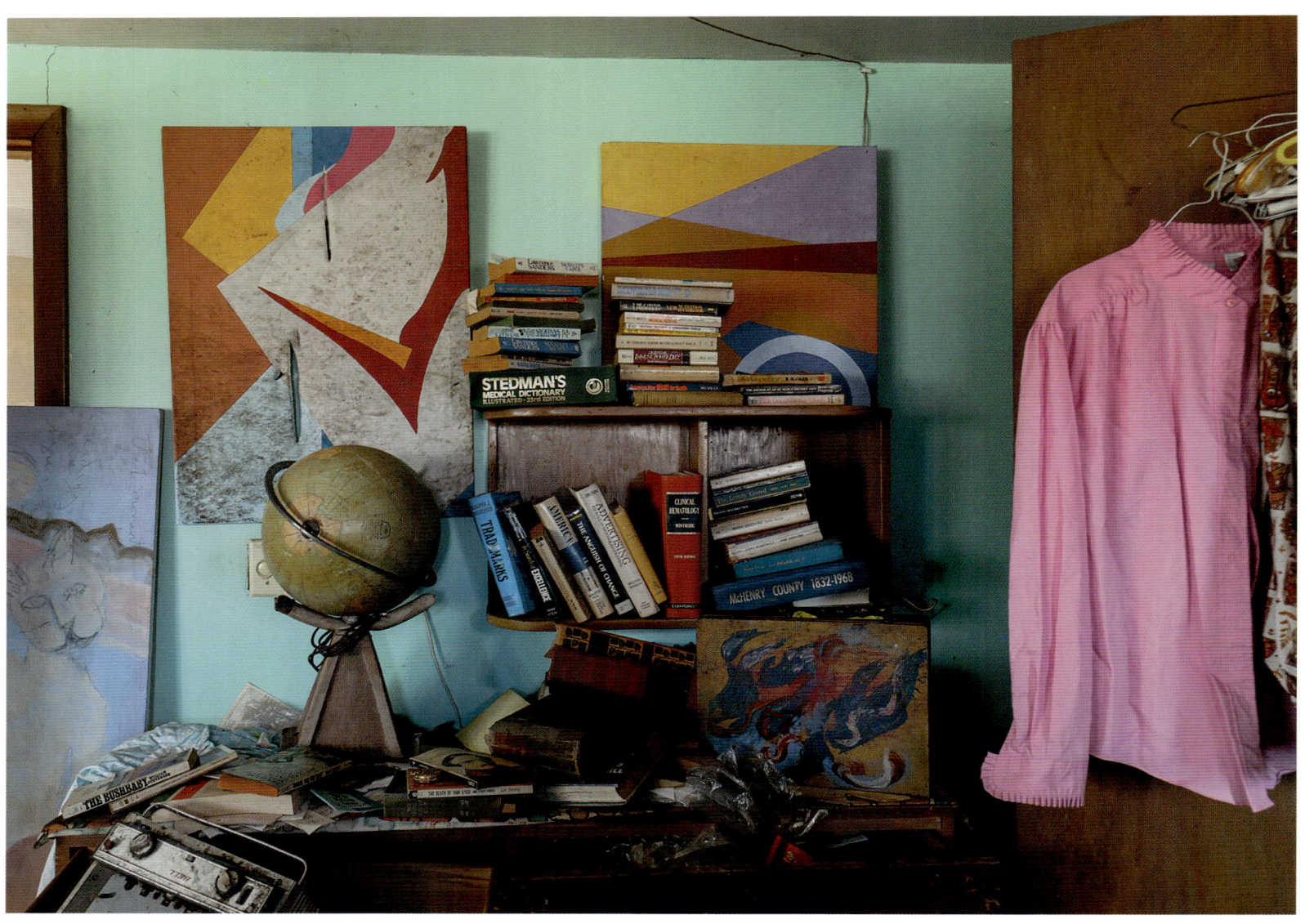

"AN ARTIST'S BEDROOM"
McHenry County, Illinois

As I made my way through this artist's house, I passed rooms filled with old books and closets filled with clothes. In the upstairs bedroom, this dresser held many objects, including the artist's painting case. Original artwork can be seen hanging on the walls.

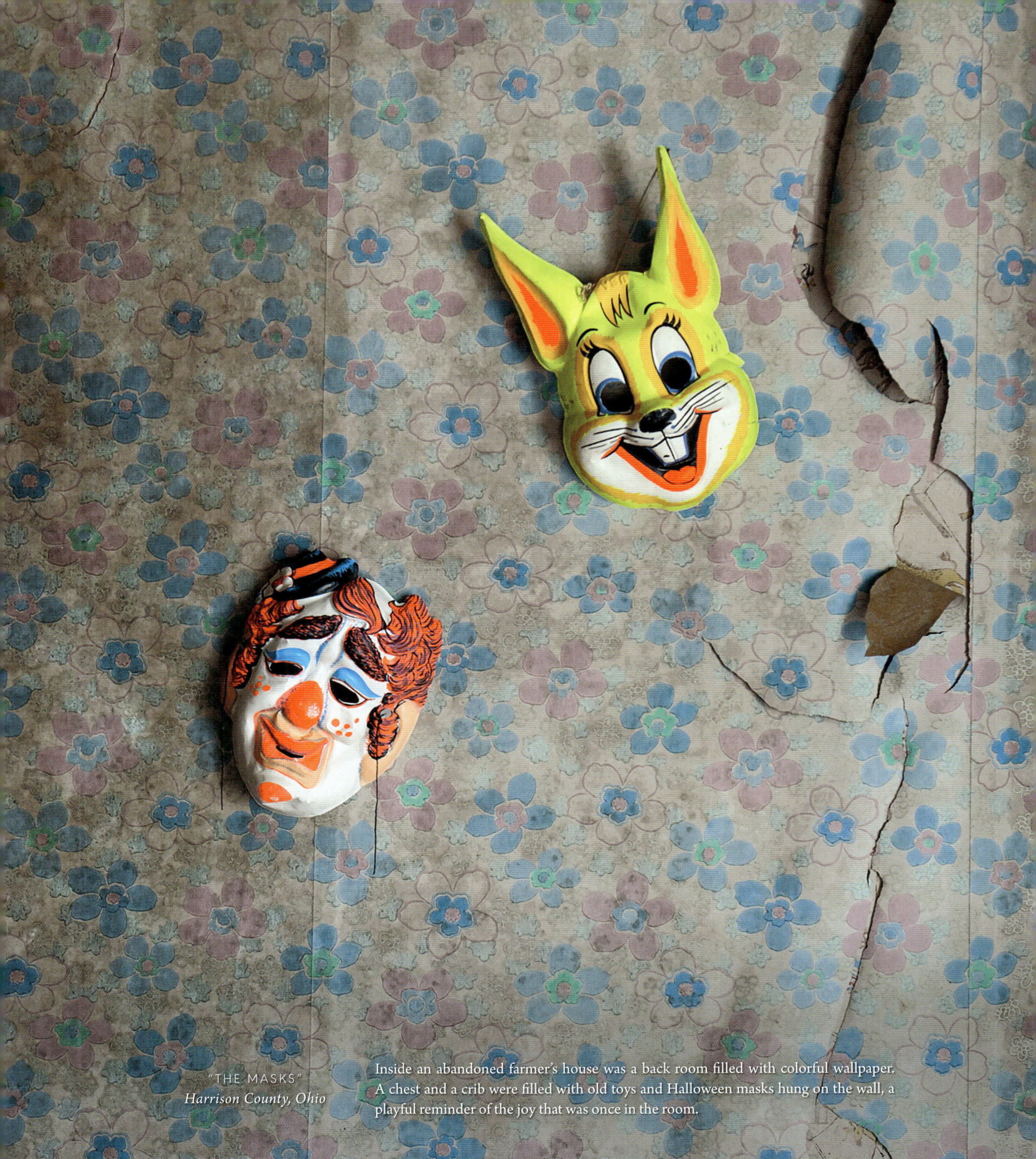

"THE MASKS"
Harrison County, Ohio

Inside an abandoned farmer's house was a back room filled with colorful wallpaper. A chest and a crib were filled with old toys and Halloween masks hung on the wall, a playful reminder of the joy that was once in the room.

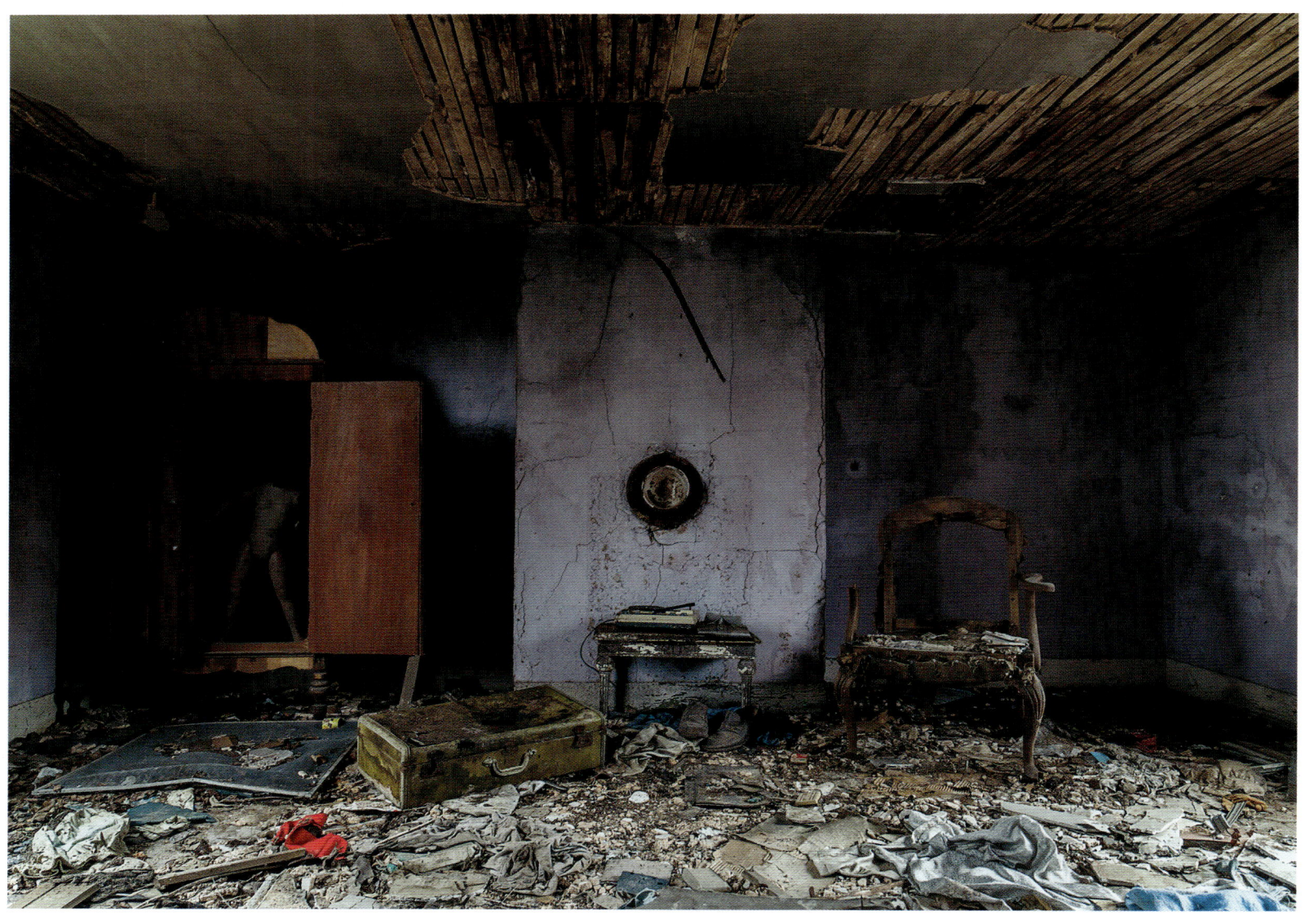

"WAITING IN THE WARDROBE"
Cumberland County, Virginia

This upstairs bedroom is scattered with falling debris. Parts of furniture remain as well as an old suitcase. A doll form stands in an open wardrobe.

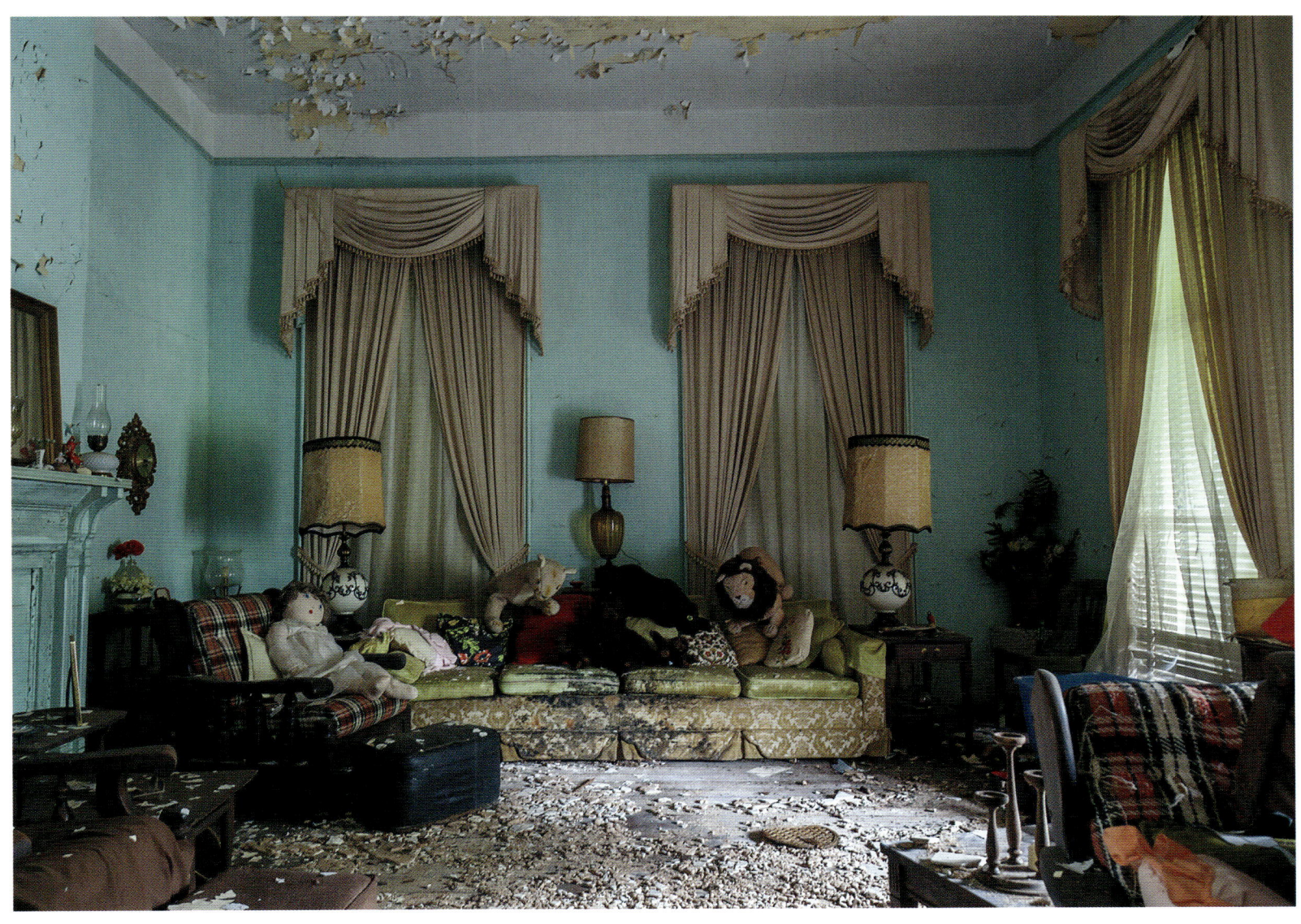

"THE STUFFED ANIMALS"
Jefferson County, Georgia

This historic house in this small town was hidden behind thick bushes, barely noticeable. The living room is a perfect representation of the architecture, with its large windows and high ceilings.

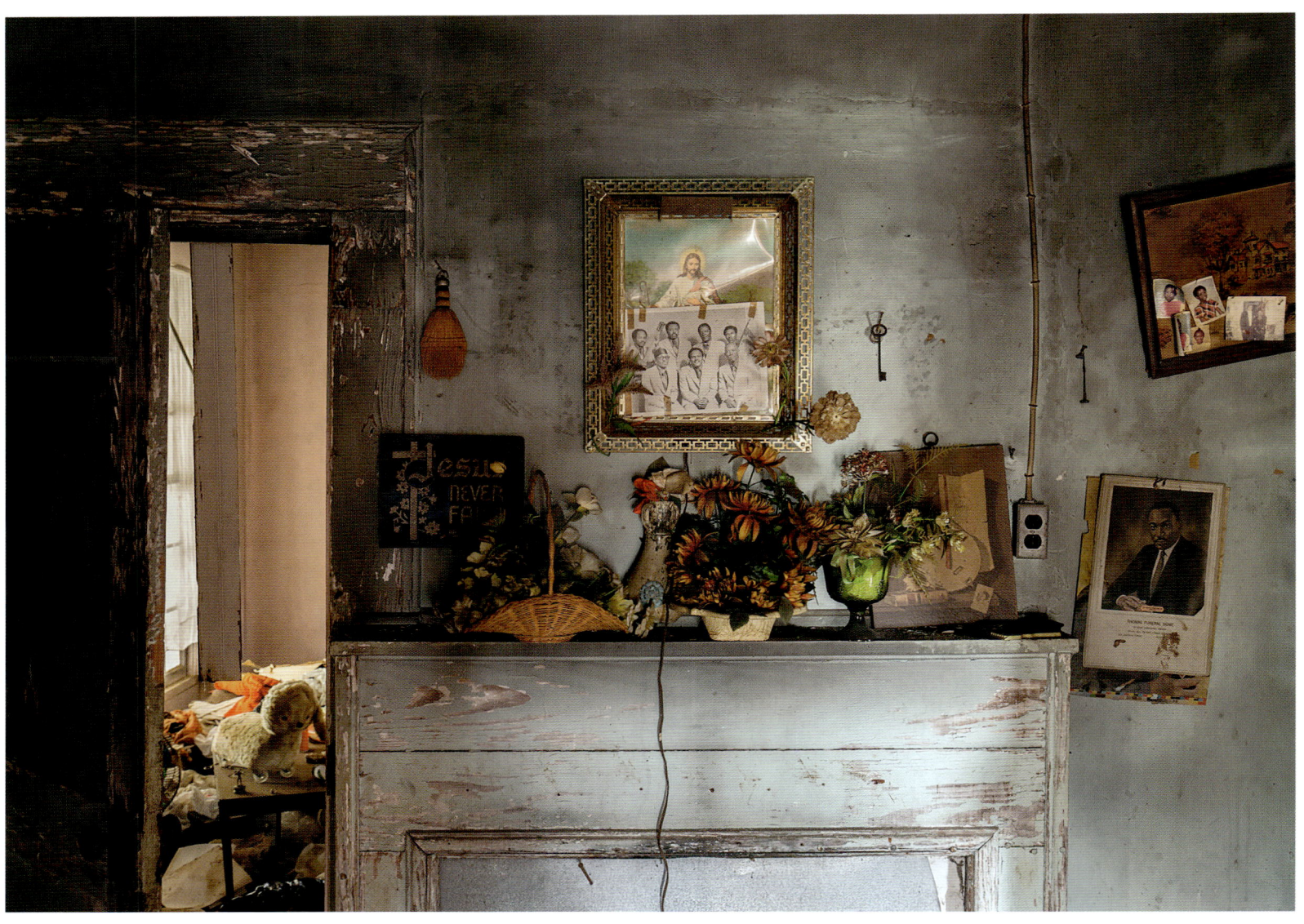

"THE HUNTER'S HEART"
Terrell County, Georgia

There is an abundance of abandoned houses in rural Georgia. While driving through, I noticed this boarded-up house (above and opposite) with an open window, not far back from the road. I believe an army veteran lived here with his churchgoing wife.

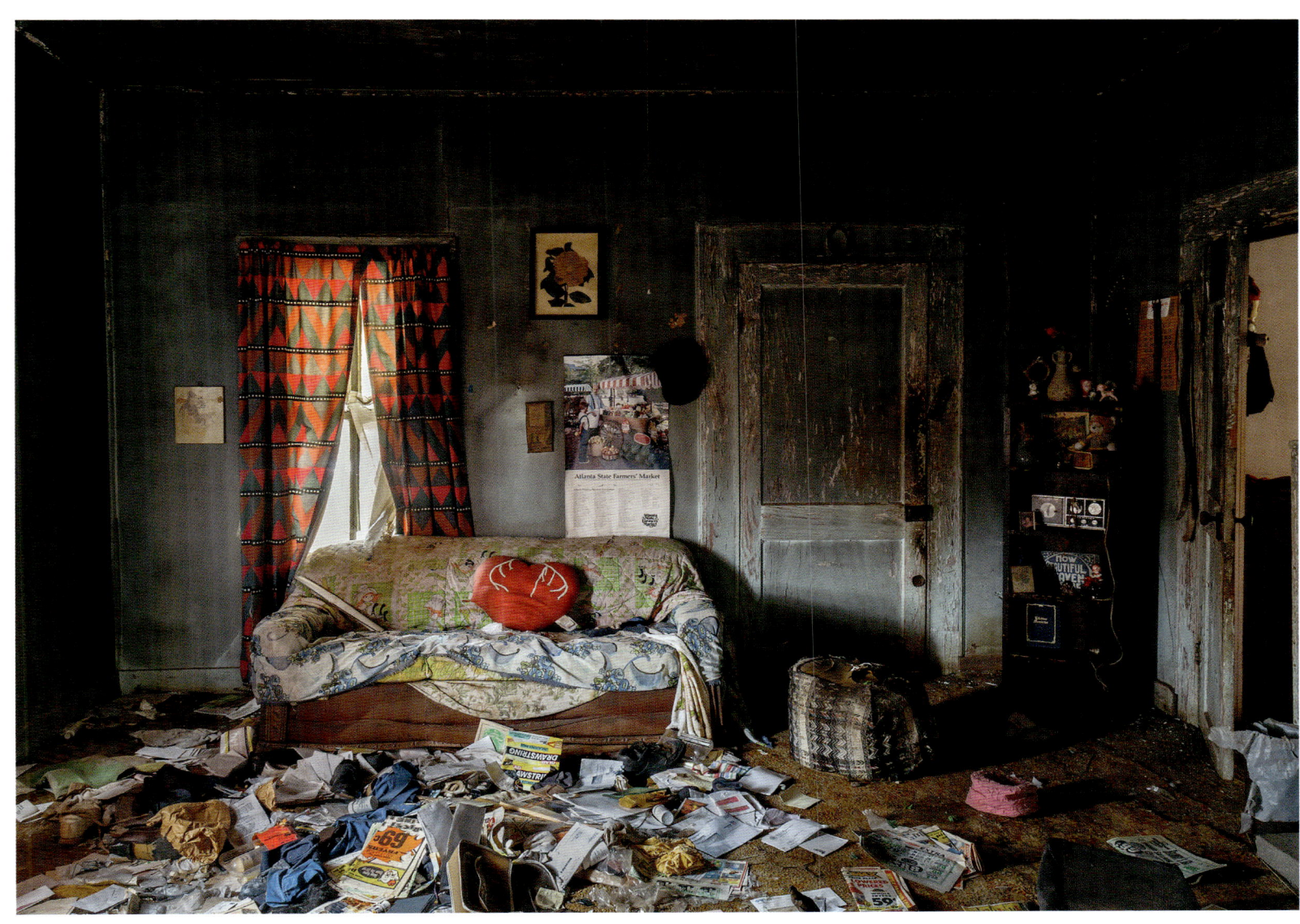

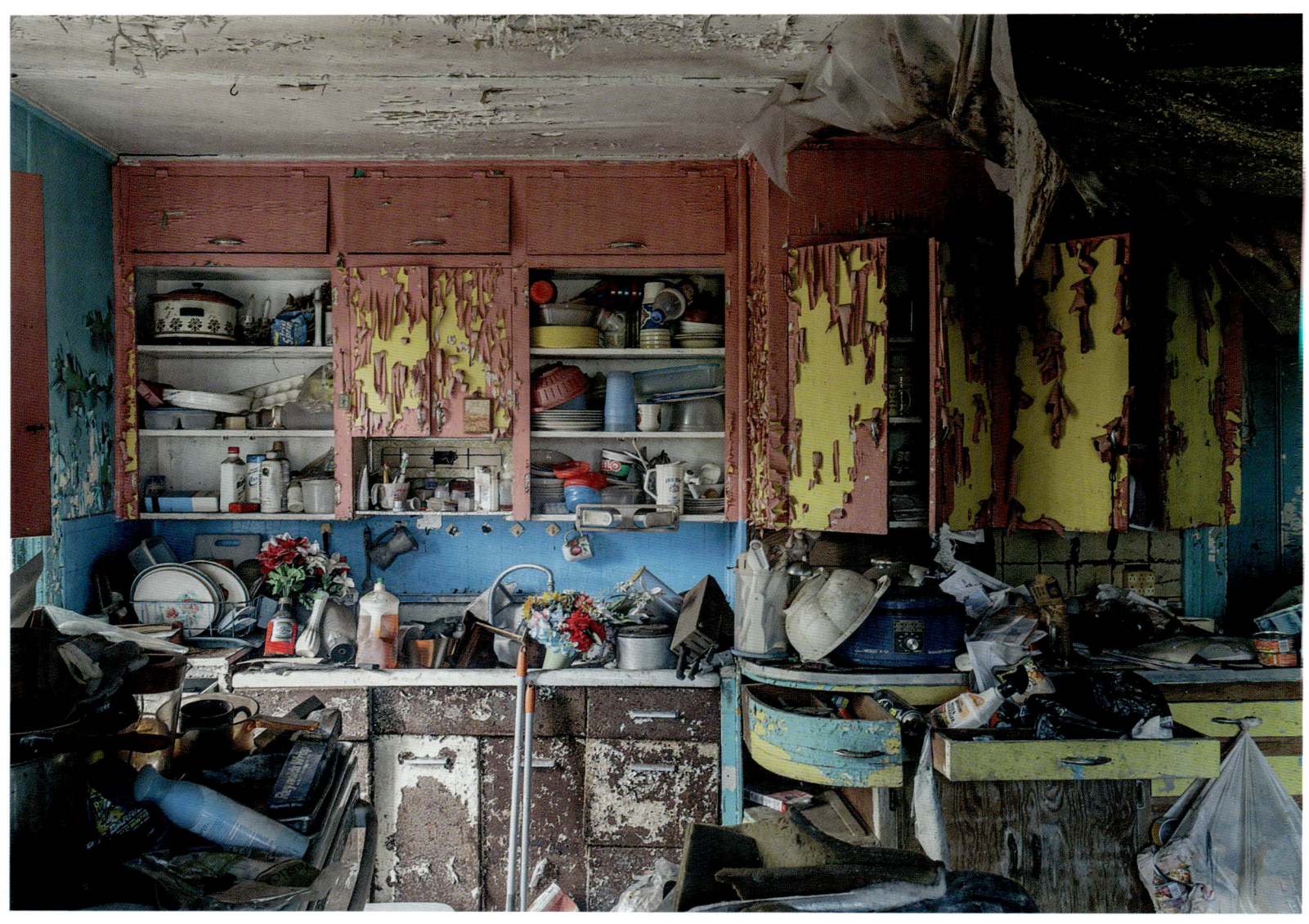

This house (above and opposite) was filled with a hoard of items and half collapsed inside. It was hard to move around, but in the kitchen I found some of the most vibrant paint decay I have ever seen. Another layer underneath is complemented by colorful kitchenware and contrasted with garbage scattered about.

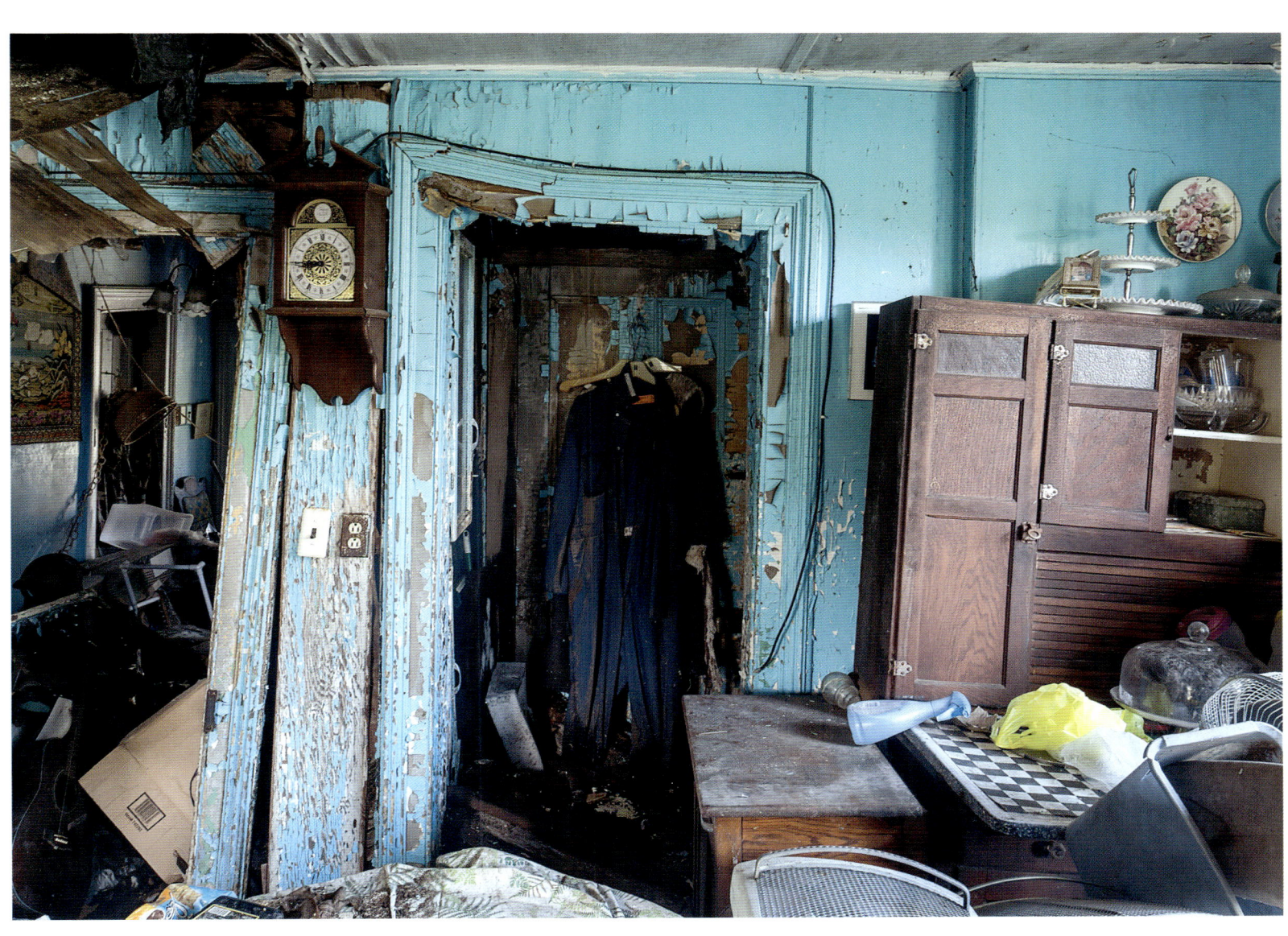

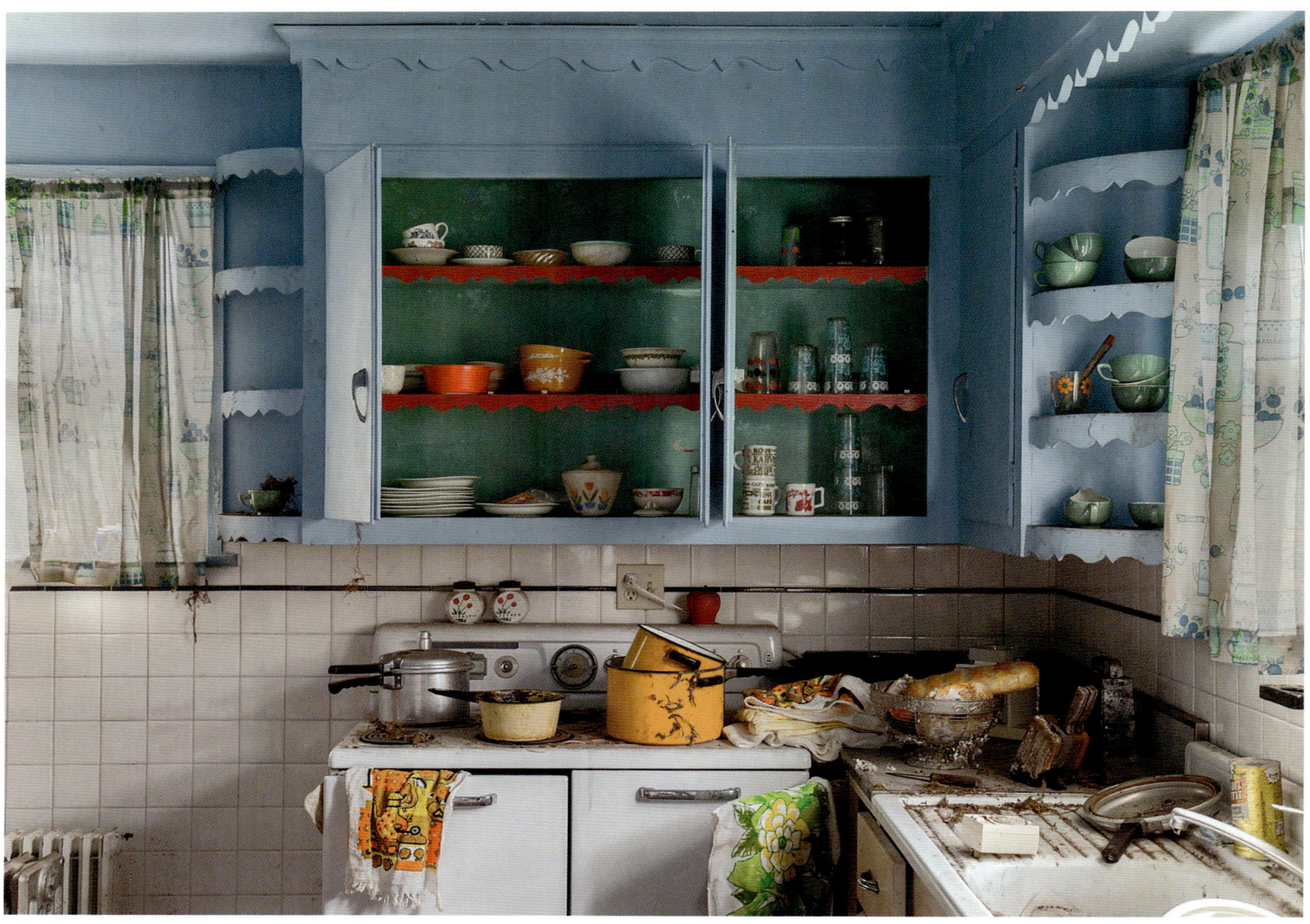

"COLORFUL KITCHENWARE"
Somerset County, New Jersey

Quite possibly the most colorful location I've photographed, this entire house was painted blue. Inside these cabinets were even more vintage bowls, glasses, and kitchenware.

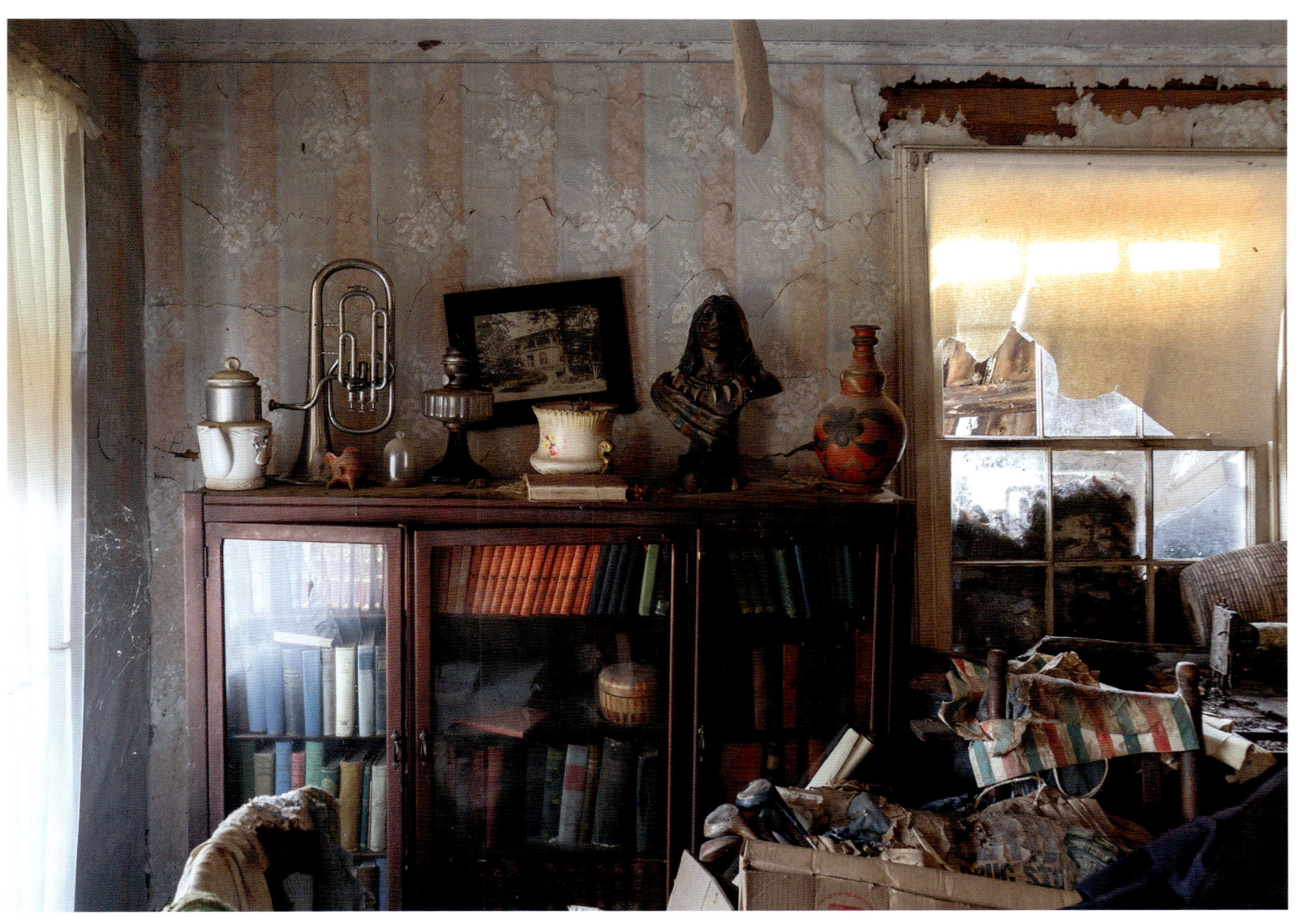

"A CURIOUS BOOKCASE"
Jefferson County, West Virginia

Driving along a winding rural road near the Appalachian Mountains in West Virginia, I saw cars up on a hill. Next to them was a large deteriorating farmhouse. My curiosity made me stop. The house was filled with antiques, each room a hoard. A calendar in the kitchen read 1984; presumably that's when the last occupants lived here.

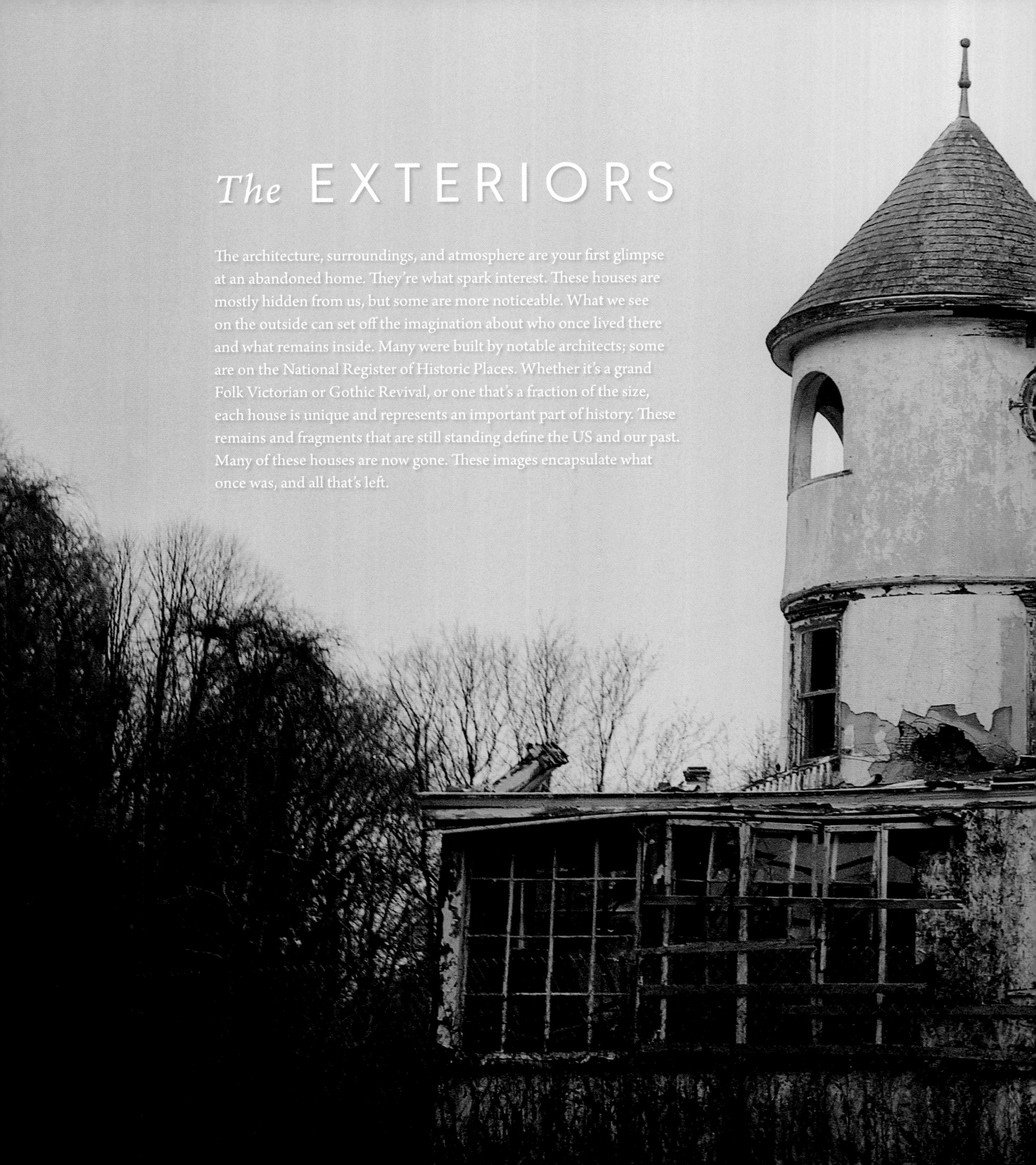

The EXTERIORS

The architecture, surroundings, and atmosphere are your first glimpse at an abandoned home. They're what spark interest. These houses are mostly hidden from us, but some are more noticeable. What we see on the outside can set off the imagination about who once lived there and what remains inside. Many were built by notable architects; some are on the National Register of Historic Places. Whether it's a grand Folk Victorian or Gothic Revival, or one that's a fraction of the size, each house is unique and represents an important part of history. These remains and fragments that are still standing define the US and our past. Many of these houses are now gone. These images encapsulate what once was, and all that's left.

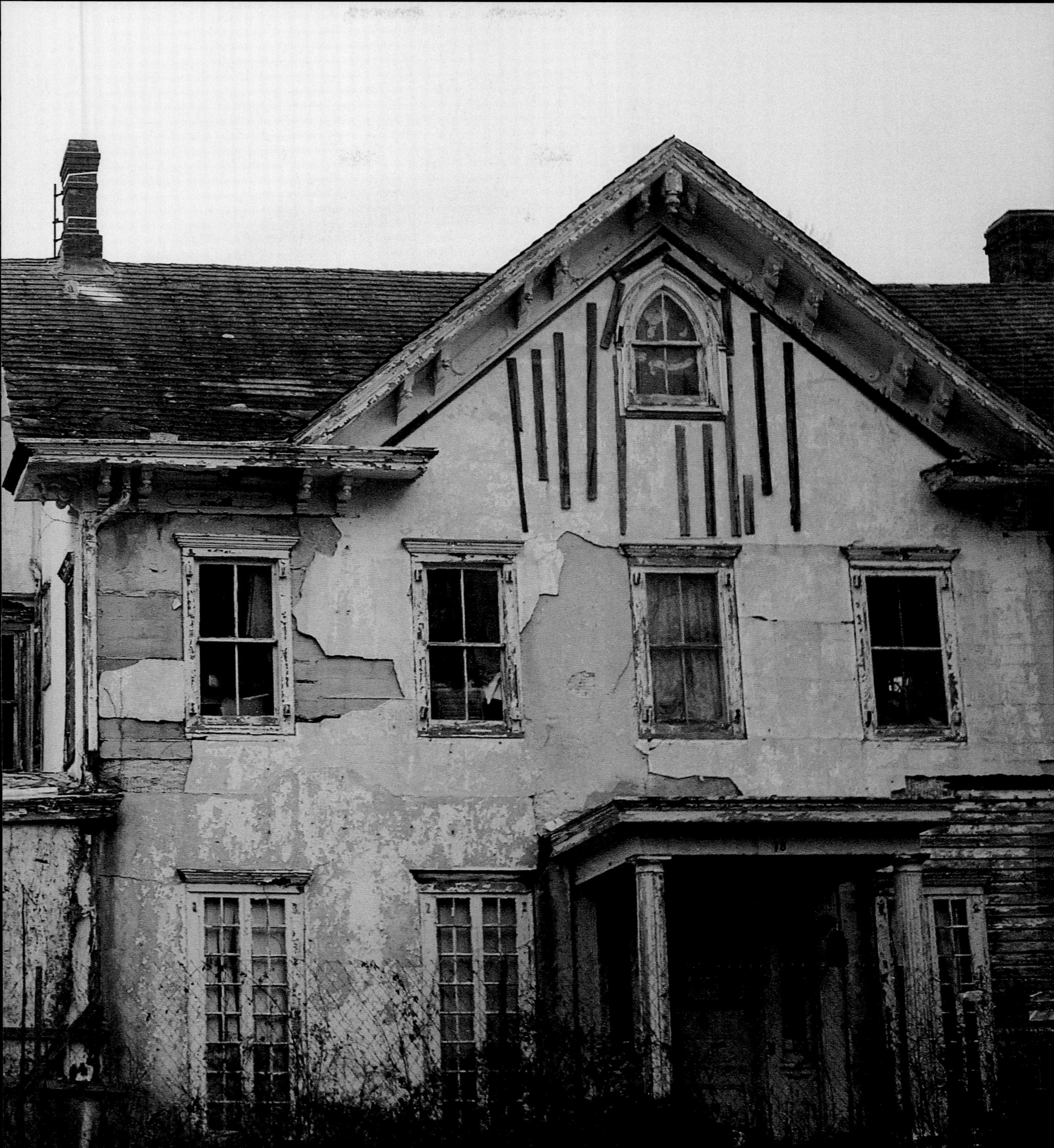

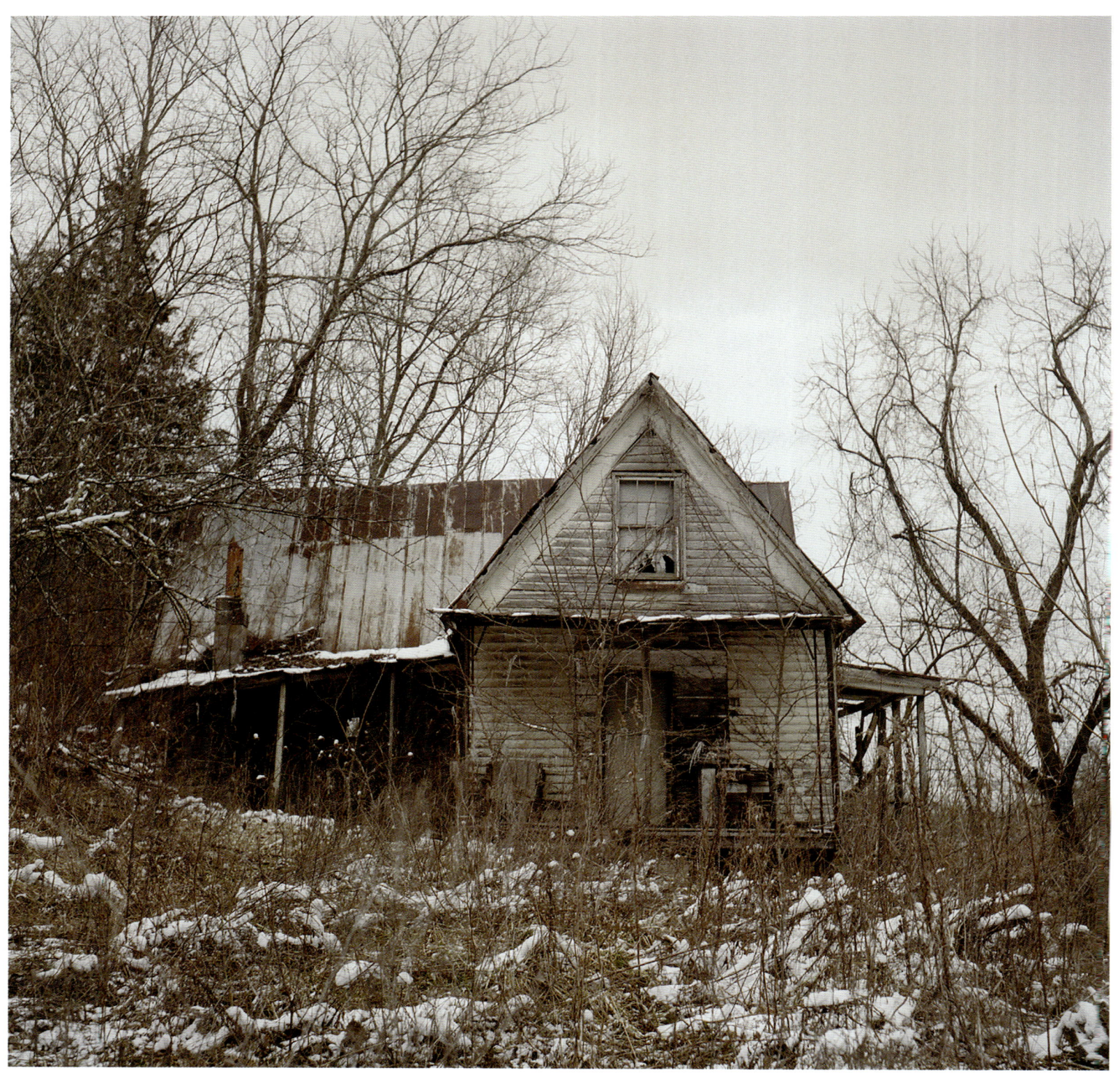

"THE GOTHIC COTTAGE"
Scott County, Kentucky

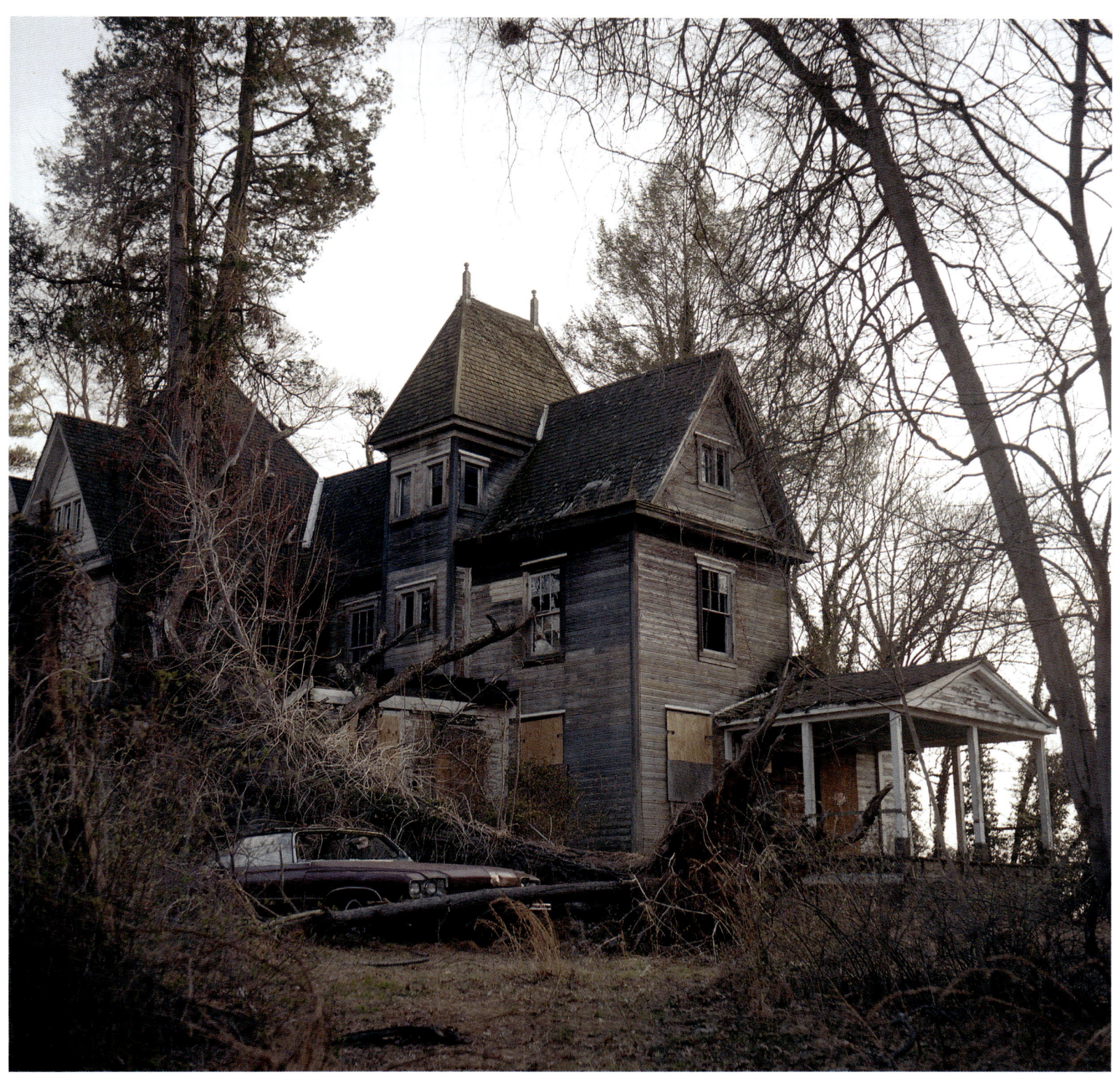

"THE WINDERBOURNE MANSION"
Boyds, Maryland

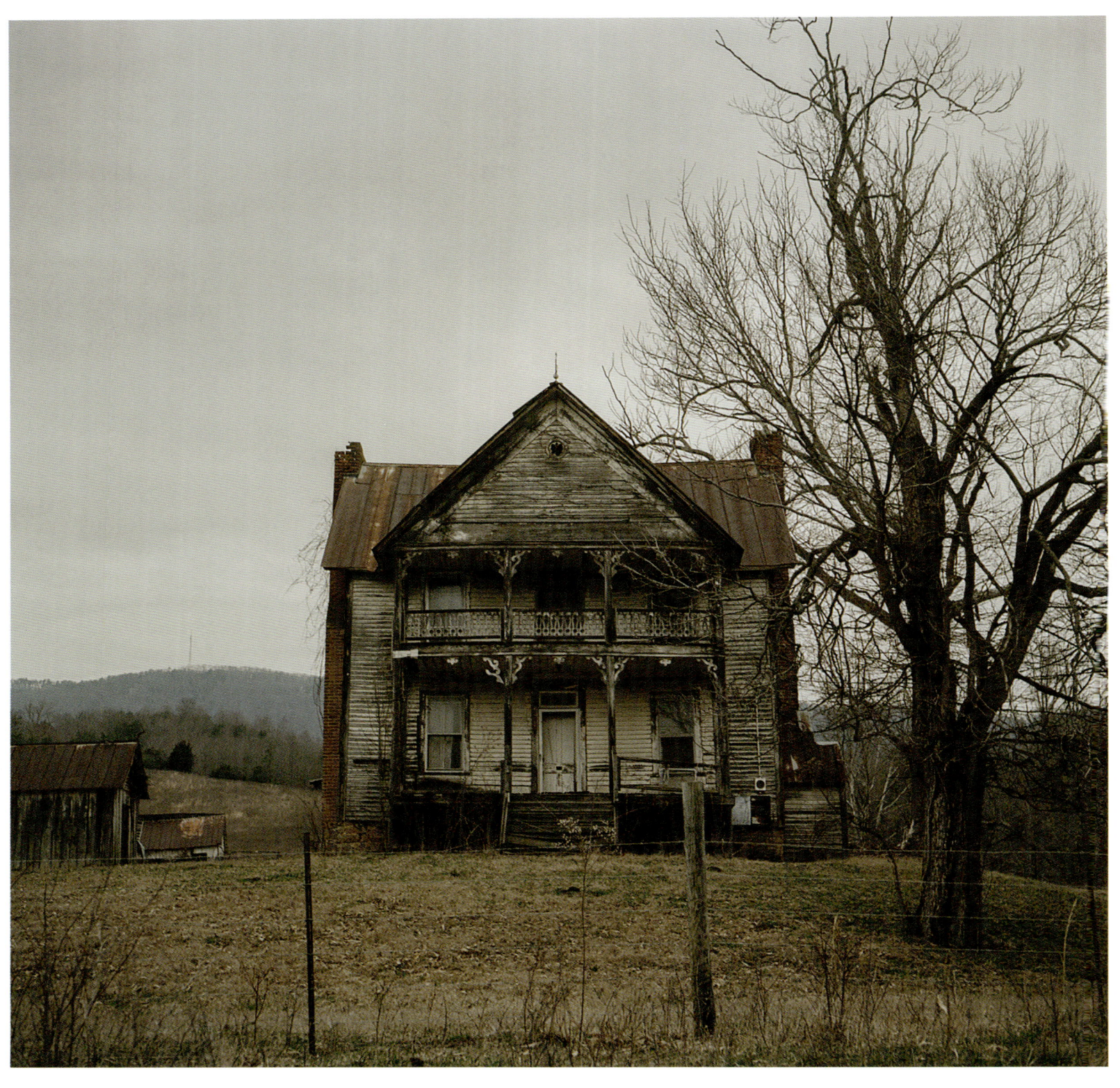

"THE JUDGE'S HOUSE"
Grainger County, Tennessee

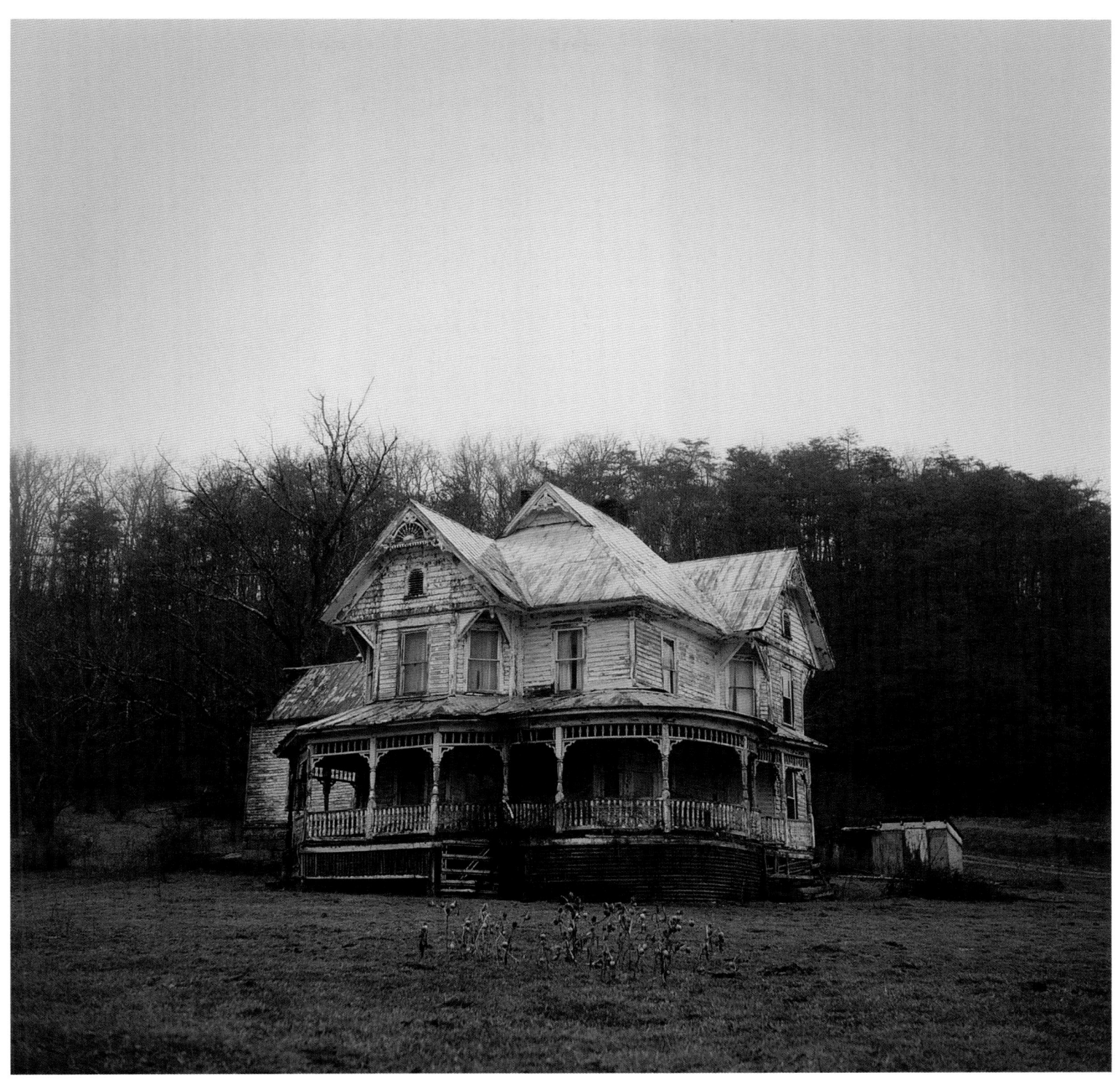

"THE INDIAN CREEK HOUSE"
Summers County, West Virginia

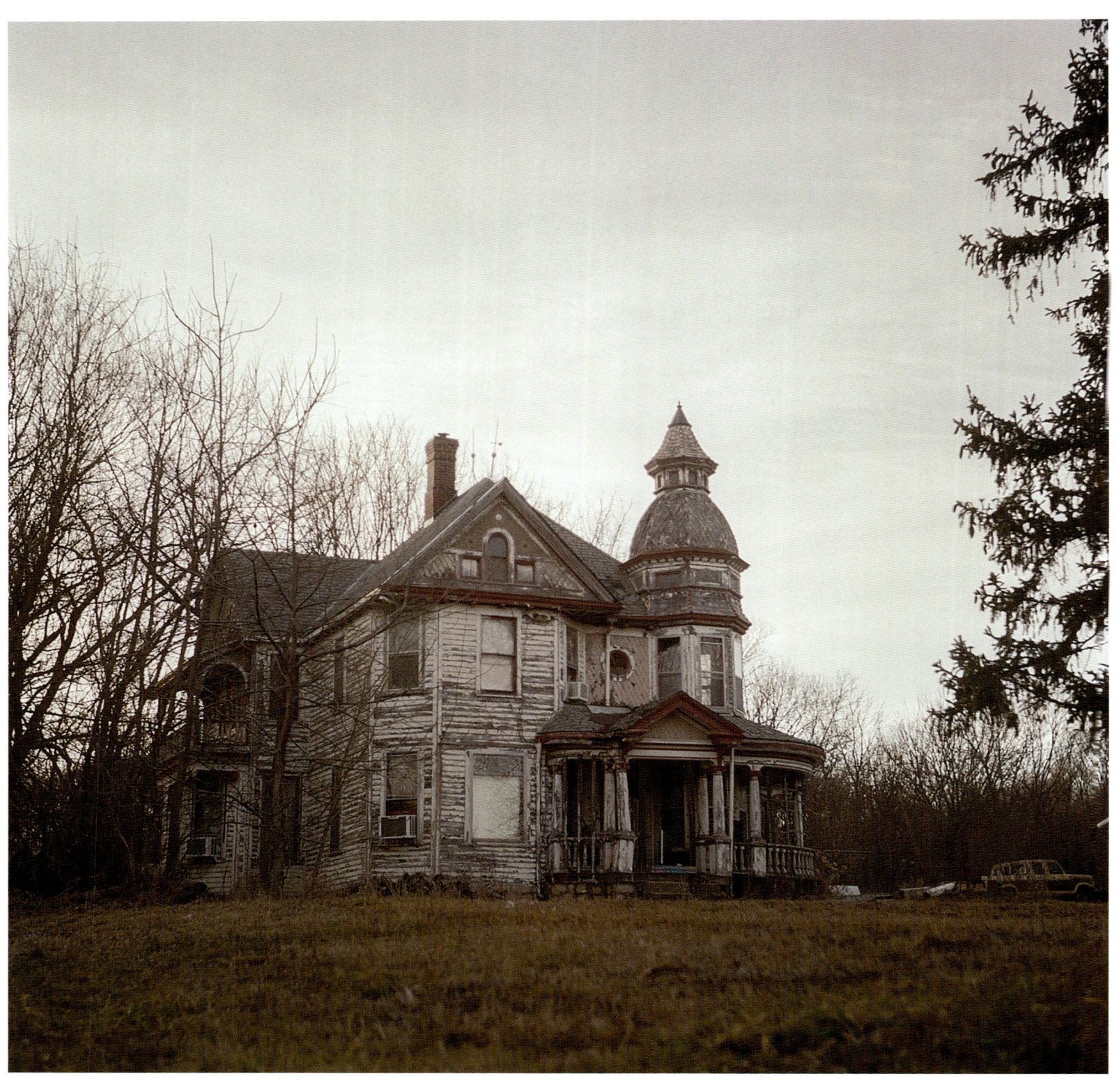

"THE HOUSE IN THE PAINTING"
Atchison County, Kansas

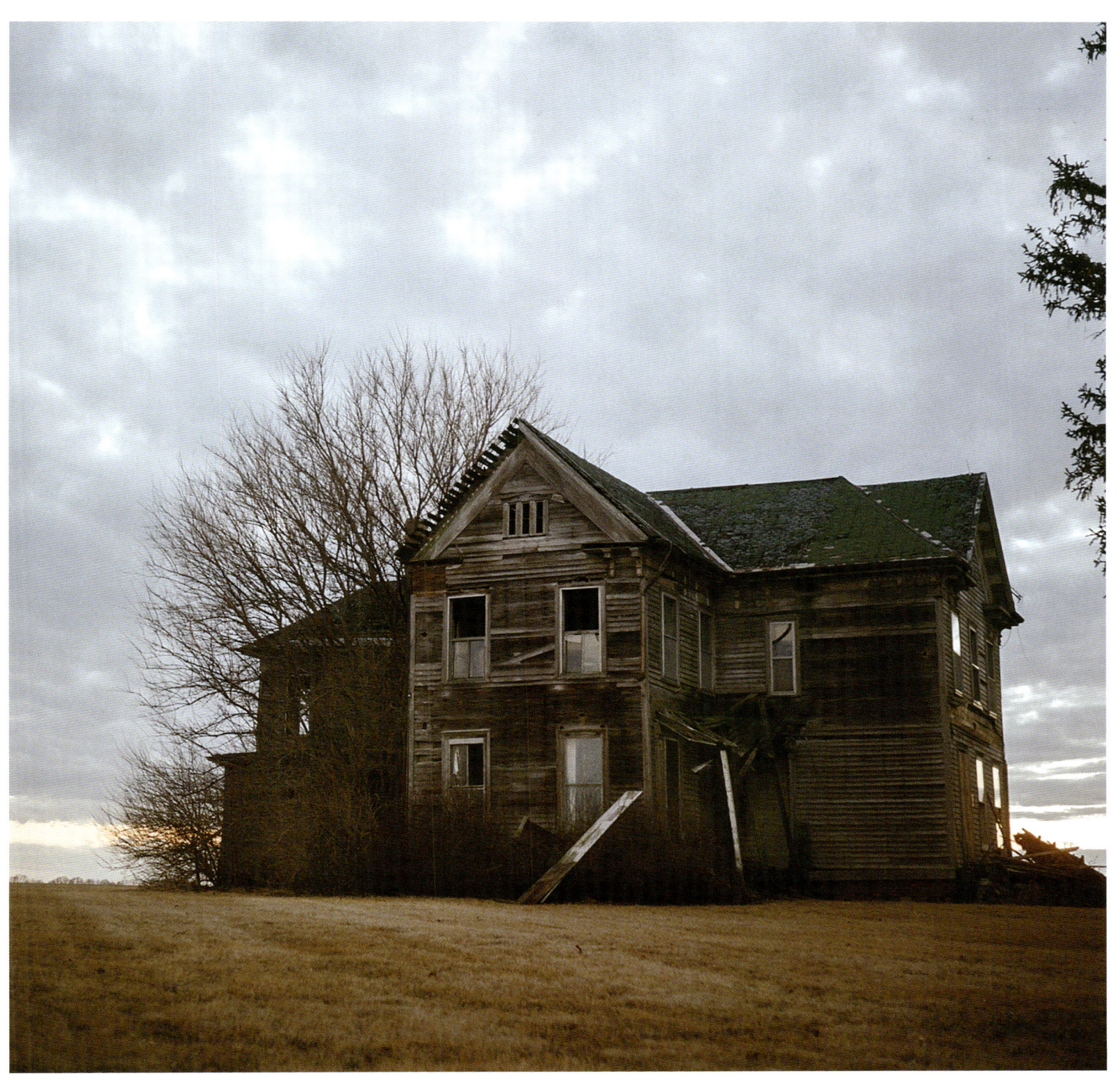

"THE ILLINOIS FARMHOUSE"
McLean County, Illinois

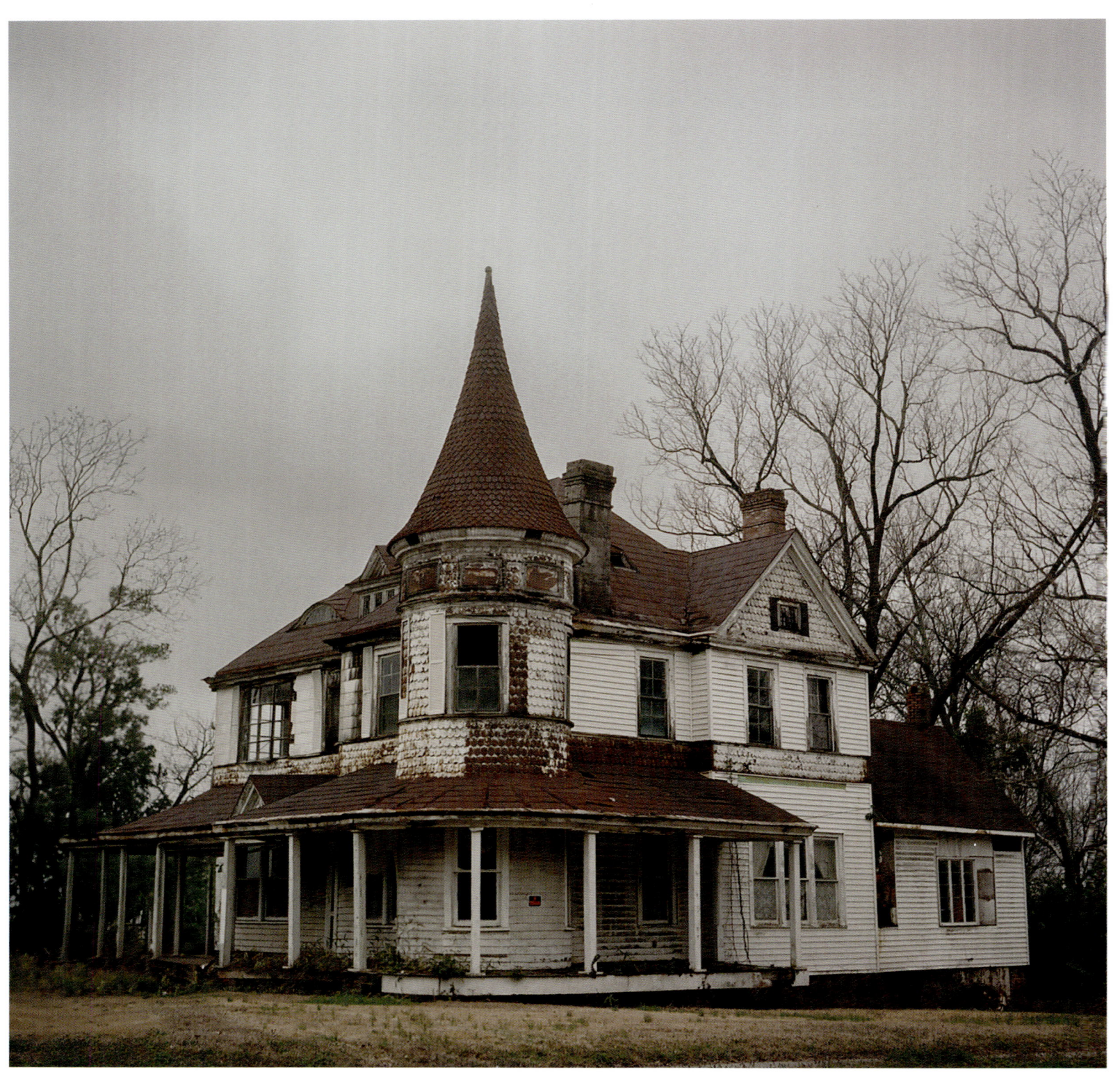

"THE QUEEN ANNE"
Chester County, South Carolina

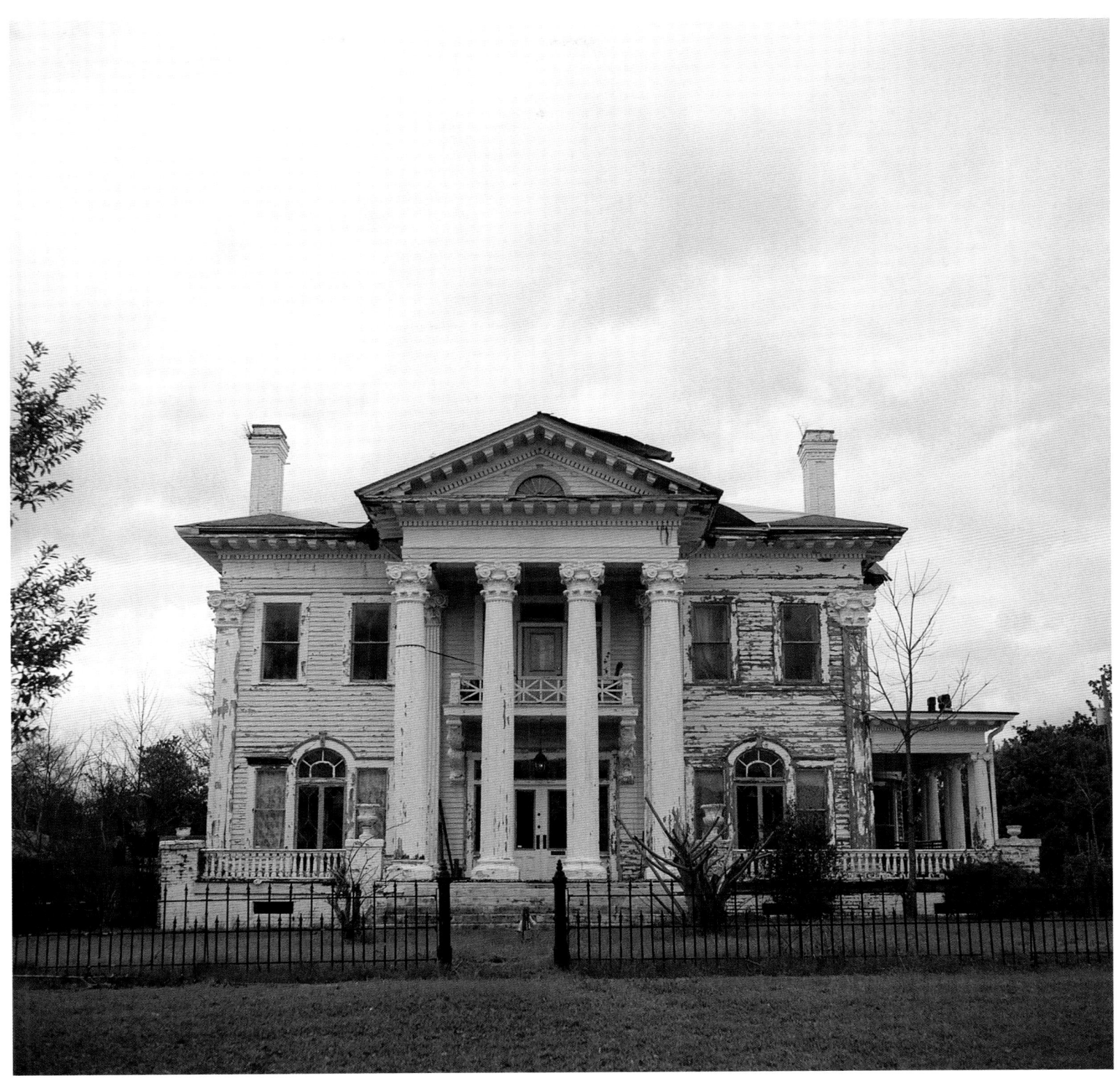

"THE RAINER-LEWIS HOUSE"
Bullock County, Alabama

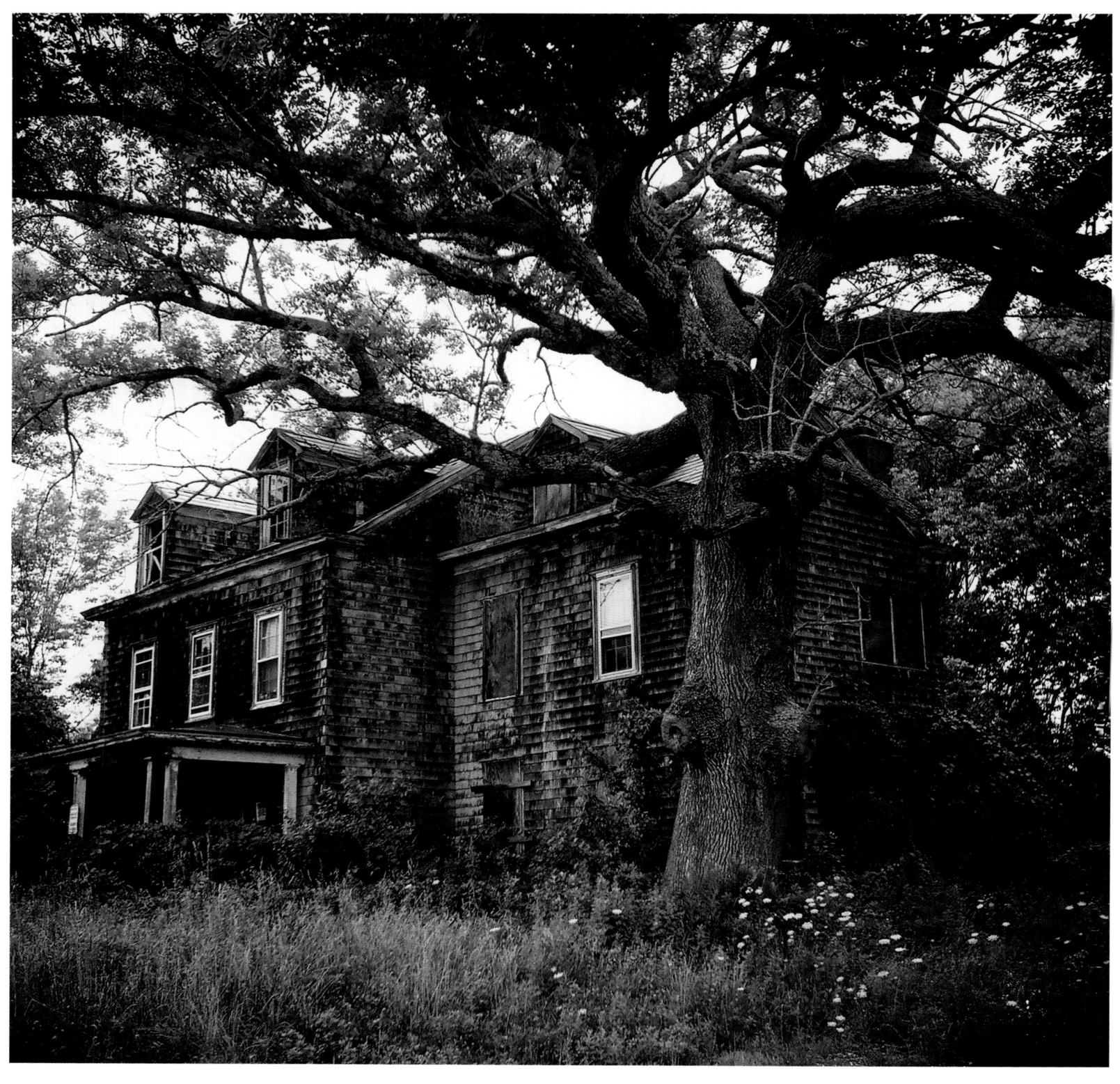

"THE POLICE STATION"
Monmouth County, New Jersey

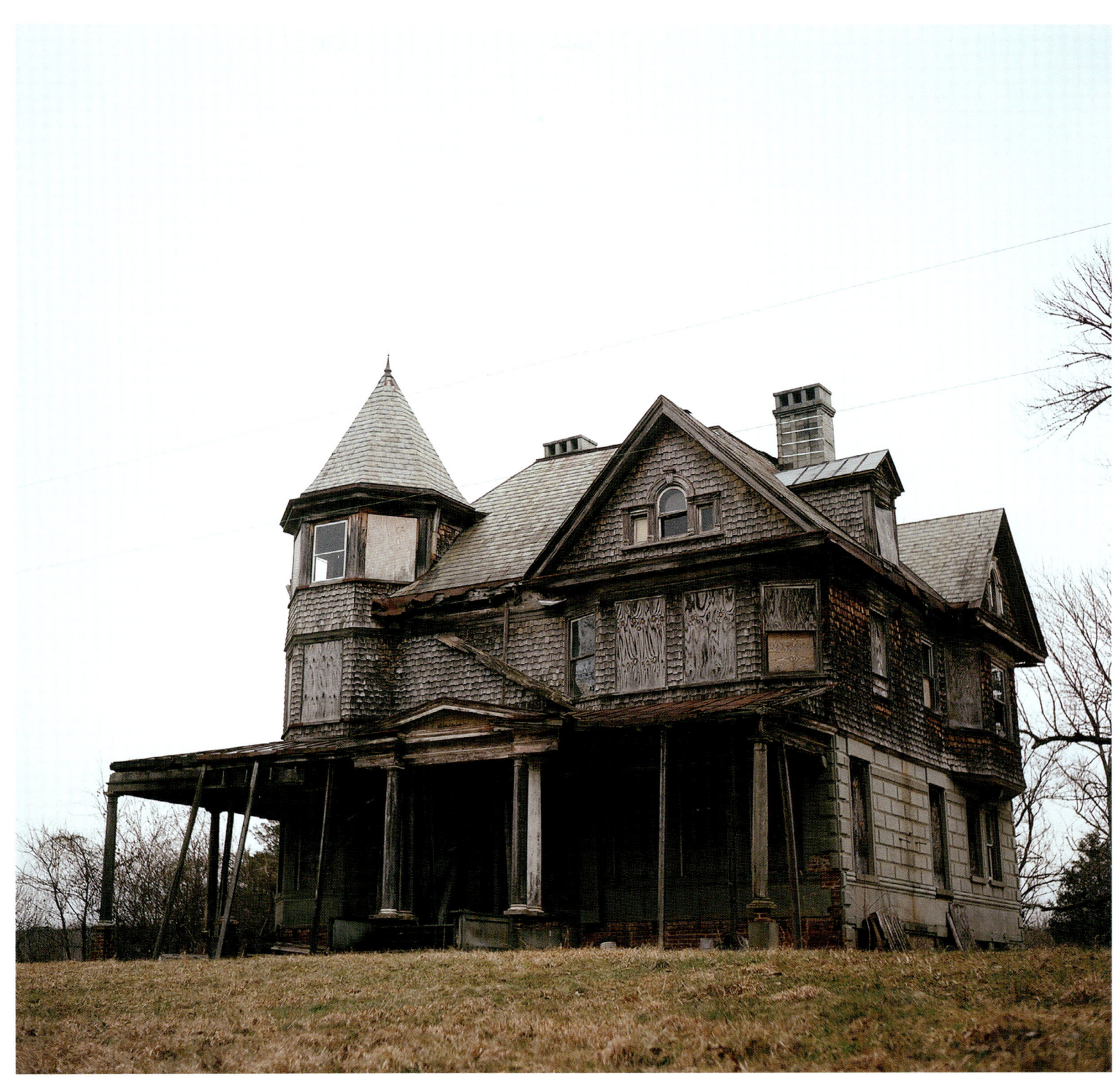

"THE SOAPSTONE VICTORIAN"
Albemarle County, Virginia

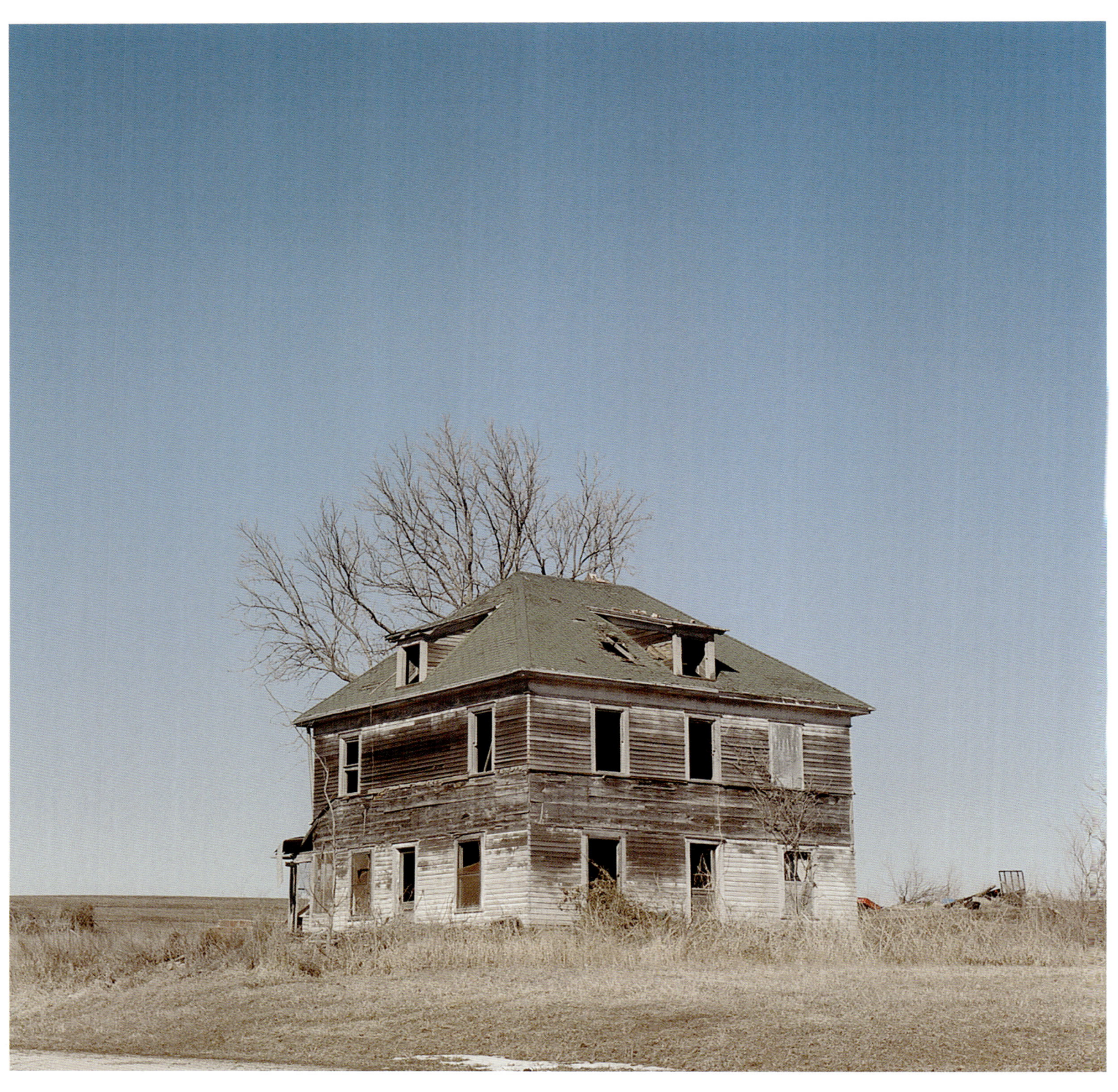

"THE PRAIRIE HALF SQUARE"
Richardson County, Nebraska

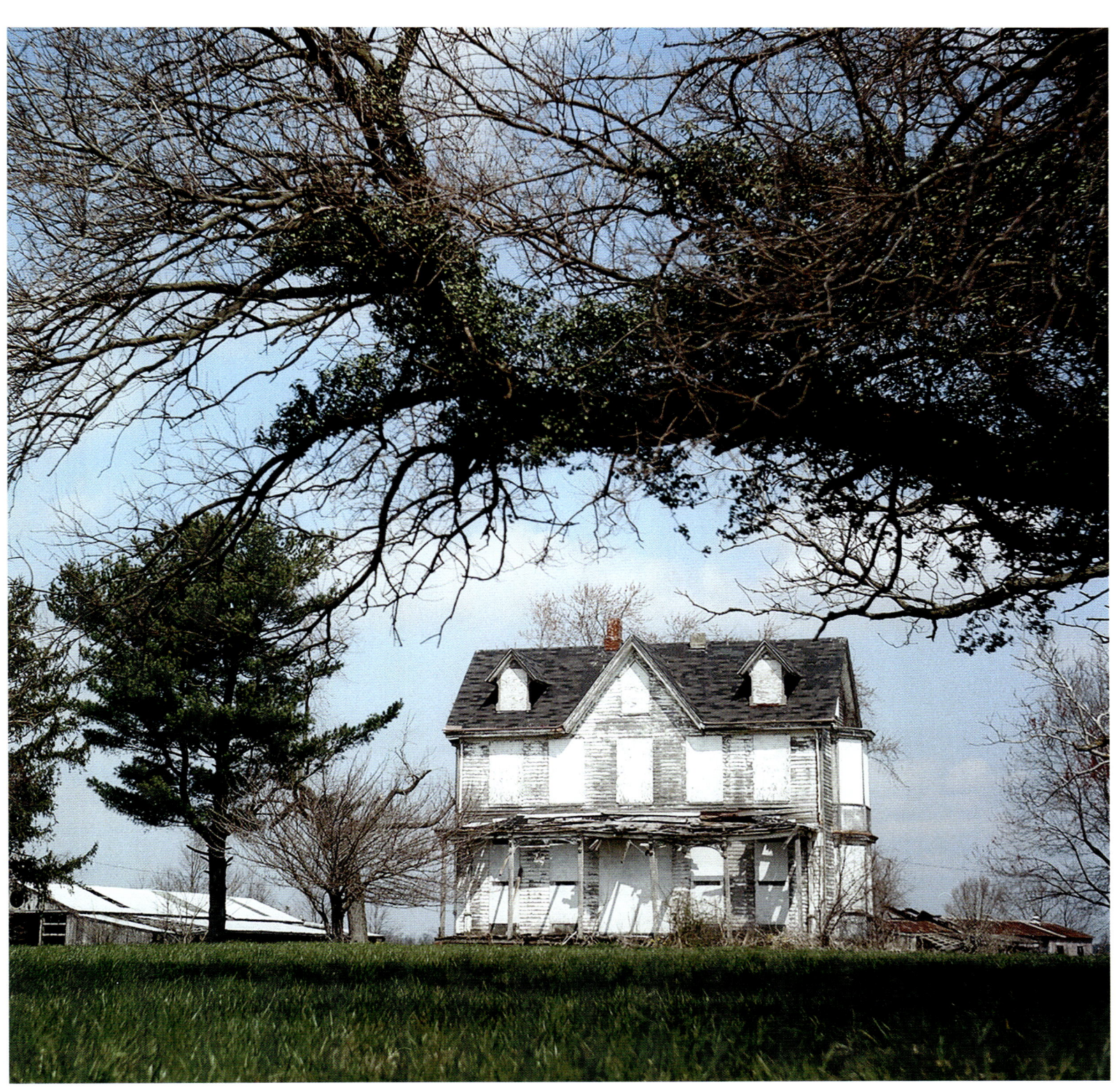

"THE FARMHOUSE PAINTED WHITE"
Kent County, Maryland

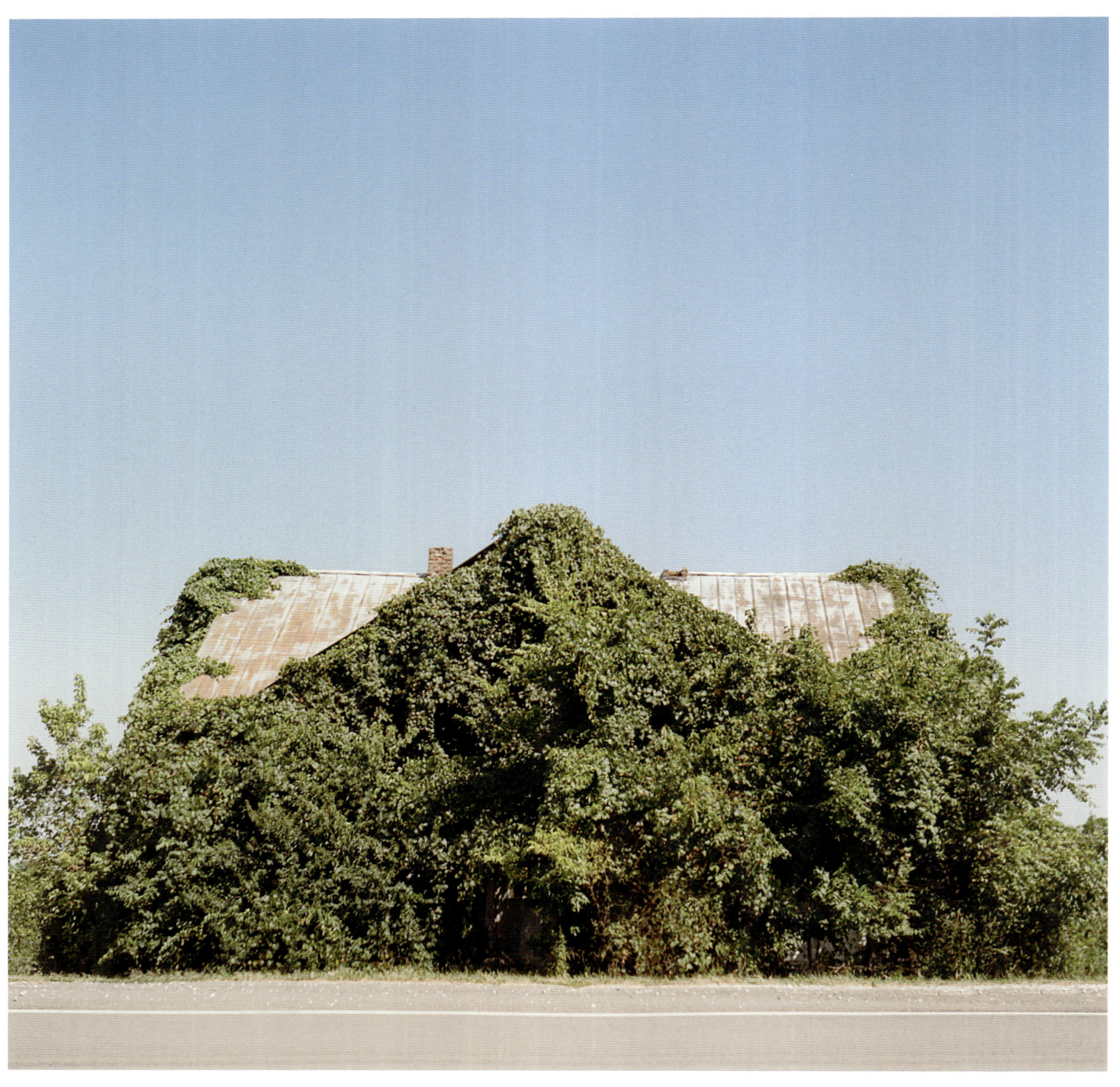

"COVERED IN VINES"
Switzerland County, Indiana

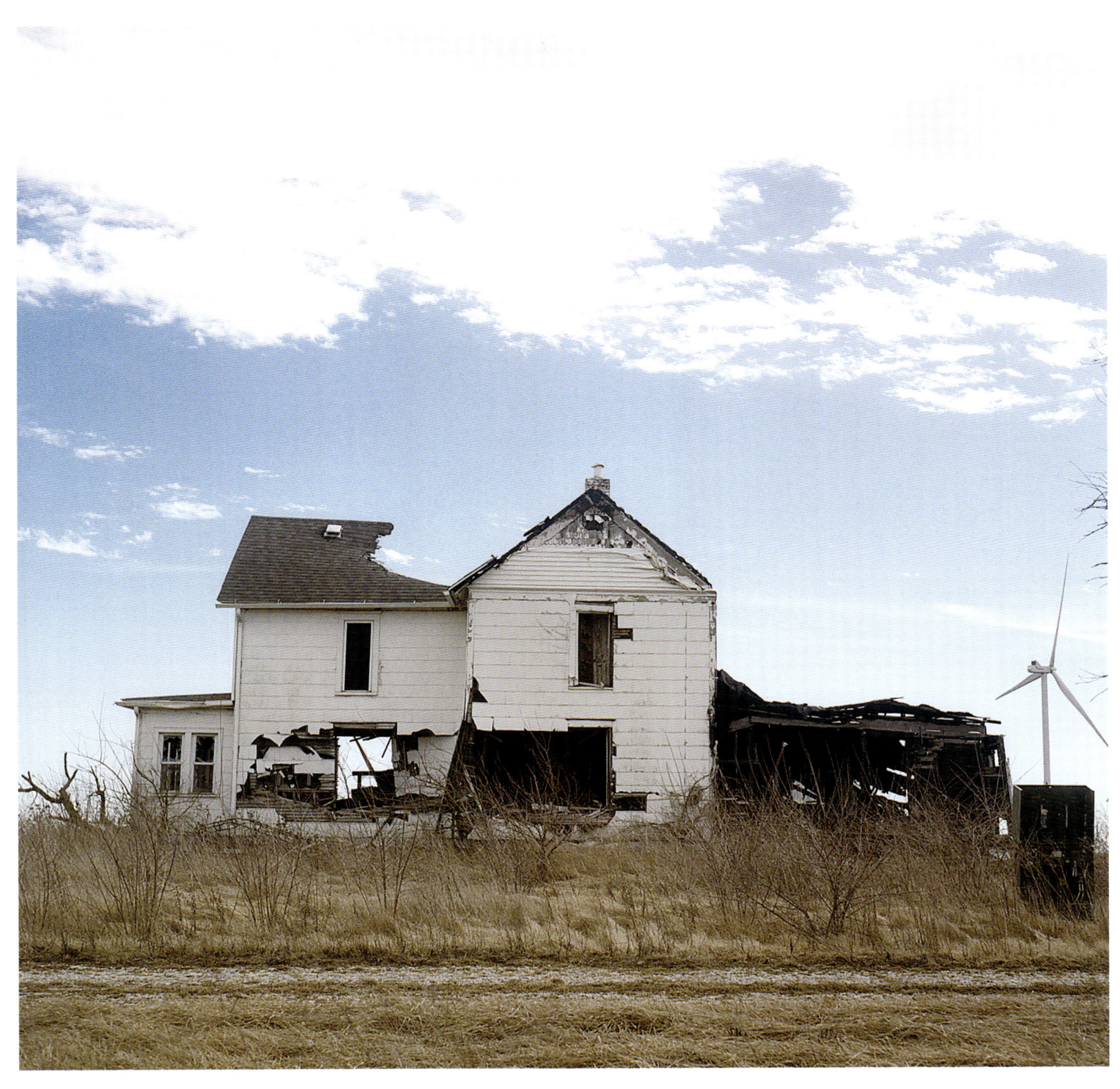

"THE HOUSE OFF THE HIGHWAY"
White County, Indiana

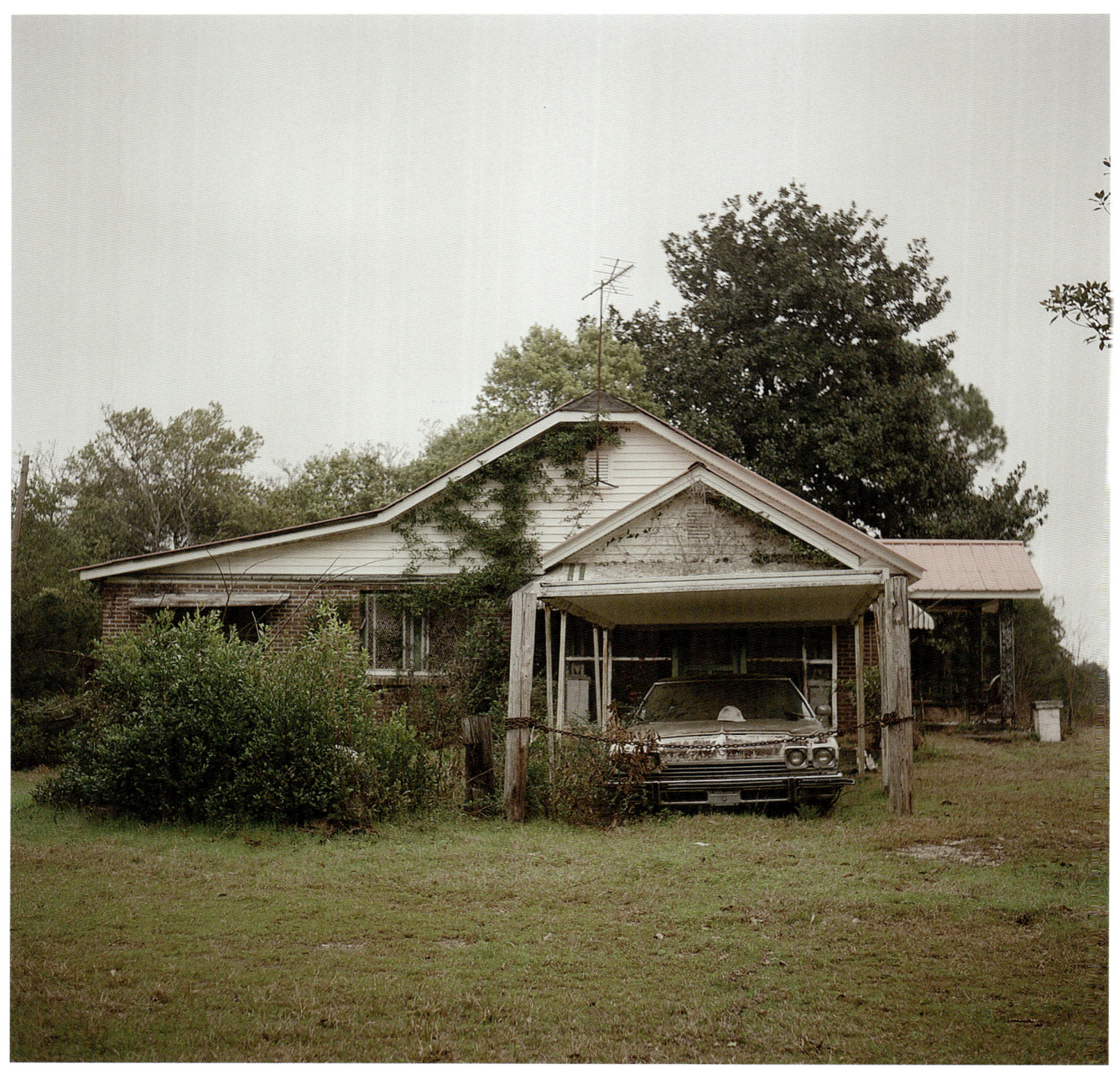

"THE MID-CENTURY RANCH"
Talbot County, Georgia

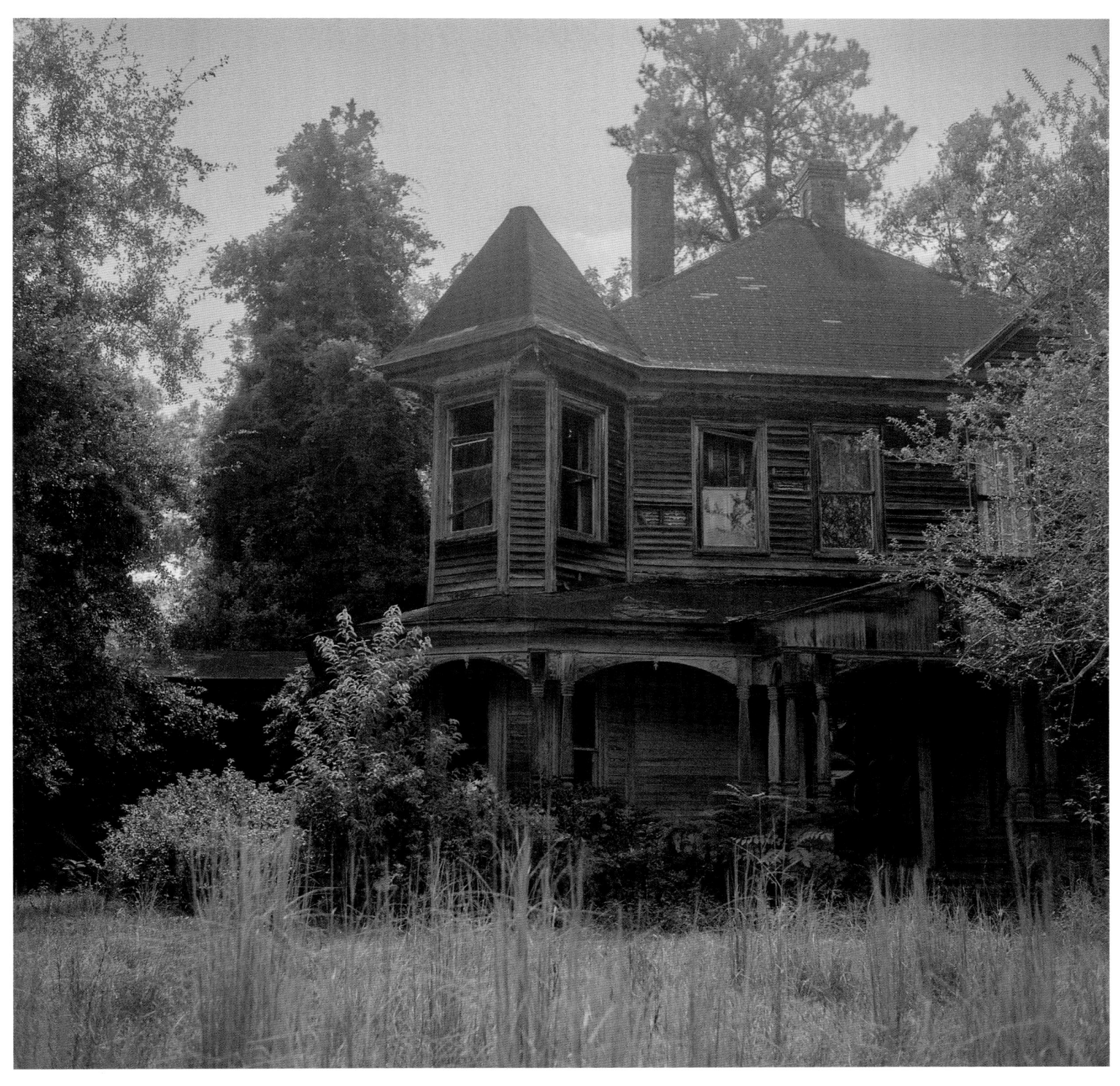

"THE CILO HOUSE"
Marlboro County, South Carolina

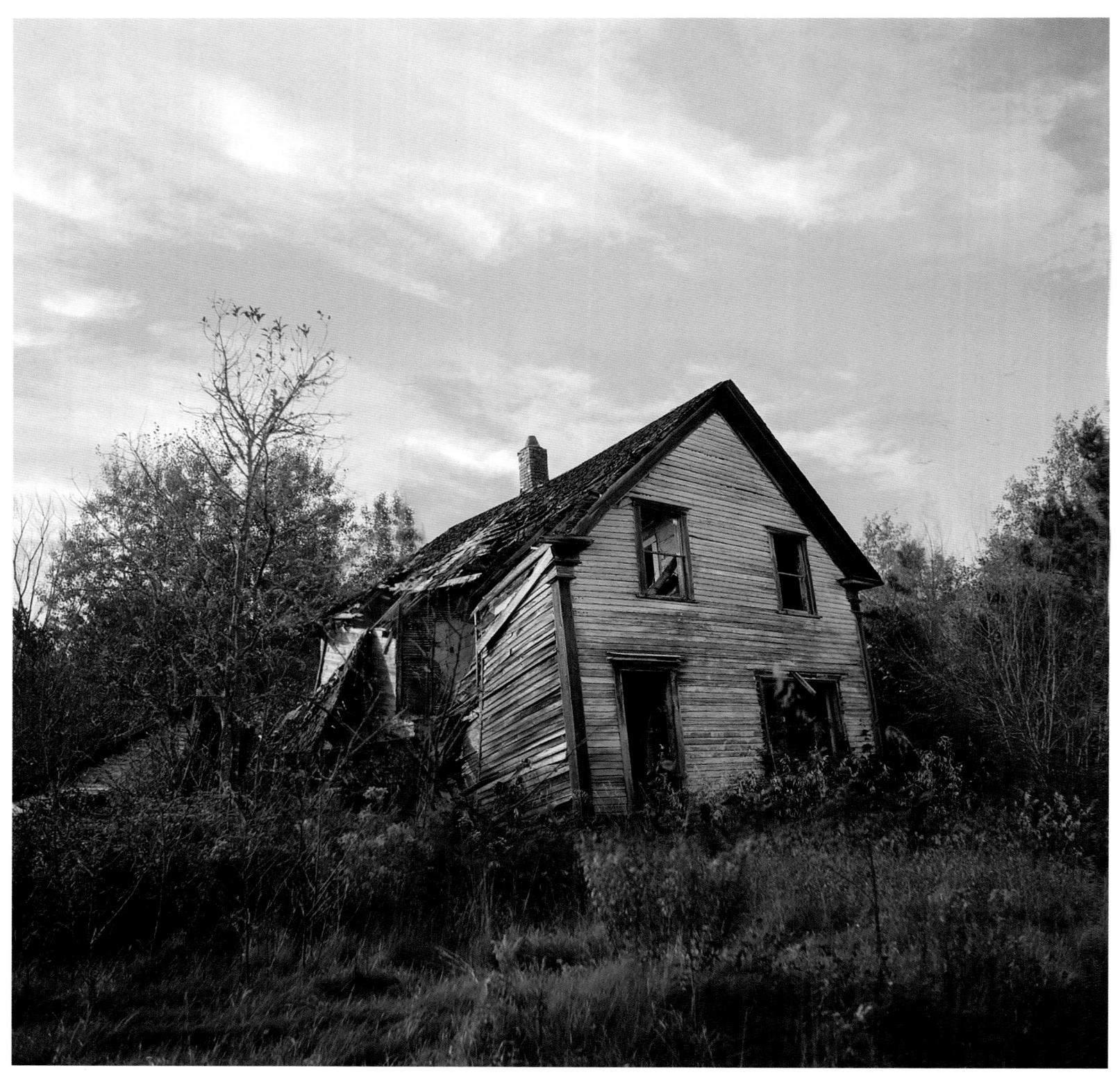

"FALLING DOWN"
Aroostook County, Maine

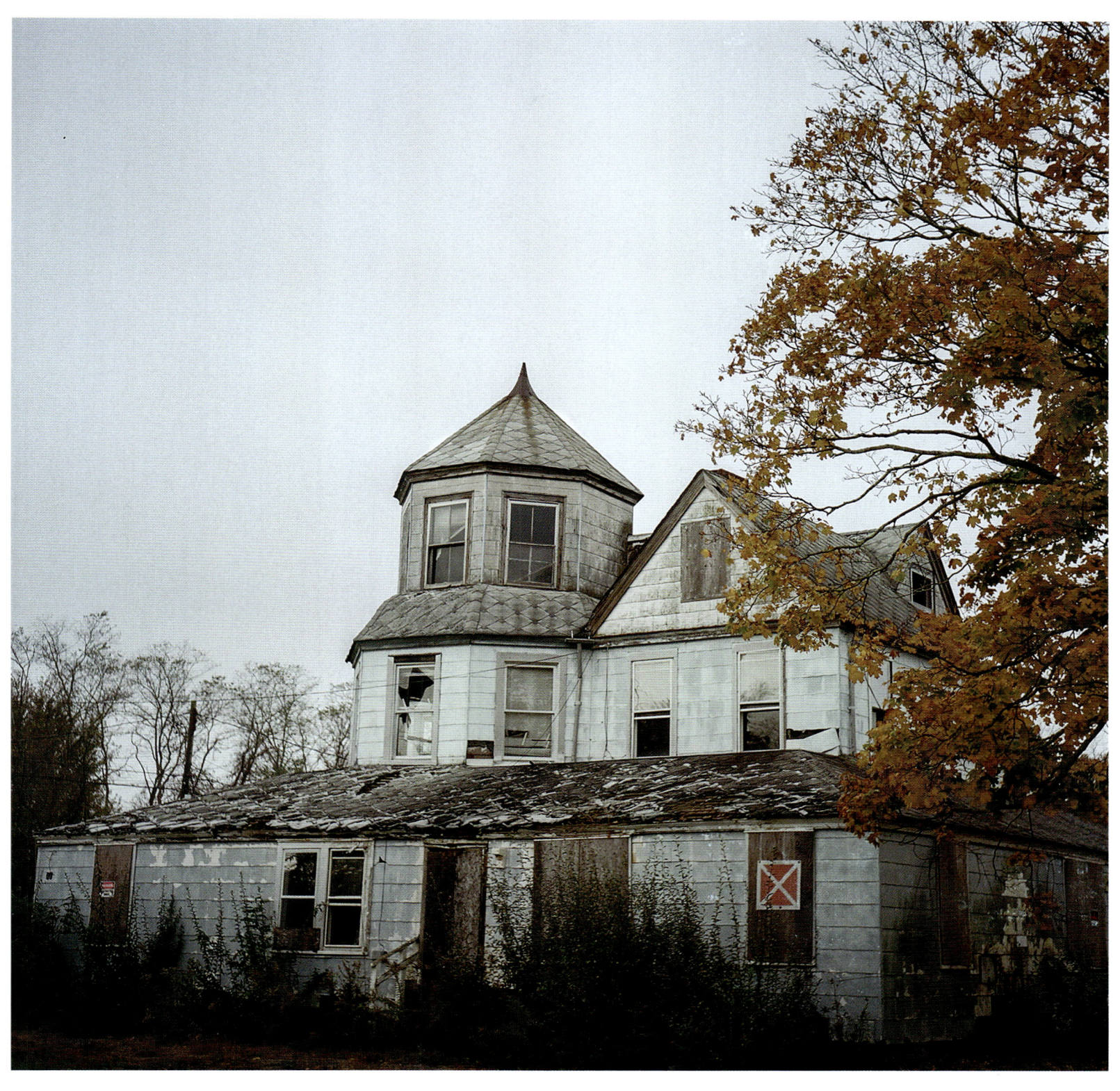

"CANNIBAL CASTLE"
Suffolk County, New York

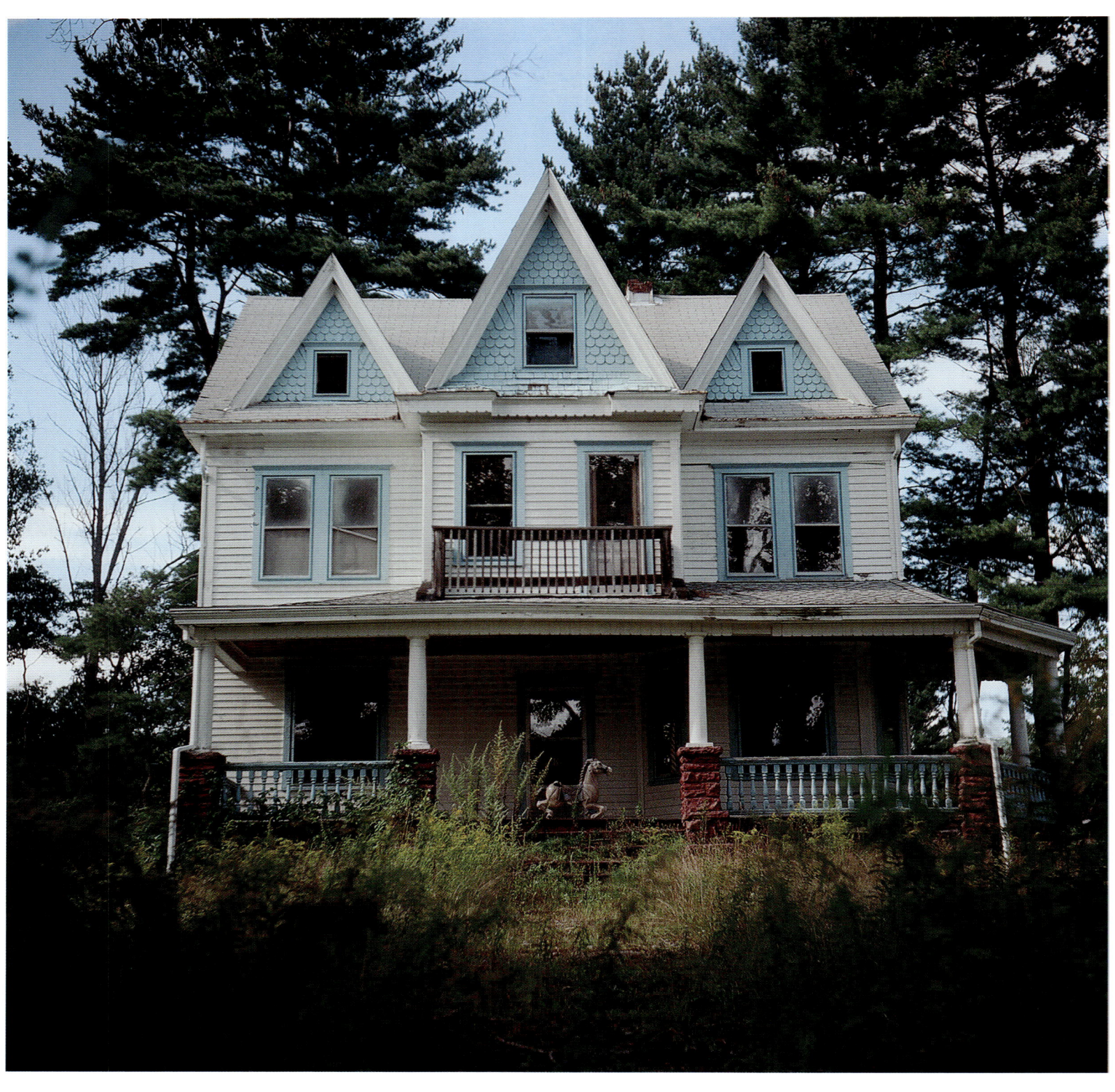

"THE MINIATURE MANOR"
Upstate New York

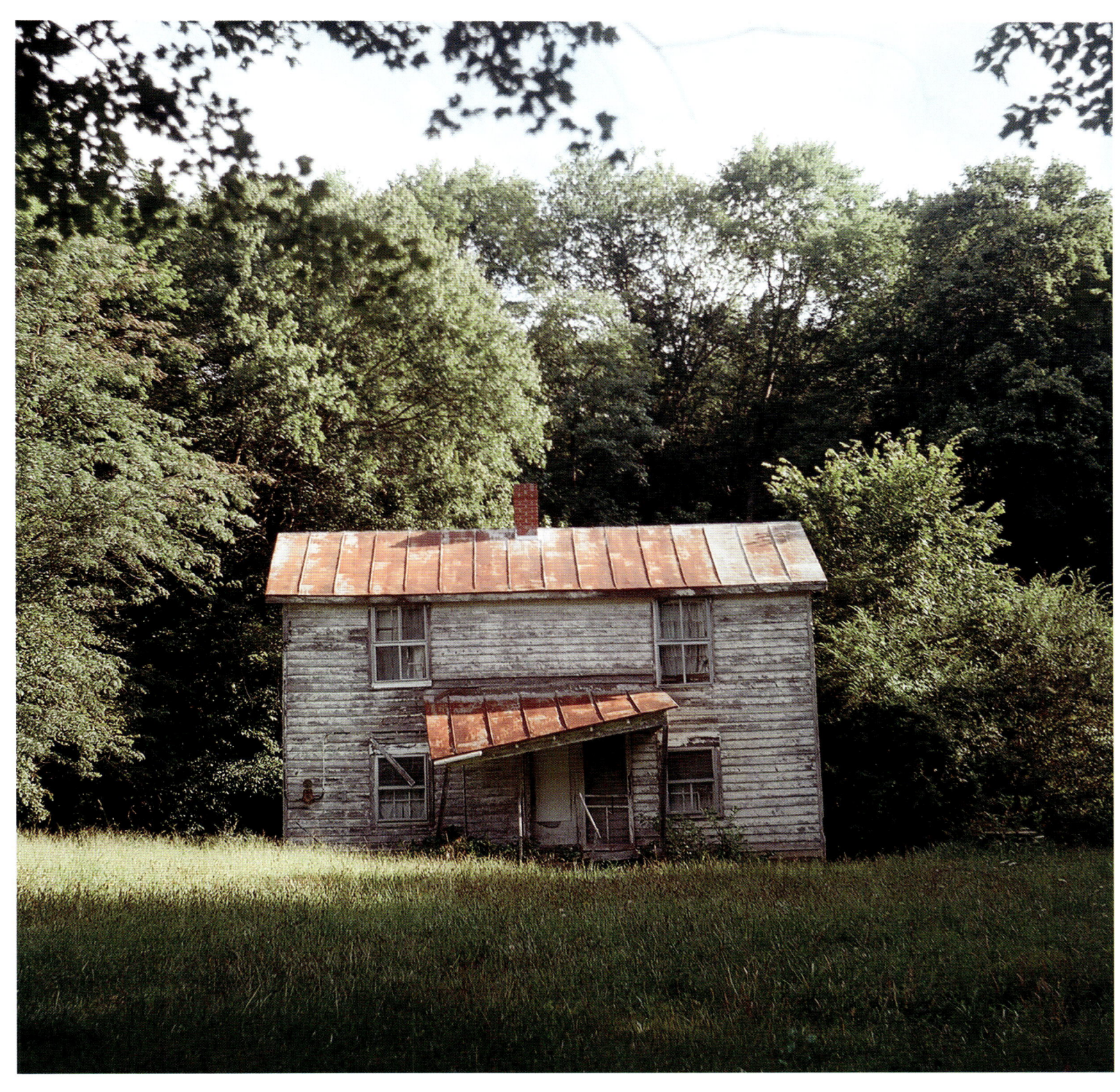

"THE HOUSE IN THE WOODS"
Amherst County, Virginia

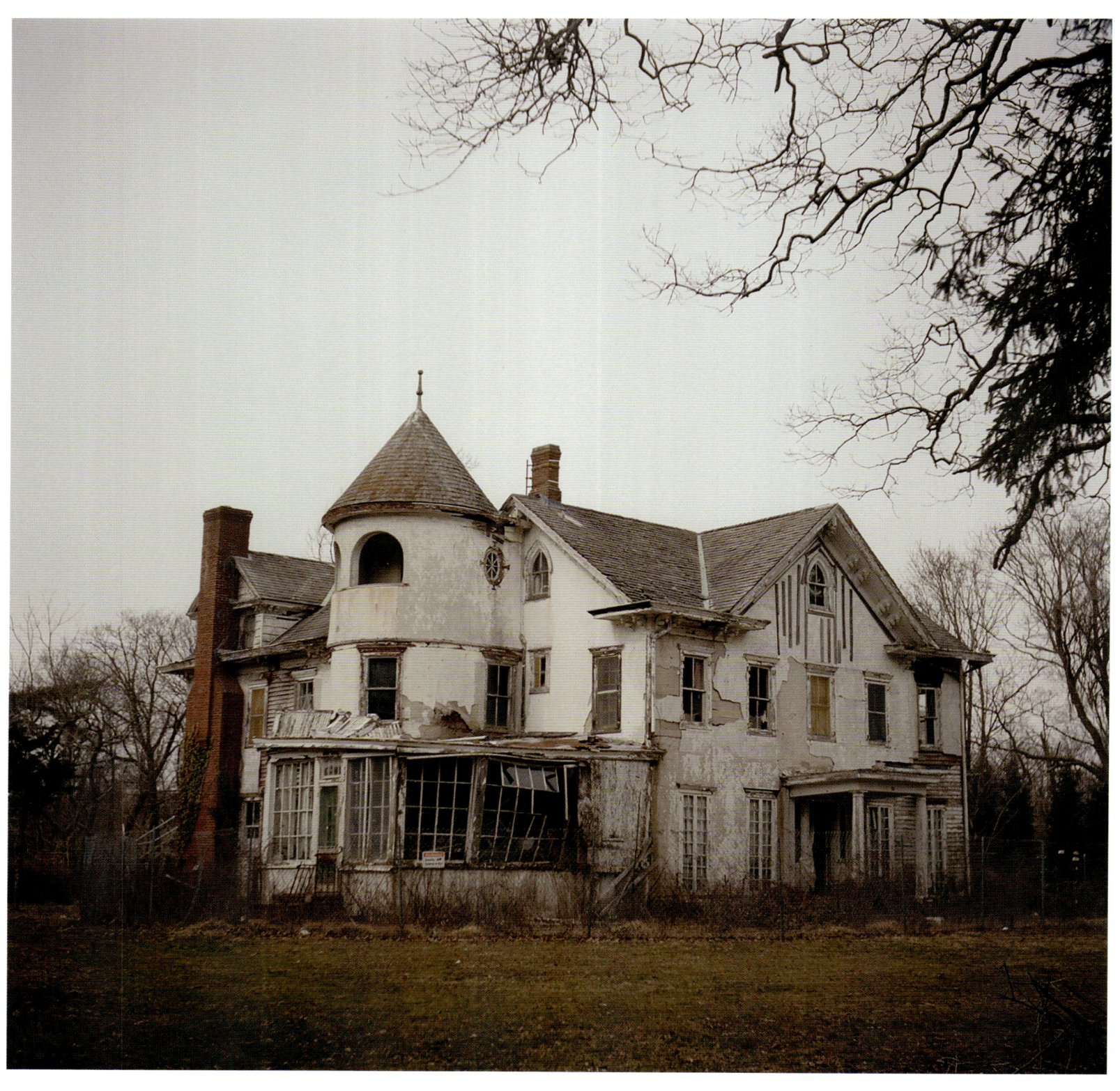

"THE BAYPORT HOUSE"
Suffolk County, New York

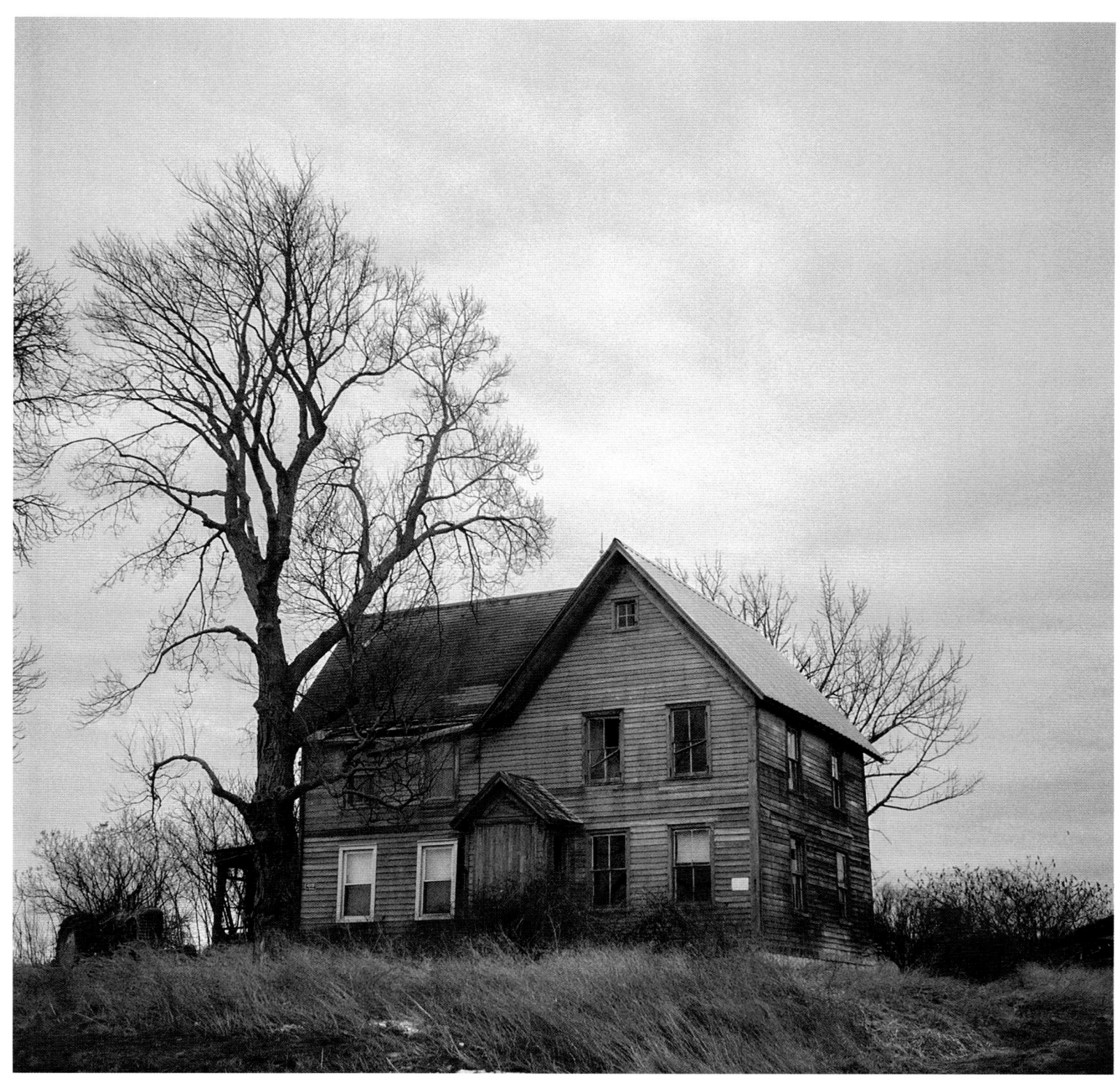

"THE HOUSE ON THE HILL"
Schohaire County, New York

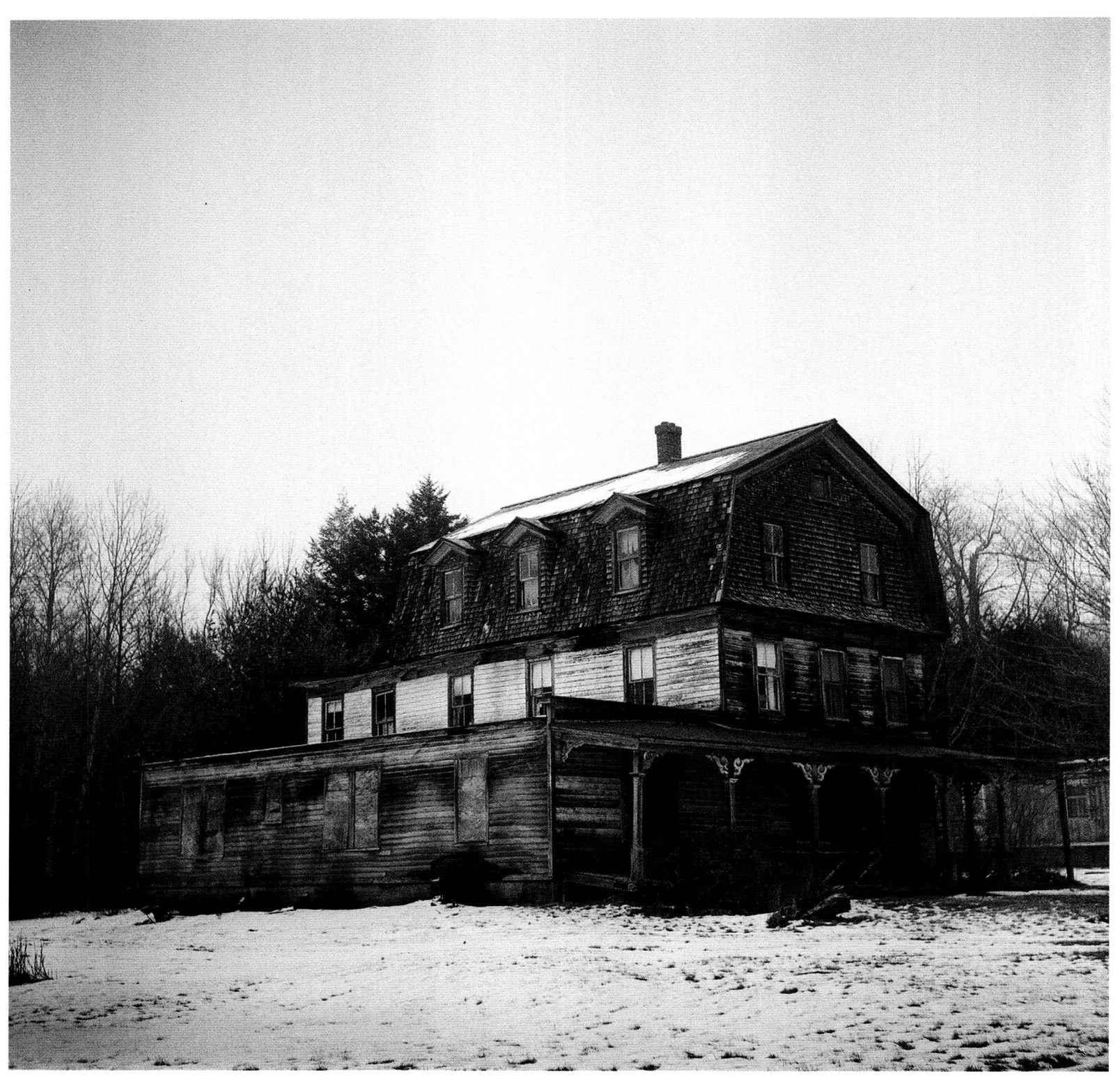

"THE NEW YORK BOARDINGHOUSE"
Greene County, New York

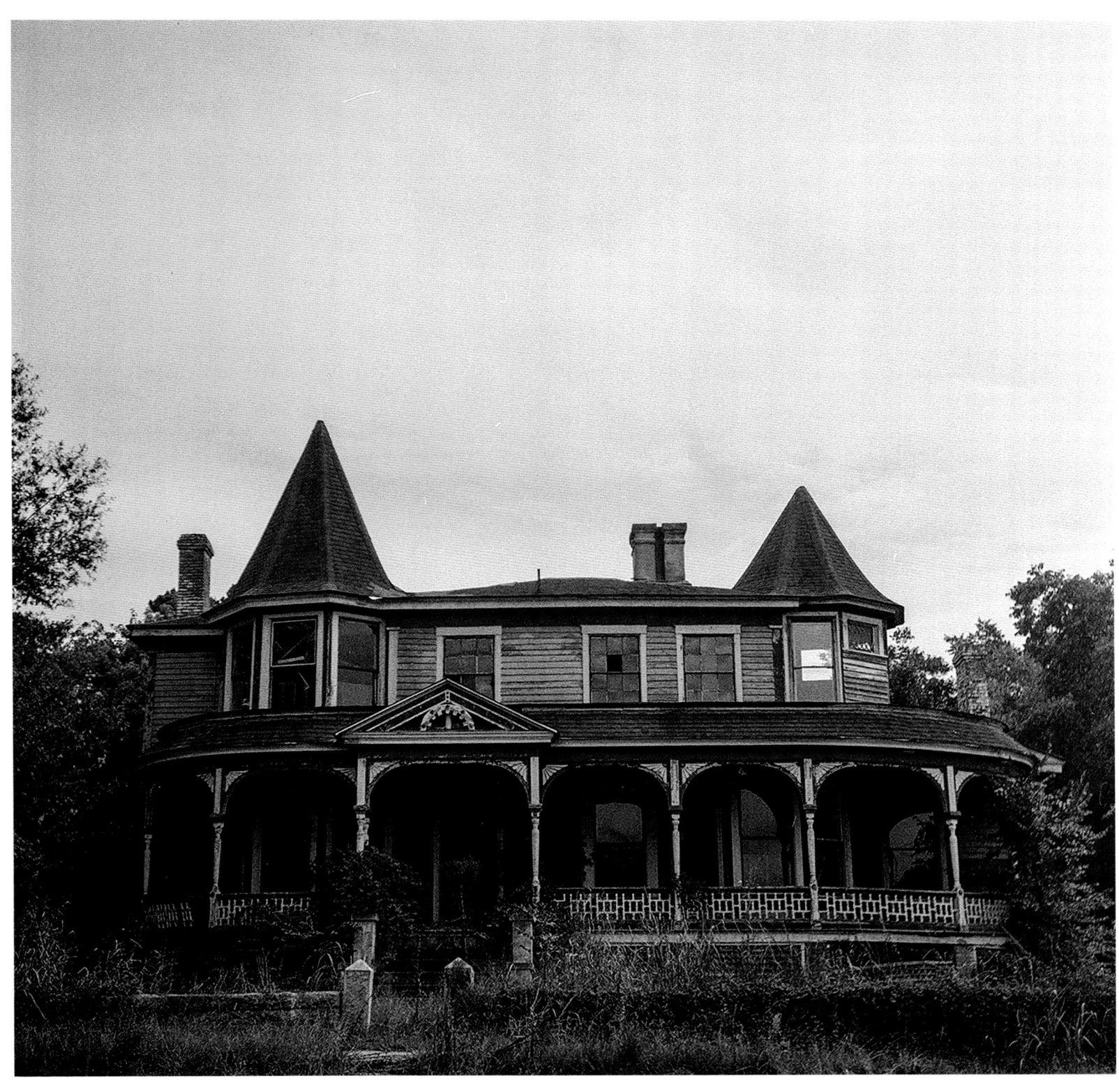

"THE PENDLETON-GRAVES HOUSE"
Hancock County, Georgia

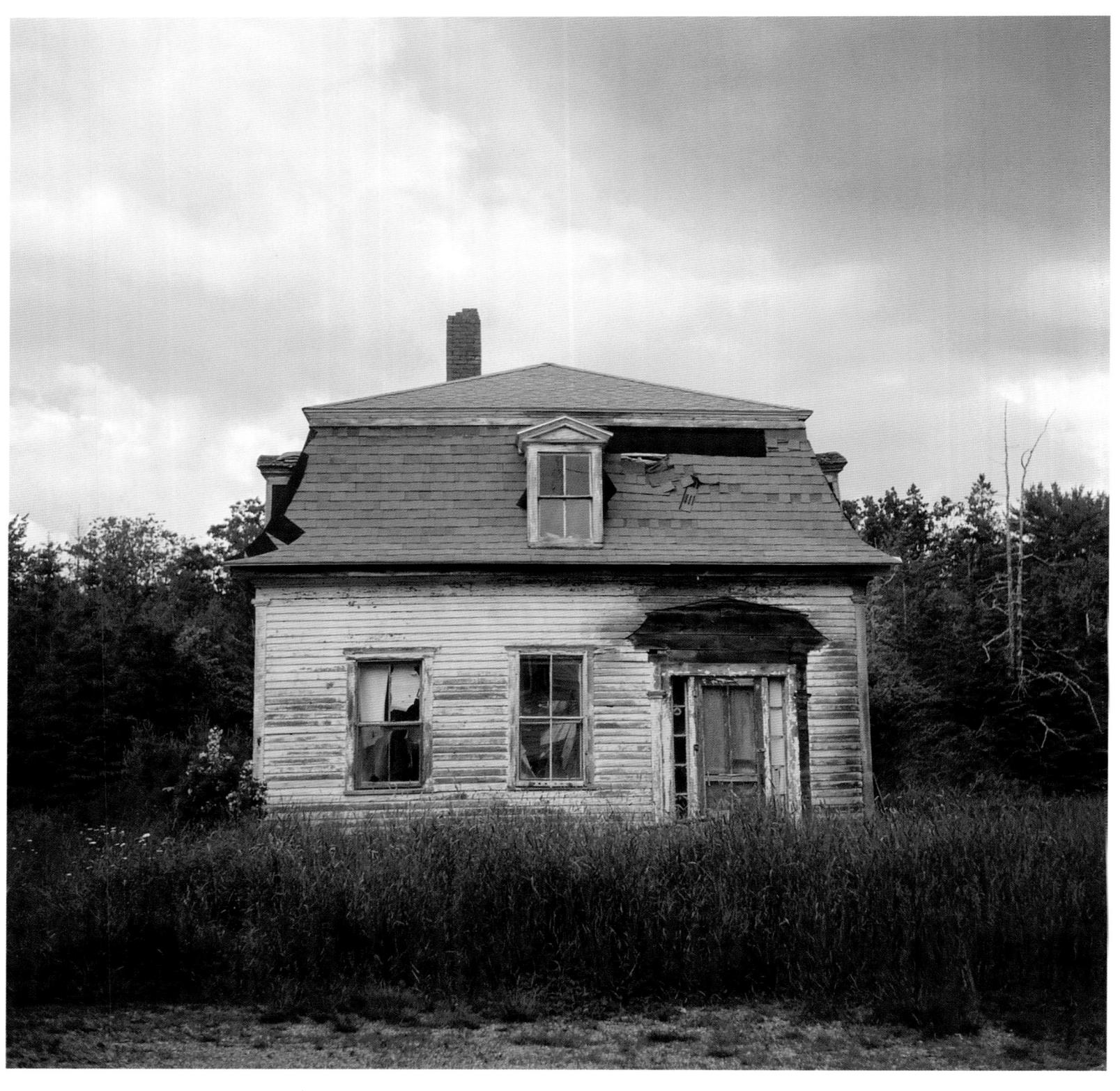

"THE MAINE MANSARD"
Hancock County, Maine

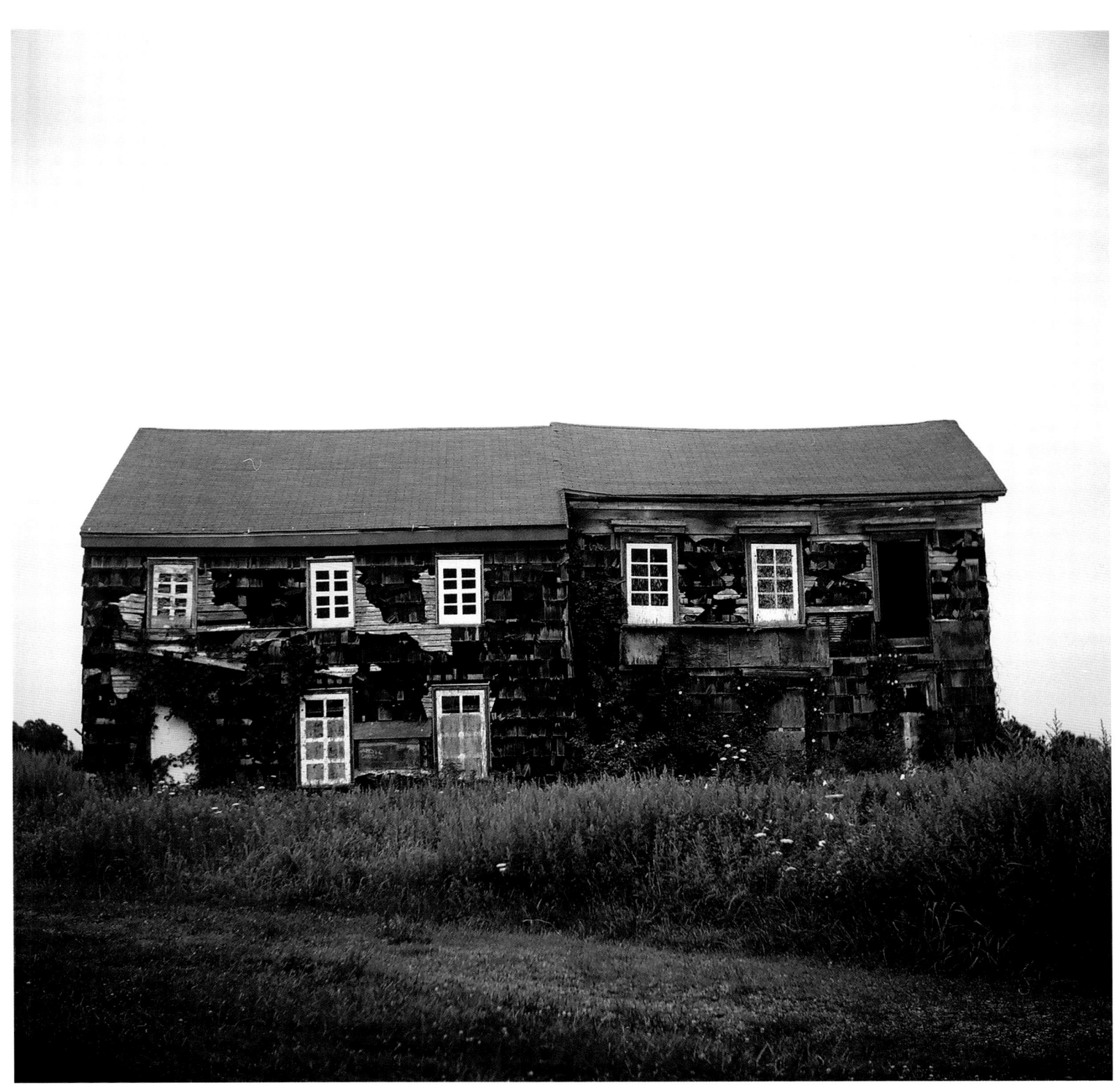

"THE FARMHOUSE ON A BATTLEFIELD"
Monmouth County, New Jersey

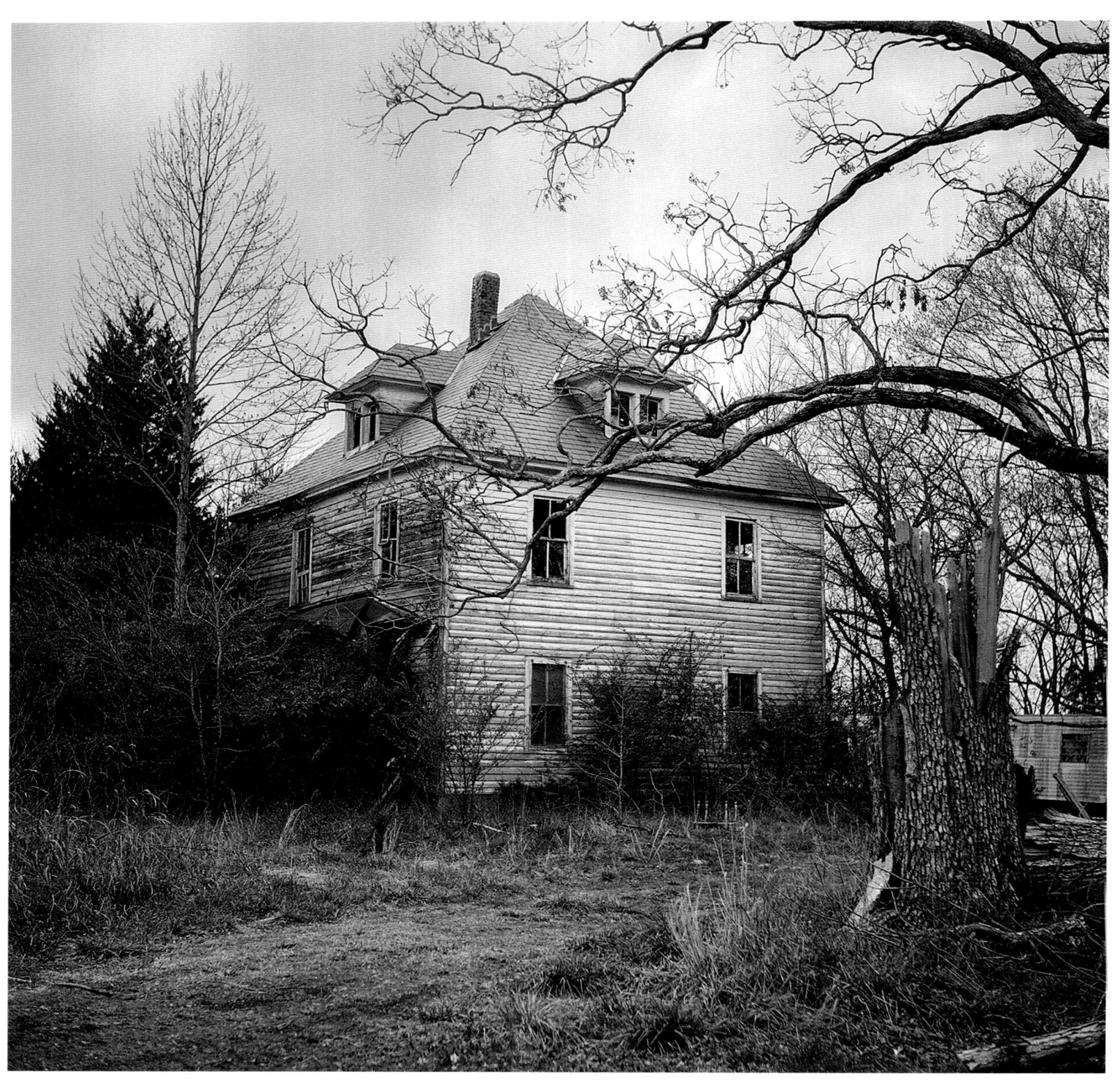

"THE ANTIQUES HOARDER'S HOUSE"
Buckingham County, Virginia

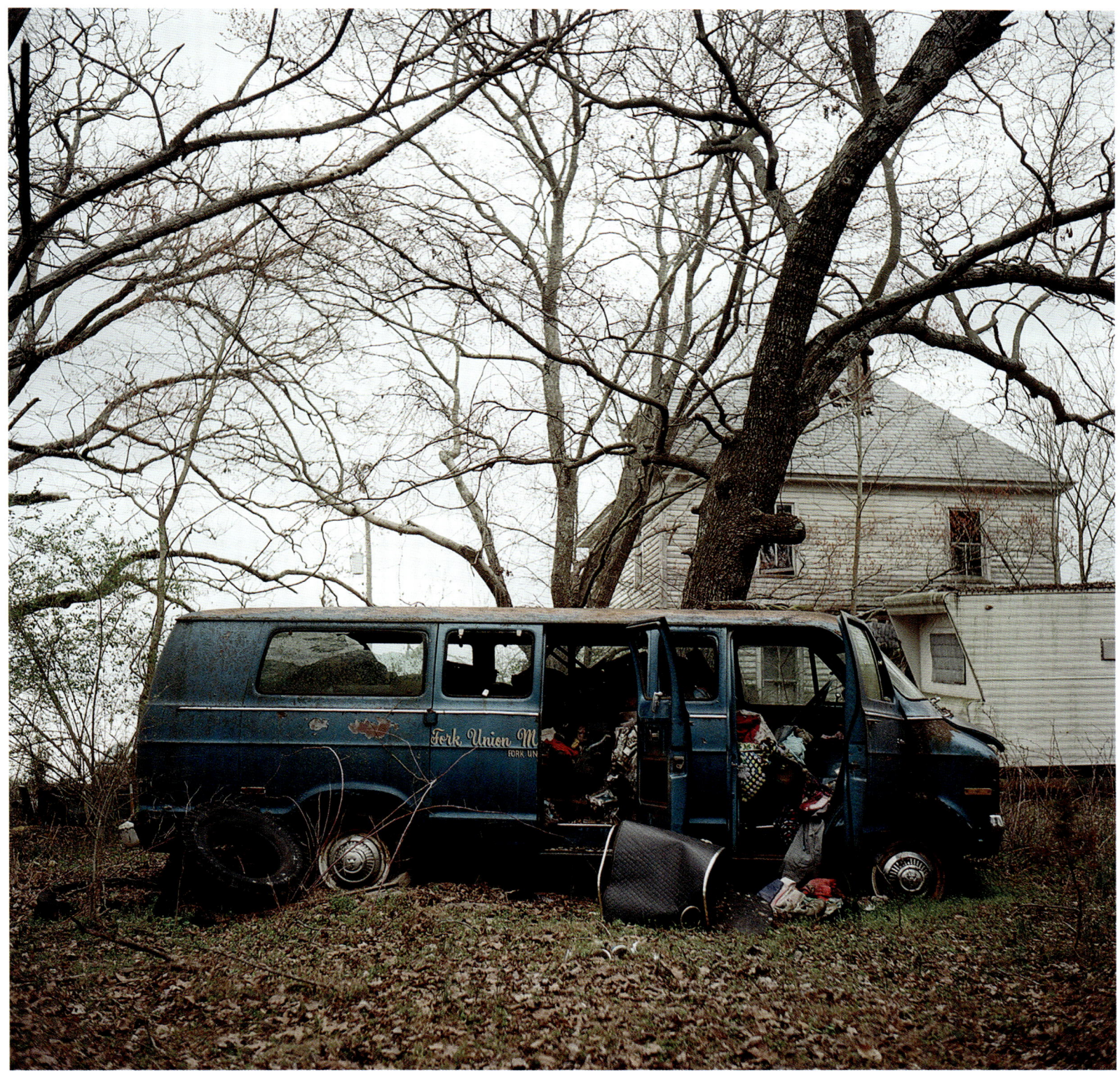

"THE VAN"
Buckingham County, Virginia

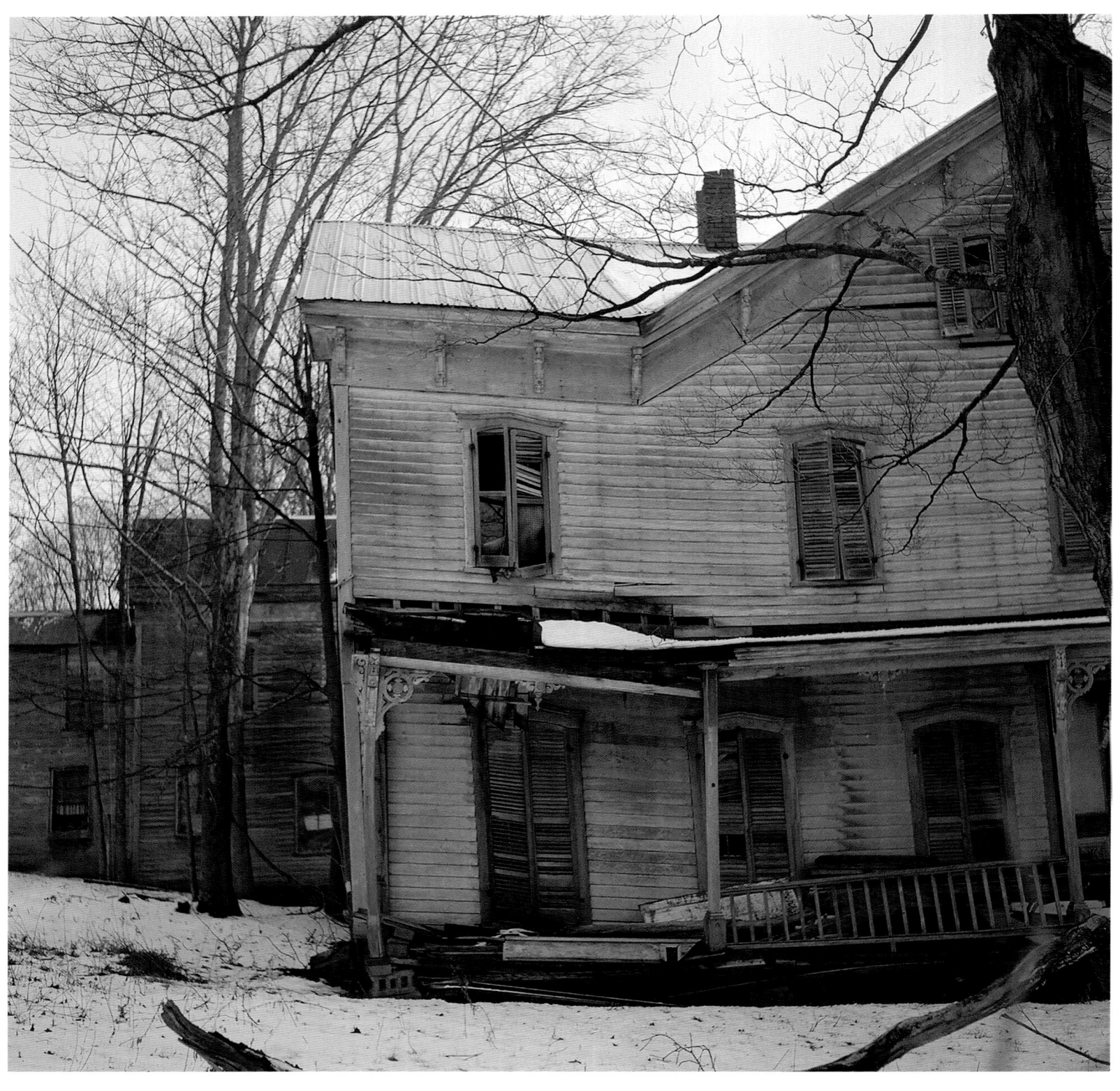

"THE OLD BOARDING HOUSE"
Sullivan County, New York

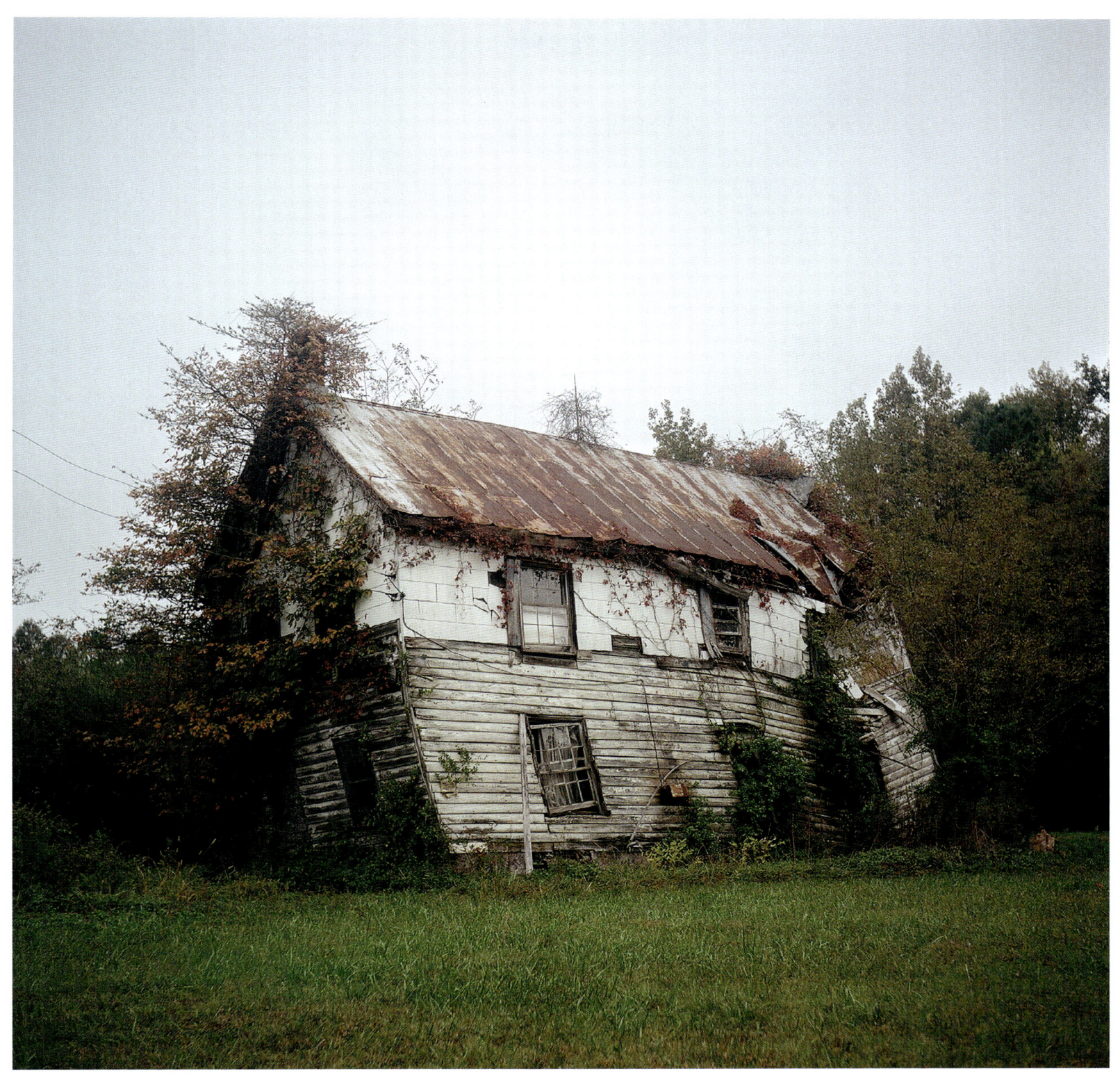

"THE LEANING HOUSE"
Westmoreland County, Virginia

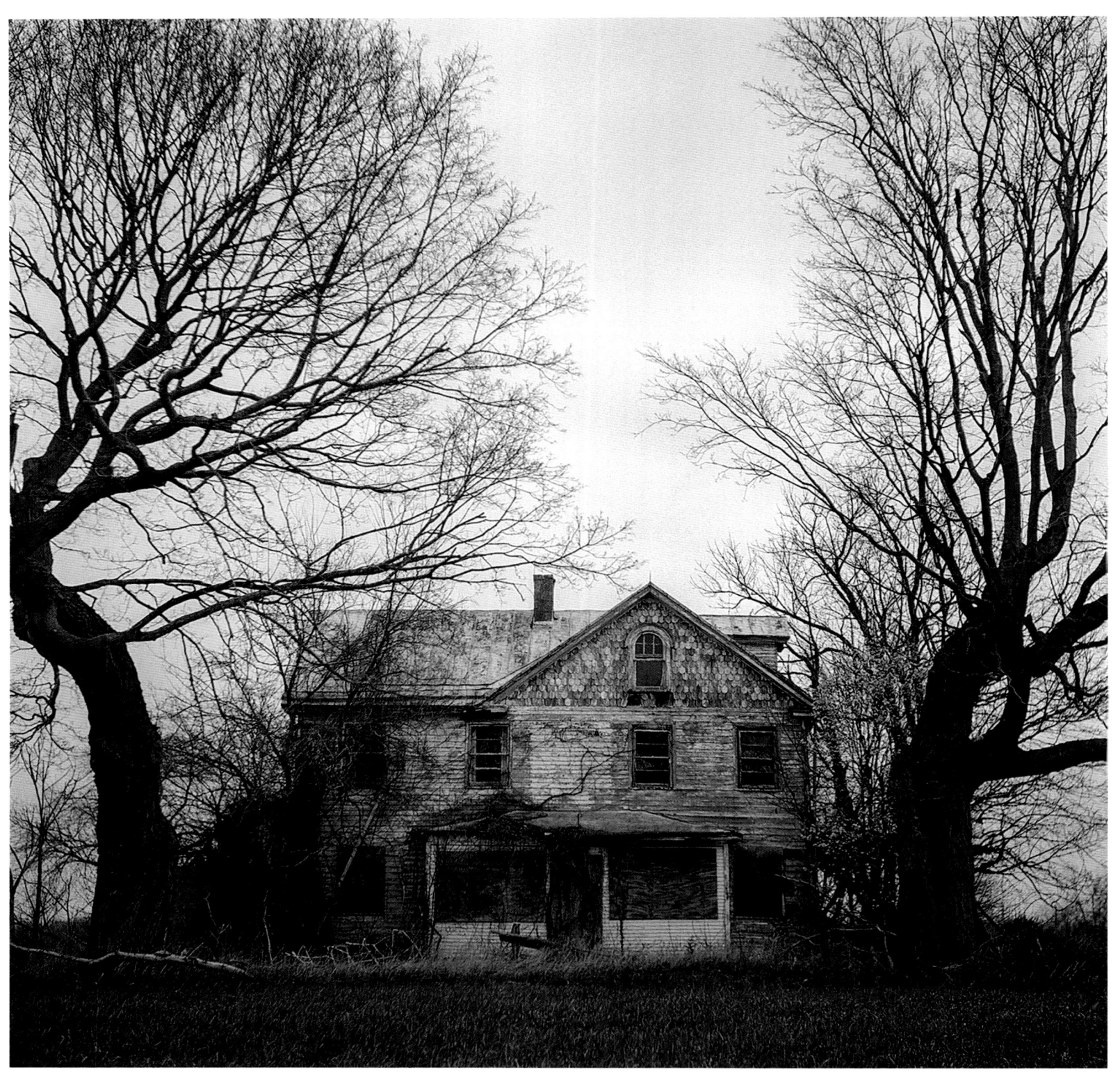

"THE ANTHROPOMORPHIC TREES"
Prince George's County, Maryland

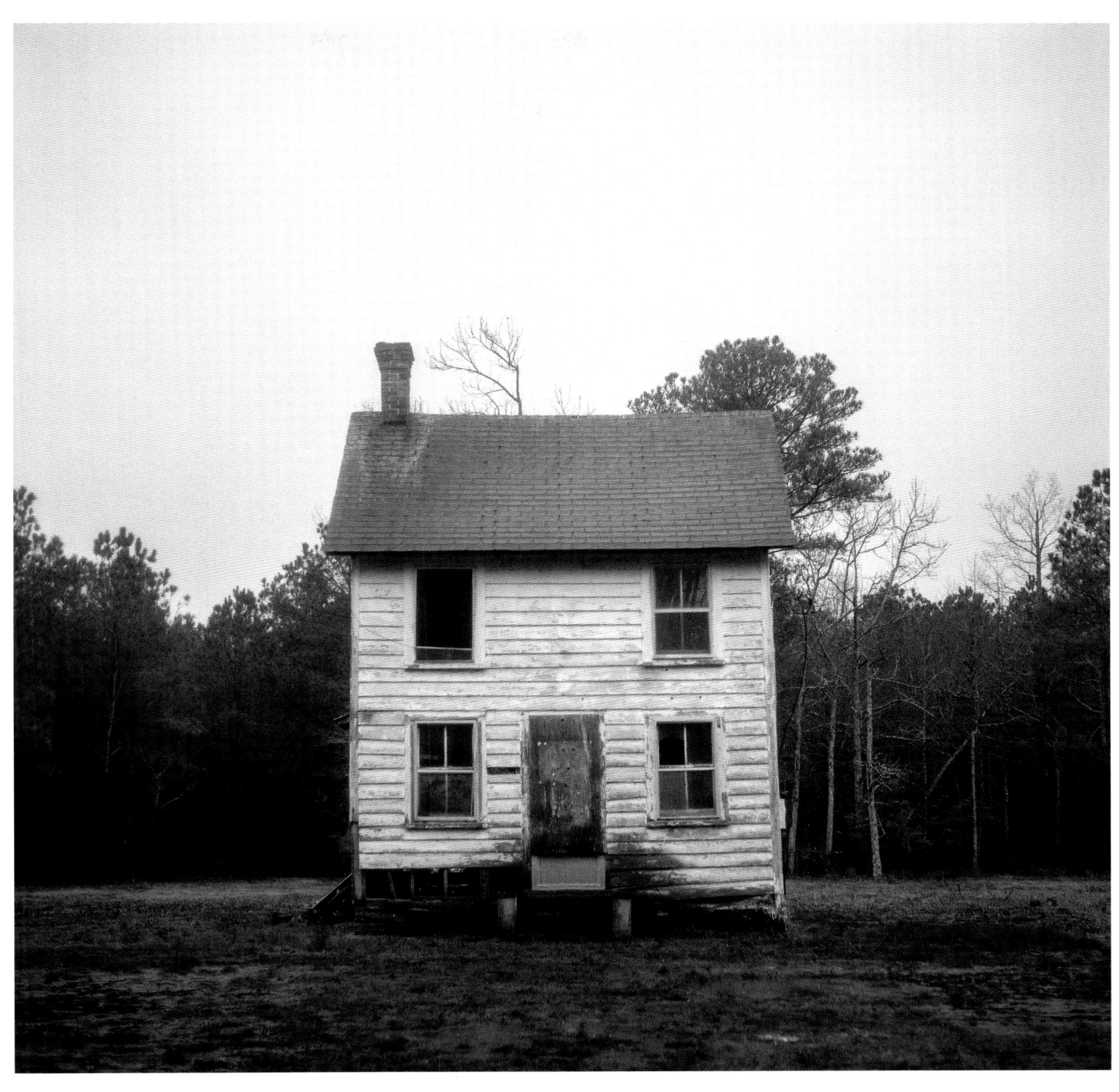

"THE OLD MAN'S HOUSE"
Somerset County, Maryland

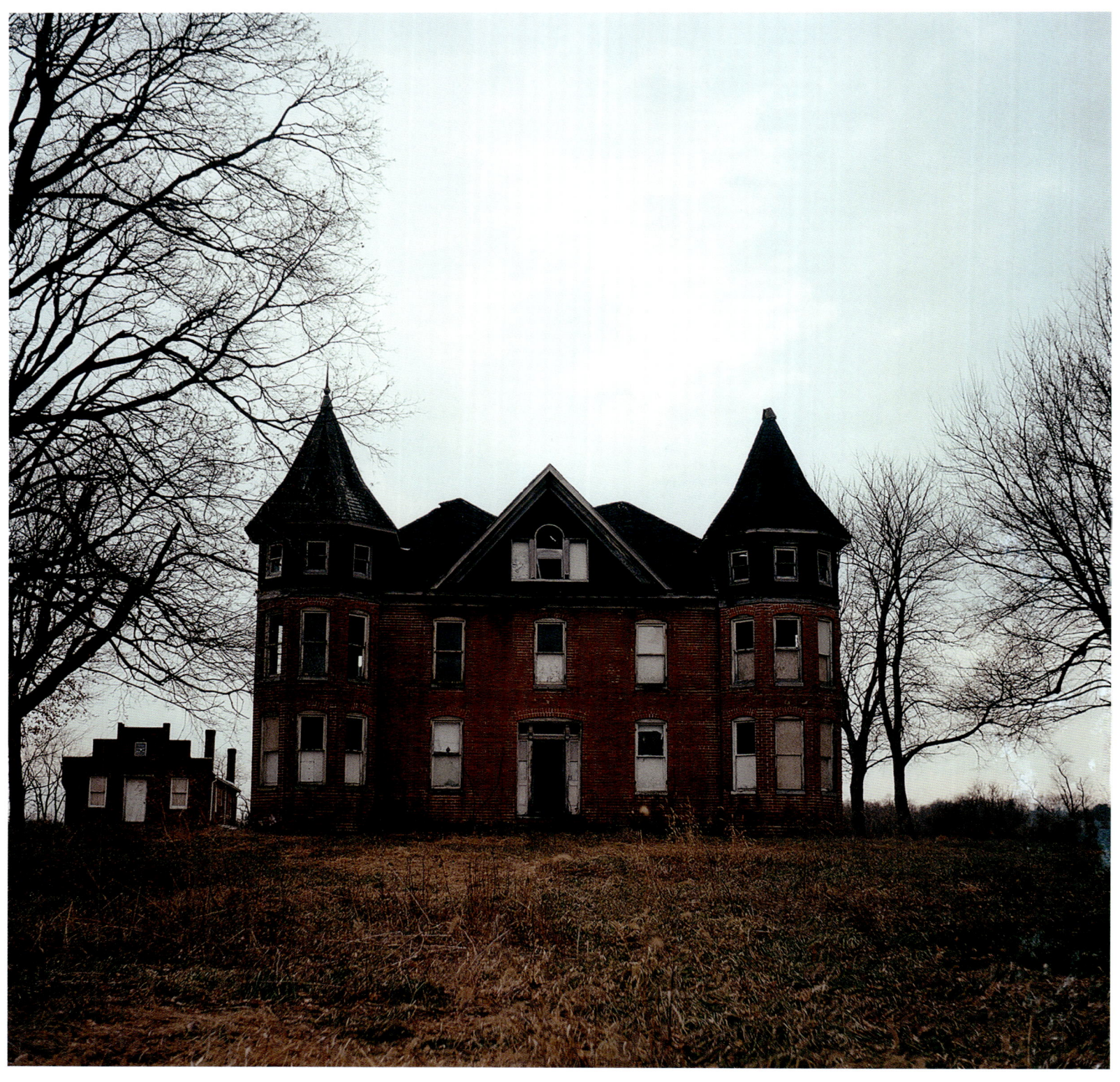

"THE BALLENGER CREEK HOUSE"
Frederick County, Maryland

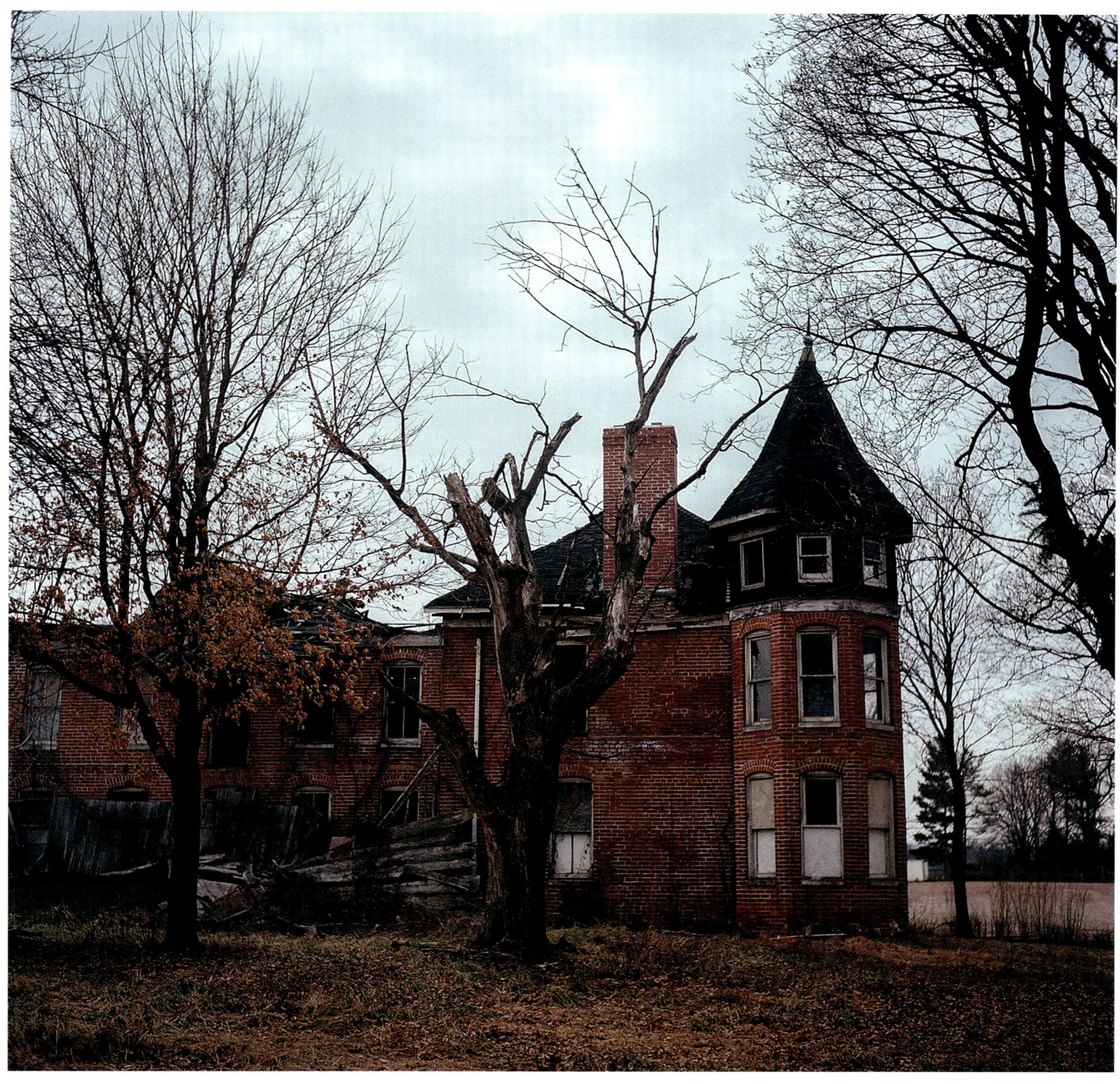

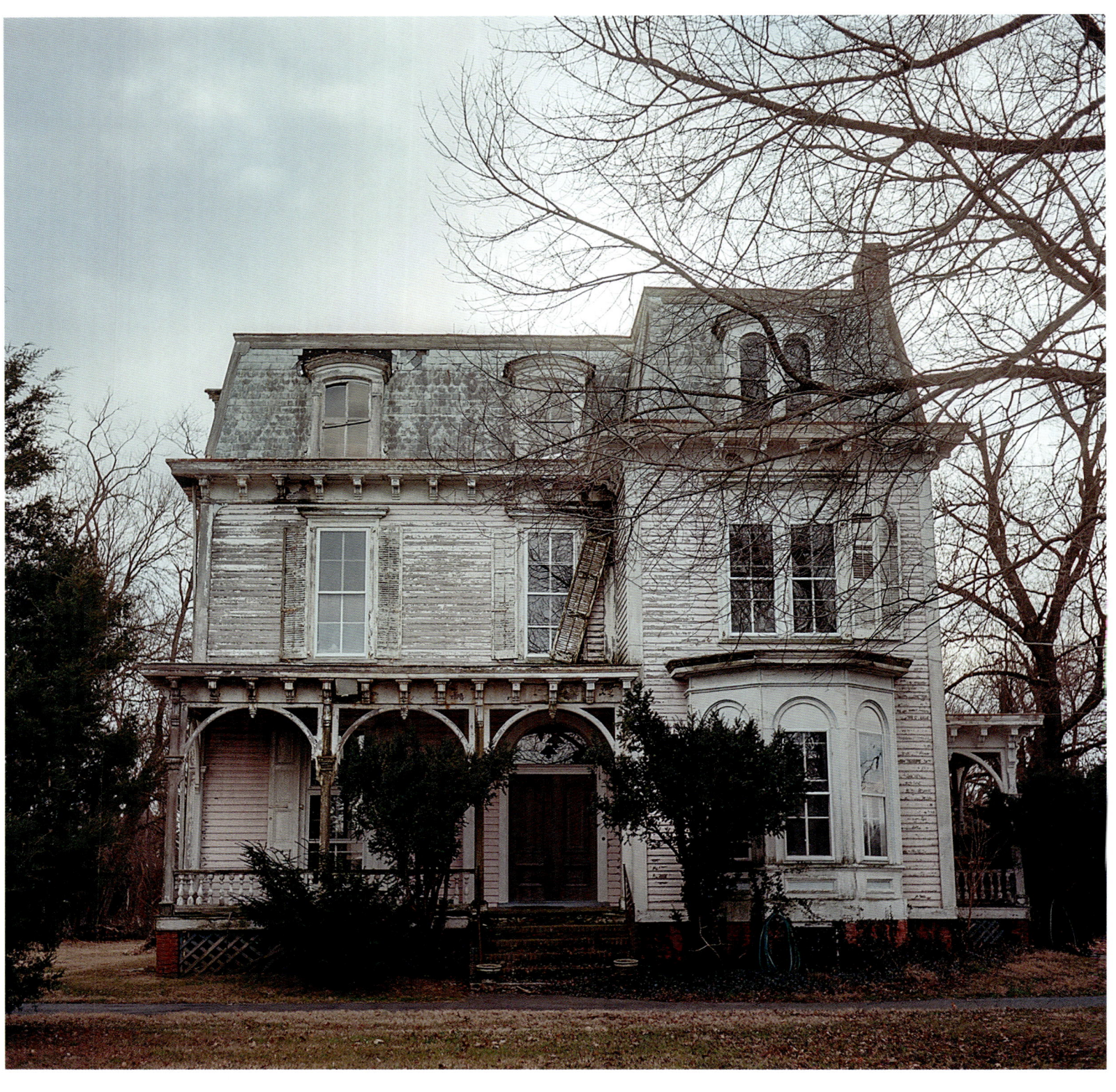

"A MARYLAND MANSARD"
Cecil County, Maryland

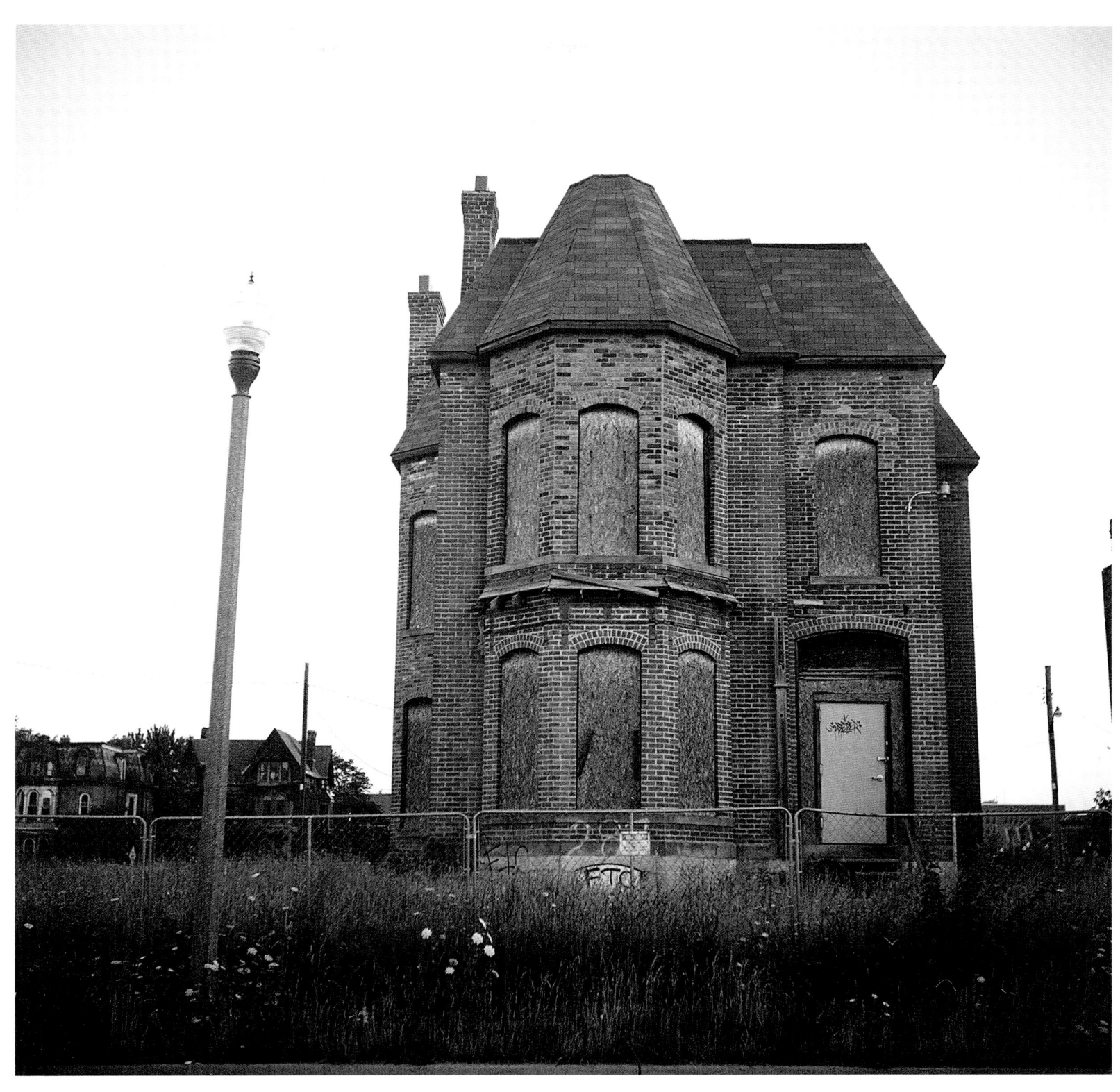

"A MANSARD TWIN"
Wayne County, Michigan

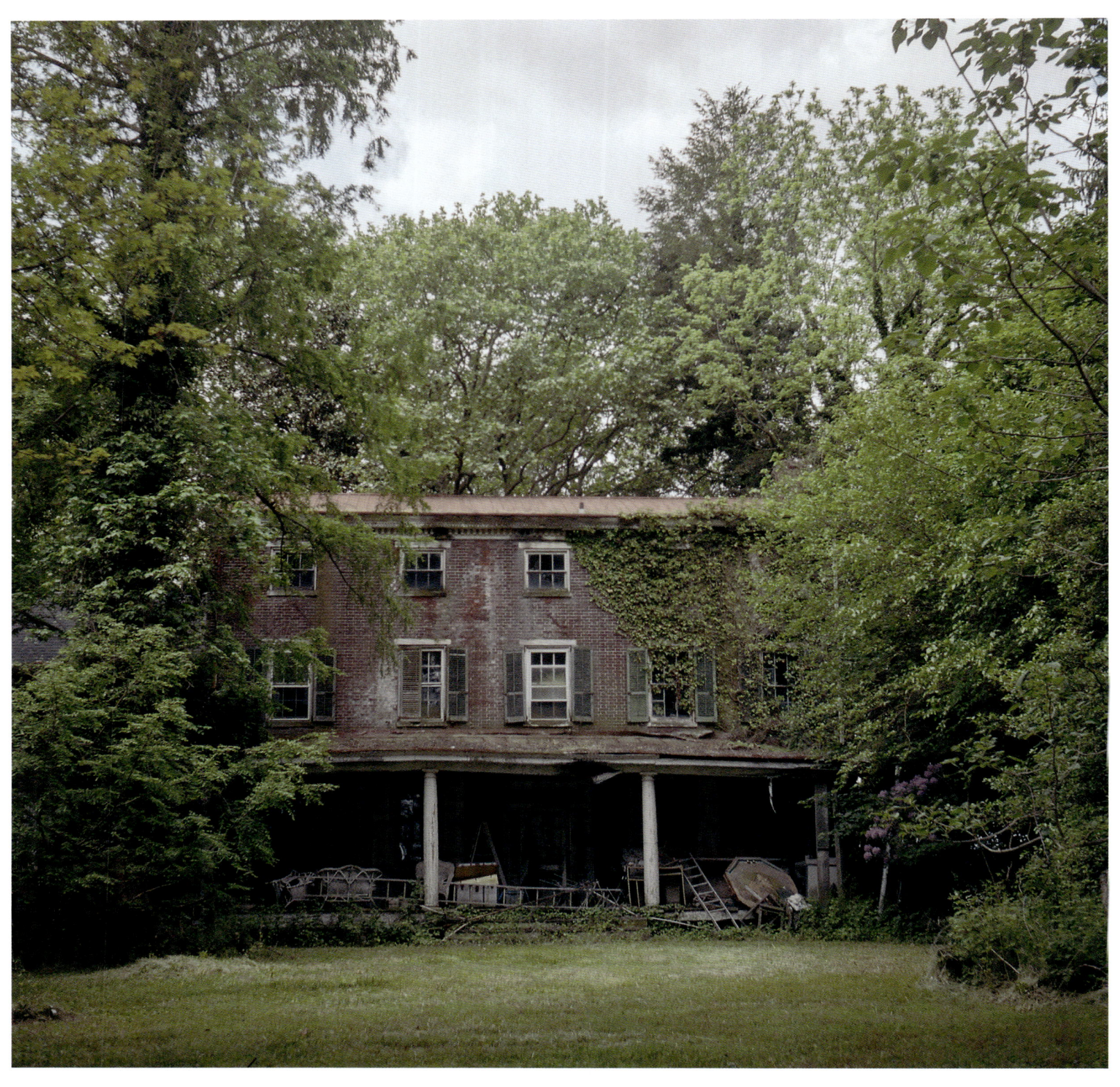

"THE POLITICIAN'S HOUSE"
New Castle County, Delaware

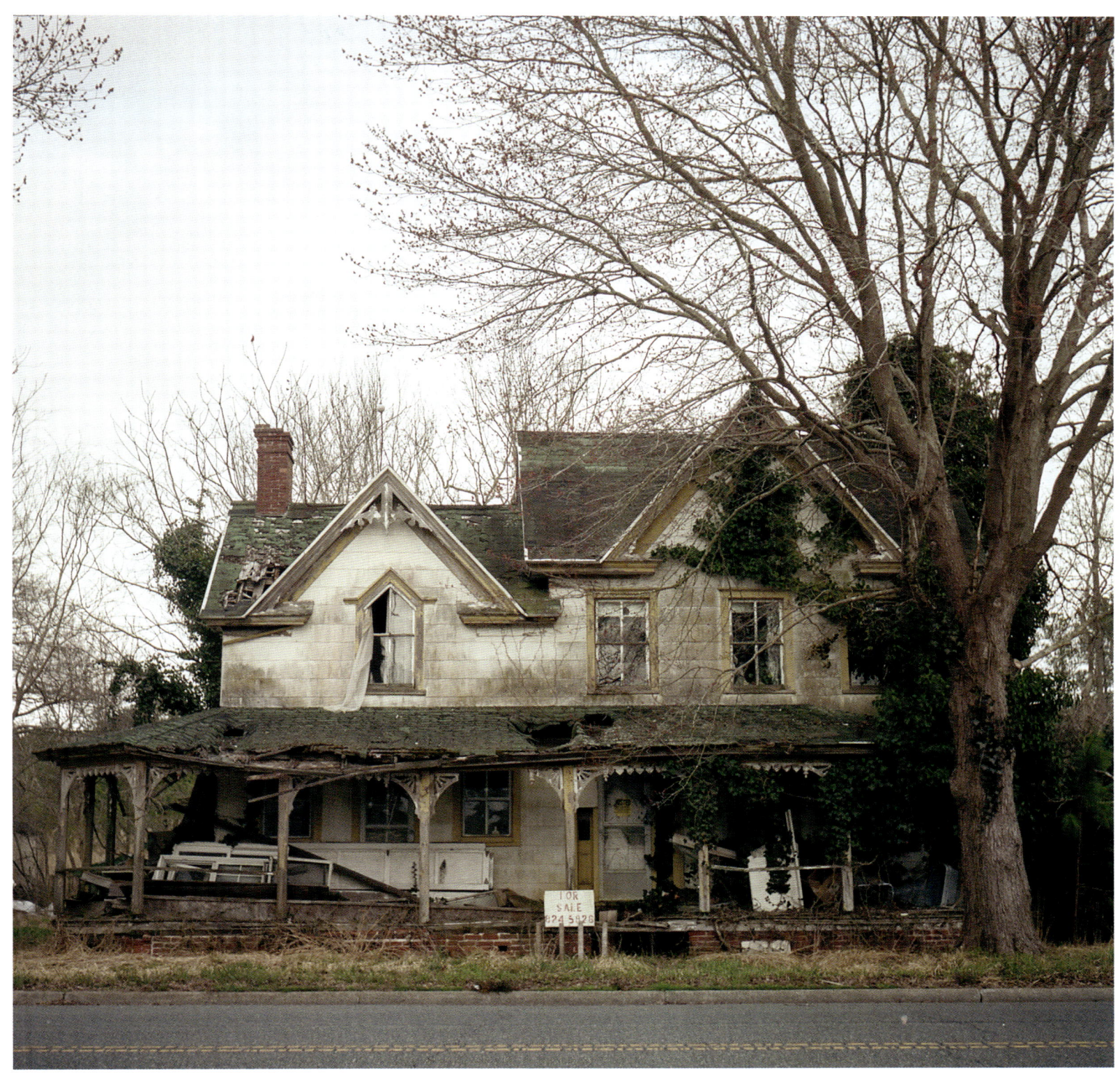

"THE HOUSE AT THE END OF THE STREET"
Accomack County, Virginia

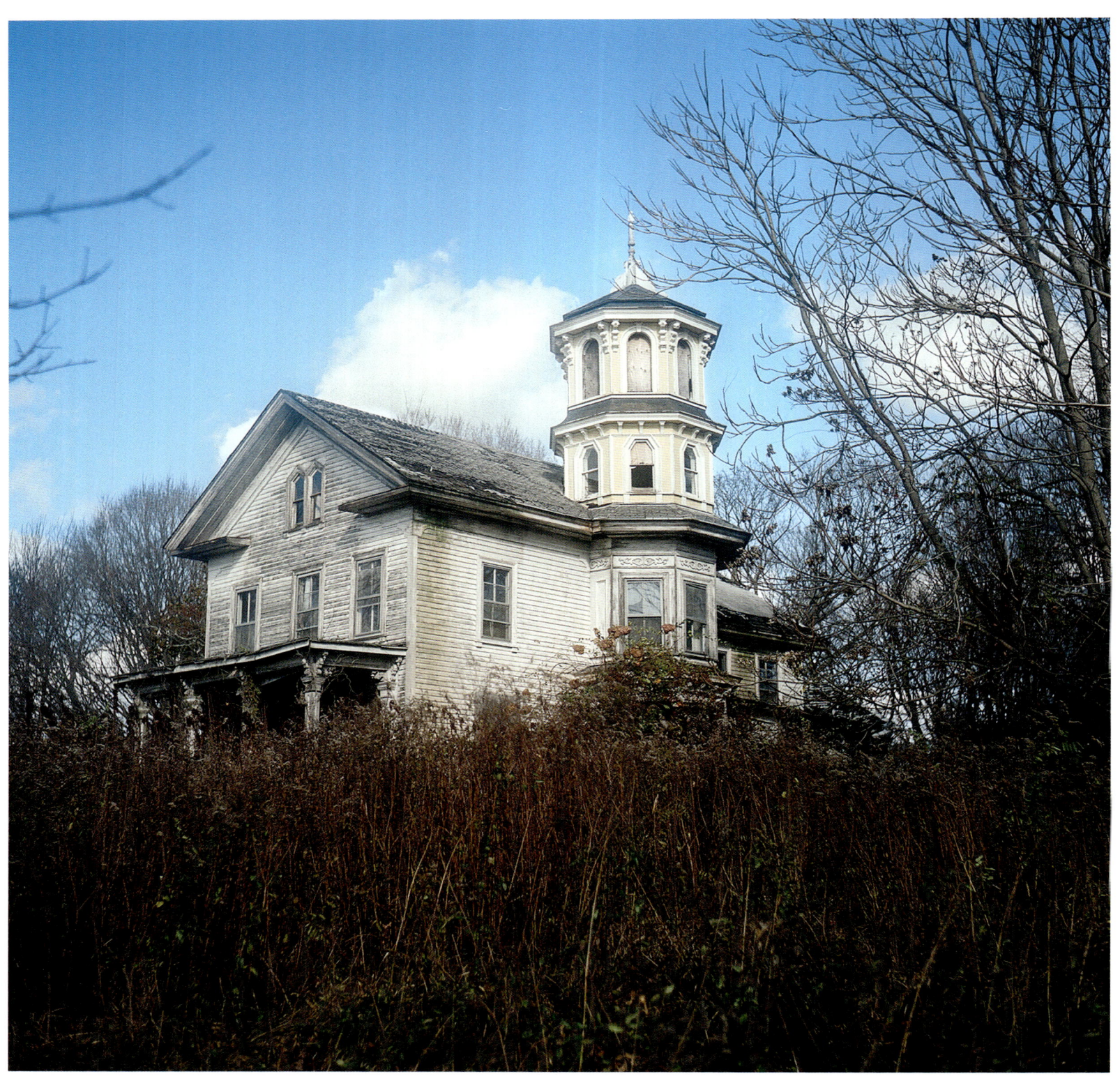

"THE OLD BISHOP HOUSE"
Middlesex County, Connecticut

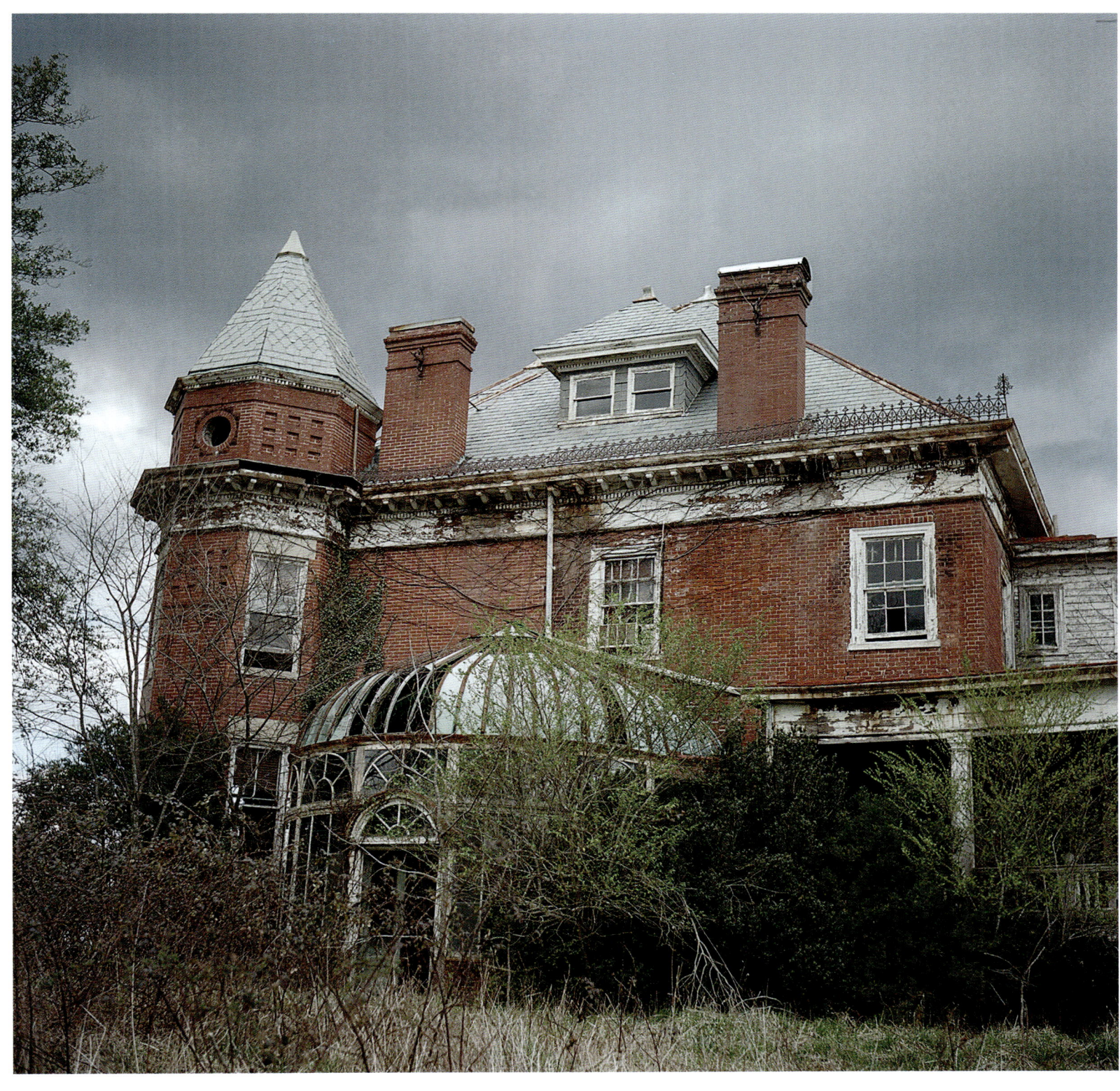

"DUNNINGTON MANSION, SIDE VIEW"
Prince Edward County, Virginia

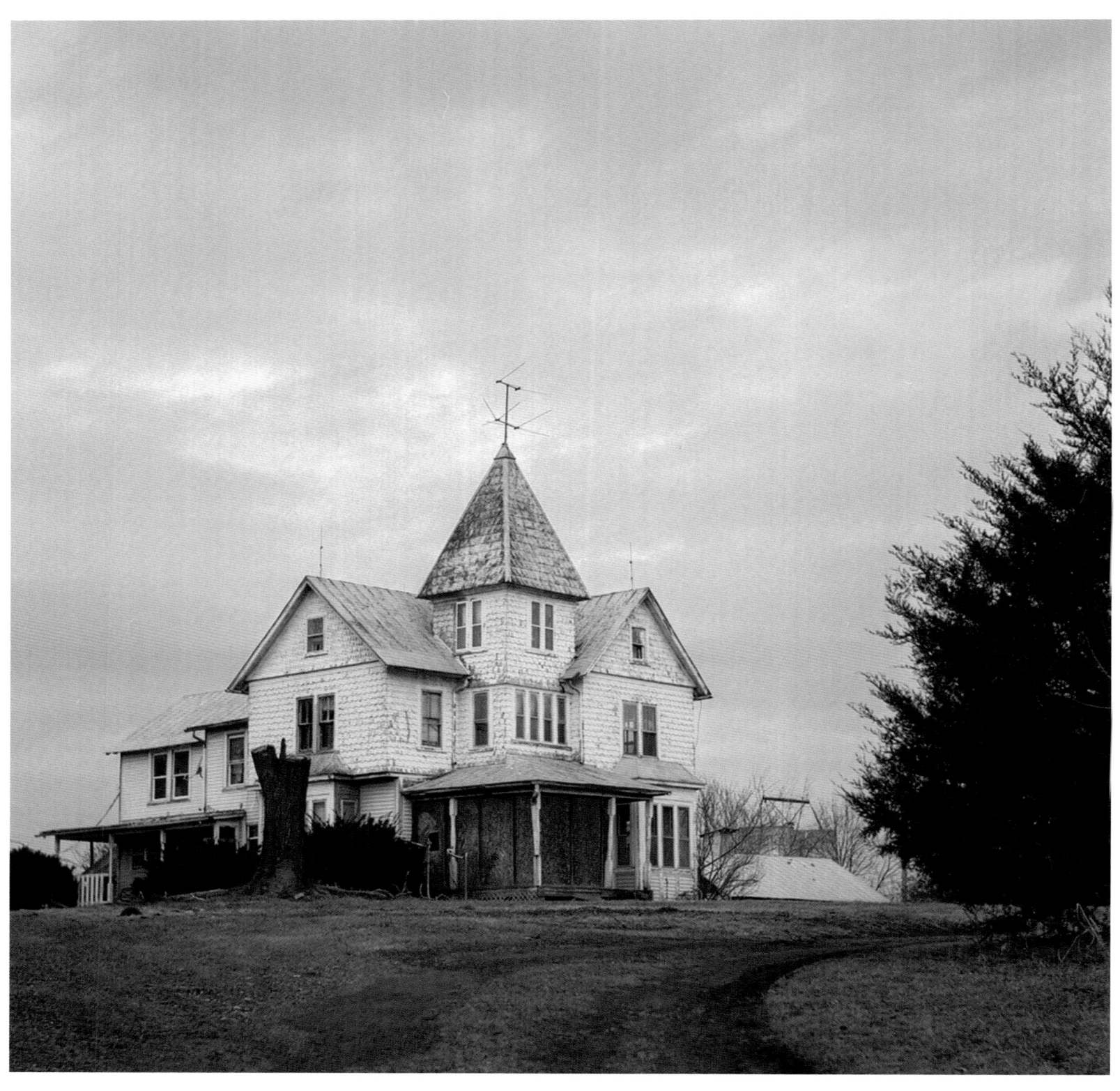

"THE FOLK VICTORIAN FARMHOUSE"
Page County, Maryland

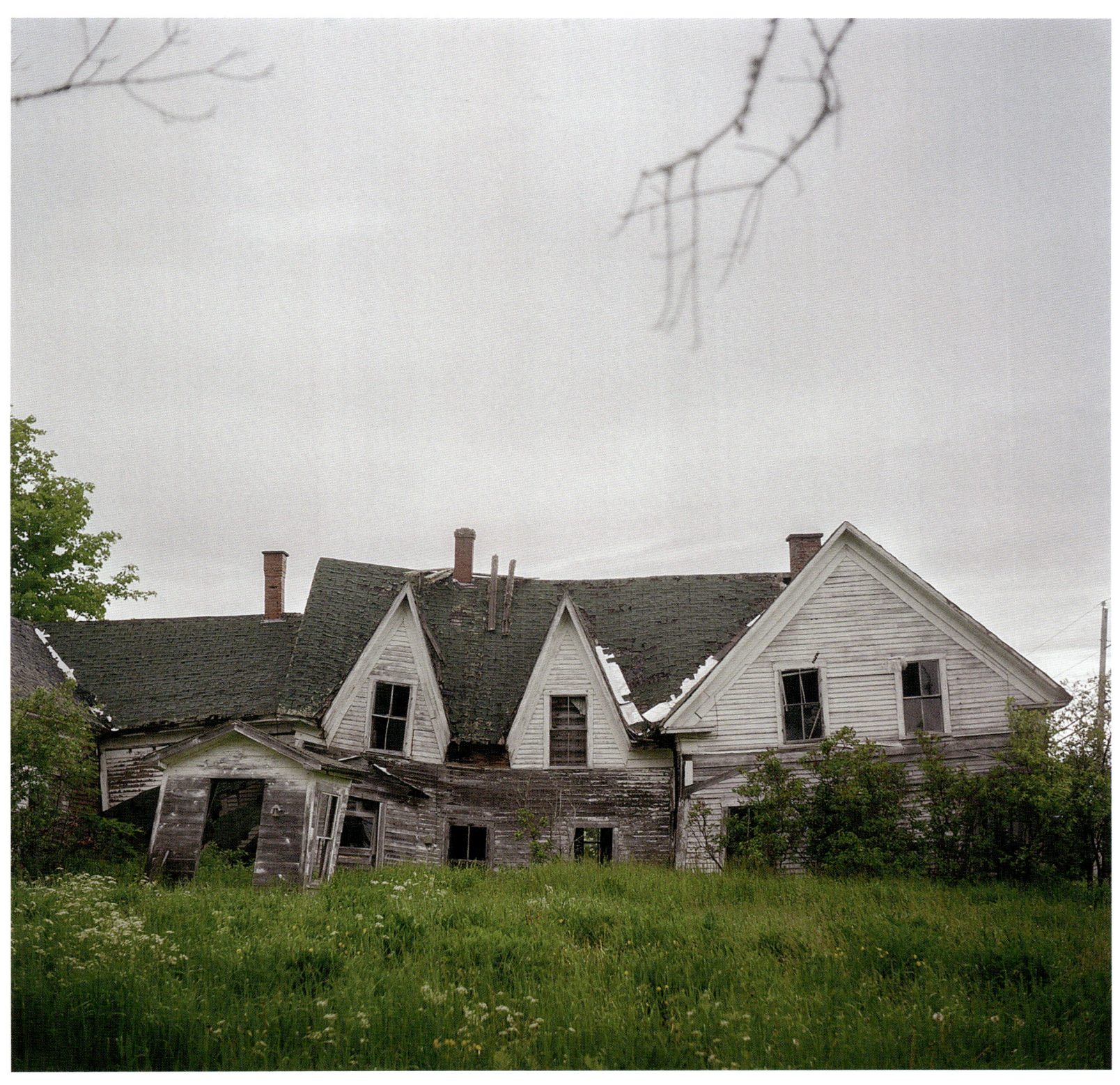

"THE CROOKED HOUSE"
Aroostook County, Maine

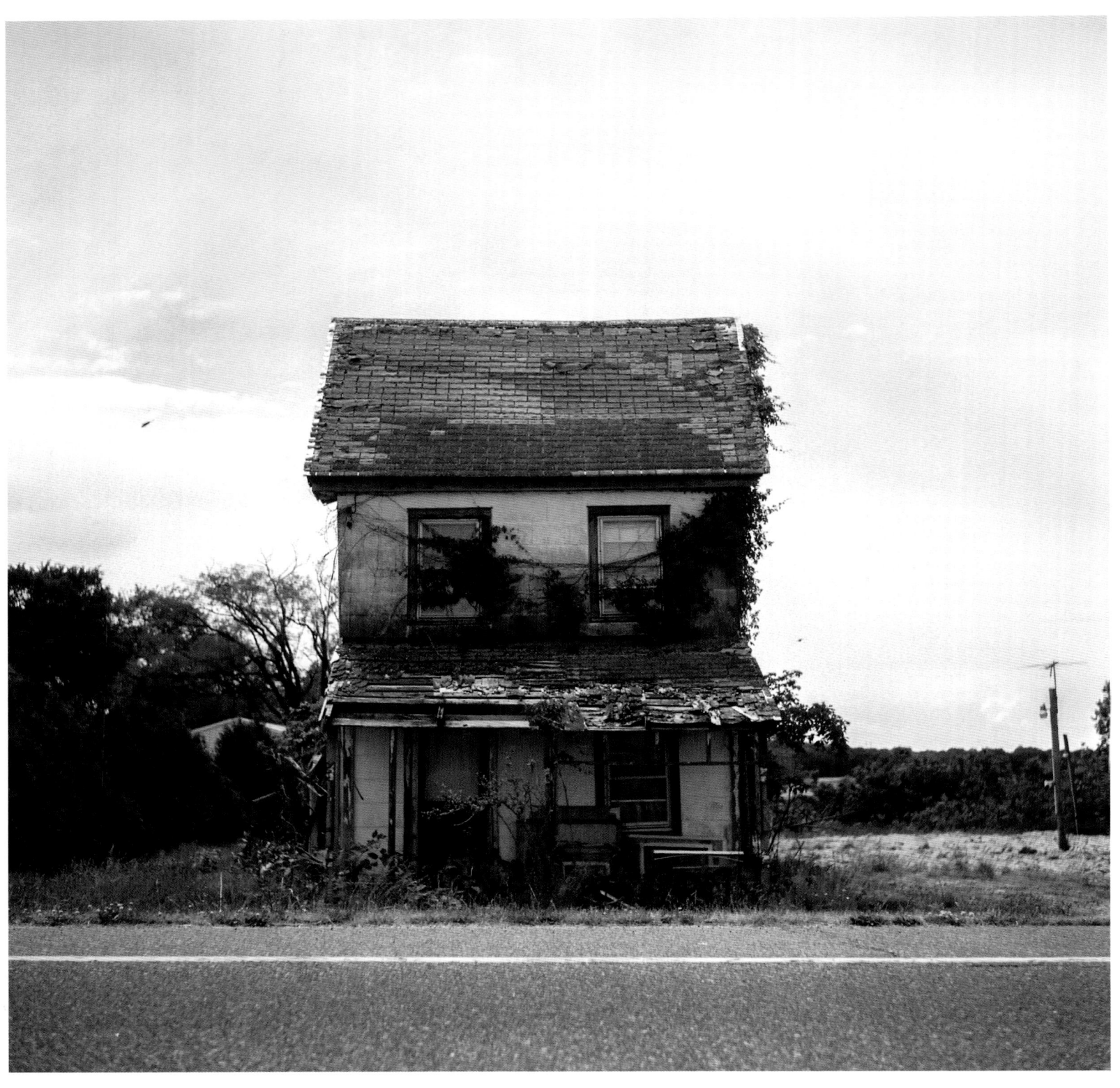

"THE TINY HOUSE BY THE SEA"
Queen Anne's County, Maryland

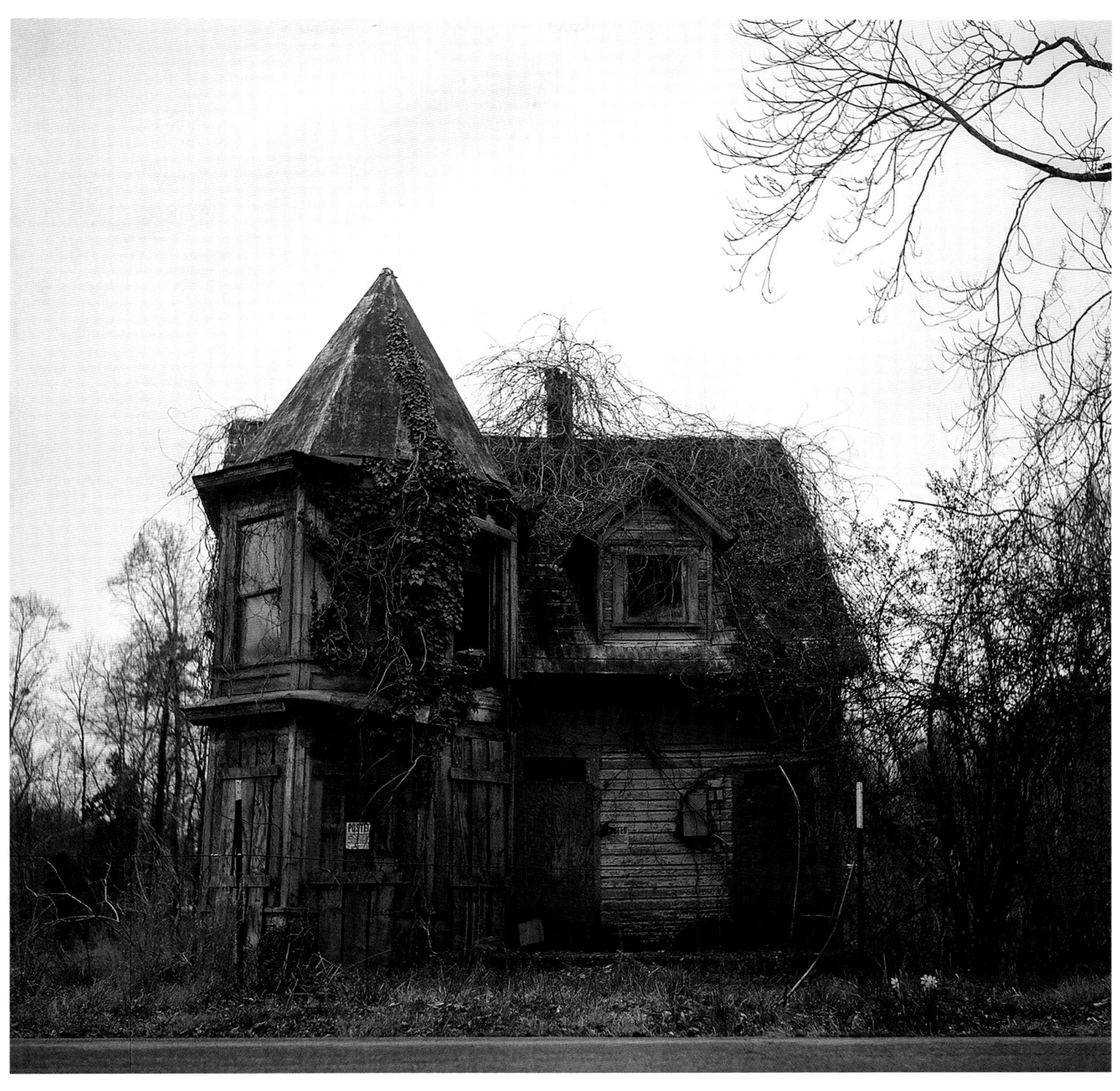

"THE WITCH'S HOUSE"
Surry County, Virginia

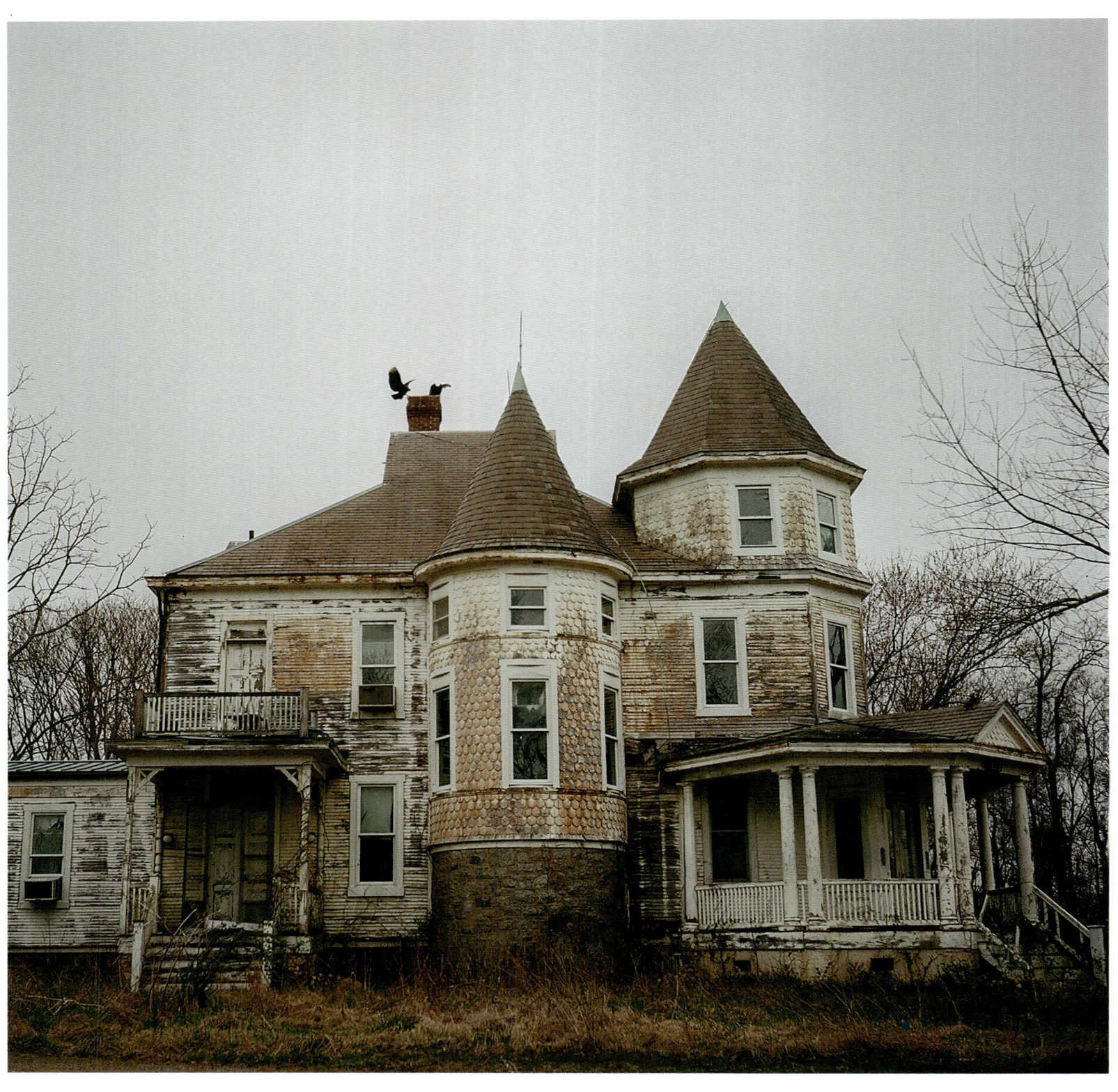

"THE MILITARY-BASE VICTORIAN"
Harford County, Maryland

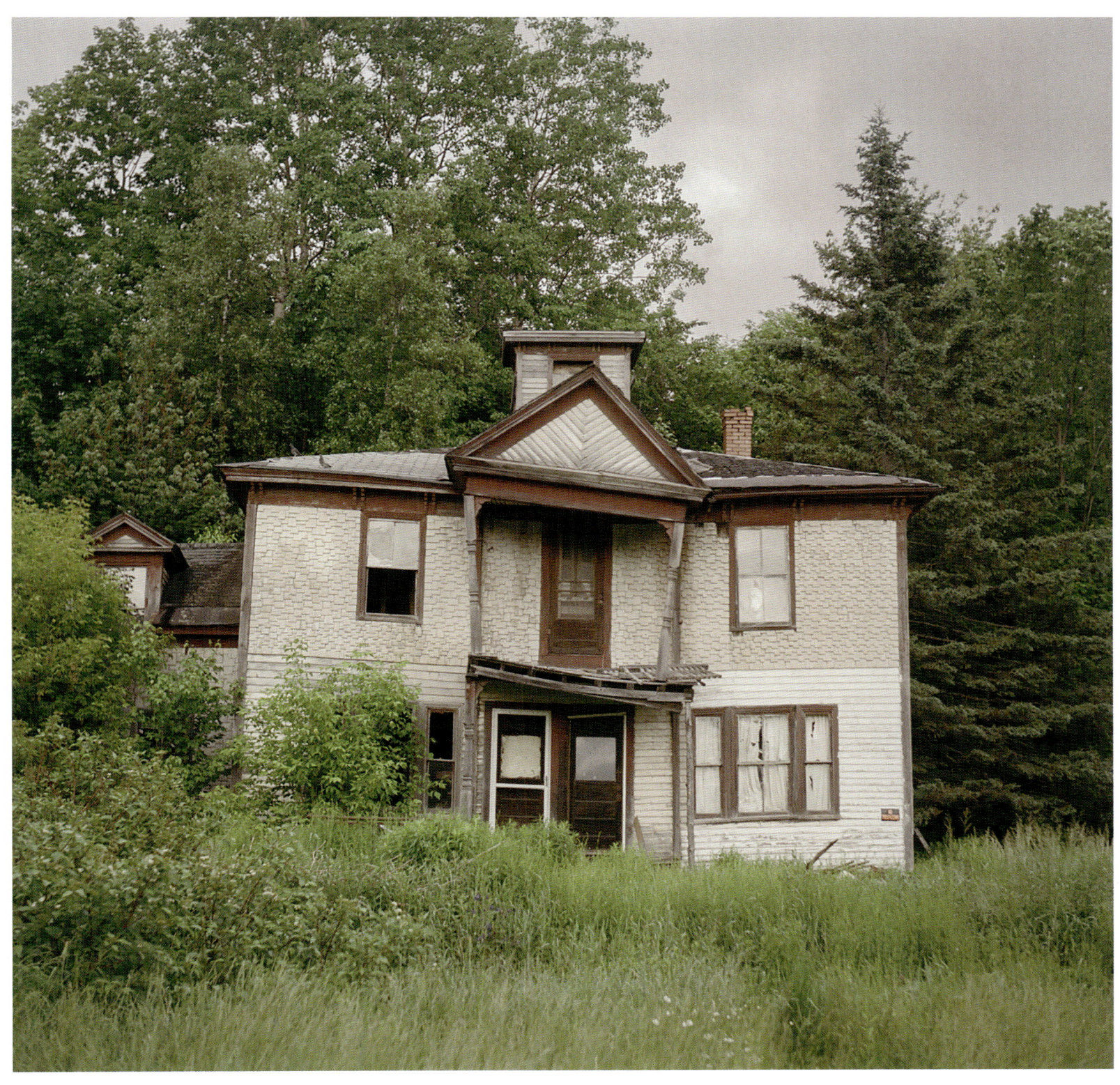

"THE TWO-TIERED PORCH"
Aroostook County, Maine

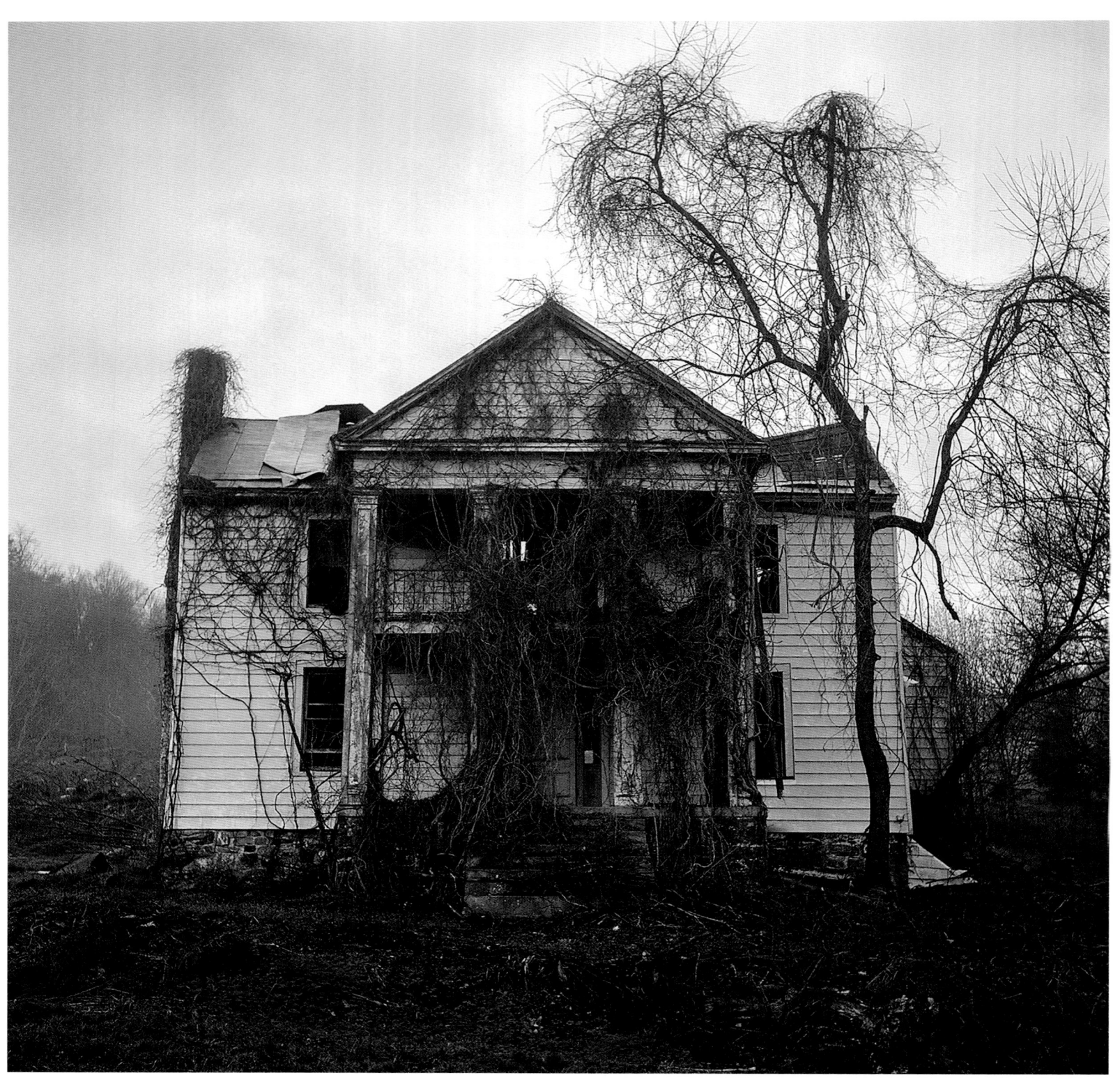

"THE DEAD VINES"
Norfolk County, Virginia

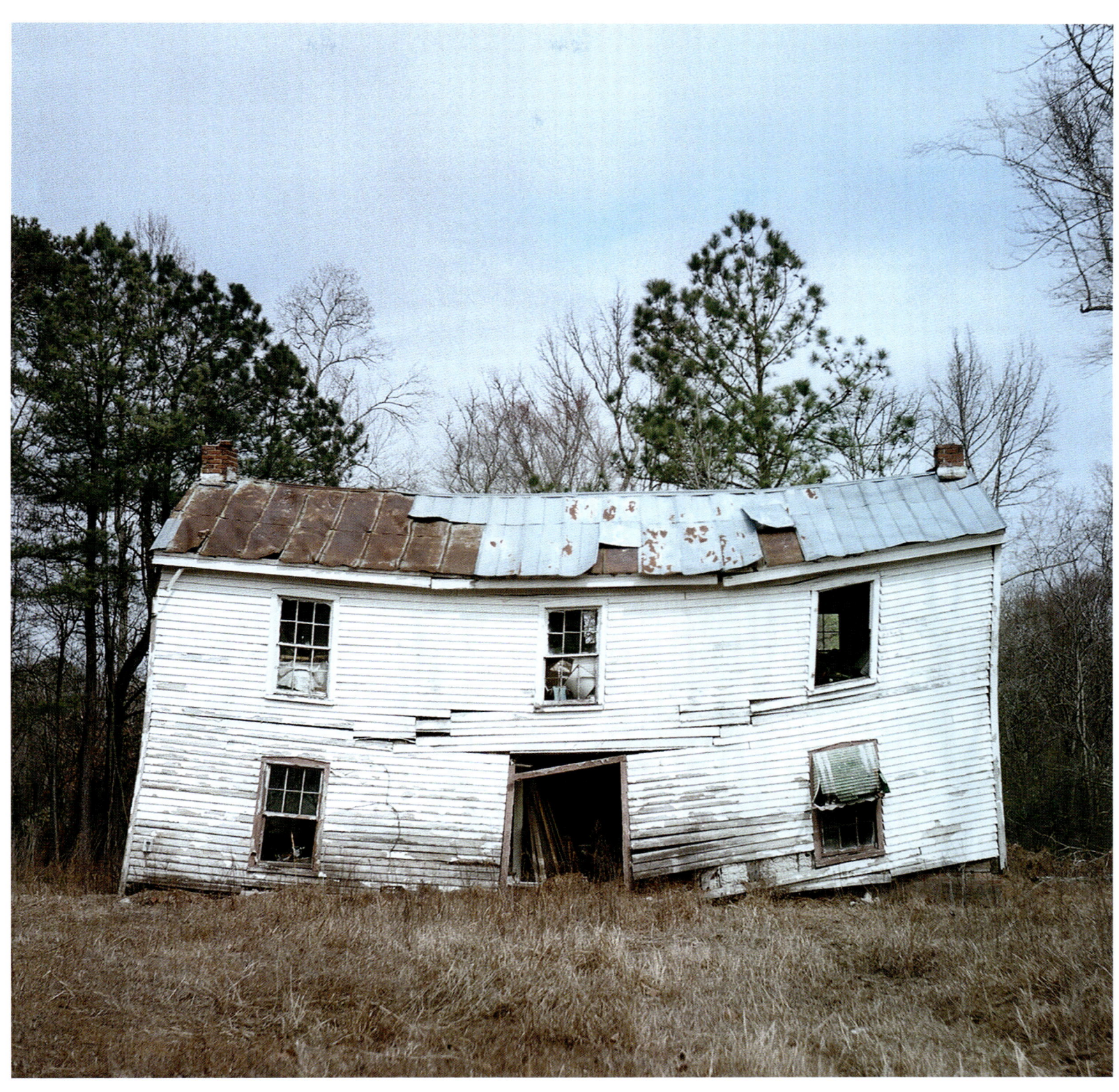

"SWALLOWED BY THE GROUND"
Surry County, Virginia

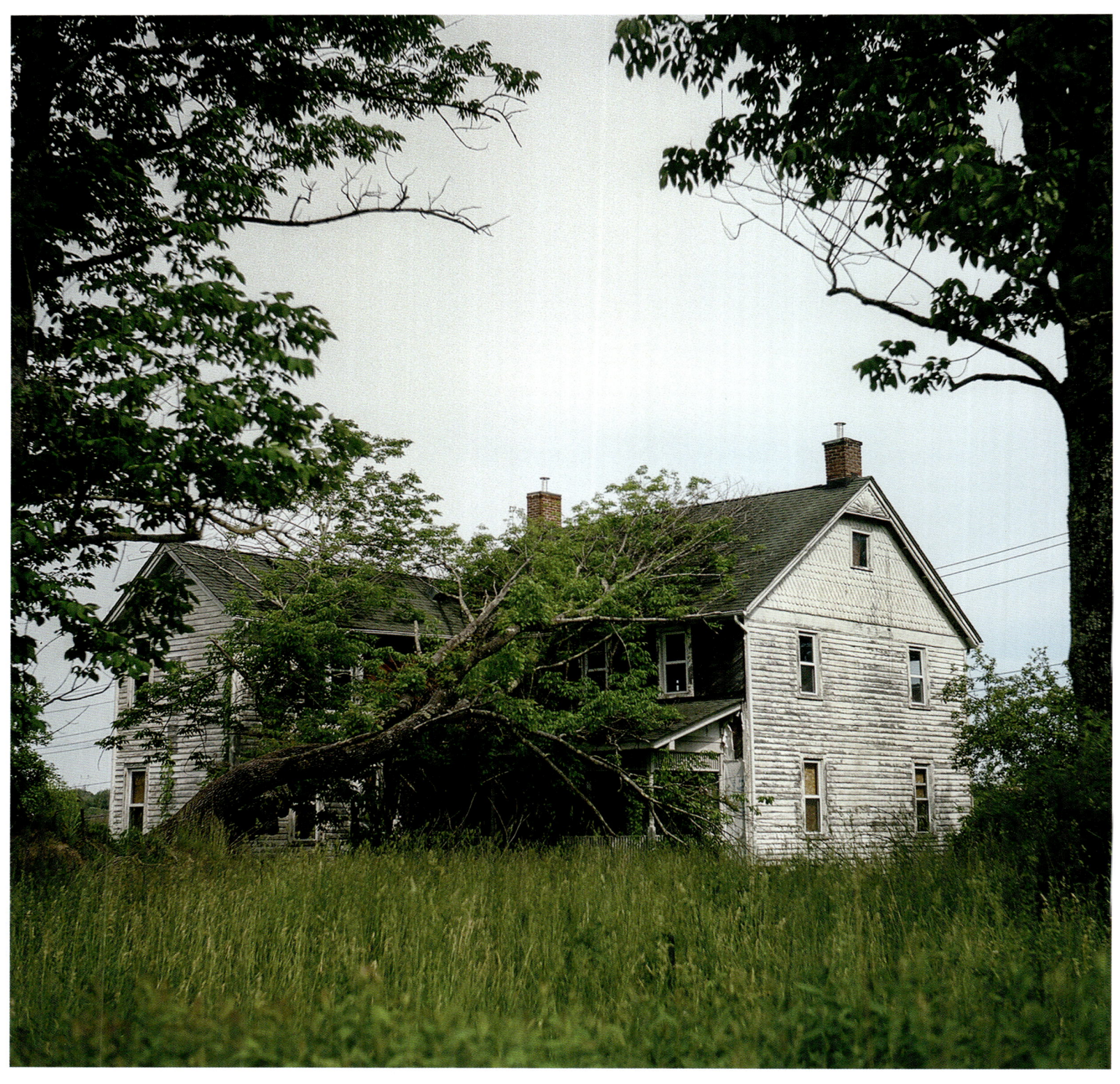

"THE FALLEN TREE"
Chester County, Pennsylvania

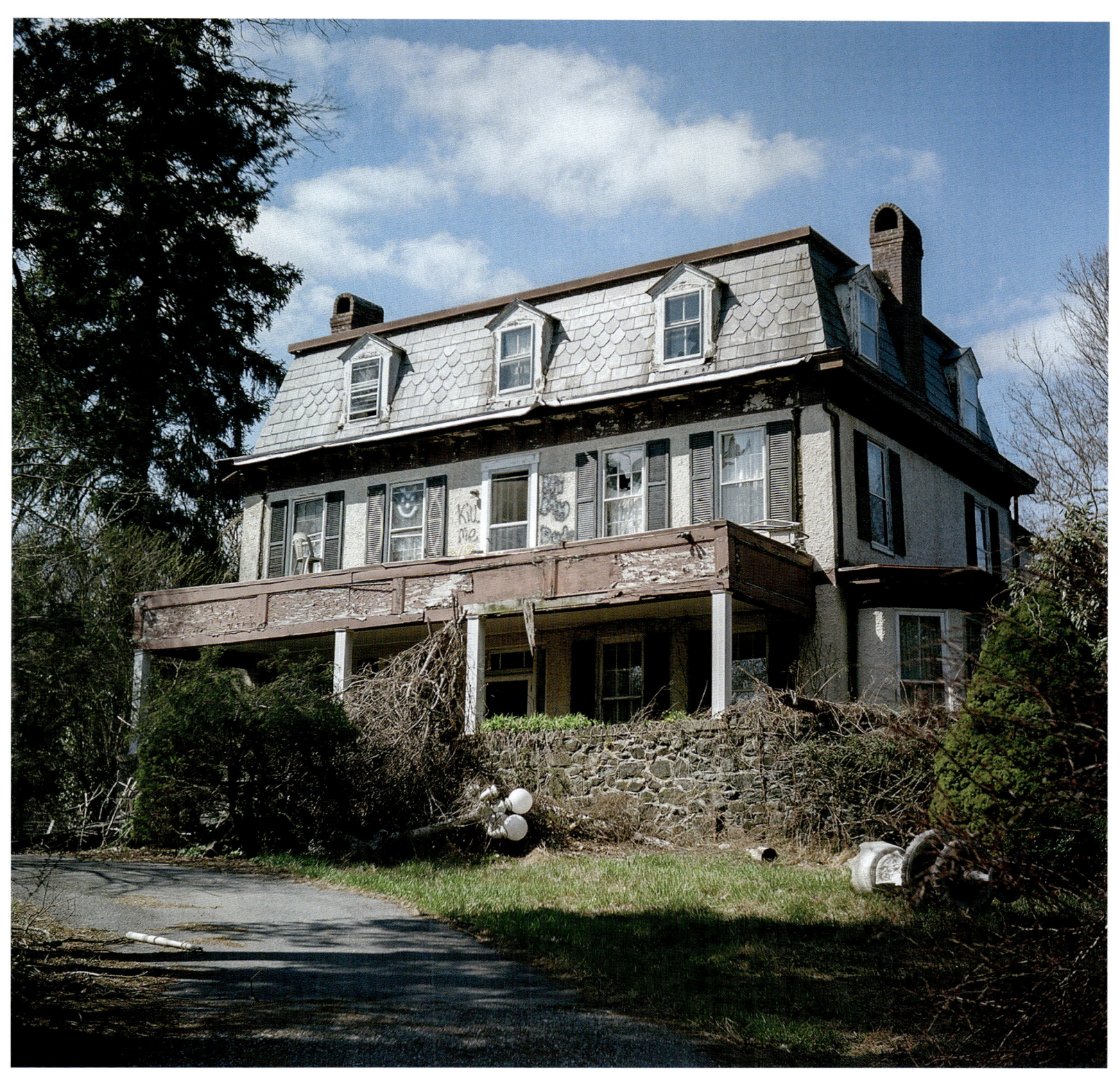

"THE GRAFITTIED HOUSE"
Baltimore County, Maryland

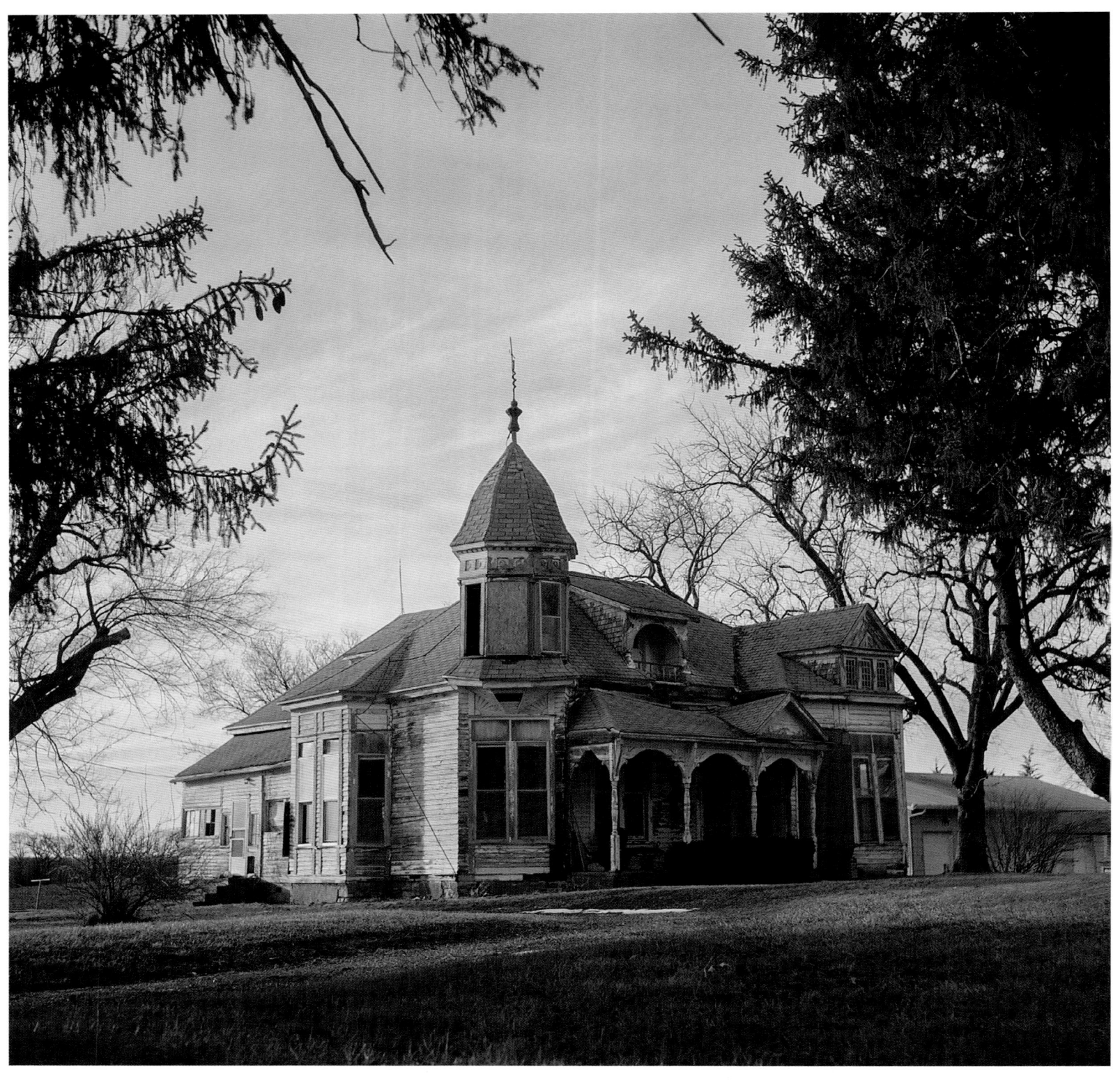

"A QUEEN ANNE IN KANSAS"
Atchison County, Kansas

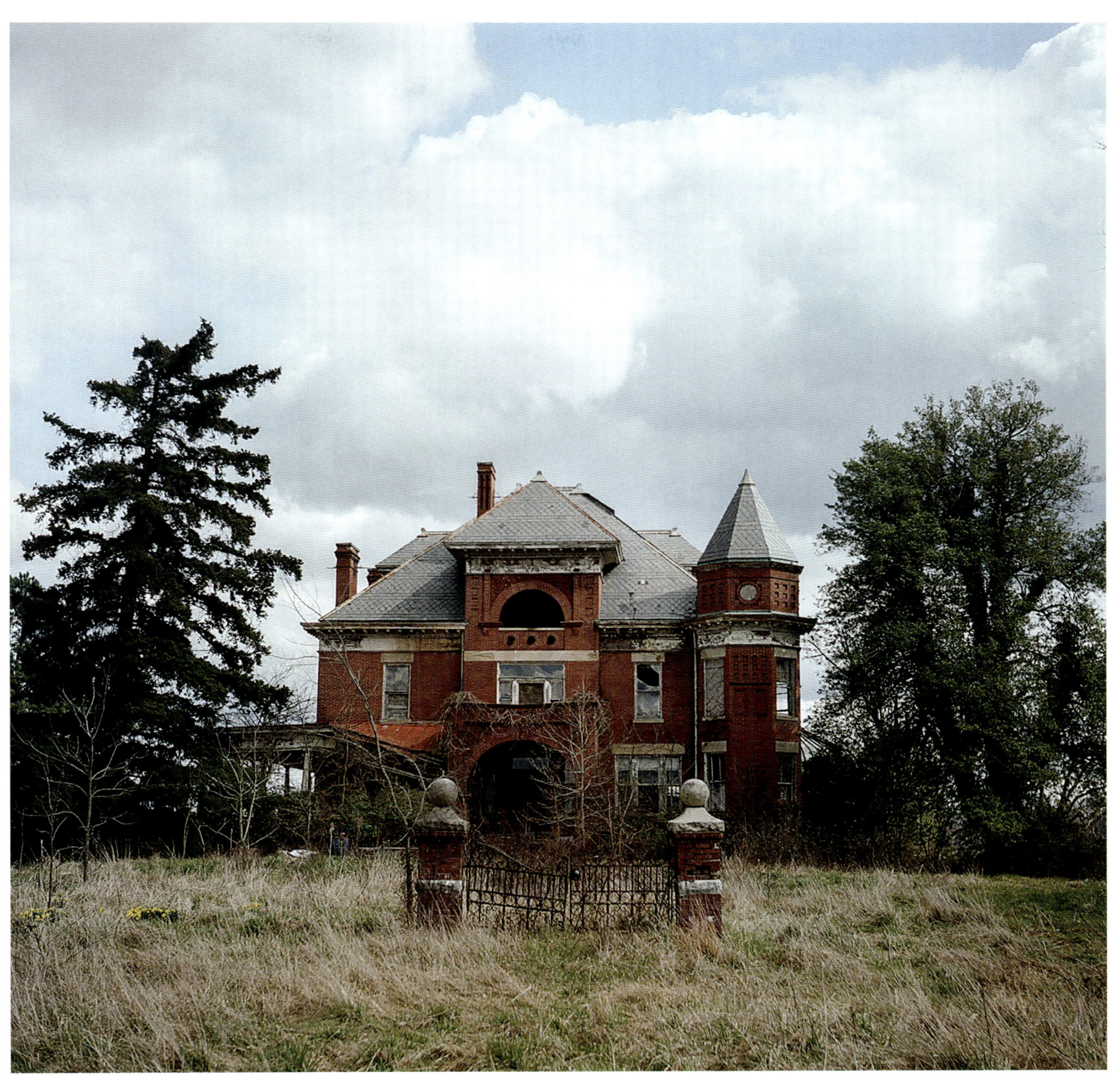

"DUNNINGTON MANSION"
Prince Edward County, Virginia

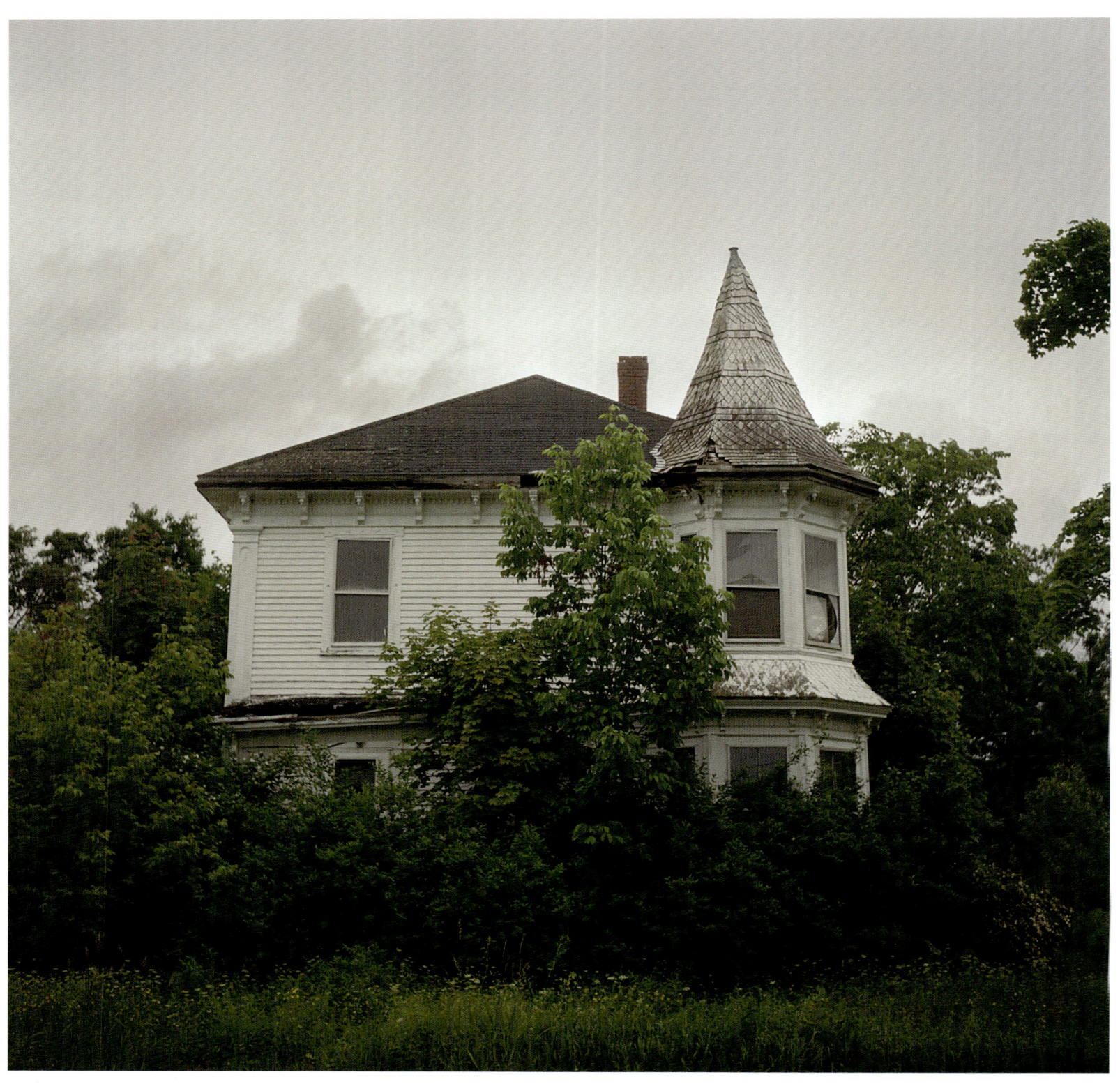

"THE MYSTERIOUS VICTORIAN"
Washington County, Maine

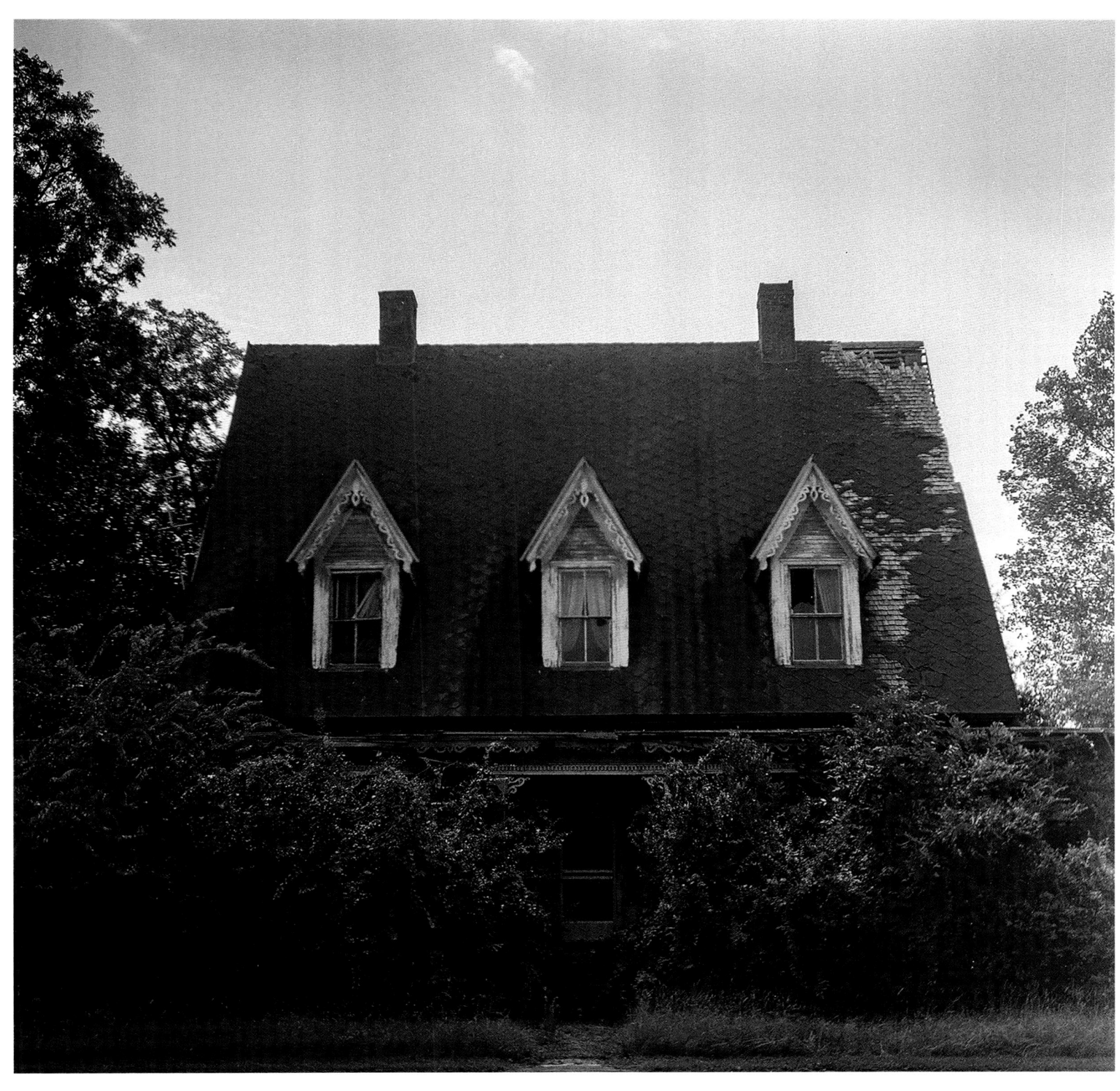

"LOUISE"
Jefferson County, Georgia

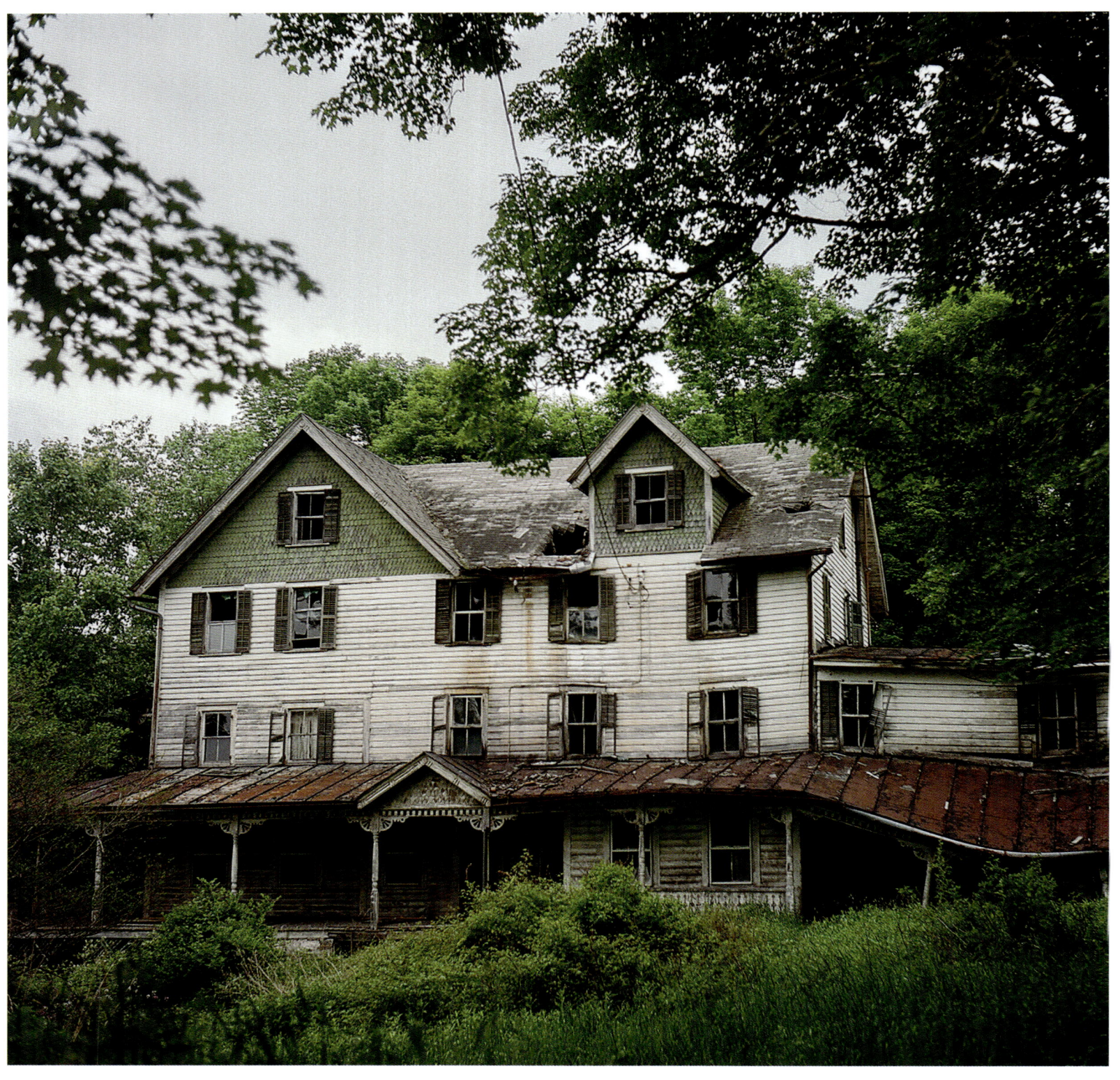

"KENOZA DELL HOUSE"
Sullivan County, New York

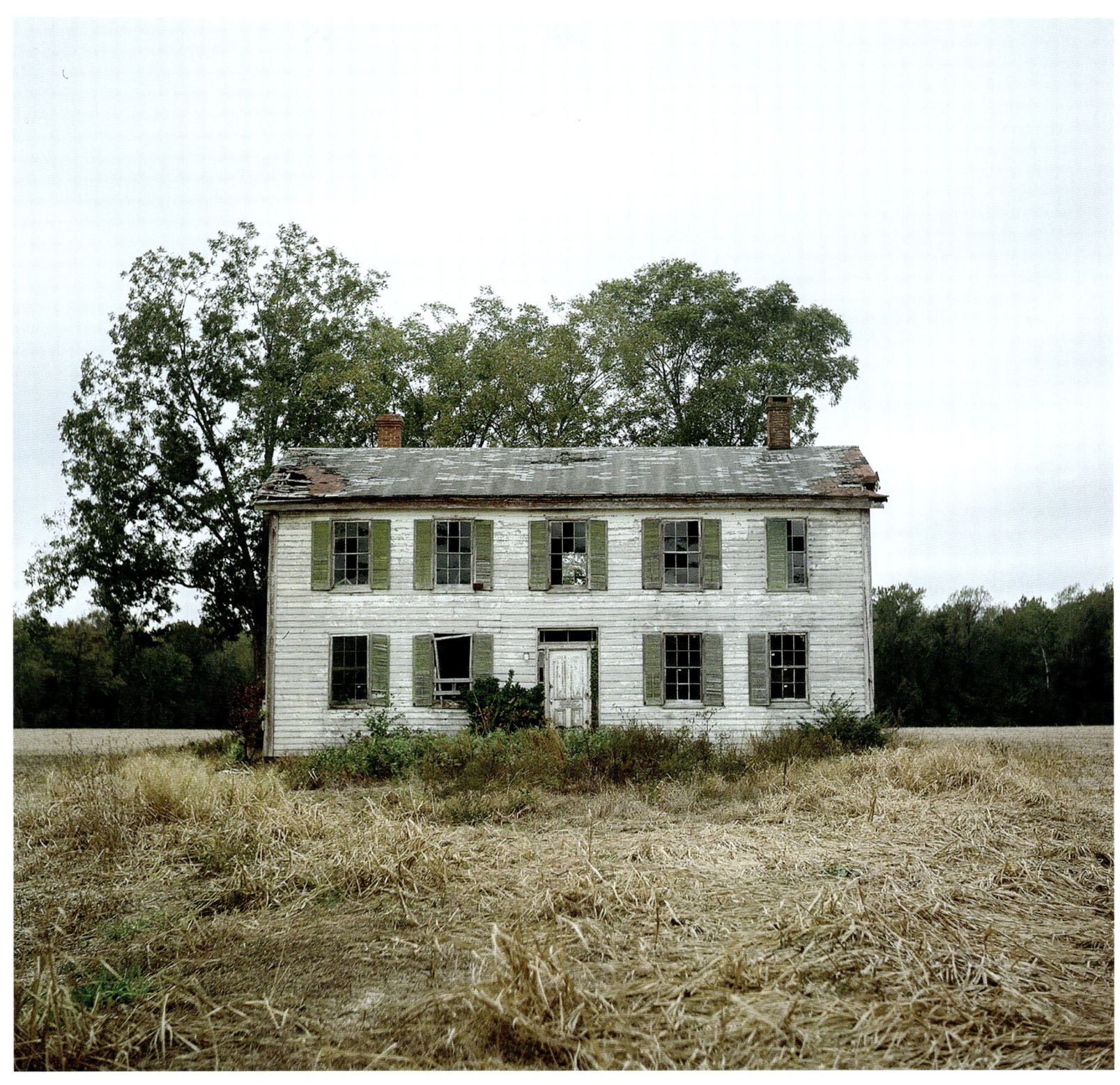

"THE COLONIAL"
Louisa County, Virginia

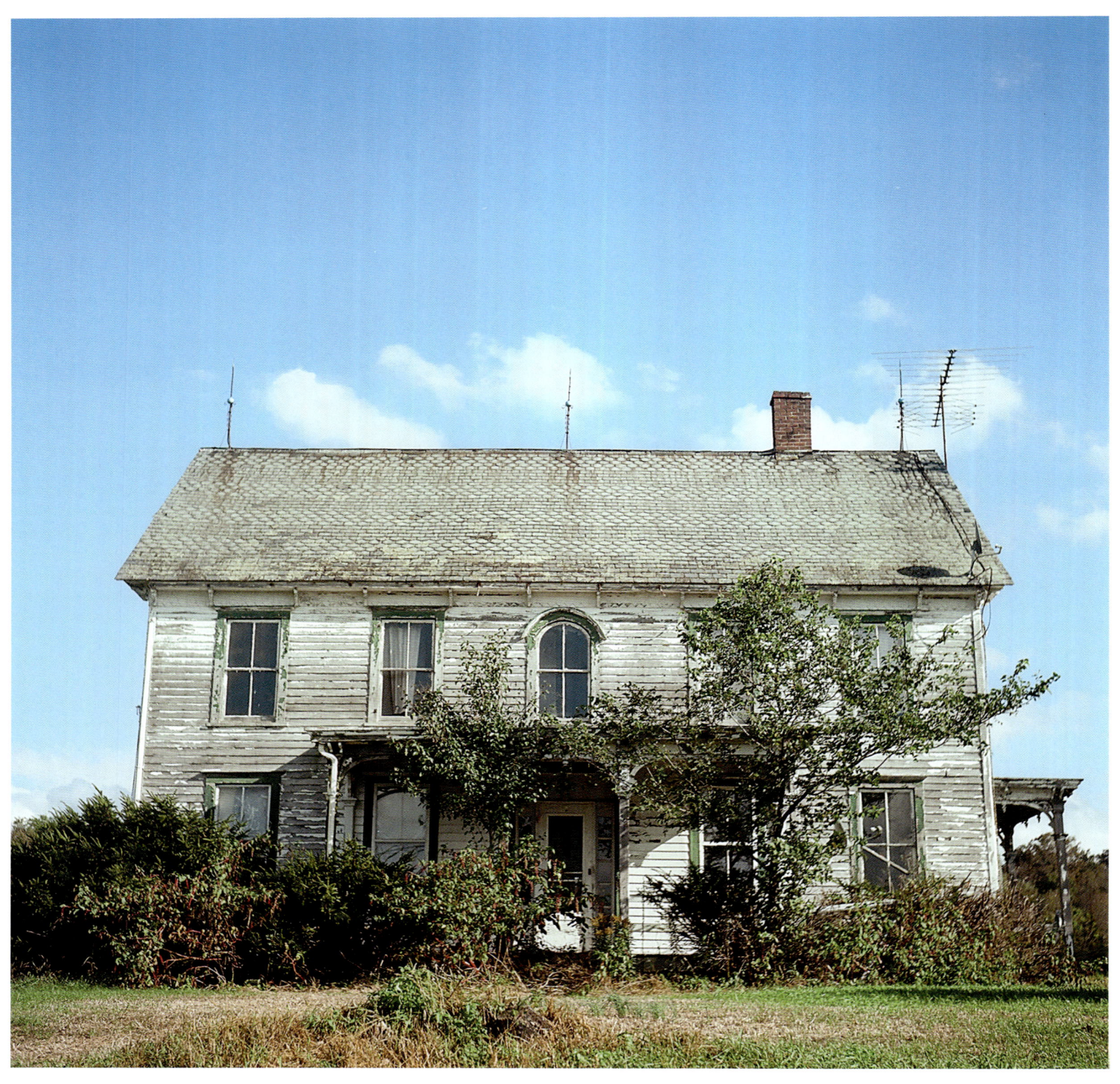

"THE NEW JERSEY FARMSTEAD"
Sussex County, New Jersey

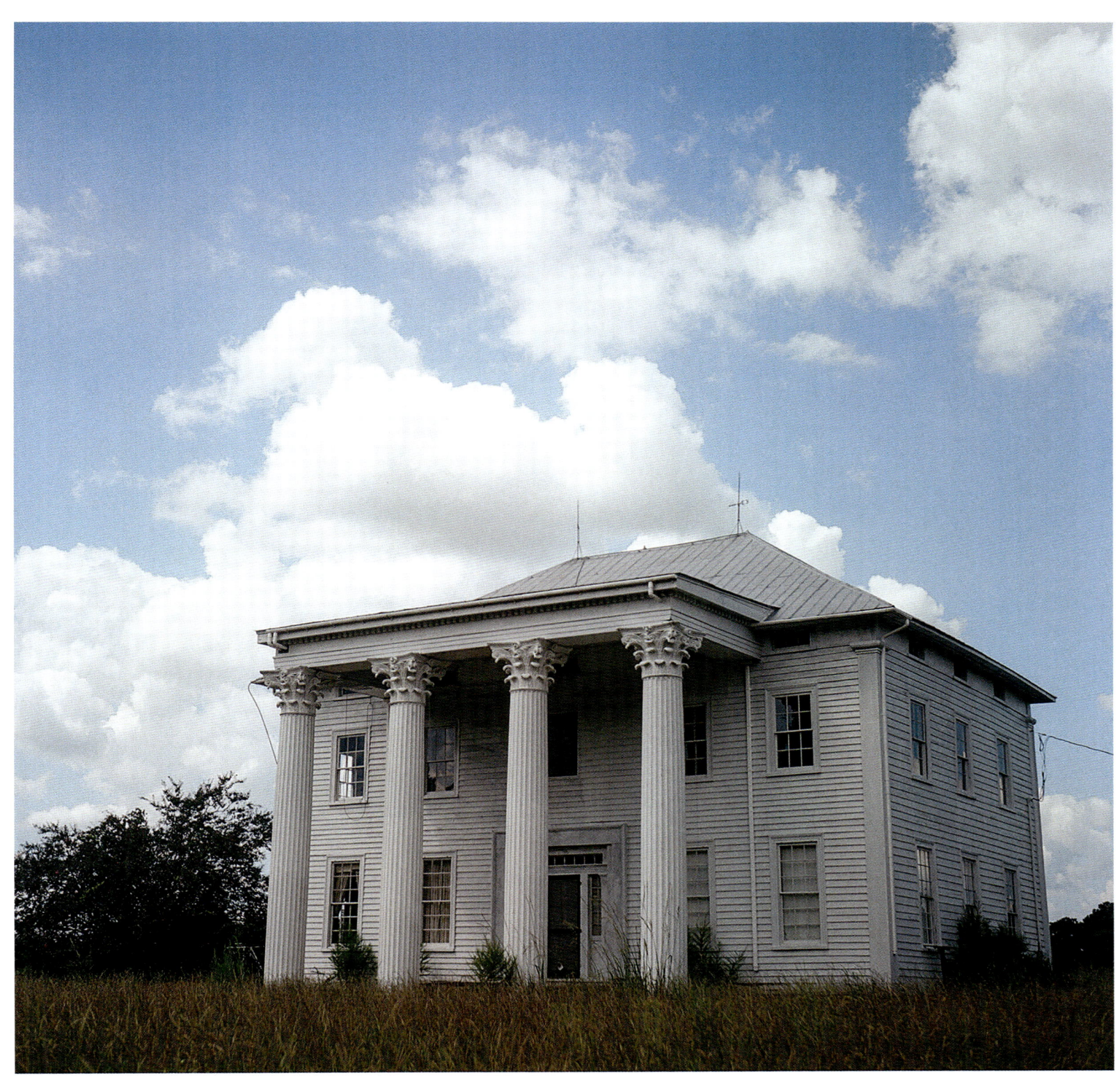

"QUEWHIFFLE PLANTATION"
Sampson County, North Carolina

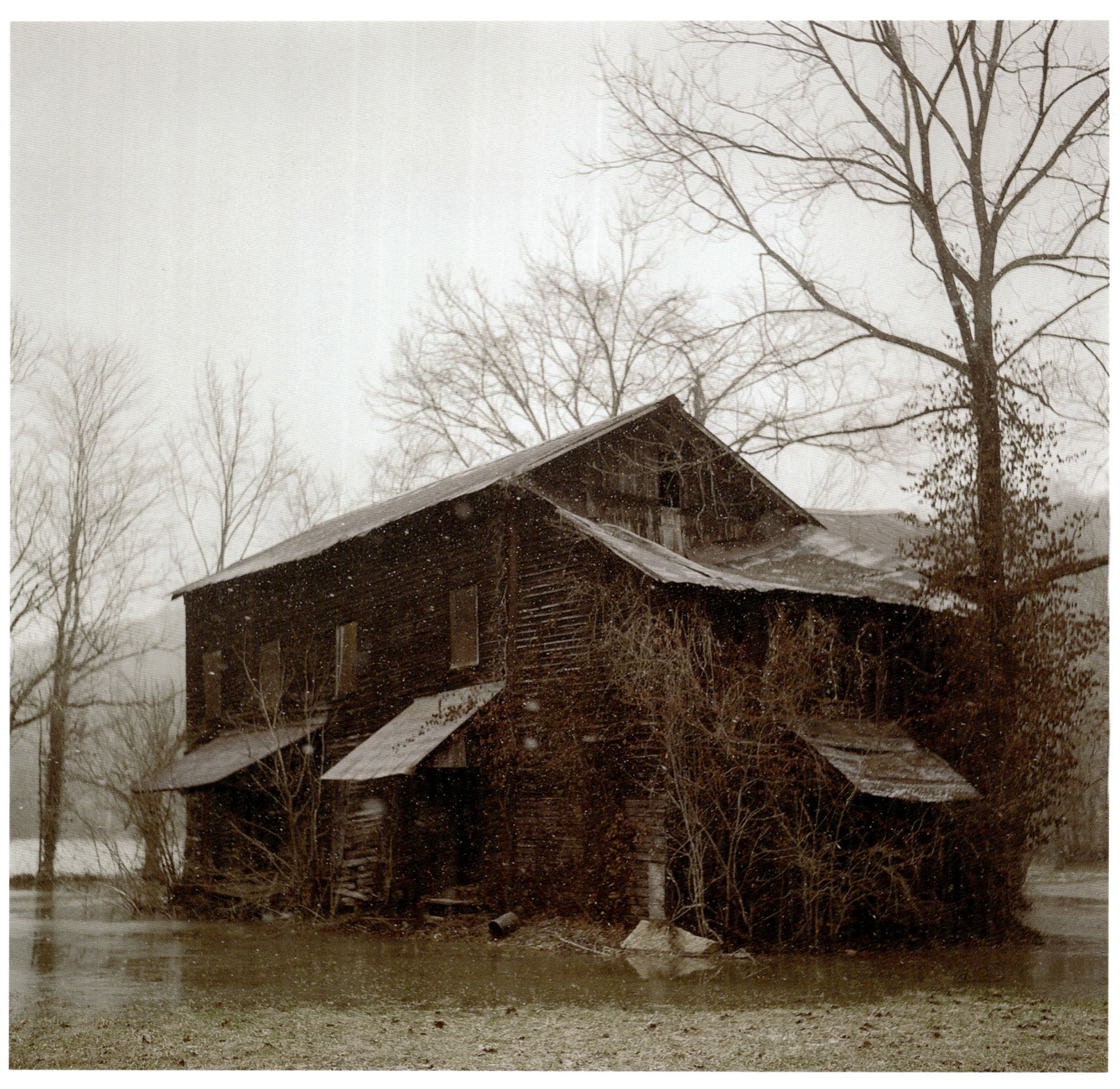

"IN THE KENTUCKY FLOOD"
Boone County, Kentucky

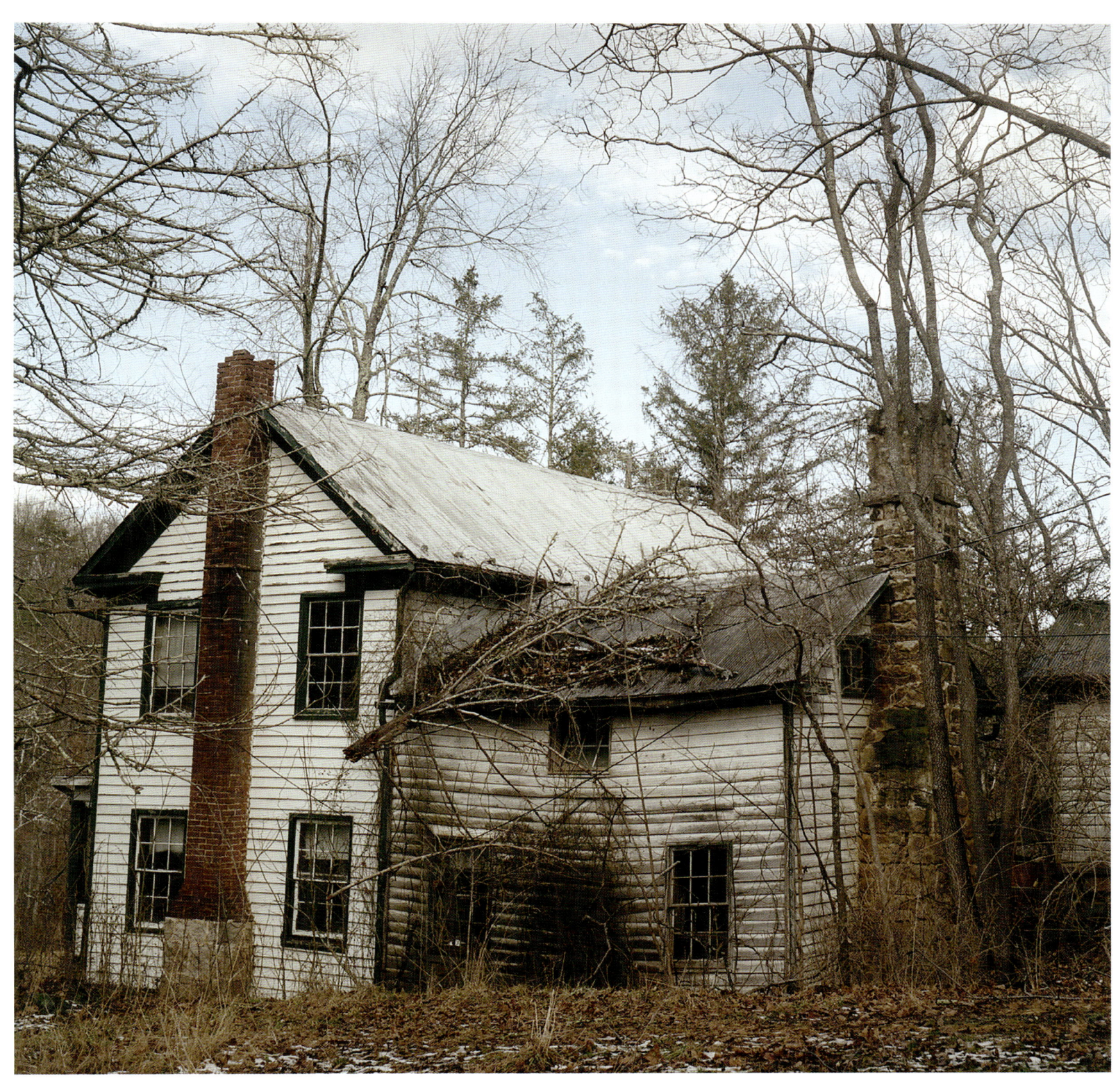

THE CAR COLLECTOR'S HOUSE
Jefferson County, West Virginia

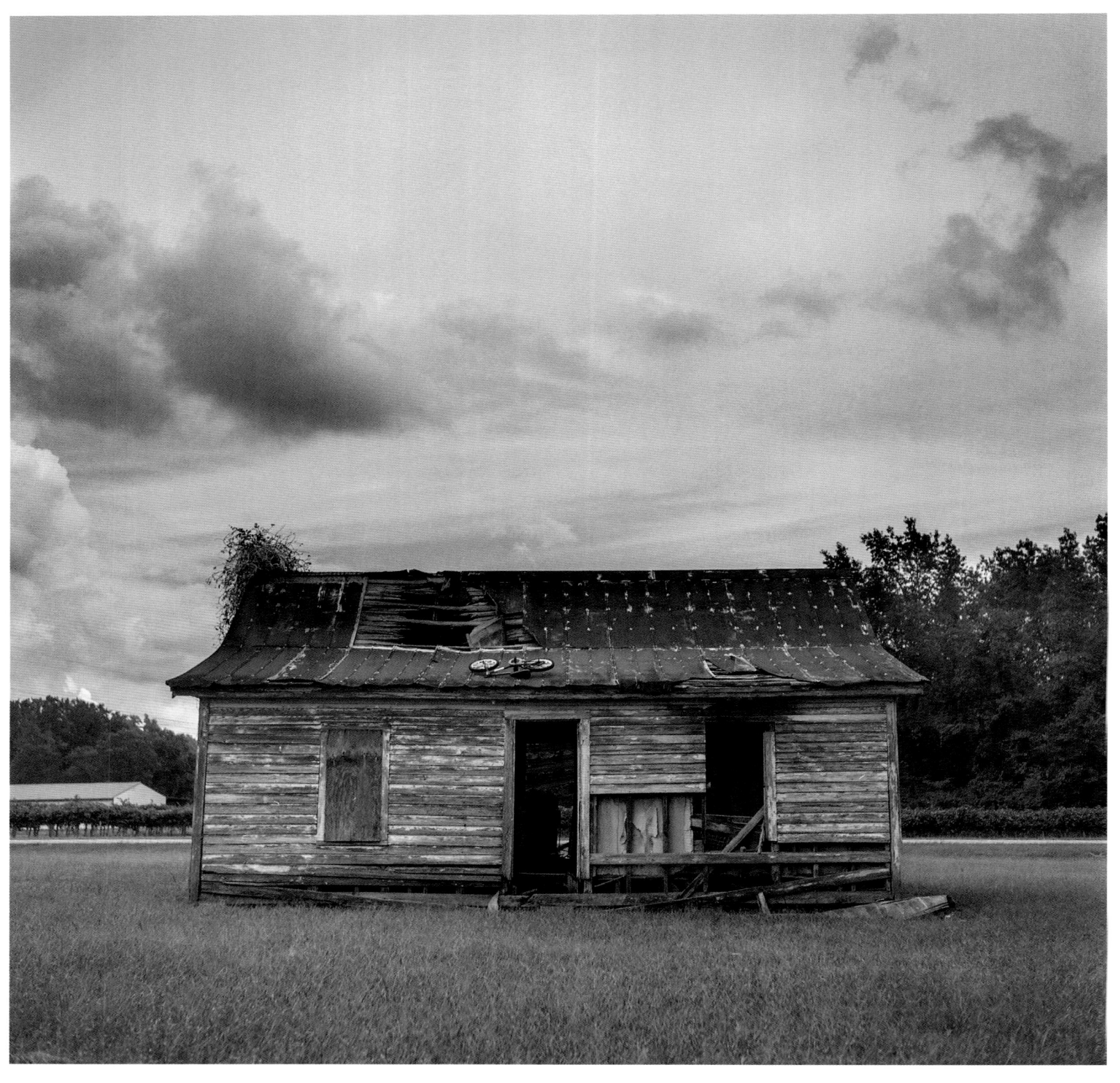

"THE BIKE ON THE ROOF"
Duplin County, North Carolina

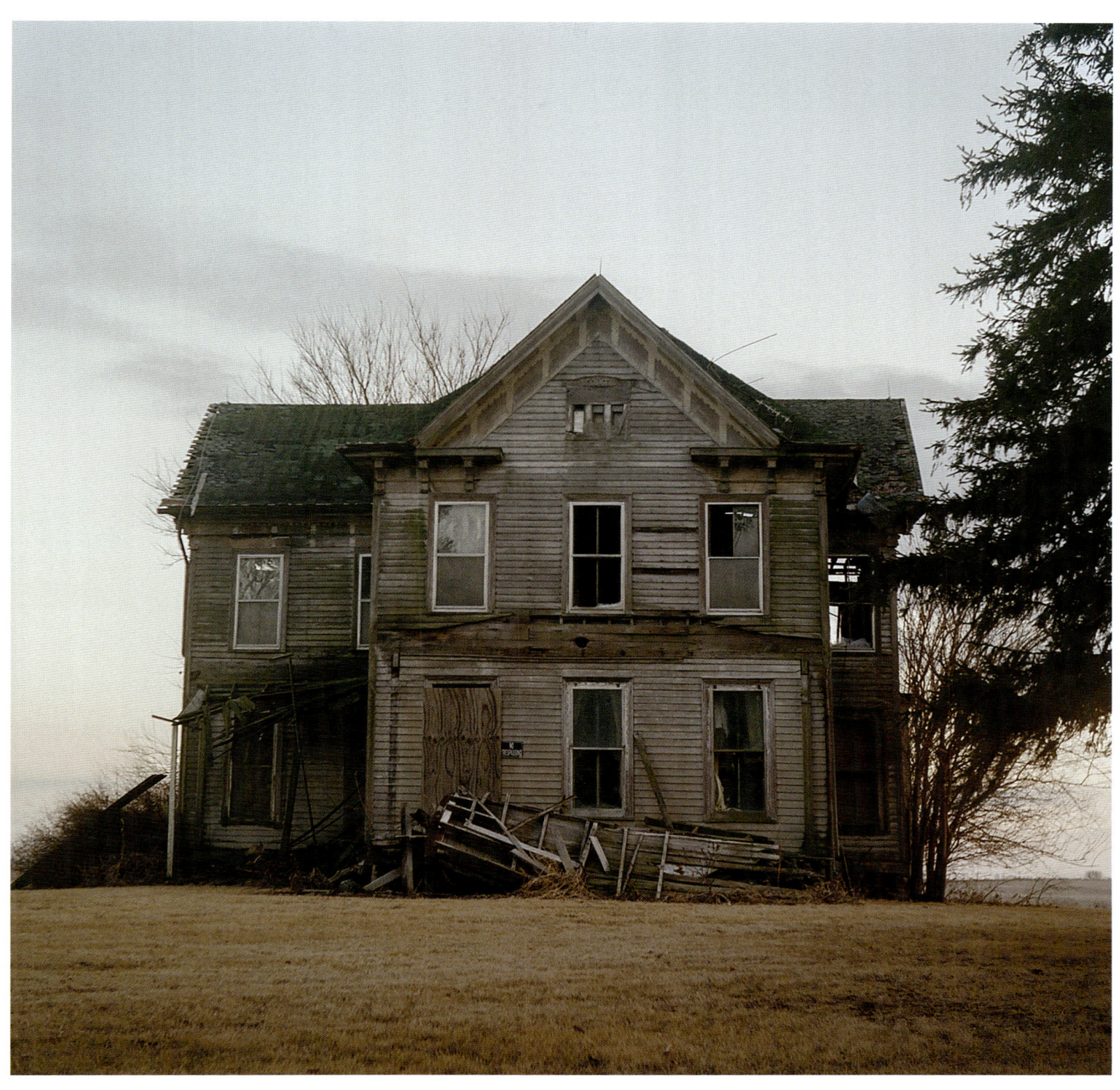

"THE MIDWEST FARMHOUSE"
McLean County, Illinois

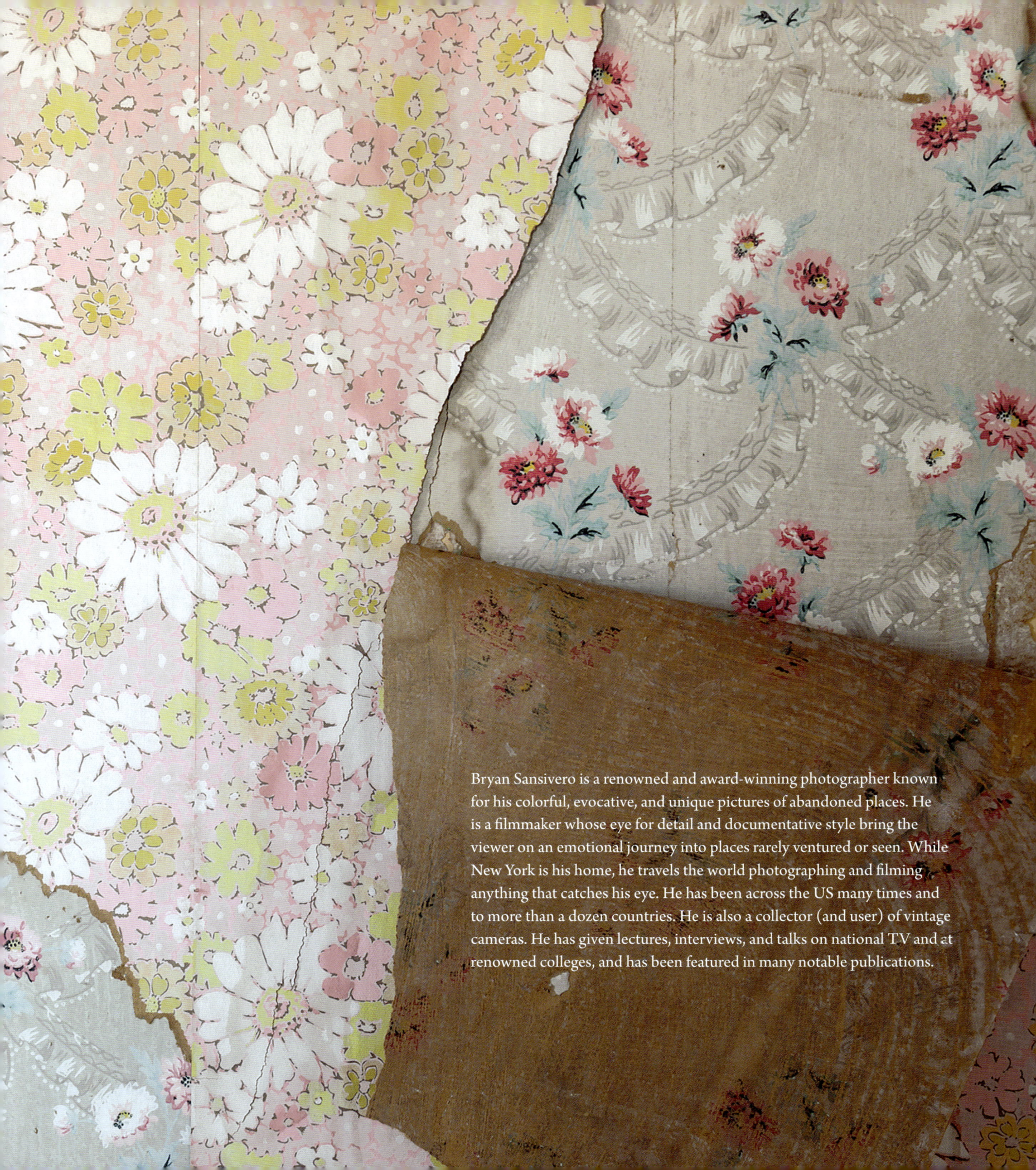

Bryan Sansivero is a renowned and award-winning photographer known for his colorful, evocative, and unique pictures of abandoned places. He is a filmmaker whose eye for detail and documentative style bring the viewer on an emotional journey into places rarely ventured or seen. While New York is his home, he travels the world photographing and filming anything that catches his eye. He has been across the US many times and to more than a dozen countries. He is also a collector (and user) of vintage cameras. He has given lectures, interviews, and talks on national TV and at renowned colleges, and has been featured in many notable publications.

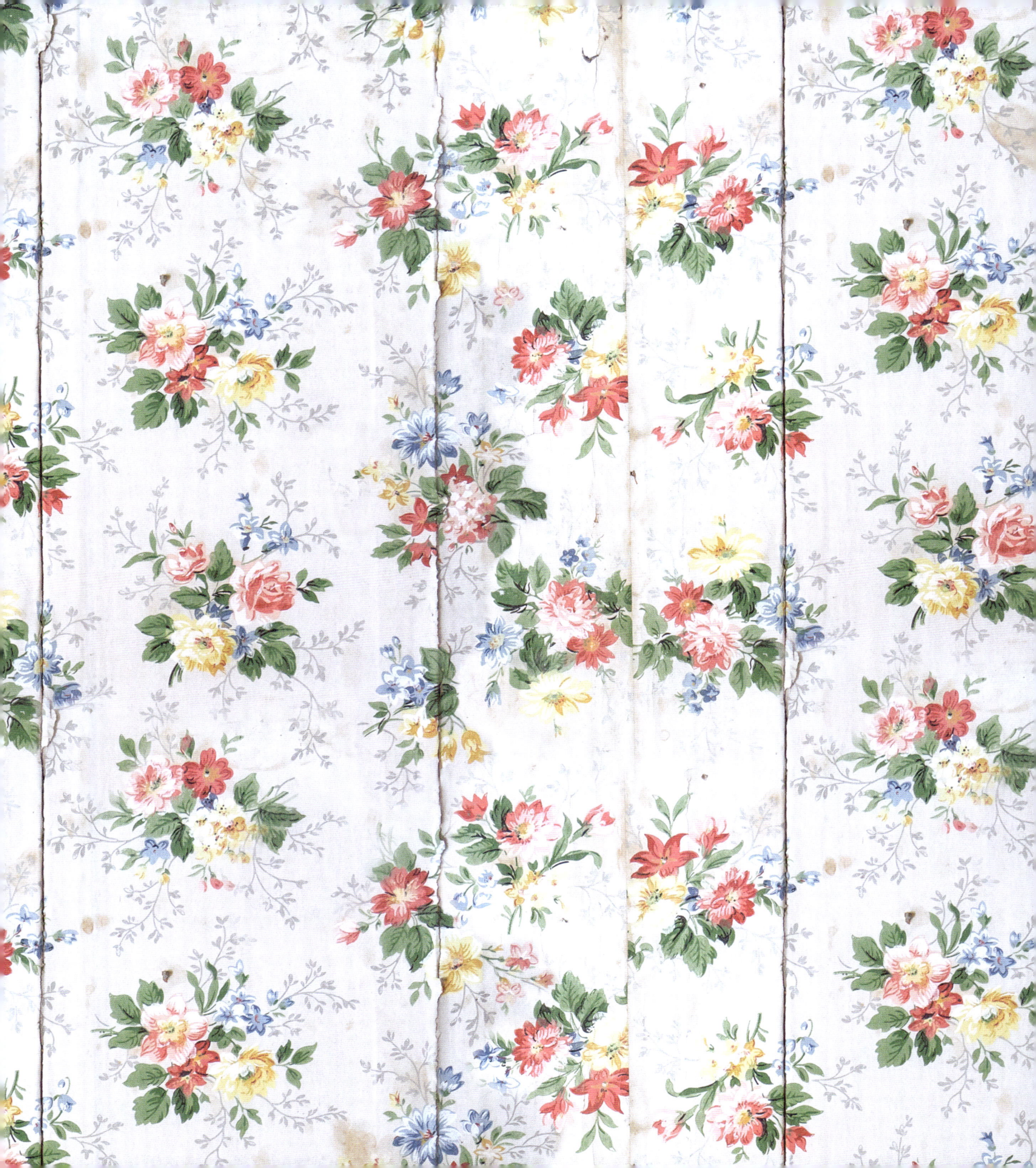

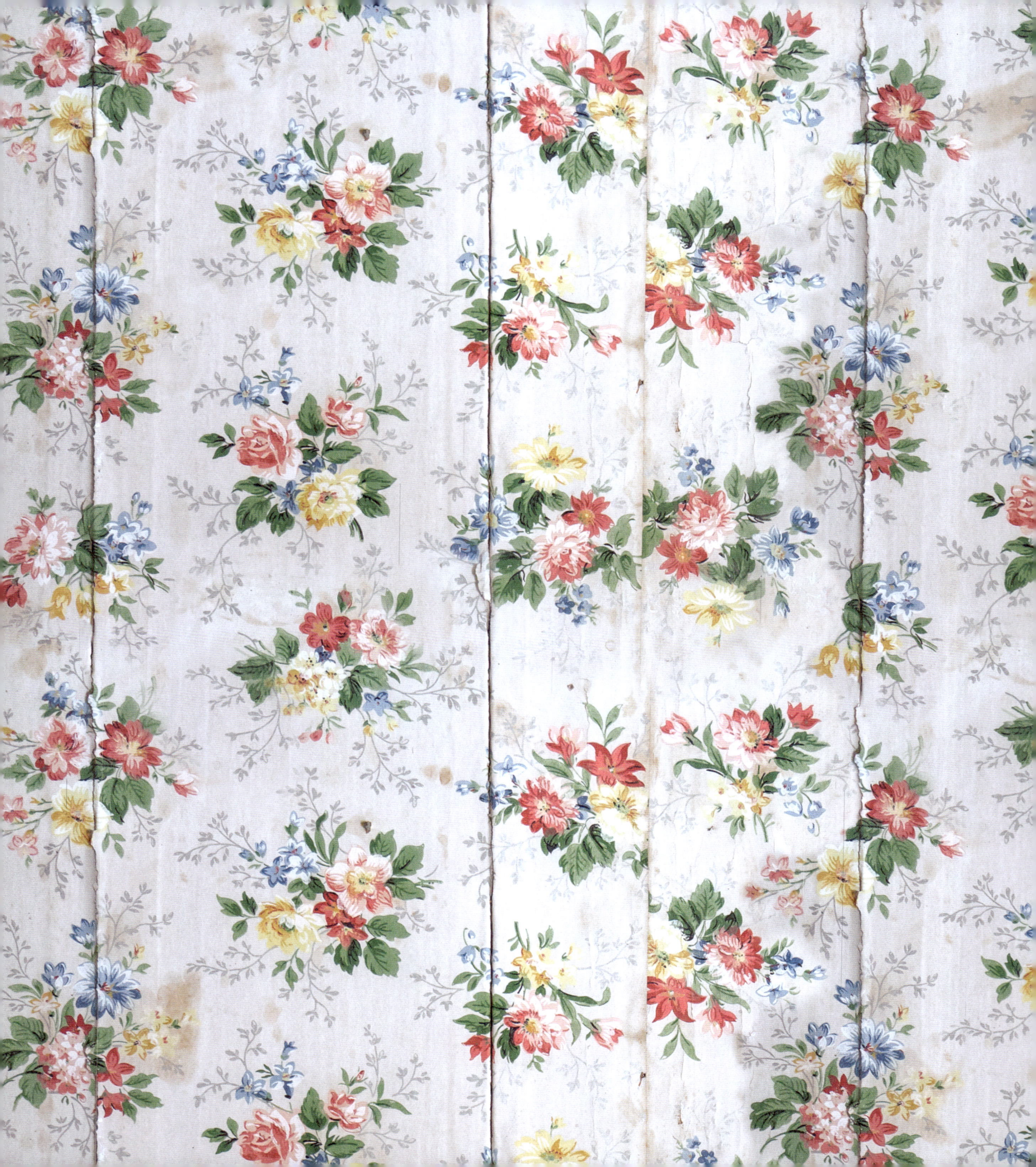